ENGINEERING ETHICS

Concepts and Cases

FIFTH EDITION

ENGINEERING ETHICS

Concepts and Cases

CHARLES E. HARRIS, Jr.
Texas A&M University

MICHAEL S. PRITCHARD
Western Michigan University

MICHAEL J. RABINS
late of Texas A&M University

RAY JAMES
Texas A&M University

ELAINE ENGLEHARDT
Utah Valley University

WADSWORTH
CENGAGE Learning·

Australia • Brazil • Japan • Korea • Mexico • Singapore • Spain • United Kingdom • United States

WADSWORTH
CENGAGE Learning

Engineering Ethics: Concepts and Cases,
Fifth Edition
Charles E. Harris, Jr., Michael S. Pritchard,
Michael J. Rabins, Ray James, and
Elaine Englehardt

Editor-in-Chief: Lyn Uhl

Publisher: Clark Baxter

Senior Sponsoring Editor: Joann Kozyrev

Development Editor: Mary Ann McHugh

Assistant Editor: Joshua Duncan

Editorial Assistant: Marri Straton

Media Editor: Philip Lanza

Brand Manager: Jennifer Levanduski

Market Development Manager:
Joshua I. Adams

Senio Marketing Communications Manager:
Linda Yip

Rights Acquisitions Specialist: Ann Hoffman

Manufacturing Planner: Sandee Milewski

Art and Design Direction, Production
Management, and Composition:
PreMediaGlobal

Cover Image: ©Hemera collection/
Thinkstock (RF)

For product information and technology assistance, contact us at
Cengage Learning Customer & Sales Support, 1-800-354-9706

For permission to use material from this text or product,
submit all requests online at **www.cengage.com/permissions**.
Further permissions questions can be emailed to
permissionrequest@cengage.com.

Library of Congress Control Number: 2012955334

ISBN-13: 978-1-133-93468-4

ISBN-10: 1-133-93468-4

Wadsworth
20 Channel Center Street
Boston, MA 02210
USA

Cengage Learning is a leading provider of customized learning solutions with office locations around the globe, including Singapore, the United Kingdom, Australia, Mexico, Brazil and Japan. Locate your local office at **international.cengage.com/region.**

Cengage Learning products are represented in Canada by Nelson Education, Ltd.

For your course and learning solutions, visit **www.cengage.com.**

Purchase any of our products at your local college store or at our preferred online store **www.cengagebrain.com.**

Instructors: Please visit **login.cengage.com** and log in to access instructor-specific resources.

Printed in the United States of America
3 4 5 6 7 16 15

CONTENTS

LIST OF CASES

WE ARE HAPPY TO OFFER the fifth edition of *Engineering Ethics: Concepts and Cases.* Much of the old material has been reorganized and new sections have been added to take account of advances in the field of engineering ethics.

This fifth edition is the first prepared without any contributions from Professor Michael Rabins. As noted in the fourth edition, Dr. Rabins passed away in 2007, but many of his ideas from the first four editions continue to be reflected in this edition. Two new coauthors have contributed to this edition; Dr. Ray W. James, P.E., Assistant Dean of the Dwight Look College at Texas A&M University and long-time engineering coordinator of the engineering and ethics course required of all engineering students at Texas A&M brings the perspective of a professional engineer. And philosopher Elaine Englehardt, Distinguished Professor of Ethics at Utah Valley University, brings to the team her expertise as a specialist in professional and practical ethics.

The authors are indebted to Professor Michael Davis for his careful review and thoughtful suggestions for improvements to the fourth edition. Some of his suggestions have stimulated some of these changes described here. His advice is gratefully acknowledged.

We acknowledge with thanks permission to adapt portions of Michael S. Pritchard's article, "Engineering Ethics," for inclusion in Chapter 1. This article is forthcoming in Hugh LaFollette, Editor, *International Encyclopedia of Ethics* (Wiley-Blackwell: forthcoming 2013).

The major changes to the fifth edition are as follows:

- The concept of "aspirational ethics," introduced in the fourth edition, gets increased emphasis, not only in the Chapter 1, but also in other places in the book.
- Chapter 2 ("A Practical Ethics Toolkit") contains new material on virtue ethics and a new discussion of moral theories understood as analogous to models in science and engineering.
- Chapter 4 (The Social and Value Dimensions of Technology) has been rewritten and now includes an application of virtue ethics to issues in social networking.
- Chapter 6 (Risk and Liability in Engineering) has been updated to reflect ethical issues arising out of several recent incidents: the terrorist attacks on the World

Trade Center, the Macondo well blowout, (also see the newly added Case 46, "The 2010 Loss of the Deepwater Horizon and the Macondo Well Blowout"), and the 2011 disaster at the Fukushima nuclear power plant. We have added a new focus on the increase of risk in innovative engineering designs and the responsibility of engineers with respect to innovative designs. Finally, the responsibilities of the engineer engaged in operation of engineering systems to identify and manage risks are discussed.

- Chapter 7 (Engineers in Organizations) now begins with a focus on the importance of integrating the values of engineers, customers, employers, and the general public. It also discusses impediments to responsible behavior (previously presented in Chapter 2 of the fourth edition) in the context of the organizational settings within which engineers typically work.
- Chapter 8 (Engineers and the Environment) has a new section on sustainability and life cycle analysis. The chapter also contains a new discussion of environmental stewardship.
- Chapter 9 (Engineering in the Global Context) has new material on the movement to establish transnational criteria for engineering education and licensure and a discussion of the possibility of an international concept of professionalism.
- A supplementary website is provided for the use of students and instructors. The website will provide practice multiple choice questions to challenge students and stimulate instructors, ideas for student essay topics, and perhaps additional case studies.

We consider these some of these ideas in more detail.

ASPIRATIONAL ETHICS

Most traditional engineering ethics has focused on the prevention of harm to the public, whether the harm is the result of professional misconduct (e.g., practicing outside one's area of expertise) or dangers from engineering products or processes. Whistleblowing by the engineers who protested the launch of the *Challenger* is one of the most dramatic manifestations of preventive ethics. During the past few years, scholars in engineering ethics have emphasized that engineering ethics should have a more positive dimension: encouragement of engineers to promote human welfare through technology. We develop this idea in Chapter 1 and elsewhere in the book.

ETHICAL THEORIES AS MODELS

Models are an integral part of science and engineering. Models aid in understanding complex phenomena and in predicting future events. Moral theories can be understood as models because they provide organizing principles that help in understanding the function of morality and why morality condemns and praises certain types of behavior. As with models in science and engineering, models in ethics have limitations. The limitations of the two major ethical theories, utilitarianism and respect for persons, however, can be a useful aid in the understanding of many ethical conflicts.

In this edition we emphasize more than before the practical and problem-solving nature of the ethical techniques we discuss, that they should be thought of as analogous to tools in a toolkit. These techniques should be used whenever they are practically useful in resolving moral problems, and only then. Moral theories or models are often not useful in resolving ethical problems faced by individual engineers, but they are often helpful in dealing with larger social and policy issues posed by technology. Virtue ethics has been introduced because it can also be a useful tool in understanding the moral dimensions of some issues.

SUSTAINABILITY AND STEWARDSHIP OF THE ENVIRONMENT

Environmental issues continue to be a challenge for engineers. For this reason we devote more time to several pioneers in environmental thought. One of the challenges for engineering is to practice sustainable engineering to the extent that it is possible. Even the definition of the term "sustainable" is controversial, and total or complete sustainability may perhaps best be thought of as an ideal. Life cycle analysis, however, is a practical attempt to implement sustainability in design and manufacture.

Engineering has more effect on the environment than does any other profession. We believe the concept of "environmental stewardship" is a practical philosophy appropriate for engineers, in part because it sidesteps many of the theoretical issues in environmental philosophy, such as the distinction between anthropocentric and nonanthropocentric ethics.

ENGINEERING AS A GLOBAL PROFESSION

As engineering becomes increasingly prominent in developing societies, the need for standardized criteria for engineering education and licensure also becomes more pressing. The Washington Accord, established in 1989, is the most important attempt so far to standardize criteria for engineering education. The development of internationally recognized ethical standards is only just beginning. In promoting further development of ethical standards, it would be useful to have a universally recognized concept of "professional." Some suggestions are made as to how this development might proceed.

THE PASSING OF CHARLES E. HARRIS

Charles E. Harris, the father of author Harris, came to college age in difficult economic times. His parents were unable to help him financially, so he worked his way through engineering school at Vanderbilt University and then spent his entire professional career as an electrical engineer with the US Corps of Engineers. He was licensed by the Tennessee State Board of Architectural and Engineering Examiners in 1947. His low certificate number (1692) indicates that his career spanned the early days of professional registration in the state. He was a member of the American Institute of Electrical Engineers, now the Institute of Electrical and Electronics Engineers (IEEE). The last twenty years of his professional career, when he designed hydroelectric projects for the Cumberland River in Tennessee, were the most satisfying for him. He was praised as an outstanding engineering manager, noted for his good judgment and compassionate attitude. He was also a devoted husband and father. He died peacefully in his sleep, in his own home and without pain, in his 101st year.

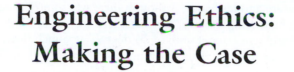

CHAPTER ONE

Engineering Ethics: Making the Case

Main Ideas in This Chapter

- This book focuses on the ethical challenges of engineers as professionals.
- Ethical commitment is central to most accounts of professionalism, including engineering.
- The codes of ethics of professional engineering societies are important resources for studying engineering ethics, but they, too, must be critically evaluated.
- Possible conflicts between professional ethics, personal ethics, and common morality raise important moral questions.
- In addition to concern about preventing disasters and professional misconduct, engineering ethics is also concerned with promoting a better life through the development and use of technology.

"WHY SHOULD I STUDY ETHICS? I am an ethical person." Engineering students often ask this question when the subject of professional ethics is raised, and the short and simple answer to it is not long in coming: "You are not being asked to study ethics in general, but your profession's ethics." Entering into a profession as an ethical person does not mean that one is well prepared for the ethical challenges that may lie ahead. Professional life presents distinctive problems of its own. It is the aim of this book to provide an introduction to many of those problems in an engineering context and to offer constructive suggestions for how they can be thoughtfully addressed.

We begin with three widely discussed stories that illustrate how ethics can come into play in engineering practice.

THE *CHALLENGER* DISASTER

On the night of January 27, 1986, the prelaunch teleconference involving Morton Thiokol and the Marshall Space Flight Center was filled with tension. Morton Thiokol engineers conveyed their recommendation against launching the *Challenger* space shuttle the next morning. This recommendation was based on their worries about the ability of O-rings to seal at low temperatures.

Chief O-ring engineer Roger Boisjoly knew the problems with the O-rings all too well. More than a year earlier he had warned his colleagues of potentially serious problems. The O-rings were part of the sealing mechanism between the segments of the booster rockets. If they lost too much of their resiliency, they could fail to seal properly. The result could be escaping hot gases, ignited fuel in the storage tanks, and a fatal explosion.

The evidence was incomplete but ominous: There appeared to be a correlation between temperature and resiliency. Although there was some leakage around the seal even at relatively high temperatures, the worst leakage was at 53 degrees Fahrenheit. With a predicted ambient temperature of 26 degrees at launch time, the O-rings were estimated to be at 29 degrees. This was much lower than the launch temperatures of any previous flight.

The teleconference was temporarily suspended. The Marshall Space Flight Center had questioned Morton Thiokol's no-launch recommendation, and Morton Thiokol had requested the suspension to allow its engineers and management to reassess their recommendation. There would be no launch without approval from Morton Thiokol, and Morton Thiokol's management would not recommend launching without approval from its managers.

Gerald Mason, senior vice-president at Morton Thiokol, knew that the National Aeronautics and Space Administration (NASA) badly needed a successful flight. He also knew that Morton Thiokol needed a new contract with NASA, and a recommendation against launch probably would not enhance the prospects of obtaining the contract. Finally, Mason was aware that the engineering data were inconclusive. The engineers could not give any firm figures as to the precise temperature at which it would be unsafe to fly. They were relying on the apparent correlation between temperature and resiliency and their tendency to be conservative on serious O-ring safety issues.

The teleconference with the space center would resume shortly, and a decision had to be made. Mason turned to Robert Lund, supervising engineer, and said, "Take off your engineering hat and put on your management hat."[1] The earlier no-launch recommendation was reversed.

Roger Boisjoly was deeply upset by this reversal of the engineers' recommendation. He did not want to be a part of something that could lead to death and destruction. More than this was involved, however. Boisjoly was not only a concerned citizen *but also an engineer*. It was his *professional* engineering judgment that the O-rings were not trustworthy in these conditions. As an engineer, he had an obligation to protect the health and safety of the public, and he evidently believed that this obligation extended to the astronauts. Now his *professional* judgment was being overridden.

Boisjoly also did not believe it was appropriate to take off one's engineering hat in such circumstances. His engineering hat was a source of pride, and it also carried with it certain obligations. He believed that *as an engineer* he had an obligation to render his technical judgment and to protect the safety of the public. So he made one last attempt to defend the no-launch recommendation, pointing out the low-temperature problems to Thiokol management. But his protests against launching were not heeded.

The next day, just 73 seconds into the launch, and witnessed by schoolchildren in their classrooms across the country, the *Challenger* exploded, taking the lives of the six astronauts and schoolteacher Christa McAuliffe. In addition to the tragic loss of human life, the disaster destroyed millions of dollars worth of equipment and severely tarnished NASA's reputation.

Roger Boisjoly failed to prevent the disaster, but he felt he had exercised his professional responsibilities. However, matters did not end there for him. He later testified before the Rogers Commission, which had been appointed by the president to investigate the causes of the accident. There he described the teleconference the night before the launch, as well as his earlier efforts to alert others to the O-ring problems. His testimony earned him the label of "whistleblower," and ultimately resulted in colleagues at Morton Thiokol regarding him as disloyal. Although he was not fired from his job, the aftermath of the disaster took a heavy toll on his physical and psychological well-being. He soon left the company, thus ending his 27-year career as a mechanical engineer in the aerospace industry.[2] He then spent many years as a low paid consultant and lecturer on ethics, visiting colleges, universities, and professional audiences all around the United States.

In 1988 Roger Boisjoly received the American Association for the Advancement of Science (AAAS) Scientific Freedom and Responsibility Award for his exemplary behavior in regard to the *Challenger*.[3] He passed away on February 3, 2012, more than 25 years after the fatal launch of the *Challenger*. His passing was noted in articles in leading newspapers across the country that provided detailed accounts of his memorable role in trying to prevent the disaster.[4]

WATER RESTORATION IN SARAJEVO

In 1993, Frederick Cuny, founder of Dallas's Intertect Relief and Reconstruction Corporation, led a team of associates to Sarajevo, Bosnia, to try to help restore heat and safe water for besieged residents of that war-torn city. When the team arrived, it found that the only source of water for many citizens was a polluted river. Those who took their pails to the edge of the river exposed themselves to sniper fire, which had already killed hundreds of residents.

Preliminary investigation of the scene led the Cuny team to conclude that there must be an inactivated water system somewhere in the city's old town. Fortunately, they discovered a network of old cisterns and channels that could be put back into good working order if a new water-filtration system could be designed and installed. Unfortunately, materials for constructing the filtration system would have to be brought in from outside.

Modules for the system were designed to fit into a C-130 airplane that was flown from Zagreb, the capital of neighboring Croatia, into Sarajevo. The storage area was packed with only three inches to spare on each side. To sneak the modules by checkpoints operated by Bosnian Serbs (Sarajevo's besiegers), the team had to unload the modules in less than 10 minutes. As a result of the Cuny team's efforts, more than 20,000 residents of Sarajevo were provided with a clean, safe source of water.[5]

Frederick Cuny founded Intertect in 1969, at age 27. In the following years, he led disaster relief projects in Bangladesh, Sri Lanka, Lebanon, Guatemala, Armenia, Cambodia, Sudan, Ethiopia, Somalia, Kurdistan, and Chechnya. Regarding his basic approach to disaster relief, Cuny's view was that focusing first on smaller features that one can understand is the key to eventually acquiring a larger picture of what is needed.[6] In Sarajevo, the main problems concerned water and heat, so this is what Cuny and his associates focused on.

In preparing for disaster relief work, Cuny was struck at the outset by the fact that medical professionals and materials are routinely flown to international disasters, but engineers and engineering equipment and supplies are not. Intertect would strive to change this.[7]

HURRICANE KATRINA

In late August 2005, Hurricane Katrina wreaked havoc along the Gulf of Mexico coastline states of Louisiana, Mississippi, and Alabama. Hardest hit was Louisiana, which endured the loss of more than 1000 lives, thousands of homes, damage to residential and nonresidential property of more than $20 billion, and damage to public infrastructure estimated at nearly $7 billion. Most severely damaged was the city of New Orleans, much of which had to be evacuated and which suffered the loss of more than 100,000 jobs.

At the request of the US Army Corps of Engineers (USACE), the American Society of Civil Engineers (ASCE) formed the Hurricane Katrina External Review Panel to review the comprehensive work of USACE's Interagency Performance Evaluation Task Force. The resulting ASCE report, *The New Orleans Hurricane Protection System: What Went Wrong and Why*, is a detailed and forceful statement of the ethical responsibilities of engineers to protect public safety, health, and welfare.[8]

The ASCE report documents engineering failures, organizational and policy failures, and lessons learned for the future. It notes:[9] "What is unique about the devastation that befell the New Orleans area from Hurricane Katrina—compared to other natural disasters—is that much of the destruction was the result of engineering and engineering-related policy failures."

From an engineering standpoint, the panel asserts, there was an overestimation of soil strength that rendered the levees more vulnerable than they should have been, a failure to satisfy standard factors of safety in the original designs of the levees and pumps, and a failure to determine and communicate clearly to the public the level of hurricane risk to which the city and its residents were exposed.

Who should be blamed for these failures and shortcomings? Noting the difficulty of assigning specific blame, the panel chose not to pursue this question. It comments: "No one person or decision is to blame. The engineering failures were complex, and involved numerous decisions by many people with many organizations over a long period of time."[10]

Rather than attempt to assign blame, the panel used the hindsight it acquired to make recommendations about the future. The report identifies a set of critical shifts in thought and action that are needed. The first is that safety should be kept at the forefront of public priorities. This requires preparing for the possibility of future hurricanes rather than allowing experts and citizens alike to become complacent about the relative unlikelihood of something like this happening soon again. Next, clear, quantifiable risk estimates should be made and communicated to the public in ways that enable nonexperts to have a real voice in determining the acceptability or unacceptability of those risks. Additionally, an organized, coherent hurricane protection system is needed, one with strong leadership and management. The report recommends that a high-level, licensed engineer, or a panel of highly qualified, licensed engineers, be appointed with full authority to oversee the system:[11]

> The authority's overarching responsibility will be to keep hurricane-related safety at the forefront of public priorities. The authority will provide leadership, strategic vision, definition of roles and responsibilities, formalized avenues of communication, prioritization of funding, and coordination of critical construction, maintenance, and operations.

The ASCE report urges the upgrading and review of design procedures. It points out that "ASCE has a long-standing policy that recommends independent external peer review of public works projects where performance is critical to public safety, health, and welfare."[12] This is especially so where reliability under emergency conditions is critical, as it clearly was when Hurricane Katrina struck. The effective operation of such an external review process, the panel concludes, could have resulted in a significant reduction in the amount of resulting destruction.

The report's final recommendation is essentially a reminder of our limitations and the ethical importance of placing safety first:[13]

> Although the conditions leading up to the New Orleans catastrophe are unique, the fundamental constraints placed on engineers for any project are not. Every project has funding and/or schedule limitations. Every project must integrate into the natural and man-made environment. Every major project has political ramifications.
>
> In the face of pressure to save money or to make up time, engineers must remain strong and hold true to the requirements of the profession's canon of ethics, never compromising the safety of the public.

The report concludes with an appeal to a broader application of the first Fundamental Canon of ASCE's Code of Ethics. Not only must the commitment to protect public safety, health, and welfare be the guiding principle for the New Orleans hurricane protection system, but also "it must be applied with equal rigor to every aspect of an engineer's work—in New Orleans, in America, and throughout the world."[14]

1.1 INTRODUCTION

These three stories illustrate the importance of engineering knowledge to the lives and well-being of the public and the consequent responsibilities that engineers bear. It is unfortunate that, despite Roger Boisjoly's efforts, the *Challenger* saga had a tragic ending. Sadly, 17 years later, another space shuttle, the *Columbia*, also met with disaster. This time, with the backing of a large number of his engineering colleagues, NASA engineer Rodney Rocha made several attempts to persuade management to ask outside agencies for photos of the damage the *Columbia* sustained when it was launched.[15] He met with firm resistance and reported that one manager said he refused to be a "Chicken Little." Although it is not clear whether the additional information could have been used to save the *Columbia*, it was important that Rocha made the effort.

The examples of Boisjoly and Rocha underline the reality that the advice of engineers is not always heeded. Yet often it is; and, in any case, given their expertise and responsibility for protecting our safety and welfare, it is needed. Boisjoly's advice for young engineers was that, whether or not their advice is accepted, engineers must be prepared to look for problems and report them to others, along with suggestions about how these problems might be addressed. Recalling a time early in his career when he was reluctant to report a problem, Boisjoly says he learned an important lesson from his supervisor. After mustering up the courage to tell him about the problem, Boisjoly was greeted with stern criticism—not for reporting the problem, but for taking so long to do so! The longer one delays, his supervisor told him, the more costly it may be to rectify the problem. Boisjoly's advice to young engineers? Develop the *habit* of looking for and reporting trouble. Also, develop positive relationships with fellow engineers who share that habit, rather than acquiring the reputation of being a "lone ranger."[16]

It is reassuring to hear stories with happier endings, like that of Fred Cuny and his associates in Sarajevo. Their work makes it clear that engineers can play a vital role in protecting and assisting the public, even in dire circumstances. This requires not only basic engineering competence and technical skills, but also imagination, persistence, and a strong sense of responsibility.

Although most engineers will never face situations involving the high drama of the *Challenger* disaster or the restoration of a water system on the battlefront, all engineers will encounter challenging situations that ethically call for reflection, expertise, advice, and good decision making. Also, unlike Roger Boisjoly and Fred Cuny, they will most likely go nameless in the public eye. The ASCE report calls for engineers to help better prepare us for future hurricanes. Many engineers have volunteered their efforts to help victims of Hurricane Katrina and to help restore devastated areas so that they can be safely inhabited. The names of these engineers are not widely known, but their work should be appreciated, not simply taken for granted.

More typical in the lives of everyday engineers are the following fictional, but realistic, cases:

- Engineer Tom Benton is conferring with a vendor who is promoting a certain type of valve for the project Tom's company is working on. Knowing that Tom is an avid golfer, the vendor suggests that they discuss matters further at a private country club that Tom has long wanted an opportunity to play. The vendor is a member and invites Tom to be his guest. Should Tom accept the offer?
- Environmental Engineer Mary Andrews discovers that her plant is discharging a substance into a local river that, although not presently regulated by the government, causes her some concern. She decides to do some reading about the substance and finds that some studies suggest it is a carcinogen. As an engineer, she believes she has an obligation to protect the public, but she also wants to be a loyal employee. Although the substance can be removed, it will likely be somewhat expensive to do so. Her supervisor says, "Forget about it until the government makes us do something. Then all the other plants will have to spend money, too; and we won't be at a competitive disadvantage." What should Mary do?
- Engineer Jim Schmidt has an in-house tool-and-die department that would like to bid on a contract that has been submitted to outside vendors. The in-house manager asks Jim for the quotes from the other vendors so he can underbid them. "After all," the department manager argues, "we are both on the same team. It's better to keep the money inside if we can. You don't have to tell the outsiders what you've done." What should Jim do?

Issues such as these arise in the professional experience of most engineers. However, it is unlikely that they will be brought to the attention of the public. We hope that this book will help students and professional engineers handle such issues more effectively. We believe that a study of professional ethics can do this and that such study should be a part of their professional education.

1.2 ENGINEERING AND ETHICS

What is *engineering*? No doubt it is easier to present examples that involve engineering of one sort or another than it is to define what engineering is. The same is true of *ethics*, and the combination, *engineering ethics*. To illustrate some of the difficulties, consider this characterization, attributed by John D. Kemper and Billy R. Sanders to the Accreditation Board for Engineering and Technology, Inc. (ABET):[17]

> Engineering is the profession in which knowledge of the mathematical and natural sciences gained by study, experience, and practice is applied with judgment to develop ways to utilize, economically, the materials and forces of nature for the benefit of mankind.

This statement has several noteworthy features. First, it quite rightly indicates that engineering has an intimate relation with the mathematical and natural sciences. It somehow employs these sciences in the practical endeavor of developing ways of making human use of the materials and forces of nature. However, second, the phrase "applied with judgment" suggests that this is not simply an algorithmic process. The exercise of *judgment* is needed, and this may allow for alternative ways of making use of the mathematical and natural sciences, and perhaps much else, as well. Kemper and Sanders succinctly put it this way:[18]

> It should be realized that not every aspect of every engineering problem is solved with the use of science and advanced mathematics. Many problems are simply not amenable to scientific solutions, and experienced judgment is used instead. Such would be the case, for example, in problems involving suitability of manufacture, assembly, and maintenance. On the other hand, many engineering projects are impossible to complete without the use of science and advanced mathematics. Some examples are projects dealing with jet aircraft, digital computers, suspension bridges, nuclear reactors, and space satellites.

Third, the engineering projects mentioned by Kemper and Sanders can help us understand connections between engineering and *benefits for humanity*. Jet aircraft, digital computers, suspension bridges, nuclear reactors, and space satellites all provide such benefits—by deliberate design. However, they might also be used for purposes that many would argue are not necessarily beneficial. In fact, some may be deliberately designed to cause serious harm and destruction (e.g., in a military setting). Also, some of these same engineering products may bring serious risks along with promised benefits even when intended to benefit humanity. Jets can crash. Bridges can collapse. Satellites can malfunction with resulting harms, and so on.

These complications help us understand how ethics and engineering are linked. What engineers do has profound effects on human well-being, for good or ill. Engineering also has profound effects on nonhuman life, and on the environment—for humans and nonhumans alike. What engineers *do*, individually or collectively, is one thing. What they *ought* to do may be another. Engineering ethics is concerned with this second question; and, for reasons that will soon become apparent, this can be as complicated and controversial as it is important.

A fourth noteworthy feature of the above characterization of engineering is its emphasis on specialized knowledge, study, and experience. Specialization of this sort is a mark of most professions. The Preamble of the National Society for Professional Engineers' (NSPE) Code of Ethics emphasizes this in framing the ethical responsibilities of engineers:

> Engineering is an important and learned profession. As members of this profession, engineers are expected to exhibit the highest standards of honesty and integrity. Engineering has a direct and vital impact on the quality of life for all people. Accordingly, the services provided by engineers require honesty, impartiality, fairness, and equity, and must be

dedicated to the protection of the public health, safety, and welfare. Engineers must perform under a standard of professional behavior that requires adherence to the highest principles of ethical conduct.

The NSPE Preamble is a *normative* statement regarding what is ethically required of engineers, not merely a statement that describes what they, in fact, do. The basis for these ethical requirements is engineering's "direct and vital impact on the quality of life for all people." That what engineers do, individually and collectively, has this impact is a factual claim. What responsibilities go with this, and what is required of engineers in fulfilling them, is the concern of engineering ethics.

The Preamble's opening sentence stresses not only that engineering is an important profession (given its "direct and vital impact" on our lives), but it is also a learned one. This lines up nicely with the idea that specialized knowledge, study, and experience are necessary for good engineering. As William F. May notes, a consequence of the increasing role of the professions in society is what he calls a "knowledge explosion."[19] However, much of this knowledge is highly specialized and, therefore, not widely shared. Even within engineering, those with different expertise may find it difficult, if not impossible, to "talk shop" in any depth. So, May concludes, the "knowledge explosion" that goes with our increased reliance on the professions is accompanied by an "ignorance explosion"—an ignorance that virtually everyone else has of the specialized knowledge possessed by those in this or that area of expertise.

May concludes: "[Professionals] had better be virtuous. Few may be in a position to discredit [them]. The knowledge explosion is also an ignorance explosion; if knowledge is power, then ignorance is powerlessness."[20] In some instances the shortcomings of an engineer or group of engineers may be quite obvious even to those who lack special engineering expertise. However, more typically, problems may surface only years after the mistakes or events leading to failures have occurred. By then, not only is the damage done, it may be difficult to determine who should be held accountable, and for precisely what. The fact that most engineers work in large organizations makes such determinations all the more difficult.

Given this, not only in engineering, but in the professions generally, May adds: "One test of character and virtue is what a person does when no one is watching. A society that rests on expertise needs more people who can pass that test."[21] It is clear that, the more we must rely on engineers doing their work well when no one is watching, the more we must place our trust in the competence and integrity of engineers. So it is not surprising that the Preamble to the NSPE Code of Ethics stresses the importance of honesty and integrity for engineers. Nor, given the impact engineering has on society, should it be surprising to see the Preamble emphasize the importance of engineers attending to public safety, health, and welfare.

However, this emphasis on public safety, health, and welfare has not always been found in engineering societies' codes of ethics. In fact, prior to 1970, most engineering codes listed engineers' first responsibility to be fidelity to their employers or clients. No explicit mention of responsibilities to the public could be found. However, for a variety of reasons, the 1970s were marked by increased public attention to ethical issues in science, engineering, medicine, and business. For example, the Environmental Protection Agency (EPA), the Occupational Safety and Health Administration (OSHA), and the Belmont Report (regarding the use of human subjects in experimentation) all emerged during this period.

1.3   GETTING STARTED

Early efforts in teaching engineering ethics made heavy use of case studies, typically depicting actual events that had received significant media coverage. A list of names familiar to engineers and nonengineers alike was available to generate initial interest: Corvair, Pinto, DC-10, Three-Mile Island, *Challenger*, Chernobyl…. Unfortunately, each of these names is associated with disasters or alleged wrongdoing of one sort or another, suggesting that the subject of engineering ethics is primarily concerned with allegations of fault, irresponsibility, and blame—or defenses against such charges.

Nearly exclusive concentration on such "big news/bad news" stories raises two worries. The first is that students might unwittingly be encouraged to conclude that ethics in engineering is only about the "newsworthy," in which case they might also conclude that they have little to worry about, as it is very unlikely that any of them will ever find themselves featured in the media, at least not for their engineering work. Like the vast majority of engineers, they will remain unnamed and unnoticed by the public in general, and the media in particular. The second is that they might be misled into thinking that engineering ethics is mainly about the negative—bad things happening, wrongdoing, or, shifting slightly to the positive, avoiding wrongdoing.

A remedy for the first worry is to present cases that are not newsworthy in the "big news" sense, but which are, nevertheless, ethically significant—such as having one's judgment compromised by accepting a gift from a vendor. However, at best this takes care of only half of the worry—the "big news" part. Cases still may dwell on the negative—only on a smaller scale.

A remedy for this second worry is to present a fair sampling of positive cases, as well—whether "big news" or not. Here it is helpful to remind ourselves that wrongdoing has a contrary. We seem not to have a word, "rightdoing," which might be contrasted with "wrongdoing."

However, we do have a number of notions that can be contrasted with wrongdoing. We might think of a spectrum of responsibility, ranging from the clearly irresponsible to the exemplary. On such a spectrum, we can find, at one end, cases that are clear instances of wrongdoing. At the other end, we can find cases that go well beyond what can reasonably be expected as a matter of duty or obligation—the supererogatory. In between we find cases of ordinary, competent, and responsible engineering work that can be expected as a matter of professional duty or obligation.

One way to begin to appreciate the positive side of engineering from an ethical point of view is to consider the larger impact that engineering has had on society. In 2000 the National Academy of Engineers (NAE) attempted to identify the 20 greatest engineering achievements of the twentieth century. Here is the list that evolved:[22]

- electrification
- the automobile
- the airplane
- water supply and distribution
- electronics (vacuum tubes, transistors, etc.)
- radio and television
- agricultural mechanization
- computers
- telephones

- air conditioning and refrigeration
- highways
- spacecraft
- the Internet
- imaging (especially in medicine)
- household appliances
- health technologies
- petroleum and petroleum technologies
- laser and fiber optics
- nuclear technologies
- high-performance materials

Of course, these innovations, whatever benefits they may have brought, also carry with them risks of harm, if not actual harms. So, for such innovations to be successful, both in the laboratory and in the public domain, acceptance of a high degree of responsibility on the part of engineers is necessary.

Bearing these accomplishments (and their accompanying risks) in mind, we can see why the opening words of the Preamble to the NSPE Code of Ethics are fitting. They place large responsibilities for public health, safety, and welfare in the hands of engineers, both collectively and individually. That honesty and integrity are central values in this regard can be seen if one considers the possible consequences of a licensed, professional engineer putting a seal of approval on a construction project without regard to whether or not it actually satisfies relevant building standards. Furthermore, those who do provide their seal of approval need to rely to at least some extent on the honesty and integrity of those whose work they monitor or supervise. Even aggressive monitoring and supervising cannot entail watching every move of those on whom the success of a project depends. Much engineering work is done in teams, composed of members who must trust each other, just as different teams on complex projects must trust each other.

So, taking into account both positive and negative aspects of engineering ethics, what are some of the leading areas of ethical concern? Here is a list (not necessarily complete) of possible topics:

- engineering design (ethical as well as technical and economic factors)
- safety, risk, and liability (both moral and legal)
- the need for trust, reliability, honesty in engineering work and communication
- conflicts of interest
- ownership of ideas (copyright, trade secrets, patents, taking your knowledge with you)
- confidentiality
- communication with managers, clients, public
- barriers to responsibility (self-interest, fear, ignorance, microscopic vision, groupthink)
- engineers in organizations (manager/engineer relations, protest, whistleblowing, loyalty)
- environmental concerns
- engineers in an international setting (different needs, laws, practices, and expectations)
- laws, regulations, standards, and ethics
- professional and personal ethics

- working with others
- acknowledging mistakes
- career choice
- roles and responsibilities of engineering societies
- public service (pro bono, disaster relief, policy advisory roles, expert witnessing)
- discrimination in the workplace (women, minorities)
- codes of ethics

1.4   CODES OF ETHICS

The last item on the list of areas of ethical concern, codes of ethics, has been the subject of some controversy. Engineering codes of ethics are products of the deliberations of members of professional societies such as the National Society for Professional Engineers, the American Society of Civil Engineers, the American Institute of Chemical Engineers, the American Society of Mechanical Engineers, the Institute for Electrical and Electronics Engineers, and so on. One concern is that only a relatively small percentage of practicing engineers actually belong to any professional society for engineers. Membership in such a professional organization is not a requirement for practice. Should the codes be regarded as addressed only to those who are members of their respective societies? If so, then what should be said about ethics in regard to nonmember engineers?

The first thing that should be said is that the prescriptions and guidelines typically found in engineering codes of ethics are grounded in concepts and principles of ordinary morality that are not the creation of a select group of professionals. The code provisions are the result of the deliberations of engineers trying to articulate the ethical dimensions of engineering practice of, say, civil, mechanical, or electrical engineers—regardless of whether the practitioners are members of the special societies in question. This is reflected both in the Preamble of NSPE's code and in the large number of professional society codes that are patterned after the NSPE code.

So, for example, the NSPE code holds that all engineers, whether NSPE members or not, ought to hold public health, safety, and welfare paramount—not because the code says so, but because of what engineers do, regardless of whether they are members of NSPE. Affirming the NSPE code by becoming a member may provide an additional reason for satisfying its requirements (a promise or commitment made), but there are reasons for accepting these requirements even without having made an explicit promise or commitment to abide by them, assuming the code is well thought out. Of course, codes of ethics do change through time. NSPE's Board of Ethical Review acknowledges that, not only does this happen, but that it should when there is good reason to change. As already noted, the provision that there is a paramount duty to protect public health, safety, and welfare was introduced to most codes only in the early 1970s. However, it does not follow that the codes thereby created, or established, that duty. Another way of regarding this is that the codes expressed a commitment to an already existing duty. (In fact, in the 1920s the American Association of Engineers had such a provision in its code, but it disappeared when AAE itself dissolved in the late 1920s.)

Much of engineering ethics focuses on the responsibilities and performance of individual engineers. There is much to discuss at this level. There are, however, other levels that warrant attention. Engineers commonly work in groups. This raises questions about how engineers should work with others on common projects. Here individual responsibility may best be understood in terms of one's role within a larger unit. As an individual, an engineer may envisage his or her problems exclusively as his or hers, even in relation to the larger group. However, it is also possible, and often desirable, to view engineering problems as "ours," rather than simply "mine" or "yours." This not only calls for joint endeavor but perhaps also for compromise (not, "my way or no way"). This, in turn, raises the question of how much (and what kinds of) compromising is compatible with maintaining one's own integrity as an individual. In the case of design, one may need to support a design that would not be one's first choice if the choice were left up to him or her. However, success on the project requires cooperation, not stubborn resistance. Teams, in turn, may need to work with, and compromise with, other teams (other engineering teams, managerial teams, or other units in the organization).

Another level that warrants careful consideration is the professional society to which an engineer may (or should) belong. Historically, engineering societies have played fundamental roles in establishing standards of acceptable design and practice. The American Society of Mechanical Engineers, for example, played a leading role in developing uniform standards in the boiler industry, in response to disastrous explosions of boilers due to inadequate safety standards. However, this can also give rise to ethical problems, as it did in the famous *Hydrolevel v. ASME* legal case that went all the way to the US Supreme Court. The Court found against ASME for failing to guard itself against conflicts of interest interfering with fair trade in the boiler industry. So even efforts to protect public health and safety can involve a professional society in ethical difficulties (and costly litigation).

The recent involvement of the American Society of Civil Engineers in the aftermath of Hurricane Katrina is a much more positive story. At the request of the US Army Corp of Engineers, ASCE formed the Hurricane Katrina External Review Panel to assess the causes of the destruction wreaked by Hurricane Katrina in 2005, and to recommend future actions that might be taken to deal more effectively with future hurricanes. As we have noted above, the resulting ASCE report, *The New Orleans Hurricane Protection System: What Went Wrong and Why*, makes a strong set of recommendations that pivot around engineers' responsibility to protect public safety, health, and welfare. These recommendations range from the replacement of what they found to be a woefully inadequate hurricane protection system with a well-organized, coordinated one to the refusal to compromise public safety, health, and welfare.

1.5   ENGINEERING AS A PROFESSION

Engineers, like doctors, lawyers, accountants, and others whose competent work requires special knowledge and expertise typically regard themselves as professionals. Historically, the term "profession" has referred to a free act of commitment to a way of life. When associated with the monastic vows of a religious order, it referred to a monk's public promise to enter a distinct way of life with allegiance to high moral ideals. One "professes" to be a certain type of person and to occupy a special social role that carries with it stringent moral requirements. By the late seventeenth century, the term had been secularized to refer to those who professed to be duly qualified.

Thus, "profession" once meant, according to the *Oxford Shorter Dictionary*, the act or fact of professing. It has come to mean "the occupation which one professes to be skilled in and to follow ... A vocation in which professed knowledge of some branch of learning is used in its application to the affairs of others or in the practice of an art based upon it." If we focus on this definition's characterization of a profession as an occupation, it is evident that a profession provides its members with a means of livelihood.

At the same time, as philosopher Michael Davis points out, a profession openly commits itself to high moral standards. Davis offers this as a definition of "profession":

> A profession is a number of individuals in the same occupation voluntarily organized to earn a living by openly serving a moral ideal in a morally permissible way beyond what law, market, morality, and public opinion would otherwise require.[23]

To this we would add two other features that most professions, including engineering, exemplify. First, entrance into these professions typically requires an extensive period of training, and much of this training is of an intellectual character. The requisite knowledge and skills are grounded in a body of theory. This theoretical base is obtained through formal education, usually in an academic institution. Today, most professionals have at least a bachelor's degree in an appropriate discipline from a college or university, and many professions require advanced degrees, which are often conferred by a professional school.

Second, professions like engineering possess knowledge and skills that are vital to the well-being of the larger society. A society that has a sophisticated scientific and technological base is especially dependent on its professional elite. We rely on the knowledge possessed by physicians to protect us from disease and restore us to health. The lawyer has knowledge vital to our welfare if we have been sued or accused of a crime, if our business has been forced into bankruptcy, or if we want to get a divorce or buy a house. The accountant's knowledge is also important for our business successes or when we have to file our tax returns. Likewise, we are dependent on the knowledge and research of scientists and engineers for our safety in an airplane, for many of the technological advances on which our material civilization rests, and for national defense.

Combining these two considerations with Davis's definition highlights several features that are important in the concept of a profession that can be applied to engineering, medicine, dentistry, law, accountancy, social work, and other standard professions:

1. A profession cannot be composed of only one person. It is always composed of a number of individuals.
2. A profession involves a public element. One must openly "profess" to be a physician or attorney, much as the dictionary accounts of the term "profession" suggests.
3. A profession is a way people earn a living and is usually something that occupies them during their working hours. A profession is still an occupation (a way of earning a living), even if the occupation enjoys professional status.
4. A profession is something that people enter into voluntarily and that they can leave voluntarily.
5. A profession commits itself to some morally desirable goal, although this goal may not be unique to a given profession. Physicians are committed to curing the sick and comforting the dying. Lawyers help people obtain justice within the law. Engineers protect public health, safety, and welfare.

6. Professionals are expected to pursue morally desirable goals by morally permissible means. For example, medicine cannot pursue the goal of health by cruel experimentation, deception, or coercion.

7. Professional standards should obligate professionals to act in ways that go beyond what law, market, morality, and public opinion would otherwise require. Physicians have a special obligation to help people (their patients) be healthy that nonphysicians do not, attorneys have a special obligation to help people (their clients) achieve justice that the rest of us do not, and engineers have a special obligation to protect the public from harms that the rest of us do not.

It should be borne in mind that it is common for professionals, and especially engineers, to be employed by corporations and other large organizations. Employers and fellow employees also have legitimate expectations of those who work for these organizations, quite apart from the moral requirements that come with an employee's professional status. Furthermore, professionals are sometimes subjected to considerable pressure to act in ways that are inconsistent with the standards of their profession, or that conflict with the moral aspirations they might have as professionals. How professionals should deal with such challenges is also a significant part of professional ethics in general, and engineering ethics in particular.

1.6 ETHICS: PROHIBITIVE, PREVENTIVE, AND ASPIRATIONAL

Understandably, much of ethics focuses on what one should *not* do, rather than on what one should do. This can be regarded as an ethics of *prohibitions*. Engineering codes of ethics exemplify this. Much of their content specifies rules that state prohibitions. For example, by one way of counting, 80 percent of the code of the National Society of Professional Engineers (NSPE) consists of provisions that are, either explicitly or implicitly, prohibitive in character. For example, "II. Rules of Practice," 1.c, states that "engineers shall not reveal facts, data, or information without the prior consent of the client or employer except as authorized by law or this Code." Although this provision seems to *permit* (as distinct from *require*) engineers to reveal facts, data, or information under some circumstances, its main intent seems clearly to be prohibitive.

Section II.1.b states that "engineers shall approve only those engineering documents that are in conformity with applicable standards." In other words, engineers shall *not* approve engineering documents that are *not* in conformity with applicable standards. This is not the same as saying that engineers *shall* approve engineering documents that are in conformity with applicable standards. Presumably, there are other criteria that would need to be satisfied for approval of an engineering document to be *required*. Section 1.b is silent about what those criteria might be. It restricts itself to a statement that specifies one of the criteria for *not* approving an engineering document.

Many provisions that are not stated in a negative form nevertheless are essentially prohibitive. The rule having to do with undisclosed conflicts of interest states: "Engineers shall disclose all known or potential conflicts of interest that could influence or appear to influence their judgment or the quality of their services." This could be restated as a prohibition against nondisclosure of known or potential conflicts of interest.

Many other provisions of the code, such as the requirement that engineers notify the appropriate professional bodies or public authorities of code violations (II.1.f), are "policing" provisions and thus essentially prohibitive in character. Even the requirement that engineers be "objective and truthful" (II.3.a) is another way of stating that engineers shall not be biased and deceitful in their professional judgments. Similarly, the provision that engineers continue their professional development (III.9.e) is another way of stating that engineers shall not neglect their professional development.

It is easy to think of several good reasons for the NSPE code's prohibitive tone. First, it makes good sense to support the idea that a first duty of moral agents, including professionals, is not to harm others—not to murder, lie, cheat, or steal, for example. Before engineers attempt to do good, they need to realize they have a responsibility not to harm others. Second, the codes are largely formulated in terms of rules that can be enforced, and it is easier to enforce rules that specify what is prohibited than rules that require, or at least encourage, more open-ended objectives. The specificity of a rule that states "avoid undisclosed conflicts of interest" is relatively easy to enforce, at least in comparison to the more open-ended requirement that engineers are to "hold paramount the welfare of the public." It is noteworthy that, insofar as this latter requirement is given more specific renderings, it is in regard to what one should do when observing others *violating* the requirement. Beyond this, there are no suggestions about what more directly and positively might contribute to holding public safety, health, and welfare paramount.

However, provision III.9.e, that engineers are to continue their professional development, does offer some promise of shading into the positive. As already noted, it could be taken simply as another way of stating that engineers are not to neglect their professional development. But trying to advance one's professional development would seemingly require attending positively to acquiring new knowledge and skills that can be put into engineering practice. This, in turn, can be seen as an invitation for engineers to reflect in more positive terms on what they think it is important or desirable to aspire to as an engineer.

Provision II.3.a and other provisions requiring engineers to be truthful and objective in their reports and representation of data can also be given a positive interpretation if one reflects on why these requirements are so important for reliable engineering, especially where risk and safety are involved.

One way to think of engineering ethics in more positive terms is to regard it to be concerned not only with *prohibiting* wrongdoing but also with *preventing* undesirable things from happening. *Preventive ethics*, as we shall call it, includes ethical prohibitions, but it can be compared favorably with the notion of preventive medicine. By attending carefully to our health needs before we become seriously ill, we may prevent such illnesses from occurring, or at least significantly reduce their likelihood or their seriousness. Similarly, by anticipating the sorts of ethical problems that could become quite serious if left unanticipated or unattended, we may prevent their occurrence or minimize their seriousness.

This requires the exercise of moral imagination before matters have already taken an unfortunate turn. One of the managers interviewed in Barbara Toffler's *Tough Choices* explains how he tries to anticipate ethical challenges:[24]

I first play out the scenario of what would happen if I did it one way and what would happen if I did it the other way. What would be the followup? What would be the next move? What would be the response back and what would be the consequences? That's the only way you can tell if you're going to make the right move or not because I think something that instinctively may feel right or wrong, if you analyze it, may not pan out that way.

Like managers, engineers are well advised to engage in such imaginative exercises. To minimize the chances of being taken by surprise (and disappointment or regret), engineers must imagine possible alternatives and their likely consequences.

It should be noted that many of the provisions under "III. Professional Obligations," actually do have a more positive tone. This is especially true of III.2: "Engineers shall at all times strive to serve the public interest." Illustrations provided include participation in civic affairs, "work for the advancement of the safety, health, and well-being of their community," and adherence to principles of sustainable development.

Despite the NSPE code's heavy emphasis on prohibitions, the significance of less enforceable, positive provisions should not be underestimated. Ethics is not necessarily lawlike, and it does not depend on enforceability for its importance. Furthermore, it should not be expected that a professional code of ethics will capture all that individual members of a profession care about morally as professionals. The NSPE code, for example, expresses what might be thought of as the highest shared ethical standards among engineers. Many engineers, however, embrace professional standards and goals for themselves that are not necessarily shared by all engineers. We will refer to this more personal side of engineering ethics as *aspirational ethics*.

Focusing on this aspirational face of engineering ethics reveals the limitations of exclusively prohibitive and preventive approaches to professional ethics. One of the limitations is the relative absence of a positive motivational dimension. Engineers do not choose engineering as a career in order to avoid professional misconduct, or even to help prevent bad things from happening. To be sure, many engineering students desire the financial rewards and social position that an engineering career promises, and there is nothing wrong with this. We have found, however, that engineering students are also attracted by the prospect of making a difference in the world, and doing so in a positive way. They are excited by projects that alleviate human drudgery through labor-saving devices, eliminate or reduce disease by providing clean water and sanitation, develop new medical devices that save lives, create automobiles that run on less fuel or on alternative sources of energy that are less polluting than fossil fuels, help reduce environmental damage with recyclable products and, in general, develop useful, sustainable ways of addressing our problems. In short, they are moved by the idea that what they will be doing may improve the quality of human life and the environment around them.

Although, as we have noted, this more positive aspect of engineering is recognized to some extent in engineering codes of ethics, nevertheless, the positive face of engineering ethics has taken second place to the more prohibitive face in most engineering ethics textbooks, including earlier editions of this one.

In addition to us, several other writers on engineering ethics have come to advocate an increased emphasis on the more positive and welfare-promoting aspects of engineering. Mike Martin, coauthor (with Roland Schinzinger) of an important textbook in engineering ethics, opens his *Meaningful Work* with the following statement:

> Personal commitments motivate, guide and give meaning to the work of professionals. Yet these commitments have yet to receive the attention they deserve in thinking about professional ethics…. I seek to widen professional ethics to include personal commitment, especially commitment to ideals not mandatory for all members of a profession.[25]

Personal commitments to ideals, Martin believes, can add an important new and positive dimension to engineering ethics.

P. Aarne Vesilind, engineer and writer on engineering ethics, has edited the book *Peace Engineering: When Personal Values and Engineering Careers Converge*. One of the essays, by Robert Textor, discusses peace in terms of global environmental management, sustainable development, seeking greater economic justice, making efforts to reduce the production and use of weapons, and fostering awareness of cultural differences.[26] Although engineering students may not share all of Textor's peace agenda, there may be many whose personal values incline them to seek engineering employment that could enable them to support some, if not all, of these concerns.

Promoting the welfare of the public can be done in many different ways, ranging from designing a new energy-saving device in the course of one's ordinary employment to using one's vacation time to design and help install a water purification system in an underdeveloped country. These are instances of engineering practice that go well beyond what others would say is professionally required, regardless of the self-assessment of the engineers(s) in question. In his special efforts to stop the fatal launch of the *Challenger* space shuttle in 1986, engineer Roger Boisjoly thought of what he did as a part of his job responsibilities. However, his admirers would probably see him as approaching his work with a level of conscientiousness and dedication above and beyond what anyone could reasonably demand of him. This also extends to his openness with the Rogers Commission that investigated the launch. His criticisms of what took place the night before the launch (and of what did *not* happen more than a year earlier when he first issued his concerns about the now infamous O-rings in the shuttle) were regarded by many of his colleagues and members of his community as company disloyalty. This required considerable courage on his part, and a willingness to face the censure and ostracism by those who strongly disapproved of his actions, including many other engineers. Even knowing that his revelations would be severely rebuked by many, Boisjoly felt that, as a responsible engineer, he should not remain silent on these matters.

A less controversial example is that of the chief design engineer in a small firm that specializes in safety belts for window washers who clean the windows of high-rise buildings. This requires going up and down the sides of buildings on scaffolding. While interviewing employees at this small firm, one of the authors of this book was told that the chief design engineer sometimes worked weekends on his own time trying to improve the design of the company's belt. He did this even though the belt was more than adequately meeting the safety standards for such belts, and it was selling very well.

Asked why he kept working on the design, he replied, "People are still getting hurt and even dying." How does this happen? He explained that, although required by law to wear belts when working on the scaffolding, some take them off when no one is looking. They do this, he said, to gain more freedom of movement. The belt was constraining them from raising or lowering the scaffolding as quickly as they would like.

Asked whether he thought that responsibility for the accidents falls on the workers who take off their belts, the engineer agreed. But, he added, "You just do the best you can, and that's usually not good enough." Although not denying that the company's current belt was a good one, he was convinced that a better one is possible; and he was determined to come up with a better design. Improving the belt was no longer a part of the chief engineer's official job responsibilities, but this did not discourage him from finding his own time to work on this project.

A third example is air bag pioneer Carl Clark's effort, even after retirement, to develop air bags for car bumpers and wearable air bags for the elderly to prevent broken hips. Much of this work was done on his own time, without pay. In the end, bumper air bags were even patented by someone else.[27]

Frederick C. Cuny's rescue efforts in Sarajevo have already been mentioned. But his disaster relief work extends far beyond this. Cuny had attended engineering school, but due to poor grades he never received his degree in engineering. In his early twenties, however, he learned how to conduct disaster relief work in such a way that the victims could recover enough to help themselves. Shortly after founding Interact Relief, he went to Biafra to help organize an airlift to rescue Biafrans after a devastating war. Later, he organized relief efforts involving engineering work in Bosnia after the war and in Iraq after Operation Desert Storm. When Cuny's work in Iraq was completed, the Kurds held a farewell celebration. He was the only civilian in a parade with the marines with whom he had worked.[28]

However, it would be a mistake to focus only on the efforts of individual engineers. For example, a group of General Electric engineers on their own time in the late 1930s developed the sealed beam headlight, which greatly reduced the number of accidents caused by night driving. There was considerable doubt as to whether the headlight could be developed, but the engineers persisted and finally achieved success.[29]

Finally, consider Engineers Without Borders, an international organization for engineering professionals and engineering students who want to use their expertise to promote human welfare. For example, engineering students from the University of Arizona chapter elected to work on a water supply and purification project in the village of Mafi Zongo, Ghana, West Africa. The project's aim was to supply 30 or more villages, with approximately 10,000 people, with safe drinking water. In another project, engineering students from the University of Colorado installed a water system in Muramka, a Rwandan village. The system provides villagers with up to 7000 liters of safe water for everyday use. It consists of a gravity-fed settling tank, rapid sand filters, and a solar-powered sanitation light.[30] The many Engineers Without Borders websites at colleges and universities around the world feature a wide range of projects aimed at providing technical and engineering assistance to impoverished areas.

1.7 ASPIRATIONAL ETHICS AND PROFESSIONAL CHARACTER: THE GOOD ENGINEER

Two features of a more aspirational approach to ethics are of special importance. First, as Mike Martin notes, this more positive approach to engineering ethics has an important *motivational* aspect (that of doing good) that is not necessarily present in an ethical perspective that focuses primarily on prohibitions and avoiding wrongdoing. Second, as Martin also suggests, there is a *discretionary* element in aspirational ethics. Engineers may have a considerable range of freedom in how they promote public welfare.

Neither of these two features can be conveyed very well in rules that specify a required course of action. "Hold paramount public welfare" is an important positive moral prescription for engineers, but it gives little direction for conduct. It does not tell engineers whether to devote time to Engineers Without Borders, or to some special projects on which they are willing to work on their own time, or to simply designing a product that is more energy efficient. These decisions are best left to engineers to decide for themselves, given their interests, abilities, commitments, and what is possible for them in their own situations.

For this reason, we suggest that the more appropriate vocabulary for talking about aspirational ethics is that of professional character rather than the vocabulary of rules. Rules are appropriate for prohibitions such as "Don't violate confidentiality." Rules are less appropriate for capturing and stimulating motivation to do good. Here the most relevant question is not "What kinds of rules are important in directing the more positive and aspirational elements of engineering work?" Rather, the question is "What types of persons, professionally speaking, will be the most likely to promote the welfare of the public through their engineering work?"

We will use the expression *professional character* to refer to those character traits that serve to define the kind of person one is, professionally speaking. Good engineers are those who have those traits of professional character that make them the best, or ideal, engineers. Here we suggest three such traits, without implying that this is by any means an exhaustive list. The first is professional pride, particularly in one's technical expertise. If engineers want their work to contribute to public welfare, they must make sure that their professional competence is at the highest possible level. This competence includes not only the obvious proficiencies in mathematics, physics, and engineering science but also those abilities and sensitivities that only come with a certain level of practical experience.

The second character trait is social awareness and concern, which is an awareness of and concern for the ways in which technology both affects and is affected by the larger social environment within which engineers work. In other words, engineers need to be alert to what we call in Chapter 4 the "social embeddedness" of technology. Engineers as well as the rest of us are sometimes tempted to view technology as isolated from the larger social context. In the extreme version of this view, technology is seen as governed by considerations internal to technology itself and as neither influencing, nor influenced by, social forces and institutions. In a less extreme view, technology powerfully influences social institutions and forces, but there is little, if any, causal effect in the other direction. However, engineers who are sufficiently aware of the social dimensions of technology understand that there are causal influences in both directions. In any case, engineers are often called on to make design decisions that are not socially neutral. This often requires sensitivities and commitments that cannot be incorporated into rules.

A third professional character trait that can support aspirational ethics is an environmental conscientiousness. Later in this book, we explore this issue more thoroughly, but here it need only be said that the authors believe that environmental issues will increasingly play a crucial role in almost all aspects of engineering. Increasingly, human welfare will be seen as integral to preserving the integrity of the natural environment that supports human and all other forms of life. Eventually, we believe, being environmentally conscious will be recognized as an important element in professional engineering character.

1.8 CASES, CASES, CASES

In this book, we frequently present and discuss cases in engineering ethics. These cases will often be about actual events involving engineers. Sometimes they will be fictional but, we hope, realistic. The importance of cases cannot be overemphasized, and they serve several important functions. First, it is through the study of cases that we learn to recognize the presence of ethical problems, even in situations in which we might have thought there are only technical issues. Second, it is by studying cases that we can most easily develop the abilities necessary to engage in constructive ethical analysis. Cases stimulate the moral imagination by challenging us to anticipate the possible alternatives for resolving them and to think about the consequences of those alternatives. Third, a study of cases is the most effective way to understand that the codes cannot provide ready-made answers to many moral questions that professional engineering practice generates and that individual engineers must become responsible agents in moral deliberation. They must both interpret the codes they have and, when desirable, consider how the codes should be revised. Fourth, the study of cases shows us that there may be some irresolvable uncertainties in ethical analysis and that in some situations rational and responsible professionals may disagree about what is right.

Each chapter is introduced with a case, which is usually referred to in the chapter. In many chapters, we present our own attempts to resolve ethical problems. We often use brief cases to illustrate various points in our argument.

Cases are of several types. Some focus on micro-level issues about the practice of individual engineers, whereas others focus more on macro-level issues related to matters of social policy and concern regarding technology.[31] Sometimes cases are simplified to focus on a particular point, but simplification risks distortion. Ideally, most cases would be given an extended rather than abbreviated description, but this is not possible here. Many extended descriptions of individual cases require a book-length account.

Two final points are important with regard to the use of cases. First, the use of cases is especially appropriate in a text on professional ethics. A medical school dean known to one of the authors once said, "Physicians are tied to the post of use." By this he presumably meant that physicians do not have the luxury of thinking indefinitely about moral problems. They must make decisions about what treatment to administer or what advice to give in a specific case.

Engineers, like other professionals, are also tied to the post of use. They must make decisions about particular designs that will affect the lives and financial well-being of many people, give professional advice to individual managers and clients, make decisions about particular purchases, decide whether to protest a decision by a manager, and take other specific actions that have important consequences for themselves and others. Engineers, like other professionals, are case oriented. They focus on the specific in making engineering decisions. The study of cases helps students understand that professional ethics is not simply an irrelevant addition to professional education but, rather, is intimately related to the practice of engineering.

Second, the study of cases is especially valuable for engineers who may move into management positions. Cases have long been at the center of management education. Many, if not most, of the issues faced by managers have ethical dimensions. Some of the methods for resolving ethical problems discussed in Chapter 2—especially finding what we call a "creative middle way" solution—have much in common with the methods employed by managers. Like engineers, managers must make decisions within constraints, and they usually try to make decisions that satisfy as many of these constraints as possible. The kind of creative problem solving necessary to make such decisions is very similar to the deliberation that is helpful in resolving many ethical problems.

1.9   CHAPTER SUMMARY

The study of engineering ethics focuses on engineers as professionals. As such, it should be distinguished from personal and social ethics outside the context of engineering practice. The codes of ethics of professional engineering societies provide a useful framework for addressing many of the ethical issues that arise in engineering. However, these codes can be expected to change through time. Earlier codes emphasized engineers' primary duties to their employers and clients. However, by the 1970s, most codes insisted that the first duty of engineers is to protect public safety, health, and welfare. More recently, many codes have begun emphasizing the importance of sustainable technology and protecting the environment.

As a profession, engineering can be expected to commit to morally desirable goals, pursued in morally acceptable ways. The public, employers, and clients depend on the responsible use of engineering expertise. Although the study of engineering ethics can be expected to concentrate much of its attention on wrongdoing and its prevention, it also should be concerned with the positive promotion of good. That is, engineering's more aspirational side should be emphasized as well.

The use of cases is an important aspect of developing sensitivity to, and skills in dealing with, significant ethical issues in engineering. Therefore, readers can expect to be invited to reflect on both actual and fictional cases throughout this text, including the special section, **Cases**, near the end of the book.

1.10   ENGINEERING ETHICS ON THE WEB

Check your understanding of the material in this chapter by visiting the companion website for *Engineering Ethics*. The site includes multiple choice study questions, suggested discussion topics, and sometimes additional case studies to complement your reading and study of the material in this chapter.

NOTES

1. Rogers Commission, *Report to the President by the Presidential Commission on the Space Shuttle Challenger Accident*, June 6, 1986 (Washington, DC), pp. 772–773.
2. For Roger Boisjoly's own account of the *Challenger* disaster, see his "The *Challenger* Disaster: Moral Responsibility and the Working Engineer," in Deborah Johnson, ed., *Ethical Issues in Engineering* (Englewood Cliffs, NJ: Prentice-Hall, 1991), pp. 6–14. After the disaster, Boisjoly spent several years giving talks at colleges, universities, and professional meetings across the United States discussing both the circumstances leading to the disaster and the ethical responsibilities of engineers, as well as how they might best be met. Much more on Roger Boisjoly can be found in the Moral Leaders section of the Online Ethics Center for Engineering and Science at http://onlineethics.org.

3. http://archives.aaas.org/inc/wrappers_new/archives_top.inc.

4. Confident that much of the general public would readily recall the fate of the *Challenger* and the role played by Roger Boisjoly, typical accounts carried titles like Douglas Martin's *New York Times* memorial, "Roger Boisjoly, 73, Dies; Warned of Shuttle Danger," (February 3, 2012). Martin reminded readers of the infamous memo Boisjoly sent to Thiokol officials months before the launch (warning that launching in unusually cold Florida weather could result in "a catastrophe of the highest order, loss of human life"). Martin noted although Boisjoly was "hailed for his [whistleblowing] by many, he was also made to suffer for it."

5. The above account is based on C. Sudetic, "Small Miracle in a Siege: Safe Water for Sarajevo," *The New York Times*, Jan. 10, 1994, pp. A1, A7. For further discussion of the work and life of Cuny, see our case, "Disaster Relief," in the Cases section of this text. See, also, the Moral Leaders section of the Online Ethics Center for Engineering and Science at http://onlineethics.org.

6. "The Talk of the Town," *The New Yorker*, 69:39, Nov. 22, 1993, pp. 45–6.

7. Ibid.

8. ASCE Hurricane Katrina External Review Panel, *The New Orleans Hurricane Protection System: What Went Wrong and Why* (Reston, VA: American Society of Civil Engineers, 2007). Available at http://www.asce.org/static/hurricane/crp.cfm.

9. Ibid., p. 47.

10. Ibid., p. 61.

11. Ibid., p. 61.

12. Ibid., p. 81.

13. Ibid., p. 82.

14. Ibid., p. 82.

15. For a detailed account of Rocha's efforts, see James Glanz and John Scwartz, "Dogged Engineer's Effort to Assess Shuttle Damage," *The New York Times*, September 26, 2003, pp. A1, A16.

16. This paragraph is based on a public presentation made by Roger Boisjoly at Western Michigan University in 1993.

17. John D. Kemper and Billy R. Sanders, *Engineers and Their Profession*, 5th ed. (New York: Oxford University Press, 2001), p. 104. This view is attributed by the authors to ABET, but we have been unable to locate this in any ABET documents.

18. Ibid., pp. 104–105.

19. William F. May, "Professional Virtue and Self-Regulation," in Joan Callahan, ed., *Ethical Issues in Professional Life* (Oxford: Oxford University Press, 1988), p. 408.

20. Ibid., p. 408.

21. Ibid., p. 408.

22. William A. Wulf, "Great Achievements and Grand Challenges," October 22, 2000, annual meeting of the National Academy of Engineering, p. 1.

23. Michael Davis, "Is There a Profession of Engineering?", *Science and Engineering Ethics*, 3:4, 1997, p. 417.

24. Barbara Toffler, *Tough Choices: Managers Talk Ethics* (New York: Whiley, 1986), p. 288.

25. Mike W. Martin, *Meaningful Work* (New York: Oxford University Press, 2000), p. vii.

26. P. Aarne Vesilind, *Peace Engineering: When Personal Values and Engineering Careers Converge* (Woodsville, NH: Lakeshore Press, 2005), p. 15.

27. For further discussion of this and other examples of good works, see Michael S. Pritchard, "Professional Responsibility: Focusing on the Exemplary," *Science and Engineering Ethics*, 4, 1998, p. 222.

28. See Pritchard, "Professional Responsibility: Focusing on the Exemplary," for more on the remarkable story of Cuny. See, also, the case study, "Disaster Relief," in the Cases section of this text.

29. For a more detailed account, see G. P. E. Meese, "The Sealed Beam Case," *Business & Professional Ethics*, 1:3, Spring 1982, pp. 1–20. We also discuss this case in more detail in Ch. 3, "Responsibility in Engineering."

30. See the Engineers Without Borders website at http://www.ewb-usa.org.

31. For a discussion of the distinction between micro- and macro-level issues, see Joseph Herkert, "Future Directions in Engineering Ethics Research: Microethics, Macroethics and the Role of Professional Societies," *Science and Engineering Ethics*, 7:3, 2001, pp. 403–414. For a critical discussion of these distinctions, see Michael Davis, "Engineers and Sustainability: An Inquiry into the Elusive Distinction between Macro-, Micro-, and Meso-Ethics," *Journal of Applied Ethics and Philosophy*, 2, 2010, pp. 12–20.

CHAPTER TWO

A Practical Ethics Toolkit

Main Ideas in This Chapter

- Professionals are problem solvers, and ethical problems are one type of problem that they often face. Practical ethics provides a series of techniques for resolving ethical problems.
- The first task of practical ethics is to analyze an ethical problem into its factual, conceptual, and application components.
- Two techniques that are often useful in ethical problem solving are line drawing and finding creative middle way solutions.
- Often, resolving ethical problems in engineering requires more than an appeal to professional codes and standards of practice. An appeal to common morality is necessary. Common morality can be formulated in several ways and has some generally accepted structural components.
- Common morality can be modeled in several ways, two of which are especially important. These models can be useful in resolving some practical ethical problems.
- Several widely recognized tests or application procedures exist for both of the models for common morality. They can be useful tools in applying the two models, especially with regard to social issues.

IN 1993, IT WAS PUBLICLY REVEALED that Germany's Heidelberg University had in the past used more than 200 corpses, including those of eight children, in automobile crash tests. This revelation drew immediate protests in Germany. Rudolph Hammerschmidt, spokesperson for the Roman Catholic Bishops' Conference objected, "Even the dead possess human dignity. This research should be done with mannequins." ADAC, Germany's largest automobile club, issued a statement saying, "In an age when experiments on animals are being put into question, such tests must be carried out on dummies and not on children's cadavers."

In reply, the university claimed that, in every case, relatives granted permission, as required by German law. It added that although it had used children in the past, this practice had been stopped in 1989. The rationale for using corpses is that data from such crash tests are "vital for constructing more than 120 types of instrumented dummies, ranging in size from infants to adults, that can simulate dozens of human reactions in a crash." These data, it claimed, have been used to save many lives, including those of children.

Similar testing has also been conducted in the United States at Wayne State University's Bioengineering Center. Robert Wartner, a Wayne State spokesperson, indicated that the testing has been done as a part of a study by the federal government's Centers for Disease Control. However, he added, "Cadavers are used only when alternatives could not produce useful safety research."

Clarence Ditlow, head of the Center for Auto Safety, a Washington, DC, public advocacy group, said that the center advocates three criteria for using cadavers in crash testing: (1) assurance that the data sought by the tests cannot be gained from using dummies, (2) prior consent by the deceased person, and (3) informed consent of the family.[1]

2.1   INTRODUCTION

This case illustrates two important ideas. First, technology raises moral and social issues of considerable importance. Second, reference to professional codes and general concepts of professionalism may not be sufficient to resolve the issues. Those making the decision in the above case may well not be engineers, even though the issue was posed because of the existence of the automobile, in which engineering plays a vital part. But even if engineers are involved in the decision in some way, engineering codes do not supply an obvious answer to the problem. The codes hold that engineers must hold paramount the safety, health, and welfare of the public, but does this important directive imply that cadavers should be used for crash testing or that they should not be used? No other provision in any of the major engineering codes provides an obvious answer. We must recognize, then, that, in addressing many issues in professional ethics, we need ethical resources that supplement the codes.

This chapter provides several methods that go beyond the codes and are useful in analyzing and then resolving moral issues. The methods should be thought of as analogous to tools in a toolbox. Suppose carpenters are building a house. They have a number of tools at their disposal: a hammer, a screwdriver, a saw, and so forth. For some tasks, the hammer is appropriate, for others the screwdriver, and for others the saw. It is up to them to assess the tools appropriate for the tasks at hand. These all-important acts of judgment are developed only with practice. Not all of the tools are useful for every task. One has to learn to determine what tools are useful in a given situation, and this takes skill, judgment, and a certain amount of experience. We begin with conceptual tools for analyzing a moral problem into its component parts. After that, several methods are considered for resolving moral issues, beginning with more common-sense ideas and proceeding to more theoretical approaches.

2.2   DETERMINING THE FACTS

We cannot discuss moral issues intelligently apart from a knowledge of the facts that are relevant to the issues. We call questions about what the facts are *factual* issues. So we must begin by considering what those facts are. However, in discussing these moral issues, people may disagree about *what* the facts are or how they are *relevant* to a moral decision. To understand the importance of facts in a moral controversy, we propose the following theses about factual issues.

First, *often, moral disagreements turn out to be disagreements over the relevant facts.* In looking at the case at the beginning of the chapter, a factual question may present itself to you: "Is it really the case that there is important factual information that will indeed save lives and that can only be gained from crash testing with cadavers? Or is it possible to gain equivalent information from either dummies or computer simulation?" Many people (but not all) would agree that if vital information can be gained *only* by the use of cadavers then cadavers should be used, but there could well be disagreement over the facts. Even if crucial data could not have been gained by other means at the time of the news story, what about today? Could computer simulation or other methods yield the same information?

Second, *factual issues are sometimes very difficult to resolve.* We can imagine that the factual issue raised above can be very difficult to resolve. It may be very difficult to determine, for example, whether a significant correlation exists between a reduction in automobile accident deaths and the data derived form crash tests using cadavers. In the absence of definitive answers, the question whether cadavers should be used will continue to raise controversy.

Third, *sometimes we must decide important moral issues in the light of irresolvable factual uncertainty.* Suppose we cannot decide in a satisfactory way whether testing without cadavers will yield data as reliable and useful as data obtained by cadaver testing. How shall we decide what to do? Should we put greater emphasis on respecting the bodies of dead human beings or obtaining data that may save lives? In this case, the controversy shifts to a more direct consideration of moral issues.

2.3   CLARIFYING CONCEPTS

Responsible moral thinking requires not only attending carefully to the facts, but also having a good grasp of the key concepts we are using. That is, we need to get as clear as we can about the meanings of key terms. For example, "public health, safety, and welfare," "conflict of interest," "bribery," "extortion," "confidentiality," "trade secret," and "loyalty" are key terms for ethics in engineering. We call questions about the meanings of terms *conceptual issues.* If people disagree about the meanings of such terms, they may well be unable to resolve an argument, even if they agree about all of the facts and moral assumptions. For example, an engineer's action might be a conflict of interest according to one definition of the term and not a conflict of interest by another definition of the same term.

It would be nice to have precise definitions of all of these terms; but like most terms in ethics, their meanings are somewhat open-ended. In many cases, it is sufficient to clarify our meaning by thinking of *paradigms* or clear-cut examples of what we have in mind. We might, for example, think of an uncontroversial case of a conflict of interest, such as a situation in which an engineer designing a product is considering specifying bolts manufactured by a firm in which he has a controlling financial interest. The engineer might be strongly tempted to specify the bolts from his firm, even if they are not the best or most appropriate for the design. From this example, we can draw out a definition of conflict of interest, such as that it involves a conflict between a professional obligation and some private interest (such as money) that might conflict with this obligation.

In the case at the beginning of the chapter, the concept of "human dignity" is crucial in determining whether "human dignity" is violated by using cadavers in crash tests. Similarly, the concepts of "consent" and "informed consent" are crucial in determining whether the cadavers were obtained by the proper kind of consent.

2.4 DETERMINING HOW CONCEPTS APPLY: APPLICATION ISSUES

When we say that the use of cadavers in crash testing violates "human dignity," we are saying that the concept of "honoring human dignity" cannot be correctly applied to the practice of using cadavers for crash testing. This is a claim about an *application issue*, that is, a claim about whether a given term or expression applies to a person, an individual action, or a general practice. Since application issues have to do with whether a concept applies to or "fits" a certain situation, disagreements over application issues can result from either disagreements over the concept to be applied or disagreements over the facts to which the concepts are applied. Application issues can be resolved by getting clear about the relevant facts and agreeing on the meaning of the relevant concepts. Disputes over application issues can therefore be seen as situations in which the determination of whether a concept fits a situation is in dispute because of a factual issue, or a conceptual issue—or both.

2.5 DECIDING MORAL ISSUES: LINE DRAWING

So far we have been looking at some analytical techniques for sorting controversies involving moral issues into appropriate categories. Now we are ready to look at some ways of resolving them. The first of these techniques can also be useful in resolving application issues. We call this technique *line drawing*.

Consider the following example. Victor is an engineer in a large construction firm. He has been assigned the task of being the sole person to recommend rivets for the construction of a large apartment building. After some research and testing, he decides to recommend ACME rivets for the job, which he determines are of the lowest cost and highest quality. On the day after Victor's decision was made, an ACME representative visits him and gives him a voucher for an all-expense-paid trip to the annual ACME Technical Forum, which meets in Jamaica. The trip will have considerable educational value, but will also provide day trips to the beach and other points of interest.

If Victor accepts, has he been bribed? In answering this question—an application issue—it is useful to first think of a clear-cut, unproblematic case of a bribe. We can refer to this as a *paradigm case* of a bribe. Suppose a vendor offers an engineer a large sum of money to recommend the vendor's product to the engineer's company. Several aspects of the situation—we shall call them "features"—are relevant in making this situation a paradigmatic bribe. The gift is substantial; it is offered before the engineer's decision on which product to use; the engineer accepts the offer for reasons of personal gain; the engineer has sole responsibility for the decision; the vendor's product is the most expensive on the market; and it is of questionable quality. This is, without question, a bribe. Table 2.1 is a useful graphic way of representing these aspects of the situation.

We can also construct a paradigm at the other extreme, which depicts a situation that is clearly *not* a bribe. In most cases, this can be done by simply negating the characteristics of the paradigm bribe. Thus, a paradigmatic nonbribe would be a situation in which the gift is very small (perhaps a pen worth two dollars); it is offered after the engineer's decision on which product to recommend; the engineer does not personally gain from the decision; the engineer shares responsibility for the decision with

TABLE 2.1 Paradigm Case of Bribery

Features of Bribery	Paradigm Instances of Features of Bribery
Gift size	Large (>$10,000)
Timing	Before recommendation
Reason	Personal gain
Responsibility for decision	Sole
Product quality	Worst in industry
Product cost	Highest in market

© Cengage Learning

others; the vendor's product is the highest quality; and its cost is the lowest of the available products.

Now we can return to Victor's situation. We can call this a *test case*, because it is a case in which the question as to its status as a bribe is in dispute and should be tested against paradigm bribes and nonbribes. In the case of each feature, we can place an X on the continuum between two paradigms to indicate whether a given feature of the test case is closer to the paradigm bribe or the paradigm nonbribe. It is also useful to circle a few of the Xs to indicate which ones have special importance in evaluating the test case. Table 2.2 provides a useful graphic representation of these issues.

As Table 2.2 suggests, the test case is by no means a paradigm bribe and should not be considered a bribe. Nevertheless, the cost of the trip is substantial and raises some concern.

So far, line drawing has been applied to an application issue, namely whether Victor's accepting the vendor's offer should be considered an instance of accepting a bribe. Victor can also use line drawing to help him decide whether he should accept the vendor's offer. Even if accepting the offer is not accepting a bribe, it might not be wise to accept it. Here a different set of features comes into play. Victor should consider the effect of accepting the offer on his own future decisions, as well as the effect on his fellow employees. Victor and his fellow employees might be influenced to make a future decision in favor of ACME because of the trip. Another feature would be the company image that the decision to accept the offer might present. Not knowing the details, other vendors, the public, and perhaps fellow employees might see the decision as confirming a belief that Victor's firm condones accepting bribes. Still another feature might be company policy. Does Victor's firm have a policy on

TABLE 2.2 Line-Drawing Test of Concepts

Feature	Paradigm (Bribery)	Test Case	Paradigm (*Not* bribery)
Gift size	Large	____Ⓧ_____	Small (<$1.00)
Timing	Before decision	_____Ⓧ__	After decision
Reason	Personal gain	_____X_____	Educational
Responsibility	Sole	__Ⓧ_____	None
Product quality	Worst	_____X__	Best
Product cost	Highest	__X_____	Lowest

© Cengage Learning

accepting gifts from vendors? If so, does accepting this gift comply with or violate those standards? Picturing the appropriate line-drawing chart in your mind, you can begin to see that accepting the offer, at least in its present form, might not be a good idea, even if it is not a bribe. A second tool, presented in the next section, might help Victor further with his decision.

2.6   CONFLICTING VALUES: CREATIVE MIDDLE WAY SOLUTIONS

In the situation described above, different considerations seemed to suggest different courses of action. On the one hand, there is a natural desire to accept a trip to Jamaica, and the technical forum might be a source of useful information. On the other hand, accepting the offer in its present form might convey at least the *appearance* of bribery, and it might influence Victor or his fellow employees to make irresponsible decisions in the future. So, if Victor is confined to these two options, he should probably not accept the offer. But why should he assume that these are the only two options available? Why should he not try to be creative and think of an option that would satisfy the considerations in favor of taking the trip and the considerations against taking the trip—or at least to satisfy as many of the competing considerations as possible?

We can call such a solution a creative middle way solution. In this example, Victor might decide that he will not take the trip himself, but that a fellow employee who did not participate in the decision whether to use the ACME rivets might want to go. He might suggest a company policy that employees may not accept vendor rewards for buying the vendor's products. He might also suggest that the conditions under which the trip was accepted be made clear to employees, other vendors, and the public, insofar as this is possible. Finally, he might suggest that his firm split the expenses with the vendor, perhaps paying for air travel and some additional expenses. This solution does not satisfy all of the considerations completely. Victor no longer gets to take the trip, but someone in the firm does. The firm gets the advantage of any valuable information, and the firm avoids the reputation of being a firm in which bribes are accepted.

Here is another example. Brad is in the second year of his first full-time job after graduating from Engineering Tech.[2] He enjoys design, but is becoming increasingly concerned that his work is not being adequately checked by more experienced engineers. He has been assigned to assist in the design of a number of projects that involve issues of public safety, such as schools and overhead walkways between buildings. He has already spoken to his supervisor, whose engineering competence he respects, and he has been told that more experienced engineers check his work. Later he discovers that his work is often not adequately checked. Instead, his drawings are stamped and passed on to the contractor. Sometimes the smaller projects he designs are under construction within a few weeks after the designs are completed.

At this point, Brad calls one of his former professors at Engineering Tech for advice. "I'm really worried that I'm going to make a mistake that will kill someone," Brad says. "I try to overdesign, but the projects I'm being assigned to are becoming increasingly difficult. What should I do?" Brad's professor tells him that he cannot ethically continue on his present course because he is engaging in engineering work that surpasses his qualifications and may endanger the public. What should Brad do?

Brad's case illustrates one of the most common conflicts faced by engineers, one in which his obligation to his employer seems to conflict with his obligation to the public. Both of these obligations are clearly mandated by the codes. The NSPE code requires engineers to "hold paramount the safety, health, and welfare of the public" (Canon 1) and also to "act in professional matters for each employer or client as faithful agents or trustees" (Canon 4). Brad also has a legitimate interest in preserving and promoting his own career. One can even say that he has an obligation to himself, his career, and his family, if he has a wife or children.

In a situation like this, Brad could attempt to find a creative middle way that would, if possible, honor or satisfy these three obligations. It is helpful to arrange courses of action in serial order, beginning with the one that would most satisfactorily honor all three of the obligations, and continuing to options that would not honor all of the obligations.

1. Brad could go to his supervisor again and suggest in the most tactful way possible that he is uncomfortable about the fact that his designs are not being properly checked, pointing out that it is not in the firm's interests to produce designs that may be flawed. If the supervisor accepted this suggestion, he would be able to resolve the problem and keep on the best of terms with his employer. Brad could thus honor his obligation to the safety of the public, to his employer, and to himself and his career. This would be an ideal creative middle way solution.

2. Brad might talk to others in the organization with whom he has a good working relationship and ask them to help him persuade his supervisor that he (Brad) should be given more supervision. This solution is almost as good, because it would resolve the problem. However, it may result in the supervisor's reputation with his other employees and perhaps the public being tarnished, because the supervisor did not give more supervision. While satisfying Brad's obligation to the public, it might not as satisfactorily honor the obligation to his employer and himself.

3. Brad could find another job and then, after his own employment is secure, reveal the information to the state registration board for engineers or others who could stop the practice. While protecting his own career and the public, this option does not promote his employer's interests.

4. Brad might tell his supervisor that he does not believe he can continue to engage in design work that is beyond his abilities and experience and that he might have to consider changing jobs. This solution involves a confrontation with his employer. This solution might not cause the employer to change his bad practices and might harm Brad's career. It might also harm the reputation of the supervisor with his other employees.

5. Brad could go to the press or his professional society and blow the whistle immediately. This would protect the public, but possibly damage his career prospects and certainly severely damage the supervisor's business.

You can think of other possibilities as well, such as continuing in his job without protest or finding another job without protest. If the first obligation is to protect the public—as the codes say—these options would also be unsatisfactory. Perhaps only the first two options could be considered really satisfactory creative middle way solutions, and the first option is the most desirable.

2.7 COMMON MORALITY

We have already pointed out that the work of the practical ethicist is analogous to the work of a carpenter who uses whatever tools are appropriate to the task at hand. A hammer is sometimes appropriate, but at other times the carpenter needs a saw or a screwdriver. Like the skilled carpenter, the practical ethicist must have a command of all of the available tools and use whatever is appropriate for the situation. The method of line drawing or attempting to find a creative middle way may be sufficient. Sometimes, however, something more is needed. To resolve some moral issues—especially those involving larger social policies—we must look into the moral basis of these policies. This requires additional resources. These resources usually come from common morality, the stock of common moral beliefs to which most of us adhere.

Formulations of Common Morality: Virtues

One of the oldest formulations of common morality is in terms of a set of "virtues," which are character traits that motivate morally desirable action. Examples of virtues important in engineering work are honesty (in professional work), courage (in protesting action that harms the public), loyalty (to clients and employers), striving for excellence (in one's professional work), respect for the natural world (in motivating environmentally friendly engineering), and compassion or benevolence (for those who can be helped by one's engineering work).

A virtue is a complex character trait, consisting of many elements. It is possible to analyze a virtue, such as the ones described above, into four components. Consider, as an example, the virtue of honesty. First, there is an affective or emotional component. An honest person, for example, will be disgusted by lying and have a positive response to honesty, especially when one may be tempted to be dishonest. Second, there is a "dispositional" component, that is, a tendency to act in a certain way rather than another. An honest person will be strongly inclined to act honestly. Third, there is a cognitive component, consisting of expectations; beliefs about things, people, and future events; and the way one interprets events. An honest person may well believe that honesty generally promotes one's self-interest, but also that the integrity of science and technology depends upon the honesty of its practitioners. Finally, there is an identity component, in that the virtues are connected with what kind of person one conceives himself to be. Thinking of oneself as an honest person is strongly connected with one's self-identity.[3]

Here are some of the ways in which the virtues may be useful in practical ethics. First, the virtues are an essential part of evaluating persons, as opposed to actions. Much of practical ethics is devoted to determining the proper course of action or "the right thing to do" in a situation of moral choice. However, sometimes it is important to morally evaluate the character of individuals, and here the vocabulary of the virtues is important. In evaluating whistleblowers, we may want to talk about their courage. In evaluating engineers and engineering students who join Engineers Without Borders, we may want to talk about their compassion or perhaps their "professional benevolence."

Second, promoting the development of the virtues is an important part of promoting ethical action, especially ethical action for which there are no legal or professional sanctions. An engineer may face reprimands or even legal penalties for taking bribes, breaking confidentiality, or engaging in other types of professional misconduct.

However, one faces no such sanctions for failure to manifest what we have called "aspirational ethics," that is, such actions as designing clean water and sanitation systems for underdeveloped areas, and designing environmentally friendly products and processes. The motivation for such activities must be rooted in character traits, and this means the virtues. Consideration of how the virtues can be nurtured and developed is an aspect of professional ethics that requires talk of the virtues.

Third, using the vocabulary of the virtues is often necessary for moral analysis. In Chapter 4, for example, we consider the possible effect of social networking on the development of the virtues necessary for genuine friendships, such as honesty and patience. In looking at the character of moral exemplars, the vocabulary of the virtues is also essential.

Formulations of Common Morality: Rules and Duties

More common formulations of common morality in the modern era are in terms of rules or duties. Here are two such accounts. The first account is by W. D. Ross, who constructed a list of basic duties or obligations, which he called "prima facie" or "conditional" duties.[4] In using these terms, Ross intended to convey the idea that although these duties are generally obligatory, they can be overridden in special circumstances. He disclaimed finality for his list, but he believed it was reasonably complete. His list of prima facie duties can be summarized as follows:

R1. Duties resting on our previous acts
   (a) Duties of fidelity (to keep promises and not to tell lies)
   (b) Duties of reparation for wrong done
R2. Duties of gratitude (e.g., to parents and benefactors)
R3. Duties of justice (e.g., to support happiness in proportion to merit)
R4. Duties of beneficence (to improve the condition of others)
R5. Duties of self-improvement
R6. Duties not to injure others

Engineers, like others, probably share these moral beliefs, and this is reflected in many engineering codes of ethics. Most codes enjoin engineers to be faithful agents of their employees, and this injunction is reflected in the duties of fidelity (R1) and gratitude (R2). Most codes require engineers to act in ways that protect the health, safety, and welfare of the public, and this obligation is reflected in the duties of justice (R3) and beneficence (R4), and especially in the duty not to injure others (R6). Finally, most codes encourage engineers to improve their professional skills, a duty reflected in (R5).

In another account of common morality, Bernard Gert has formulated a list of ten "moral rules" that he believes capture the basic elements of our common morality.

G1. Don't kill.
G2. Don't cause pain.
G3. Don't disable.
G4. Don't deprive of freedom.
G5. Don't deprive of pleasure.

G6. Don't deceive.

G7. Keep your promise (or don't break your promise).

G8. Don't cheat.

G9. Obey the law (or don't disobey the law).

G10. Do your duty (or don't fail to do your duty).[5]

Ross's prima facie duties and Gert's moral rules overlap considerably. G1–9, for example, might be seen as specifications of Ross's duty not to injure others. The wrongness of lying and promise breaking appear on both lists. R2–R5 seem to be of a more positive nature than Gert's moral rules, which focus on not causing harm. However, Gert also provides a list of ten "moral ideals," which focus on preventing harm. In fact, the moral ideals can be formulated by introducing the word "prevent" and changing the wording of the rules slightly. Thus, the moral ideal corresponding to "Don't kill" is "Prevent killing." For Gert, the moral rules specify moral requirements, whereas the moral ideals are aspirational. So, while Gert believes that the primary requirements of common morality are negative and prohibitive, Ross gives preeminence to positive duties.

For both Ross and Gert, moral precepts are not "absolute" in the sense of being without exception. Exceptions to moral duties and rules, however, must have a justification.[6] Usually it is wrong to lie, but if the only way to save an innocent person from being murdered is to lie to the assailant about that person's whereabouts, then lying is justified. The main point is not that moral rules and principles have no exceptions; it is that taking exception to them requires having a justification, or good reason, for doing so. Deciding whether to take a walk, go to the movies, or read a book does not call for a justification. Breaking a promise, however, does call for a justification, as does injuring others.

Evaluating Actions vs. Evaluating the Person

Common morality distinguishes between evaluating an action and evaluating the person who performed the action. Actions are evaluated in terms of moral rules and duties of the type described above. A person is evaluated primarily in terms of the intent behind the action. Intent is important because common morality holds that one should never do what he or she believes to be wrong, even if the action is not wrong by the precepts of common morality. To perform an action believed to be wrong would be to intend to do something wrong, even if the action is not wrong by the standards of common morality. As we often say, a person doing what he believes is wrong would be "violating his conscience." Thus it is possible to condemn a person's action for doing something contrary to the precepts of common morality, but not condemn the person himself. Or we might condemn the person for violating his conscience, even though his action is in accord with common morality.

The distinction between action and intention can raise significant issues in professional ethics. Engineering codes say little about intent, and intent is seldom central in discussions of professional ethics. Yet when actions are evaluated from the standpoint of common morality, intent is of paramount importance. This is because requiring someone to act in a way that he believes is wrong requires him to act contrary to his best moral judgment and thus to "violate his conscience." Since violating one's conscience by doing something one understands to be wrong is a serious moral issue, some ethicists believe that a provision regarding a "right of conscience" (a right to refuse to do something that violates one's conscience) should be a part of engineering codes. Here are two examples that illustrate the need for the "right of conscience" provision. Suppose Engineer Joe is asked to build a capability into a web browser to collect certain personal information. Even though similar capabilities are a part of some other browsers and the client has asked for this capability, Joe objects because of his concerns about protecting privacy. According to the right of conscience, Joe should have the right to refuse the client's request. Or suppose Engineer Jane is asked to develop a medical device for monitoring fetal health that can also, with modifications, facilitate abortions. She objects to developing this device because of its capacity to facilitate abortions. According to the right of conscience, Jane should have the right to refuse this request. To date, no right of conscience provision is a part of any engineering code, insofar as the authors are aware.

2.8   THE STRUCTURE OF COMMON MORALITY

Ethicists usually think of common morality as having certain structural elements. Two of these elements are listed below.

Judgments in Common Morality

Judgments in common morality can be of four types. We can say that something is permissible, impermissible, obligatory, or supererogatory. An action or practice is *permissible* if one is morally permitted to do it but also morally permitted not to do it. An engineer might decide to design a parking lot for a nonprofit organization free of charge, but it would also be morally acceptable not to do it. An action is *impermissible* if is not morally acceptable to perform the action. It is impermissible to have an undisclosed conflict of interest. An action or practice is *obligatory* if one is morally required to do it. Disclosure of a conflict of interest is obligatory. An action or practice is *supererogatory* if it is praiseworthy if one does it, but one cannot be condemned if he or she does not do it. Designing a parking lot for a nonprofit organization is supererogatory. Thus, supererogatory actions or practices are a special class of permissible actions, but, because of their praiseworthy nature, it is useful to have a special term.

Levels of Common Morality

It is also usually held that common morality has several levels of generality, ranging from the more general to the more specific.

The first level is the general moral statements of the type illustrated by Gert's rules and Ross's prima facie duties. "Don't lie" falls into this category.

The second level is moral judgments about general practices or classes of actions. These are often called "mid-level moral judgments" or "intermediate moral judgments." Examples are: "Engineers should never engage in undisclosed conflicts of interest" and "Engineers should always use environmentally friendly materials if cost and availability permit." Moral judgments about such practices as slavery, contraception, homosexual conduct, or the permissibility of euthanasia also fall into this second category.

The third level is moral judgments about particular actions. Examples are: "Engineer Mike should not have specified bolts manufactured by a firm in which he had a vested interest" and "Engineer Mary should have used more environmentally friendly materials in her design." We should note that another and perhaps more common type of moral judgment about actions involves applying descriptive evaluative terms to actions, as in "James was cruel when he said that," or "The actions of Company X amounted to exploitation," or "Sally's statement was simply a lie." In all of these cases, we are morally condemning actions, even though we do not use such terms as "wrong" or "impermissible." However, these statements can be converted to statements of the earlier type simply by adding premises such as "Cruelty is wrong," "Exploitation is wrong," or "Lying is wrong." Then we can produce the statements that cruelty, exploitation, and lying are wrong.

2.9 MODELING COMMON MORALITY

Modeling in Ethics

Modeling is a common practice in science and engineering. Most people are familiar with climate models, which enable climate scientists to understand and predict climate phenomena. Engineers use models to understand products and structures and to anticipate problems which can then be corrected before the products are put into manufacture or the structures are built. Engineers know that models are never perfect, and that it is their responsibility to be aware of a model's limitations and to use it only within those limits.

The concept of modeling can be useful in ethics as well. Just as in science and engineering, an ethical model can enhance our ability to understand ethical concepts and to apply them more effectively. Specifically, an ethical model should answer three questions. First, is there a moral standard or criterion that can be used to identify right actions and summarize the main idea in morality? Second, what is the function or purpose of morality in society? Why is it that every society appears to have something like a moral code? Third, what kinds of reasons or evidence are relevant in justifying a moral claim?

Two Models of Common Morality

Probably the two most widely discussed models of common morality are the *utilitarian model* and the *respect for persons model*. The moral standard of the utilitarian model is: *those actions or practices should be followed that maximize human well-being*. Given this standard, we can say that the function of morality is to promote human welfare or well-being. Moral precepts should be judged in the light of this consideration: if precepts promote human welfare they should be endorsed, and if they do not further this end, they should not. Finally, the reasons that are most relevant for a utilitarian in evaluating an action or practice are suggested by tests that guide in the identification of actions and practices that promote human well-being.

The moral standard of the respect for persons model is: *those actions or practices should be followed that protect and respect the moral agency of human beings*. We can define moral agency as the capacity to choose goals or purposes of one's own, that is, to direct one's own life. In terms of this standard, the primary function of morality is first and foremost negative: to provide rules that safeguard the moral agency of people, and, especially, protect them from unwarranted interference from others. The best reasons for actions are identified by tests that point out ways in which the moral agency of individuals can be protected.

Limitations of the Two Models

There is reason to believe, however, that both of these models, as powerful and impressive and useful as they are, have limitations in their ability to account for all aspects of common morality. We can begin by looking at some limitations of the utilitarian model. First, although intent is a crucial idea in common morality, as we have seen, it is difficult to account for the importance of intent in utilitarian terms. From a utilitarian perspective, it is the consequences of an action, not the intent behind it, that matter. While utilitarians can maintain that good intent is more likely to produce actions that have positive utility, this seems to fail to get at the true reason that intent is important, namely that doing what one perceives as wrong is violating one's moral agency. Second, the utilitarian perspective is often thought to have difficulty giving a proper account of justice. While a utilitarian can say that just actions are more likely to produce utility, this may again seem not to account for the most basic reason for valuing just actions, namely that they respect the equal dignity of all people as moral agents. Finally, utilitarian thinking is often thought to have difficulties in accounting for supererogatory actions. If an action maximizes utility, it would seem to be obligatory from the utilitarian standpoint, even if it imposes great sacrifices on the agent and would ordinarily be thought of as supererogatory. Giving most of one's income to the poor, for example, would seem to be required from the utilitarian standpoint if it maximizes utility overall, even though common morality would consider such action supererogatory. By contrast, respect for persons model can justify the category of supererogatory actions by saying that we must be careful not to demand highly sacrificial acts by making them obligatory. This can subordinate our own moral agency to that of others.

The respect for persons model, however, has its own set of limitations. Many of its difficulties have to do with this approach's tendency—because of its great concern to protect the moral agency of individuals—to disallow actions that common morality might permit. For example, it is often understood to disallow an abortion that directly results in the death of the fetus, even if otherwise the mother and fetus will both die. It is often also taken to disallow the direct killing of the innocent in war, even if many more lives will thereby be saved, and to resist social policies (such as economic policies) that harm some citizens in order to help the majority.

A second problem is that the respect for persons model is often difficult to apply, in part because of the problems encountered in defining and applying crucial terms. One source of the difficulties is the so-called Principle of Double Effect, a principle often thought to be implied by the concern of respect for persons theory to protect the moral agency of individuals. In simplified form, the principle says that it is morally permissible to perform an action that has two effects, one good and the other bad, if four conditions are met: (1) The act, considered apart from its consequences, is allowable; (2) the bad consequence of the act cannot be avoided if the good effect is to be achieved; (3) the bad effect is not the means of producing the good effect, but only the unintended side effect; (4) the good effect is at least as significant as the bad effect.[7]

The major difficulties in applying this principle are probably associated with the third and fourth requirements. Sometimes determining when an act is or is not a "means," as opposed to an unintended side effect, is controversial, especially when the bad effect is known to occur. Suppose a plant emits a suspected carcinogen through its stack which may affect some people in the vicinity, but the plant provides jobs and many other benefits in the same area. In this case, are the deaths due to cancer a mere side effect or a means to the good of others? With regard to the fourth criterion, are the good effects to the area worth the deaths of some due to cancer?

Convergence and Divergence of the Two Models

We can call the problems that utilitarian and respect for person models have in explaining all aspects of common morality the *problem of incomplete extension*. Neither theory, taken by itself, is able to "extend" over, or fully explain, the whole range of content of common morality. While it is possible to continue the quest for a fully comprehensive theory, many ethicists have concluded that such a search is futile. Rather, the incomplete extension points to a highly important fact about common morality itself, namely that common morality has two fundamental strands of thought in it, one focusing on promoting overall human well-being and the other on protecting the moral agency of individuals. Neither strand, if followed consistently, can yield all of the content of common morality.

In light of the inability of the two most popular moral theories or models to explain all of common morality satisfactorily, we can say that there is no *one single* theory of common morality but the two theories, taken together, can explain the major features of common morality in a reasonably satisfactory way. Keeping in mind these two strands of moral thinking enables us to understand many moral conflicts, for many moral problems involve conflicts between utilitarian and respect for persons considerations. The case at the beginning of this chapter illustrates the conflict between utilitarian considerations having to do with the promotion of automobile safety and respect for persons considerations having to do with respecting the human person, including respecting the body.

The two models—utilitarian and respect for persons—can either converge on the same solution to a moral problem or give different solutions. If the two models lead to the same solution, we have reason to believe that the solution is correct. If they lead to different solutions, we must decide which line of reasoning is more convincing in the circumstances. Even when the two lines of reasoning lead to the same solution, the two models help us to understand more clearly the differences in the types of moral approaches to the issue.

Here is an example. David Parkinson is a member of the Madison County Solid Waste Management Planning Committee (SWMPC). State law requires that one of the committee members be a solid waste expert, David's area of specialization. SWMPC is considering recommending a specific plot of land in a sparsely populated area of Madison County for a needed public landfill. However, next to this site is a large tract of land that a group of wealthy Madison County residents wish to purchase to develop a private golf course surrounded by luxury homes. Although small, this group is well organized and has managed to gather support from other wealthy residents in the county, including several who wield considerable political power. Informally recognized as the Fairway Coalition, this influential group has bombarded the local media with expensive ads in its public campaign against the proposed landfill site, advocating instead a site that borders on one of the least affluent areas of Madison County. The basic argument is that a landfill at the site SWMPC is considering will destroy one of Madison County's most beautiful areas. Although as many as 8000 of Madison County's 100,000 residents live within walking distance of the site proposed by the Fairway Coalition, they lack the political organization and financial resources to mount significant opposition. When

SWMPC meets to discuss the respective merits of the two landfill sites, members of the committee turn to David for his views on the controversy.

In this fictional case, David Parkinson is in a position of public trust, in part because of his engineering expertise. It is evident that one of his responsibilities is to use his expertise in ways that will aid the committee in addressing matters of broad public concern—and controversy. How might he try to take into consideration what is at stake? First, it might occur to him that locating the landfill in the more heavily populated area will benefit a relatively small group of wealthy people at the expense of risking the health and well-being of a much larger number of people. Although there may be many other factors to consider, this is a utilitarian concern to promote, or at least protect, the greatest good for the greatest number of people. Second, it might occur to David that favoring the urban site over the rural site would be basically unfair because it would fail to respect the rights of the poor to a reasonably healthy environment while providing even more privilege to a wealthy minority. This is basically an appeal to the notion of equal respect for persons.

Thus far, utilitarian and respect for persons considerations seem to lead to the same conclusion. It is important to realize that different moral principles often do converge in this way, thereby strengthening our conclusions by providing support from more than one direction. Nevertheless, even when they do reach the same conclusion, two rather distinct approaches to moral thinking are involved—one taking the greater total good as the primary concern, and the other taking protection of the equal moral standing of all members of the community as the primary concern. Also, as we shall see, sometimes these two approaches are in serious tension with one another.

The next section presents several tests or application procedures that can assist in applying the two models. Keep in mind that they are tools to be used when and only when they are helpful in understanding and resolving moral issues.

2.10   TESTS OR APPLICATION PROCEDURES FOR USING THE TWO MODELS

Utilitarian Thinking

In its broadest sense, taking a utilitarian approach in addressing moral problems requires us to focus on the idea of bringing about "the greatest good for the greatest number." We refer to the population over which the good is maximized as the *audience*. One problem is determining the scope of this audience. Ideally, it might be thought, the audience should include all human beings, or at least all human beings who might be affected by the action to be evaluated. Some utilitarians think even animals clearly able to experience pain or pleasure should be included in the audience. But then it becomes virtually impossible to calculate which actions produce the most good for so large an audience. If we limit the audience so that it includes only our country, our company, or our community, then we face the criticism that others have been arbitrarily excluded. Therefore, in practice, those with utilitarian sympathies need to develop acceptable ways of delimiting their range of responsibility.

Even if we determine the audience, we must know which course of action will produce the most good in both the short- and the long-term. Unfortunately, this knowledge is sometimes not available at the time decisions must be made. For example, we do not know whether permitting advertising and competitive pricing for professional services in engineering will lead to some of the problems suggested by those who oppose it. Therefore, we cannot say for sure whether these are good practices from the utilitarian perspective. Sometimes all we can do is try a certain course of action and see what happens. This may be risky in some situations.

We have already pointed out that the utilitarian standard sometimes seems to favor the greater aggregate good at the expense of a vulnerable minority. Imagine the following: a plant discharges a pollutant into the local river, where it is ingested by fish. If humans eat the fish, they experience significant health problems. Eliminating the pollutant will be so expensive that the plant will become, at best, only marginally profitable. Allowing the discharge to continue will save jobs and enhance the overall economic viability of the community. The pollutant will adversely affect only a relatively small proportion of the population—the most economically deprived members of the community who fish in the river and then eat the fish.

Under these conditions, allowing the plant to continue to discharge the pollutant might seem justifiable from a utilitarian perspective, even though it would be unjust to the poorer members of the community. Thus, there is a problem of justly distributing benefits and burdens. Many would say that the utilitarian solution should be rejected for this reason. In such cases, utilitarian reasoning seems, to some, to lead to unacceptable moral judgments, as measured by common morality.

Despite these inherent problems of utilitarian reasoning, it can be enormously useful in many situations. Let's turn to three different formulations of how utilitarian reasoning can be implemented.

The Cost-Benefit Approach

How are we to determine what counts as the greater good? One approach that has appeal from the engineering perspective is *cost-benefit analysis*, according to which the course of action that produces the greatest benefit relative to cost is the one that should be chosen. In using this method, one must translate negative and positive utilities into monetary terms. Cost-benefit analysis is sometimes referred to as *risk-benefit analysis*, because much of the analysis requires estimating the probability of certain benefits and harms. It is possible to determine the actual cost of installing equipment to reduce the likelihood of certain health problems arising in the workplace. However, this does not guarantee that these health problems (or others) will not arise anyway, either from other sources or from the failure of the equipment to accomplish what it is designed to do. In addition, we do not know for sure what will happen if the equipment is not installed; perhaps money will be saved because the equipment will turn out not to have been necessary, or perhaps the actual consequences will turn out to be much worse than predicted. So factoring in probabilities greatly complicates cost-benefit analysis.

Cost-benefit analysis involves three steps:

1. Identify the available options.
2. Assess the costs (measured in monetary terms) and the benefits (also measured in monetary terms) of each option. The costs and benefits must be assessed for the entire audience of the action, however the audience is determined.
3. Make the decision that is likely to result in the greatest benefit relative to cost; that is, the course of action chosen must not be one for which the cost of implementing the option could produce greater benefit if spent on another option.

As we should expect, there are serious problems with using cost-benefit analysis as a sole guide for moral thinking. One problem is that the cost-benefit approach assumes that economic measures of cost and benefit override all other considerations. Consider the pollution case presented above. Cost-benefit analysis encourages the elimination of a pollutant only when it can be done in an economically efficient manner. However, suppose the chemical plant we have been considering is near a wilderness area that is damaged by one of the plant's emissions. It might not be economically efficient to eliminate the pollutant from the cost-benefit standpoint. Of course, the damage to the wilderness area must be included in the cost of the pollution, but the quantified cost estimate might still not justify the elimination—or even reduction—of the pollution. Yet it is not necessarily irrational to hold that the pollutant should be eliminated, even if the elimination is not justified by the analysis. The economic value that anyone would place on saving the wilderness is not a true measure of its value.

Cost-benefit analysis might seem to justify many practices in the past that we have good reason to believe were morally wrong. In the nineteenth century, many people opposed child labor laws, arguing that they would lead to economic inefficiencies. They pointed out, for example, that tunnels and shafts in coal mines were too small to accommodate adults. Many arguments in favor of slavery were also based on considerations of economic efficiency. When our society finally decided to eliminate child labor and slavery, it was not simply because they became economically inefficient but because they came to be considered unjust.

Another problem is that it is often difficult to ascertain the costs and benefits of the many factors that should enter into a cost-benefit analysis. The most controversial issue is how to ascertain in cost-benefit terms the loss of human life or even serious injury. How, we may ask, can a dollar value be placed on a human life? Aside from the difficulty of determining the costs and benefits of known factors (such as immediate death or injury), it is also difficult to predict what factors will be relevant in the future. If the threat to human health posed by a substance is not known, then it is impossible to execute a definitive cost-benefit analysis. This problem becomes especially acute if we consider long-term costs and benefits, most of which are impossible to predict or measure. In addition, cost-benefit analysis does not take into account the distribution of costs and benefits. Using our previous example, suppose a plant dumps a pollutant into a river in which many poorer members of the community fish to supplement their diets. Suppose also that after all of the known costs and benefits are calculated, it is concluded that the costs of eliminating the pollutant outweigh all of the health costs to the poor. Still, if the costs are paid by the poor and the benefits are enjoyed by the rich, then the costs and benefits are not equally shared. Even if the poor are compensated for the damage to their health, many would say that an injustice has still been done. After all, the wealthy members of the community do not have to suffer the same threats to their health.

Despite these problems, cost-benefit analysis can make an important contribution to moral problem solving. We can hardly imagine constructing a large engineering project, such as the Aswan High Dam in Egypt, without performing an elaborate cost-benefit analysis. Although cost-benefit analysis may not always succeed in quantifying values in ways that do justice to them, it can play an important role in utilitarian analysis. Its ability to evaluate many conflicting considerations in terms of a single measure, monetary value, makes it invaluable in certain circumstances. As with all other tools for moral analysis, however, we must keep its limitations in mind.

The Act Utilitarian Approach

Utilitarian approaches to problems do not necessarily require that values always be measured in strictly quantitative terms. However, they do require trying to determine what will, in some sense, maximize good consequences. If we take the *act utilitarian* approach of focusing our attention on the consequences of particular actions, we can ask, "Will this course of action result in more good than any alternative course of action that is available?" To answer this question, the following procedure is useful:

1. Identify the available options in this situation.
2. Determine the appropriate audience for the options, keeping in mind the problems in determining the audience.
3. Decide which available option is likely to bring about the greatest good for the appropriate audience, taking into account the harms as well as benefits.

This act utilitarian approach is often helpful in analyzing options in situations that call for making moral decisions. For example, assuming the economic costs are roughly equal, the choice between two safety devices in an automotive design could be decided by determining which is more likely to reduce the most injuries and fatalities. Also, road improvements might be decided on the basis of the greater number of people served. Of course, in either case, matters could be complicated by considerations of fairness to those who are not benefited by the improvements or might be put at even greater risk. Nevertheless, the utilitarian analyses seem to carry considerable moral weight even if, in some particular cases, they turn out not to be decisive. How much weight these determinations should be given cannot be decided without first making careful utilitarian calculations.

The Rule Utilitarian Approach

James works for Precision Parts, which supplies high-quality components for large machines. Precision Parts has a substantial in-house manufacturing operation, but also contracts with other manufacturers to make some of the components it supplies to customers. James has called for bids from some of its trusted manufacturers for Part X. After the bids have been submitted, Wendell, head of the in-house manufacturing operation, comes into James's office and says, "I know the bids are supposed to be secret, but why don't you tell me what the lowest bid was and I will try to come in under that bid. We are all in this together, and it would help Precision Parts to be able to make Part X in-house."

Looking at Wendell's request, James decides that it makes good sense. The outside manufacturer that made the lowest bid is large and will not be hurt by the loss of this contract. Precision Parts is not able to keep its own employees busy because of decreased business, and its profits are down. It seems like everyone will be better off if James honors Wendell's request. But then James asks himself, "What if Precision Parts made a general practice of breaking the confidentiality of bids and other firms did the same thing?" In other words, suppose Precision Parts and other firms adopted a general rule, "Whenever it is in a firm's interest, it may break the confidentiality of bids." Would this rule or policy, if generally practiced, benefit Precision Parts, or other firms, or the public? Now James is looking at things from a very different perspective. Instead of trying to determine the consequences of one action—violating the confidentiality of bids in this one case—he is thinking about the consequences of a general policy, as outlined in the rule. What would happen if all firms made it a general practice to violate the confidentiality of bids? If this happened, it would be general knowledge that the confidentiality of bids would not be honored, and the integrity of the whole bidding process might unravel. Every firm would be trying to become a favored bidder and might well resort to bribery or other methods to obtain favored status. Firms might well be reluctant to even submit bids to firms with in-house manufacturing facilities, such as Precision Parts, knowing that their bids would not be successful, at least not without bribes.

This fictional case illustrates the difference between act and rule utilitarian approaches. It is one thing to ask about the utility of the consequences of a single action, and another thing entirely to ask about the utility of the consequences of a general practice, as this practice is enshrined in a rule. In the case under discussion, while breaking the confidentiality of bids might have seemed to have something in its favor, at least from the act utilitarian perspective, the general practice appears to be clearly wrong, even from the utilitarian perspective. It is not necessarily the case that an action that might seem justified from an act utilitarian perspective is always wrong from a rule utilitarian perspective, but this is the case here.

Determining the consequences of a general practice is sometimes more difficult than determining the consequences of a single act, because the number of people affected by a general practice—the audience—is usually much larger. However, this is not necessarily the case. Sometimes the consequences of a general policy are so obvious that little imagination is needed to know how the policy would affect human well-being. Suppose you pull up to a red traffic light late at night. On the one hand, from an act utilitarian perspective, you might say that there is no one around, that no one would be harmed, and that it would be more convenient to violate the law and go through the red light. On the other hand, from a rule utilitarian perspective, there is no question that general disobedience of traffic lights, stop signs, yield signs, and other conventions of the road would be disastrous for everyone, including you. You might conclude that, in general, it is better for all of us that we guide our driving by conforming to these rules and conventions rather than trying in each circumstance to determine whether, for example, it is safe to go through a red light.

From a rule utilitarian perspective, then, in situations covered by well-understood, generally observed rules or practices that serve utilitarian ends, one should justify one's actions by appealing to the relevant rules or practices. The rules or practices, in turn, are justified by their utility when generally observed. In the vast majority of cases, we should probably just abide by the general rules and not even consider whether their violation in a particular case could be justified.

There are complications, however. If there are widespread departures from rules or practices, then it is less clear whether overall utility is still promoted by continuing to conform to the rules or practices. To preserve the beauty of a grassy campus quad, a "Please Use Sidewalks" sign may be posted. As long as most comply with this request, the grassy area may retain its beauty. But if too many cut across the grass, a worn path will begin to form. Eventually, the point of complying with the sign may seem lost from a utilitarian standpoint—the cause has been lost.

Another problem with the rule utilitarian approach is that determining the precise nature of the rule to be followed is sometimes difficult and controversial. Suppose James, in considering whether to violate the confidentiality of bids, considers this rule: "An employee should always and without any exceptions act so as to maximize the firm's profits." This rule is too broad and would lead to disaster if implemented. Another rule might be, "If your name is James and you work for Precision Parts, you should violate the confidentiality of the bidding process in Situation X (the situation James faces in the case described above)." This rule is too specific and seems to reduce the rule utilitarian perspective to that of the act utilitarian. Other rules, however, might be more controversial. Suppose James considers this rule: "If one's firm is facing severe economic distress or even bankruptcy, one may violate the confidentiality of the bidding process if this would promote the firm's survival." How would you raise objections to this rule?

This last rule illustrates—interestingly enough—one of the great strengths and weaknesses of the rule utilitarian approach. It is obviously dangerous for individuals to take it upon themselves to violate reasonable and generally observed social rules. Yet there might be cases in which the violation of such rules is justified. And what better way to decide when widely respected moral rules should be justified than by considering whether it would promote the general well-being if everyone violated the rules in similar situations?

Despite the complications involved in the rule utilitarian approach, it can be enormously useful in thinking about some decisions, especially those legal and social policy issues having broad social consequences. Consider again the question about whether professions should be allowed to advertise and to what extent they should be allowed to advertise. On the one hand, some believe that advertising diminishes the esteem in which the public holds a profession, places a premium on the business acumen of professionals rather than their professional competence, and can mislead the public. On the other hand, some believe that advertising provides information to the public that it would not otherwise have and promotes competition that keeps down prices for professional services. All of these arguments are rule utilitarian arguments, because they pose the question, "Which general practice followed by all professionals best promotes the well-being of the public, all things considered?"

Given that sometimes the rule utilitarian approach is useful, here are the steps that should be followed in applying this type of ethical analysis.

1. Identify the particular action or general policy to be evaluated and the available options.
2. Formulate the rules that describe the actions or policies to be evaluated.
3. Identify the audience to which the rules apply and the consequences to that audience of the rules in question.
4. Select the rule that has the best consequences for human well-being, all things considered.
5. If a rule is justified, apply the rule to the situation or social policy in question.

Applying this procedure requires answering many questions. One must formulate the relevant rules, identify the audience and the consequences of various rules to that audience, determine what "well-being" should mean in those circumstances, and so forth. Nevertheless, the method of rule utilitarian thinking can be very useful in practical ethics.

Respect for Persons Approach

The moral standard of the ethics of respect for persons requires treating each person as worthy of respect as a moral agent. This equal regard for moral agents can be understood as a basic requirement of justice. A moral agent must be distinguished from things, such as knives or airplanes, which can only fulfill goals or purposes that are imposed externally. Inanimate objects cannot evaluate actions from a moral standpoint. A paradigm example of a moral agent is a normal adult human being who, in contrast to inanimate objects, can formulate goals or purposes of his or her own. Insofar as we can do this, we are said to have *autonomy*.

From the standpoint of respect for persons, the precepts of common morality protect the moral agency of individual human beings. Maximizing the welfare of the majority must take second place to this goal. People cannot be killed, deceived, denied their freedom, or otherwise violated simply to bring about a greater total amount of utility. As with our treatment of utilitarian thinking, we consider three approaches to respect for persons thinking.

The Golden Rule Approach

Like utilitarian approaches to moral thinking, respect for persons approaches employ the idea of universalizability. Universalizability is grounded in an idea that is familiar to all of us. Most of us would acknowledge that if we think we are acting in a morally acceptable fashion, then we should find it morally acceptable for others to do similar kinds of things in similar circumstances. This same insight can lead us to ask questions about fairness and equal treatment, such as "What if everyone did that?" and "Why should you make an exception for yourself?"

Reversibility is a special application of the idea of universalizability, because the idea of universalizability implies that my judgment should not change simply because the roles are reversed. In thinking about treating others as I would have them treat me, I need to ask what I would think if I were in their position. If I am tempted to tell a lie to escape a particular difficulty, then I need to ask what I would think if the lie were told to me. Universalizing our thinking by applying the idea of reversibility can help us realize that we may be endorsing treating others in ways that we would object to if done to us. This is the basic idea behind the Golden Rule, variations of which appear in the religious and ethical writings of most cultures.

Suppose a manager orders a young engineer to remain silent about the discovery of an emission from the plant that might cause a minor health problem for people who live near the plant. For this order to satisfy the Golden Rule, the manager must be willing to have his supervisor give a similar order to him if he were a young engineer. The manager must also be willing to place himself in the position of the people who live near the plant and would experience the health problem if the emission were not eliminated.

This example reveals a significant problem in using the Golden Rule to resolve a moral problem. Suppose the manager attempts to imaginatively put himself in the position of the young engineer. We can call the engineer the *recipient* of the action. Perhaps the manager believes that people should obey their superiors without question, especially if their superiors are—as he is—professionals with many years of experience. Or he may believe that people are overly sensitive to minor health threats, especially when protecting people from them is very expensive, is detrimental to the economy, and may cost jobs. If he puts himself in the position of the recipient with these values and beliefs, he may conclude that his order is completely legitimate. On the other hand, the manager may think that people have a right to question their superiors, that industries are too prone to impose health risks on others when it is to their benefit, and that these risks are often imposed on the most economically vulnerable elements of the population because they tend to live nearer to industrial facilities. In this case, the manager may conclude that his order is not justifiable by the Golden Rule. The results of using the Golden Rule as a test of morally permissible action may vary, then, depending on the values and beliefs of the actor.

One way of trying to avoid these problems is to interpret the Golden Rule as requiring not only that the actor place himself in the position of the recipient of the action but that the actor also adopt the values of the recipient and assume his or her particular circumstances. If the recipient is in fact troubled by the order and has the second set of values, the manager must not order the young engineer to remain silent.

Unfortunately, this tactic does not resolve all of the problems. Suppose I am an engineer who supervises other engineers and I find that I must dismiss one of my supervisees because he is lazy and unproductive. The engineer whom I want to dismiss, however, believes that "the world owes me a living" and does not want to be punished for his irresponsibility. Dismissing the young engineer fails this interpretation of the Golden Rule, even though most of us would probably believe that irresponsible employees should be dismissed, even if we are the irresponsible employee.

This is not the end of problems with applying the Golden Rule. So far we have assumed that the class of recipients consists of only one person, the young engineer or the employee who does not want to be dismissed. But of course others are affected by the action. The decision whether to remain silent about a pollutant can affect those near the plant, and the decision whether to dismiss the irresponsible employee can affect many people, including other employees. If we enlarge the class of recipients to all those affected by the action, we have an almost impossible task on our hands. The recipients will almost certainly not all agree to the same decision, and then applying the Golden Rule yields no answer.

Although these problems need to be pointed out, they are often not as severe as we might suppose. In many situations, the effects of our action fall primarily on one person. Furthermore, when the effects fall on many, we can often make reasonable assumptions about what others would want, and, in many situations where the wants and desires of people are probably similar everywhere (such as for health, safety, and equal treatment), we can have a fairly high degree of certainty about these assumptions. If we have reason to believe these assumptions cannot be made, we may have to use the insights of the Golden Rule in a more general way. What it really requires is that we consider matters from a more general perspective, one in which we strive to treat others in accordance with standards that we can share.[8] We must keep in mind that whatever standards are adopted, they must respect all affected parties. Viewing oneself as, potentially, both agent and recipient is required. This perspective mandates that we understand the perspectives of agents and recipients, and the Golden Rule serves the useful function of reminding us of this.

The Self-Defeating Approach

The Golden Rule does not by itself provide all the criteria that must be met to satisfy the standard of respect for persons. But its requirements of universalizability and reversibility are vital steps in satisfying that standard. Next, we consider additional features of universalizability as they apply to the notion of respect for persons.

Another way of applying the fundamental idea of the universalizability principle is to ask whether I would be able to perform the action in question if everyone else performed the same action in the same or similar circumstances. If everyone else did what I am doing, would this undermine my ability to do the same thing?[9] If I must say "yes" to this question, then I cannot approve others doing the same kind of thing that I have done, and thus universalizing my action would be *self-defeating*. To proceed anyway, treating myself as an exception to the rule, is to pursue my own good at the expense of others. Thus, it fails to treat them with appropriate respect.

A universalized action can be self-defeating in either of two ways. First, sometimes the action itself cannot be performed if it is universalized. Suppose John borrows money, promising to pay it back at a certain time but having no intention of doing so. For this lying promise to work, the person to whom John makes the promise must believe that he will make good on his word. But if everyone borrowed money on the promise to return it and had no intention of keeping the promise, promises would not be taken seriously. No one would loan money on the basis of a promise. The very practice of promising would lose its point and cease to exist. Promising, as we understand it, would be impossible.

Second, sometimes the purpose I have in performing the action is undermined if everyone else does what I do, even if I can perform the action itself. If I cheat on an exam and everyone else cheats too, then their cheating does not prevent me from cheating. My purpose, however, may be defeated. If my purpose is to get better grades than other students, then it will be undermined if everyone else cheats, because I will no longer have an advantage over them.

Consider an engineering example. Suppose engineer Jane decides to substitute an inferior and cheaper part in a product she is designing for one of her firm's large customers. She assumes that the customer will not check the product closely enough to detect the inferior part or will not have enough technical knowledge to know that the part is inferior. If everyone practiced this sort of deception and expected others to practice it as well, then customers would be far more inclined to have products carefully checked by experts before they were purchased. This would make it much less likely that Jane's deception would be successful.

It is important to realize that using the self-defeating criterion does not depend on everyone, or even anyone, actually making promises without intending to keep them, cheating on exams, or substituting inferior and cheaper parts. The question is, What *if* everyone did this? This is a hypothetical question—not a prediction that others actually will act this way as a result of what someone else does.

As with other approaches, the self-defeating criterion also has limitations. Some unethical actions might avoid being morally self-defeating. Engineer Bill is by nature an aggressive person who genuinely loves a highly competitive, even brutal, business climate. He enjoys an atmosphere in which everyone attempts to cheat the other person and to get away with as much deception as they can, and he conducts his business in this way. If everyone follows his example, then his ability to be ruthless in a ruthless business climate will not be undermined. His action is not self-defeating, even though most of us would consider his practice immoral.

Engineer Alexa, who has no concern for preserving the environment, could design projects that were highly destructive to the environment without her actions being self-defeating. The fact that other engineers knew what Alexa was doing and even designed environmentally destructive projects themselves would not keep her from doing so or destroy the goal she had in designing such projects, namely to maximize her profit.

However, as with the Golden Rule, we need to remember that the universalizability principle functions to help us apply the respect for persons standard. If it can be argued that Bill's ruthlessness fails to respect others as persons, then it can hardly be universalized; in fact, Bill would have to approve of being disrespected by others (because, by the same standard, others could treat him with disrespect). Still, the idea of universalizability by itself does not generate the idea of respect for persons; it says only that if some persons are to be respected, then this must be extended to all. We turn to a consideration of rights to determine if this can give further support to the idea of respect for persons.

The Rights Approach

Many theorists in the respect for persons tradition have concluded that respecting the moral agency of others requires that we give them the rights necessary to exercise their moral agency and to pursue their well-being. A right may be understood as both an entitlement to act and an entitlement to have another individual act in a certain way. Because of this dual aspect, rights are often thought of as existing in a correlative relationship with duties. Thus, if Kelly has a right to life, others have a duty not to kill Kelly. If Kelly has a right to bodily integrity, others have a duty not to cause bodily harm to Kelly. Other suggested rights are the right to free action, to free speech, not to be deceived, not to be cheated, not to be stolen from, not to be disrespected, not to have promises broken, not to have one's privacy invaded, and to nondiscrimination and property.

As we have described them, rights serve as a protective barrier, shielding individuals from unjustified infringements of their moral agency by others. We can call these "negative rights." Beyond this, rights are sometimes asserted more positively as requiring the provision of food, clothing, and education. Thus, if Kelly has a right to food, others have a correlative duty to provide her with at least minimal food for survival. We can call these "positive rights." Because such positive rights are much more controversial in our culture and, in general, somewhat more difficult to apply, we focus on "negative rights," those requiring only noninterference with another person, not active support of that person's interests.

Even determining just what negative rights people have and what they require from others can be controversial, but the general underlying principle is that an individual should not be deprived of certain things if this deprivation interferes seriously with one's moral agency. If someone takes your life, then you cannot exercise your moral agency at all, so this right is relatively uncontroversial, but some of the other proposed rights do not negate your moral agency, although they diminish your power to exercise it effectively. So their status as rights may be more subject to dispute.

One problem any account of rights must face is how to deal with conflicting rights. Suppose a plant manager wants to save money by emitting a pollutant from his plant that is carcinogenic. The manager, acting on behalf of the firm, has a right to free action and to use the plant (the firm's property) for the economic benefit of the firm. But the pollutant threatens the right to life of the surrounding inhabitants. Note that the pollutants do not directly and in every case kill surrounding inhabitants, but they do increase the risk of the inhabitants getting cancer. Therefore, we can say that the pollutant *infringes* on the right to life of the inhabitants, but does not directly *violate* that right. In a rights violation, one's ability to exercise that right in a certain situation is essentially wholly denied, whereas in a rights infringement, one's ability to exercise a right is only diminished. This diminishment can occur in one of two ways. First, sometimes the infringement is a *potential* violation of that right, as in the case of a pollutant that increases the chance of death. Second, sometimes the infringement is a partial violation, as when some, but not all, of a person's property is taken.

The problem of conflicting rights requires that we prioritize rights, giving greater importance to some than to others. A useful way of doing this is offered by philosopher Alan Gewirth.[10] He suggests a three-tiered hierarchy of rights, ranging from more basic to less basic. The first tier includes the most basic rights, the essential preconditions of action: life, physical integrity, and mental health. The second tier includes rights to maintain the level of purpose fulfillment an individual has already achieved. This category includes such rights as the right not to be deceived or cheated, the right to informed consent to unusual risks and other areas, the right not to have possessions stolen, the right not to be defamed, and the right not to suffer broken promises. The third tier includes those rights necessary to increase one's level of purpose fulfillment, including the right to try to acquire property and wealth.

Using this hierarchy, it would be wrong for a plant manager to attempt to save money by emitting a pollutant that is highly carcinogenic because the right to life is a first-tier right and the right to acquire and use property and wealth for one's benefit is a third-tier right. Sometimes, however, the hierarchy is more difficult to apply. How shall we balance a slight infringement of a first-tier right against a much more serious infringement or outright violation of a second-tier or third-tier right?

The hierarchy of rights provides no automatic answer to such questions. Nevertheless, it provides a framework for addressing them. We suggest a set of steps that could be taken.

1. Identify the basic obligations, values, and interests at stake, noting any conflicts.
2. Analyze the action or rule to determine what options are available and what rights are at stake.
3. Determine the audience of the action or rule (those whose rights would be affected).
4. Evaluate the seriousness of the rights infringements or violations that would occur with each option, taking into account both the tier level of rights and the number of violations or infringements involved.
5. Make a choice that seems likely to produce the least serious rights infringements or violations, all things considered.

2.11 CHAPTER SUMMARY

Practical ethics is devoted to resolving ethical conflicts. In accomplishing this aim, the first task is to analyze a problem into its primary components. The first component is factual issues. Disagreements over facts may be difficult to resolve and can be the major center of controversy. What may appear to be a moral conflict may actually be a disagreement over morally relevant facts. Conceptual issues are controversies over the meanings of terms that are crucial in an ethical debate. If parties to a moral controversy are assuming different definitions of crucial terms, their disagreements cannot be resolved. Ethical disagreement can also arise over the question of how and whether crucial terms in an ethical debate are applicable in a given situation.

After important analytical issues are settled, the moral controversy itself must be resolved. Two useful techniques are line drawing and finding a creative middle way. In the line-drawing technique, one compares a controversial case to cases that are non-controversial, because they are clearly morally permissible or impermissible. The controversial case is decided in accordance with the paradigm that it most resembles.

Finding a creative middle way involves finding a solution that satisfies as many of the competing moral demands in a situation of moral conflict as possible.

Resolving practical moral problems sometimes requires an appeal to common morality, which is the generally accepted stock of moral beliefs in a culture, many of which appear to be almost universal. Common morality can be formulated in terms of a set of virtues, and sometimes moral analysis in terms of the virtues can be useful. In the modern era, the more common formulations are in terms of rules or duties, such as the ten moral rules of Bernard Gert and the prima facie duties of W.D. Ross. Common morality also places great importance on the intent of the moral agent.

Ethicists usually identify certain structural components in common morality. Actions can be classified as permissible, impermissible, obligatory, and supererogatory. The last category refers to actions that are praiseworthy if done (sometimes requiring heroism or courage), but not morally obligatory. Common morality is also often divided into high-level rules or duties, such as those identified by Gert and Ross, mid-level principles, such as the principle that engineers should be loyal to their employers, and specific moral judgments about actions or people.

It is sometimes useful to construct overall models of common morality. Such models can answer questions about the criterion for right and wrong, the function or purpose of morality, and the kinds of evidence and reasoning that are appropriate in resolving moral issues. Two models are especially useful in thinking about larger social issues, as opposed to moral decisions facing an individual engineer. The two most prominent models are the utilitarian perspective, whose criterion is promoting human well-being, and the ethics of respect for persons, whose criterion is protecting the moral agency of individuals. These two models have characteristic strengths and weaknesses. Sometimes they give the same answers to a moral issue—although from different perspectives—but sometimes they give different answers. In the latter case, one must evaluate the strengths of the two different perspectives with regard to the issue at hand and make a decision about the issue. The two models suggest several tests that can be helpful in resolving moral issues.

2.12 ENGINEERING ETHICS ON THE WEB

Check your understanding of the material in this chapter by visiting the companion website for *Engineering Ethics.* The site includes multiple choice study questions, suggested discussion topics, and sometimes additional case studies to complement your reading and study of the material in this chapter.

NOTES

1. This account is based on Terrence Petty, "Use of Corpses in Auto-Crash Test Outrages Germans," *Time*, Dec. 6, 1993, p. 70.
2. This case is suggested by the experience of a former engineering student at Texas A&M University.
3. These ideas are suggested by Rosalind Hursthouse's "Virtue Ethics" in the *Stanford Encyclopedia of Philosophy*. Retrieved from http://plato.stanford.edu/entries/ethics-virtue/.
4. W. D. Ross, *The Right and the Good* (Oxford: Oxford University Press, 1930), pp. 20–22.
5. Bernard Gert, *Common Morality: Deciding What to Do* (New York: Oxford University Press, 2004).

6. Ibid., p. 9.

7. C. E. Harris, Jr., *Applying Moral Theories*, 5th. ed. (Belmont, CA, 2007), p. 96.

8. For a defense of this interpretation, see Marcus G. Singer, "Defense of the Golden Rule," in Marcus G. Singer, ed., *Morals and Values* (New York: Scribners, 1977).

9. This version of the universalizability criterion is suggested by Immanuel Kant. See his *Foundations of the Metaphysics of Morals, with Critical Essays* (Robert Paul Wolff, ed.), (Indianapolis: Bobb-Merrill, 1969). For another exposition of it, see Harris, *Applying Moral Theories*, 4th ed.

10. Alan Gewirth, *Reason and Morality* (Chicago: University of Chicago Press, 1978), especially pp. 199–127 and 338–354.

CHAPTER THREE

Responsibility in Engineering

Main Ideas in This Chapter

- Responsibility has to do with accountability, both for what one does in the present and future and for what one has done in the past.
- The obligation-responsibilities of engineers require not only adhering to regulatory norms and standard practices of engineering but also satisfying the standard of reasonable care.
- Beyond this, "good works" are both possible and desirable.
- Engineers can expect to be held accountable, if not legally liable, for intentionally, negligently, and recklessly caused harms.
- Responsible engineering practice requires good judgment, not simply following algorithms.
- A good test of engineering responsibility is the question: "What does an engineer do when no one is looking?" This makes evident the importance of *trust* in the work of engineers.

ON JANUARY 16, 2003, AT 10:39 A.M. Eastern Standard Time, the *Columbia* lifted off at Kennedy Space Center, destined for a 16-day mission in space.[1] The seven-person *Columbia* crew, which included one Israeli pilot, was scheduled to conduct numerous scientific experiments and return to earth on February 1. Only 81.7 seconds after liftoff, a briefcase-size piece of the brownish-orange insulating foam that covered the large external tank broke off and hit the leading edge of the orbiter's left wing. Unknown to the *Columbia* crew or the ground support staff, the foam knocked a hole in the leading edge of the wing that was approximately 10 inches across.

Cameras recorded the foam impact, but the images provided insufficient detail to determine either the exact point of impact or its effect. Several engineers, including Rodney Rocha, requested that attempts be made to get clearer images. There were even requests that the *Columbia* crew be directed to examine the wing for possible damage. It had become a matter of faith at NASA, however, that foam strikes, although a known problem, could not cause significant damage and were not a safety-of-flight issue, so management rejected this request. The astronauts were not told of the problem until shortly before reentry, when they were informed that the foam strike was inconsequential, but that they should know about it in case they were asked about the strike by the press on return from their mission.

Upon reentry into the Earth's atmosphere, a snaking plume of superheated air, probably exceeding 5000 degrees Fahrenheit, entered the breach in the wing and began to consume the wing from the inside. The destruction of the spacecraft began when it was over the Pacific Ocean and grew worse when it entered US airspace. Eventually, the bottom surface of the left wing began to cave upwards into the interior of the wing, finally causing *Columbia* to go out of control and disintegrate, mostly over east Texas. The entire crew, along with the spacecraft, was lost.

3.1　INTRODUCTION

This tragic event, which has many striking similarities with the *Challenger* disaster 17 years earlier, illustrates many of the issues surrounding the notion of responsibility in the engineering profession. Engineers obviously played a central role in making the *Columbia* flight possible and in safeguarding the spaceship and its travelers. From the outset of the launch, engineers had a special eye out for possible problems. Rodney Rocha and other engineers on NASA's Debris Assessment Team became concerned about flying debris. Noticing and assessing such details was their responsibility. If they did not handle this well, things could go very badly. Even if they did handle this well, things could go very badly. The stakes were high.

The concept of responsibility is many faceted. As a notion of accountability, it may be applied to individual engineers, teams of engineers, divisions or units within organizations, or even organizations themselves. It may focus primarily on legal liabilities, job-defined roles, expectations of professional engineering societies, or self-imposed moral standards.

As professionals, engineers are expected to commit themselves to high standards of conduct.[2] As noted in Chapter 1, the Preamble of NSPE's Code of Ethics emphasizes the importance of engineers being committed to honesty, integrity, fairness, and the protection of public safety, health, and welfare. This is based on the special roles engineers assume in their work and the crucial impact that this work has on our lives. We can refer to this as *role responsibility*.

Our dependence on the responsible exercise of engineering expertise points to the need to place our *trust* in the reliable performance of engineers, both as individuals and as members of teams of engineers who work together. In turn, when given opportunities to provide services to others, it is important for engineers to conduct themselves in ways that do not generate *distrust*. This has important implications for a professional's approach to his or her responsibilities. In general, we can think of possible approaches to responsibility along a spectrum. At one end of the spectrum is the attitude of doing as little as one can get away with and still stay out of trouble, keep one's job, and the like. At the other end of the spectrum are attitudes and dispositions that may take one "above and beyond the call of duty." This does not mean that one self-consciously aims at doing more than duty requires. Rather, it involves a thoroughgoing commitment to a level of excellence that others regard as supererogatory, or "going the extra mile."

In the professional domain, the attitude of doing only what is needed to stay out of trouble and keep one's job falls far short of what is regarded as minimally acceptable, both by responsible professionals themselves and those for whom they provide services. However, given William S. May's point (discussed in Chapter 1) that professionals cannot be constantly "watched," behavior that falls short of satisfying even minimally acceptable standards often can go unnoticed, at least in the short run, if not the long run. Supererogatory behavior may also go unnoticed, or at least be underappreciated. The professional's attitude might be "I'm just doing my job." But if others were to take a close look at this professional's "work ethic," they might well conclude that this is someone who exhibits an extraordinarily high level of dedication and performance.

Bearing in mind this somewhat imprecise spectrum of possible approaches to one's work, we can ask what sorts of attitudes and dispositions employers might look for if they were hoping to hire a responsible engineer.[3] We would expect integrity, honesty, and a willingness to make some self-sacrifice, and some degree of civic-mindedness to make the list. In addition to displaying basic engineering competence, a responsible engineer would also be expected to exhibit imaginativeness and perseverance, to communicate clearly and informatively, to be committed to objectivity, to be open to acknowledging and correcting mistakes, to work well with others, to be committed to quality, and to be able to see the "big picture" as well as more minute details. No doubt there are other items that could be added to the list. What all these characteristics have in common is that they contribute to the reliability and trustworthiness of engineers.

3.2 ENGINEERING STANDARDS

One way in which engineers can try to gain the trust of those they serve and with whom they work is to commit themselves to a code of ethics that endorses high standards of performance. Like other engineering codes of ethics, the NSPE code requires that the work of engineers satisfies "applicable engineering standards." These may be regulatory standards that specify technical requirements for specific kinds of engineering design—for example, that certain standards of safety be met by bridges or buildings. As such, they focus primarily on the results of engineering practice—on whether the work satisfies certain standards of quality or safety. Engineering standards may also require that certain procedures be undertaken to ascertain that specific, measurable levels of quality or safety are met; or they may require that whatever procedures are used be documented, along with their results.

Equally important, engineering codes of ethics typically insist that engineers conform to standards of competence, standards that have evolved through engineering practice and presumably are commonly accepted, even if only implicitly, in ordinary engineering training and practice.[4] Regulatory standards and standards of competence are intended to provide some assurance of quality, safety, and efficiency in engineering. It is important to realize, however, that they also leave considerable room for professional discretion in engineering design and practice. There are few algorithms for engineers to follow here. So, the need for engineering judgment must be emphasized.[5]

Although the NSPE Code of Ethics is the product of the collective reflection of members of one particular professional society of engineers, it seems intended to address the ethical responsibilities of all practicing engineers. Given this, the standards endorsed by the code should be supportable by reasons other than the fact that NSPE members publically commit themselves to those standards. That is, the standards should be supportable by reasons that are binding on even those engineers who are not members of NSPE. Are they?

In answering this question it is important to note that the Preamble does not single out NSPE members, as distinct from other engineers, when prescribing how engineers ought to conduct themselves. Instead, it depicts the general role that engineering plays in society, along with more specific standards of conduct suitable for fulfilling that role responsibly. Presumably, this depiction is apt regardless of whether engineers are members of NSPE.

Engineers and nonengineers alike can readily agree that engineers do play the sort of vital societal role depicted by the Preamble, which emphasizes that engineers are expected to use their specialized knowledge and skills in ways that benefit employers, clients, and the public and that do not betray the trust placed in them. This is a matter of, we will say, *obligation-responsibility*. Assessments of how well engineers handle their obligation-responsibilities are typically in terms of praise and blame. Unfortunately, we seem more inclined to blame shortcomings and failures than to praise everyday competent, if not exceptional, engineering practice. (We *expect* our cars to start, the elevators and trains to run, and the traffic lights to work.) In any case, we speak of an engineer as "being responsible" for a mistake or as being one of those "responsible" for an accident. This is a fundamentally negative and backward-looking concept of responsibility. Let us refer to it as *blame-responsibility*. However, it is important not to forget that assessments can be positive as well as negative.

We shall next discuss obligation-responsibility in relation to what is commonly called the *standard of care*, a standard of engineering responsibility accepted both in law and engineering practice. Then we will turn to the more negative notion of blame-responsibility and its relation to the standard of care. We shall consider issues of responsibility in regard to failures in the design or functioning of engineered products. These issues are complicated by the organizational structures within which most engineers work. Whether organizations themselves (as distinct from individuals) can sensibly be held morally responsible for harms is a controversial question. However, they can (and are) held liable in law, and this can have important implications for the moral responsibilities of their employees, including engineers.

3.3 THE STANDARD OF CARE

Engineers have a professional obligation to conform to the standard operating procedures and regulations that apply to their profession and to fulfill the basic responsibilities of their job as defined by the terms of their employment. Sometimes, however, it is not enough to follow standard operating procedures and regulations. Unexpected problems can arise that standard operating procedures and current regulations are not well equipped to handle. In light of this, engineers are expected to satisfy a more demanding norm, the *standard of care*. To explain this idea, we can first turn to codes of ethics.

Codes of ethics of professional engineering societies attempt to identify in a structured, comprehensive way standards its members believe should govern their conduct as engineers. However, because particular situations cannot be anticipated in all their relevant nuances, applying these standards requires professional *judgment*. For example, although sometimes it is obvious what would constitute a failure to protect public, health, and safety, often it is not. Not actively protecting public safety will fail to satisfy the public safety standard only if there is a responsibility to provide that level of safety. But, since no engineering product can be expected to be "absolutely" safe (at least, not if it is to be a useful product) and there are economic costs associated with safety improvements, there can be some uncertainty about what a reasonable standard of safety is for this or that product.

Rather than leave the determination of what counts as safe solely in the hands of individual engineers and their employers, safety standards are set by government agencies (such as the National Institute of Standards and Technology, the Occupational Safety and Health Administration, and the Environmental Protection Agency) or nongovernmental organizations (such as professional engineering societies and the International Organization for Standardization). Nevertheless, standards of safety, as well as standards of quality, may still leave room for considerable engineering discretion. Although some standards have a high degree of specificity (e.g., minimal requirements regarding the ability of a structure to withstand winds of a certain velocity that might strike that structure at, say, a 90 degree angle), some simply require that unspecified standard processes be developed, followed, and documented.[6]

Engineering codes of ethics typically make more general statements about engineers being required to conform to accepted standards of engineering practice. What such standards come to in actual practice depends, of course, on the area of engineering practice in question, along with whatever formal regulatory standards may be in place. However, underlying all of this is a broader standard of care in engineering practice, a standard appealed to in law and about which experienced, respected engineers can be called upon to testify in the courts in particular cases.

Joshua B. Kardon characterizes this standard of care in this way.[7] Although some errors in engineering judgment and practice can be expected to occur as a matter of course, not all errors are acceptable:

> An engineer is not liable, or responsible, for damages for every error. Society has decided, through case law, that when you hire an engineer, you buy the engineer's normal errors. However, if the error is shown to have been worse than a certain level of error, the engineer is liable. That level, the line between non-negligent and negligent error is the "standard of care."

How is this line determined in particular cases? It is not up to engineers alone to determine this, but they do play a crucial role in assisting judges and juries in their deliberations. Kardon continues:

> A trier of fact, a judge or jury, has to determine what the standard of care is and whether an engineer has failed to achieve that level of performance. They do so by hearing expert testimony. People who are qualified as experts express opinions as to the standard of care and as to the defendant engineer's performance relative to that standard.

For this legal process to be practicable and reasonably fair to engineers, it is necessary that there be an operative notion of accepted practice in engineering that is well understood by competent engineers in the areas of engineering under question. As Kardon puts it:[8]

> A good working definition of the standard of care of a professional is: that level or quality of service ordinarily provided by other normally competent practitioners of good standing in that field, contemporaneously providing similar services in the same locality and under the same circumstances.

Given this, we should not expect to find a formal statement of what specifically satisfies the standard. Rather, an appeal is being made to what is commonly and ordinarily done (or not done) by competent engineers. However, it should be recalled that the

Preamble of the NSPE Code of Ethics calls for engineers to adhere to "the highest principles of ethical conduct." For many engineers, these standards might well demand more than the legally recognized standard of care does. So from the standpoint of engineering ethics, the standard of care seems to represent a minimally acceptable standard—but the highest *shared* standard among competent, responsible engineers in the relevant areas of practice.

3.4 RESPONSIBLE OVERSIGHT

Engineers who have responsible charge for a project are expected to exercise careful oversight before putting their official stamp of approval on the project. However, what careful oversight requires will vary with the project in question in ways that resist an algorithmic articulation of the precise steps to be taken and the criteria to be used. In general, what is expected is what is often called *reasonable*, or *due*, care.

Two well known cases are instructive. In the first instance, those in charge of the construction of the Kansas City Hyatt Regency hotel were charged with professional negligence in regard to the catastrophic walkway collapse in 1981. (This is discussed in greater detail in Case 17 in Cases.) Although those in charge did not authorize the fatal departure from the original design of the walkway support, it was determined that responsible monitoring on their part would have made them aware of the proposed change. Had it come to their attention, a few simple calculations could have made it evident to them that the resulting structure would be unsafe.

In this case it was determined that the engineers in charge fell seriously short of acceptable engineering practice, resulting in a failure to meet the standard of care. Satisfying the standard of care cannot guarantee that failure will not occur. However, failure to satisfy the standard of care itself is not acceptable. In any particular case, there may be several acceptable ways of meeting the standard. Much depends on the kind of project in question, its specific context, and the particular variables that (sometimes unpredictably) come into play.

The second case involved a departure from the original design not noted by William LeMessurier, the chief structural engineer of Manhattan's 59-story Citicorp Building.[9] LeMessurier was surprised to learn after the building was completed that its major structural joints were bolted rather than deep-welded together, as called for in the original design. However, initially he was confident that the building still more than adequately satisfied the New York City building code's requirement that winds striking the structure from a 90 degree angle would not pose serious danger to the building. The code did not specify whether welds or bolts should be used to secure the joints, only that the resulting structure must satisfy the 90 degree wind test.

Fortunately, LeMessurier did not rest content with the thought that bolted joints still satisfied the city building code. Now he decided to calculate what might happen if winds struck the building diagonally at a 45 degree angle. This question seemed sensible, since the first floor of the building is actually several stories above ground, with the ground support of the building being four pillars placed in between the four corners of the structure rather than at the corners themselves. Further calculations by LeMessurier determined that bolted joints rendered the structure much more vulnerable to high winds than had been anticipated. Despite satisfying the city code, LeMessurier concluded that the building was not safe enough and that corrections were needed. The code could not be relied on to set reliable criteria for the standard of care in all cases.

From this it should not be concluded that there could be only one acceptable solution to the joint problem. LeMessurier's plan for reinforcing the bolted joints worked. But the original plan for deep welds apparently would have, as well. Many other acceptable solutions may have been possible. So a variety of designs for a particular structure could satisfy acceptable engineering standards. The Hyatt Regency case is a clear illustration of culpable failure. The original design itself failed to meet building code requirements. The design change made matters worse. The Citicorp case is a clear illustration of how the standard engineering practice of meeting code requirements may not be enough.

No doubt William LeMessurier was dismayed at finding a serious problem with the Citicorp Building. However, there was much about the structure in which he could still take pride. A particularly innovative feature was a 400-ton concrete damper placed near the top of the building. LeMessurier claims to have introduced this feature, not to improve safety, but to reduce the sway of the building—a matter of comfort to residents. Of course, this does not mean that the damper has no effect on safety. Although designed for comfort, it is possible that it also enhances safety. Or, especially since its movement needs to be both facilitated and constrained, it is possible that, without other controls, it could have a negative effect on safety. In any case, the effect that a 400-ton damper near the top of a 59-story structure might have on the building's ability to handle heavy winds is something that requires careful attention.

Supporting the structure on four pillars midway between the corners of the building is another innovation—one that might explain why it eventually occurred to LeMessurier that it was worthwhile to try to determine what effect 45 degree winds might have on the structure's stability. Both innovations could fall within the range of accepted engineering practice, provided that well conceived efforts are made to determine what effect they might have on the overall integrity and utility of the structure. The risk of relying exclusively on the particular directives of a building code is that its framers are unlikely to be able in advance to take into account all of the relevant effects of innovations in design. That is, it is quite possible for regulations to fail to keep pace with technological innovation.

3.5 BLAME-RESPONSIBILITY AND CAUSATION

Now let us turn to the more negative concept of responsibility, blame-responsibility. We can begin by considering the relationship of responsibility for harm to causation of harm. When the Columbia Accident Investigation Board looked at the *Columbia* tragedy, it focused on what it called the "causes" of the accident. It identified two principal causes: the "physical cause" and the "organizational causes." The physical cause was the damage to the leading edge of the left wing by the foam that broke loose from the external tank. The organizational causes were defects in the organization and culture of NASA that led to an inadequate concern for safety.[10] The board also made reference to individuals who were "responsible and accountable" for the accident. The board, however, did not consider its primary mission to be the identification of individuals who should be held responsible and perhaps punished.[11] Thus, it identified three types of explanations of the accident: the physical cause, organizational causes, and individuals responsible or accountable for the accident.

The concept of cause is related in an interesting way to that of responsibility. Generally speaking, the more we are inclined to speak of the physical cause of something, the less we are inclined to speak of responsibility—and the more we are inclined to speak of responsibility, the less inclined we are to focus on physical causes. When we refer only to the physical cause of the accident—namely, the damage produced by the breach in the leading edge of the orbiter's left wing—it is inappropriate to speak of responsibility. Physical causes, as such, cannot be responsible agents. The place of responsibility with respect to organizations and individuals raises more complex issues. Let us turn first to organizations.

The relationship of organizations to the concepts of causation and responsibility is controversial. The Columbia Accident Investigation Board preferred to speak of the organization and culture of NASA as a cause of the accident. With respect to the physical cause, the board said:[12]

> The physical cause of the loss of the *Columbia* and its crew was a breach in the Thermal Protection System on the leading edge of the left wing, caused by a piece of insulating foam which separated from the left bipod ramp section of the External Fuel Tank at 81.7 seconds after launch, and struck the wing in the vicinity of the lower half of Reinforced Carbon-Carbon panel number 8.

With respect to the organizational causes of the accident, the board said:[13]

> The organizational causes of this accident are rooted in the Space Shuttle Program's history and culture, including the original compromises that were required to gain approval for the Shuttle, subsequent years of resource constraints, fluctuating priorities, schedule pressures, mischaracterization of the Shuttle as operational rather than developmental, and lack of an agreed national vision for human space flight. Cultural traits and organizational practices detrimental to safety were allowed to develop, including: reliance on past successes as a substitute for sound engineering practices (such as testing to understand why systems were not performing in accordance with requirements); organizational barriers that prevented effective communication of critical safety information and stifled professional differences of opinion; lack of integrated management across program elements; and the evolution of an informal chain of command and decision-making processes that operated outside the organization's rules.

With respect to the relative importance of these two causes, the board concluded:[14]

> In the Board's view, NASA's organizational culture and structure had as much to do with this accident as the External Tank form. Organizational culture refers to the values, norms, beliefs, and practices that govern how an institution functions. At the most basic level, organizational culture defines the assumptions that employees make as they carry out their work. It is a powerful force that can persist through reorganizations and reassignments of key personnel.

If organizations can be causes, can they also be morally responsible agents, much as humans can be? Some theorists believe it makes no sense to say that organizations (such as General Motors or NASA) can be morally responsible agents.[15] An organization is not, after all, a human person in the ordinary sense. Unlike human persons, corporations do not have a body, cannot be sent to jail, and have an indefinite life. On the other hand, corporations are described as "artificial persons" in the law. According to *Black's Law Dictionary*, "the law treats the corporation itself as a person which can sue and be sued. The corporation is distinct from the individuals who comprise it (shareholders)."[16] Corporations, like persons, can also come into being, pass away, and be fined.

Philosopher Peter French argues that corporations can, in a significant sense, be morally responsible agents.[17] Although French focuses on corporations, his arguments can also be applied to governmental organizations such as NASA. Corporations have three characteristics that can be said to make them very similar to moral agents. First, corporations, like people, have a decision-making mechanism. People can deliberate and then carry out their decisions. Similarly, corporations have boards of directors and executives who make decisions for the corporation, and these decisions are then carried out by subordinate members of the corporate hierarchy. Second, corporations, like people, have policies that guide their decision making. People have moral rules and other considerations that guide their conduct. Similarly, corporations have corporate policies, including, in many cases, a corporate code of ethics. In addition to policies that guide conduct, corporations also have a "corporate culture" that tends to shape their behavior, much as personality and character shape the actions of individuals. Third, corporations, like people, can be said to have "interests" that are not necessarily the same as those of the executives, employees, and others who make up the corporation. Corporate interests include making a profit, maintaining a good public image, staying out of legal trouble, and so forth.

Consider an example of a corporate decision. Suppose an oil corporation is considering beginning a drilling operation in Africa. A mountain of paperwork will be forwarded to the CEO, other top executives, and probably the board of directors. When a decision is made, according to the decision-making procedure established by the corporation, it can properly be called a "corporate decision." It was made for "corporate reasons," presumably in accordance with "corporate policy," to satisfy "corporate interests," and guided by "corporate ethics."

Regardless of whether organizations, as such, are seen as moral agents or merely causes of harm, organizations can be held responsible in at least three senses.[18] First, they can be criticized for causing harms, just as the Columbia Accident Investigation Board criticized NASA. Second, an organization that harms others can be asked to make reparations for wrong done. Finally, an organization that has harmed others is in need of reform, just as the board believed NASA needs reform.

One worry about treating organizations as morally responsible agents is the fear that individual responsibility might be displaced. However, there need be no incompatibility in holding both organizations and the individuals within them morally accountable for what they do. We will now turn to the responsibilities of individuals.

3.6 LIABILITY

Although engineers and their employers might try to excuse apparent failure to provide safety and quality by pointing out that they have met existing regulatory standards, it is evident that the courts will not necessarily agree. The standard of care in tort law (which is concerned with wrongful injury) is not restricted to regulatory standards. The expectation is that engineers will meet the standard of care as expressed in Coombs v. Beede:[19]

> The responsibility resting on an architect is essentially the same as that which rests upon the lawyer to his client, or upon the physician to his patient, or which rests upon anyone to another where such person pretends to possess some special skill and ability in some special employment, and offers his services to the public on account of his fitness to act in the line of

business for which he may be employed. The undertaking of an architect implies that he possesses skill and ability, including taste, sufficient enough to enable him to perform the required services at least ordinarily and reasonably well; and that he will exercise and apply, in the given case, his skill and ability, his judgment and taste reasonably and without neglect.

As Joshua B. Korden points out, this standard does not hold that all failure to provide satisfying services is wrongful injury. But it does insist that the services provide evidence that reasonable care was taken. What counts as reasonable care is a function of both what the public can reasonably expect and what experienced, competent engineers regard as acceptable practice. Given the desirability of innovative engineering design, it is unrealistic for the public to regard all failures and mishaps to be culpable; at the same time, it is incumbent on engineers to do their best to anticipate and avoid failures and mishaps.

It should also be noted that Coombs v. Beede does not say that professionals need only conform to the established standards and practices of their field of expertise. Those standards and practices may be in a state of change, and they may not be able to keep pace with advancing knowledge of risks in particular areas. Furthermore, as many liability cases have shown, reasonable people often disagree about precisely what those standards and practices should be taken to be.

A practical way of looking at moral responsibility is to consider the related concept of legal liability for causing harm. Legal liability in many ways parallels moral responsibility, although there are important differences. To be legally liable for causing harm is to warrant punishment for, or to be obligated to make restitution for, harms. Liability for harm ordinarily implies that the person caused the harm, but it also implies something about the conditions under which the harm was caused. These conditions are ordinarily "mental" in nature and can involve such things as malicious intent, recklessness, and negligence. Let us look at these concepts of liability and moral responsibility for harm in more detail, noting that each connotes a weaker sense of liability than the other.[20] We shall also see that, although the concept of causing harm is present, the notions of liability and responsibility are the focus of attention.

First, a person can *intentionally*, or knowingly and deliberately, cause harm. If one person stabs another in the back to take his or her money, the assailant is both morally responsible and legally liable for injury or death. The causal component in this case is the physical assault, and the mental component is the intention to do serious harm.

Second, a person can *recklessly* cause harm by not aiming to cause harm but by being aware that harm is likely to result. If I recklessly cause you harm, the causal factor is present, so I am responsible for the harm. In reckless behavior, although there is not an intent to harm, there is an intent to engage in behavior that is known to place others at risk of harm. Furthermore, the person may have what we could call a reckless attitude, in which the well-being of others, and perhaps even of himself, is not uppermost in his mind. The reckless attitude may cause harm, as in the case of a person who drives twice the speed limit and causes an accident. He may not intend to do harm or even to cause an accident, but he does intend to drive fast, and he may not be thinking about his own safety or that of others. If his reckless action causes harm, then he is responsible for the harm and should be held legally liable for it.

Third, a still weaker kind of legal liability is associated with *negligently* causing harm. Unlike recklessness, where an element of deliberateness or intent is involved (such as a decision to drive fast), in negligent behavior the person may simply overlook something, or not even be aware of the factors that could cause harm. Furthermore, there may not be any direct causal component. The person is responsible because she has failed to exercise due care, which is the care that would be expected of a reasonable person in the circumstances. In law, a successful charge of negligence must meet four conditions:

1. A legal obligation to conform to certain standards of conduct is present.
2. The person accused of negligence fails to conform to the standards.
3. There is a reasonably close causal connection between the conduct and the resulting harm.
4. Actual loss or damage to the interests of another results.

These four elements are also present in moral responsibility, except that in the first condition, we must substitute "moral obligation" for "legal obligation." Professions such as engineering have recognized standards of professional practice, both technical and moral. Professional negligence, therefore, is the failure to perform duties that professionals have implicitly or explicitly assumed by virtue of being professionals. If an engineer does not exercise standard care according to the recognized standards of his profession, and is therefore negligent, then he can be held responsible for the harm done.

One concept of legal liability has no exact parallel in moral responsibility. In some areas of the law there is *strict liability* for harms caused; there is no attribution of fault or blame, but there is a legal responsibility to provide compensation, make repairs, or the like. Strict liability is directed at corporations rather than individual engineers within the organization. However, insofar as they have a duty to be faithful and loyal employees, and perhaps even as a matter of specifically assigned duties, engineers can have responsibilities to their employer to help minimize the likelihood that strict liability will be imposed on the organization. So even strict liability at the corporate level can have moral implications for individual engineers.

Finally, even if certain engineers were not responsible in any of the above ways for harms attributable to their organization, their managers may assign them responsibility for fixing the problems that were none of their making.

Although the standard of care plays a prominent role in law, it is important to realize that it reflects a broader notion of moral responsibility as well. Dwelling on its role in law alone may suggest to some a more calculative, "legalistic" consideration of reasonable care. In calculating the case for or against making a full effort to meet the standard of care, the cost of doing so can be weighed against the chances of facing a tort claim. This involves estimating the likelihood that harm will actually occur—and, if it does, that anyone will take it to court (and that they will be successful). Liability insurance is already an expense, and those whose aim is simply to maximize gains and minimize overall costs might calculate that a less than full commitment to the standard of care is worth the risk. From this more narrow perspective of self-regard, care is not so much a matter of reasonable care as it is taking care not to get caught.

3.7 GOOD WORKS

Regarding the standard of care as only a guide to protecting *oneself* (or one's employer) from legal liability hardly does justice to its moral underpinnings. Ideally, the standard of care reflects a concern to protect *others* from harm and wrongdoing.

This captures a sense of at least minimal moral concern for others. However, the spectrum of responsibility we introduced earlier in this chapter can embrace much more.

Sometimes we say that a person has gone "above and beyond the call of duty," or that he or she has gone "the extra mile." We regard such *good works* as admirable, if not exemplary. If obligation-responsibility consists first and foremost of reasonable care, good works are something more. A simple example outside an engineering context illustrates what we have in mind.[21]

Ralph wakes up at his usual time and prepares to go to work. When he looks out the window, he is shocked to see his long driveway drifted over with snow; this was not in last night's weather forecast. He has only a snow shovel, not a plow. He realizes he will be very late to work—and very tired. As he bundles up to go out and shovel, Ralph is surprised to see his driveway being cleared by a neighbor with a snowplow attached to his pickup. Although they are neighbors, they have never actually met each other.

No doubt Ralph appreciates what his neighbor is doing. What would he think if his neighbor had done nothing to help? Would he fault him, think he had failed to do his duty, or think his neighbor had some sort of moral deficiency? These responses are unlikely. His neighbor has gone "above and beyond the call of duty." His is not a saintly or heroic act, but it is a good one.

Such things happen in professional life as well. Two examples were given in Chapter 1. The first is the engineer who keeps working on improving the safety belt for high-rise window washers who risk their lives on scaffolding that goes up and down the sides of tall buildings. The second is air bag pioneer Carl Clark, who continued after retirement, and without pay, to try to develop air bags for car bumpers and wearable air bags for the elderly to prevent broken hips when they fall. Here is a third example: Statistician Michael Stoline agreed to help analyze data to determine whether it was safe for residents in Love Canal, near Buffalo, New York, to return to their homes after being ordered to leave because of the likelihood that toxic wastes in the area posed a serious health risk. Although modestly compensated for his services, he realized that there were many more lucrative consulting opportunities. Asked why he accepted this task instead, he said: "Analyzing data just for the money doesn't mean anything to me. I want it to do some good."[22]

These three examples differ in interesting and important ways. The first is an example of someone whose dedication to work in his regular employment takes him beyond ordinary working hours, as well as beyond the reasonable expectations of his company and fellow employees. He may see this as "just doing my job"—staying with it until he is satisfied that he has done his best. However, although he might fault himself if he quit working on the safety belt and simply stuck to other tasks during ordinary work hours, it is unlikely that others would fault him for doing so. The second is someone who retired, but who continued to employ his imagination and skills on projects that he hoped would help others. The third is someone, otherwise fully employed, who took on a new set of responsibilities that were not part of his regular work—not so much to make more money as to do some good for others.

Despite their differences, these three examples illustrate dedication that goes well beyond what can be ordinarily, and rightfully, expected by others, whether in their regular place of employment or elsewhere. Although we appreciate the fact that these individuals have taken on additional responsibilities, we do not think that they had a *duty* to assume them in the first place. Even though *they* might say to themselves, "This is what I ought to be doing," it is unlikely that we would feel it is appropriate for *us* to tell them that they ought to be doing what they are doing. Instead, we praise them for their good works and admire their enlarged sense of responsibility.

Good works can be undertaken by groups as well as individuals. In the late 1930s, a group of General Electric engineers worked together to develop the sealed beam headlamp, which promised to reduce sharply the number of fatalities caused by night driving.[23] To accomplish this it was necessary to involve engineers in research, design, production, economic analysis, and governmental regulation. Although the need for headlight improvement was widely acknowledged, there was also widespread skepticism about its technical and economic feasibility. By 1937, the General Electric team proved the technical feasibility of the sealed beam headlamp. However, the remaining task was to persuade car builders and designers to cooperate with each other in support of the innovation, as well as to convince regulators of its merits.

There is little reason to suppose that the General Electric engineers were simply doing what they were told—namely to come up with a more adequate headlamp. Apparently, the virtual consensus was that this could not be done, so the engineers had to overcome considerable resistance. This was no ordinary task, as evidenced by the remarks of another engineer of that era:

> The reaching of the consensus embodied in the specifications of the Sealed Beam Headlamp is an achievement which commands the admiration of all who have any knowledge of the difficulties that were overcome. It is an achievement not only in illuminating engineering, but even more in safety engineering, in human engineering, in the art of cooperation.[24]

The difficulties faced by this group of engineers reminds us that enthusiasm for good works needs to be tempered with realism. Other demands and constraints may discourage undertaking such projects. Nevertheless, looking for opportunities to do good works, as well as taking advantage of these opportunities when they arise, are desirable traits in an engineer.

How should we understand good works within the context of engineering responsibility? Whereas we hold each other responsible for certain things, it is also possible for us to assume, or take on, certain responsibilities. The design engineer who has taken on the task of improving the quality of the safety belt is assuming additional responsibilities. These are self-imposed. The statistician, otherwise fully employed, agrees to additional consulting responsibilities only when convinced they will "do some good"—a commendable but self-imposed requirement. Finally, as the sealed beam headlamp project illustrates, such efforts need not be solitary; engineers can undertake good works together.

It is easy not to notice that what we are calling "good works" commonly occur in engineering practice. Those involved may view themselves as simply doing what needs to be done. They may see important tasks that we fail to notice, and they quietly do them. Or we may grow accustomed to how they approach their work and simply take their dedication and accomplishments for granted. Furthermore, once they take on a responsibility and the work is underway, it often is appropriate to hold them accountable for completing the work. What we may overlook is that taking on the responsibility in the first place was fully optional.

We might ask if it really is important to emphasize good works in engineering. Why not assume that, if only engineers would meet their basic obligations, they would fulfill the basic needs of those whom engineering societies acknowledge they should serve? To see why not, consider the implications of the absence of good works. Disasters are averted and assistance in recovering from them is provided, not only by professionals fulfilling their duties, but also by doing more than this requires. Relief from less severe, but nevertheless unwelcome, harms can also be provided by those willing to do more.

Whether something should be regarded as an instance of good works does not depend on the magnitude of its consequences. An improved safety belt for high-rise window washers might make a real contribution to saving lives and preventing injuries, but its magnitude pales in comparison with the number of lives saved or immeasurably improved by Frederick Cuny's disaster relief work. Good works may focus on a specific community, as in the case of the Love Canal statistician, or they may focus on an entire industry, as in the case of the engineers working on the sealed beam headlamp.

It should be noted that good works may not always be welcome. In fact, sometimes they are discouraged, intentionally or not. We need to ask to what extent the organizations within which engineers work present obstacles to doing good works. For example, an organization may define tasks and responsibilities too narrowly, actively discouraging do-gooders or rewarding only those who do not rock the boat. Good works may also be discouraged by the need to meet tight time schedules, by limited budgets, and by the press of other matters at hand. Some of these obstacles are simply realistic and justifiable limitations (particularly if good works can be accomplished only by neglecting basic duties).

However, creative efforts can sometimes overcome these limitations. A case in point is the 3M/3P plan initiated by 3M (Minnesota Mining and Manufacturing Company). Once regarded a major polluter, 3M launched a program in the 1970s that continues to save them money through an aggressive, environmentally friendly program that sets objectives that are far more demanding than current governmental regulations. In publicizing its efforts, 3M asserts, "Conventional controls are temporary and do not eliminate the problem. 3P seeks to eliminate pollution at the source through product reformulation, process modification, equipment redesign, and the recycling and reuse of waste materials."[25] Its projects are designed to combine reducing pollution with saving money, and it claims to have successfully completed thousands of projects over the last three decades. Clearly, engineers play a substantial role in these projects, which are reviewed by the 3P Coordinating Committee, which consists of representatives from engineering, manufacturing, and health and safety units at 3M. All projects, it is claimed, are proposed by 3M employees, who voluntarily participate in the program.

3.8 APPLICATIONS: A CASE STUDY

Although fictional, the following case illustrates how some of the concepts of responsibility we have been considering in this chapter can come into play in engineering practice. Carl Lawrence was alarmed by Kevin Rourke's urgent, early afternoon message: "All supervisors immediately check for open caustic valves. Supply tank is empty. Pump still running—either an open valve or a leak. Emergency order of caustic supply on the way." In only the first year of his work as a supervisor of one of Emerson Chemical's acid- and caustic-distribution systems, Lawrence had never had to deal with anything like this before. He knew he should move quickly to see if his unit was the source of the problem.

Much to his dismay, Lawrence found that the problem had originated in his unit. One of his lead operators discovered that a seldom-used caustic valve was open. Although the valve was immediately closed, Lawrence knew the cleanup remedy would be costly. Minimally, several hundred gallons of caustic would have to be replaced, and as many as 30 drums of hydrochloric acid might be needed to reduce the pH level of effluent rushing out of the plant toward the local publicly owned wastewater-treatment works.

Eventually, Lawrence would have to try to determine if someone was at fault (blame-responsibility) for the accident. No doubt he should look for the cause of the accident—the mechanical failure that produced the problem. Because the valve was opened, it is likely that a responsible agent was involved. This does not mean that someone intentionally left the valve open. It could be a case of negligence—but whose?

Lawrence discovers, let us suppose, that Rick Duffy, a lead operator from the early shift, forgot to make sure the valve was closed before leaving. Because that particular valve is in a remote and seldom-used section of Lawrence's unit, no one noticed the open valve until after Kevin Rourke sent out his emergency notice. Does this settle the question of responsibility (blame-responsibility)? It might seem so. As lead operator, Duffy has the responsibility (role-responsibility) to monitor the opening and closing of valves in his area at the appropriate time. He failed to make sure that the seldom-opened valve was closed.

Let us suppose, however, that Carl Lawrence reflects further. He recalls his first day on the job. After taking Lawrence around the facilities, Kevin Rourke asked Rick Duffy to show Lawrence how the distribution systems work. As Lawrence and Duffy moved from the acid- to the caustic-distribution system, Lawrence noted a striking difference. The acid-distribution piping had spring-loaded valves that close automatically when not in use. To pump acid into a remote receiving tank, a pump switch must be activated at the remote location. The operator has to hold the pump switch on when the tank is filling. Duffy mentioned that the penalty for propping the switch on by other means is immediate dismissal. In contrast, no similar precautions applied to the caustic system. The caustic valves have to be manually opened and closed.

Lawrence now remembers asking Duffy why the caustic system was so different. Duffy replied with a shrug: "I don't really know. It's been this way at least as long as I've been here. I suppose it's because the acid-distribution system is used so much more." Lawrence also asked Duffy if the lead operators have written procedures for filling the caustic tanks. Duffy answered that he had never seen any—nor did he recall any review of the practice during the four years he had been an operator. Lawrence then asked Duffy if he was satisfied with this. Duffy replied, "Well, I don't have any problems with it. Anyway, that's someone else's concern, not mine. I suppose they don't want to put out the money to change it. 'Don't fix the wheel if it's not broken' seems to be their attitude."

Lawrence recalls not being impressed with this line of reasoning and wondering if he should ask his supervisor, Kevin Rourke, about the caustic valve. However, not wishing to make a stir at the start of his work with Emerson, Lawrence simply dropped the matter. He now wonders if he bears some of the responsibility for the caustic overflow. Perhaps he should have persisted. Further, he begins to wonder about Rourke's responsibility. Should people in Rourke's position be looking out for potential problem areas and encouraging others, including Lawrence and Duffy, to do likewise?

We can ask these questions as part of the query about who might be to blame, or at fault, for the accident. But we need not dwell on this. We might ask, instead, what responsibilities engineers, technicians, and others should assume in their workplace—especially in working environments in which such accidents can occur. In this case, Carl Lawrence can reflect on the variety of factors that, taken together, might decrease the likelihood that such an accident could happen again. Looking back, he might well conclude that responsibility for the accident was *shared*. There were constructive things that several people might have done. More important, there are lessons to be learned for the future.

3.9   DESIGN STANDARDS

As we have noted, most engineering codes of ethics insist that, in designing products, engineers are expected to hold considerations of public safety paramount. However, there is likely more than one way to satisfy safety standards, especially when stated broadly. But if there is more than one way to satisfy safety standards, how are designers to proceed?

If we are talking about the overall safety of a product, there may be much latitude, a latitude that, of course, provides space for considerations other than safety (e.g., overall quality, usability, cost). For example, in the late 1960s, operating under the constraints of coming up with an appealing automobile that weighed under 2000 pounds that would cost consumers no more than $2000, Ford engineers decided to make more trunk space by putting the Pinto's gas tank in an unusual place.[26] This raised a safety question regarding rear end collisions. Ford claimed that the vehicle passed the current standards. However, some Ford engineers urged that a protective buffer should be inserted between the gas tank and protruding bolts. This, they contended, would enable the Pinto to pass a more demanding standard that it was known would soon be imposed on newer vehicles. They warned that, without the buffer, the Pinto would fail to satisfy the new standard, a standard that they believed would come much closer to meeting the standard of care enforced in tort law.

Ford decided not to put in the buffer. It might have been thought that satisfying the current safety standard ensured that courts and their juries would agree that reasonable care was exercised. However, this turned out to be a mistaken view. As noted above, the courts can determine that existing technical standards are not adequate, and engineers themselves are sometimes called upon to testify to that effect.

Given the bad publicity Ford received regarding the Pinto and its history of subsequent litigation, Ford might regret not having heeded the advice of those engineers who argued for the protective buffer. This could have been included in the original design, or perhaps there were other feasible alternatives during the early design phases. However, even after the car was put on the market, a change could have been made. This would have involved an expensive recall, but this would not have been an unprecedented move in the automotive industry.

These possibilities illustrate a basic point about regulatory standards, accepted standards of engineering practice, and engineering design. Professional standards for engineers underdetermine design. In principle, if not in practice, there will be more than one way to satisfy the standards. This does not mean that professional standards have no effect on practice. As Stuart Shapiro points out:[27]

> Standards are one of the principal mechanisms for managing complexity of any sort, including technological complexity. Standardized terminology, physical properties, and procedures all play a role in constraining the size of the universe in which the practitioner must make decisions.

For a profession, the establishment of standards of practice is typically regarded as contributing to professionalism, thereby enhancing the profession in the eyes of those who receive its services. At the same time, standards of practice can contribute both to the quality and safety of products in industry. Still, standards of practice have to be applied in particular contexts that are not themselves specified in the standards. Shapiro notes:[28]

> There are many degrees of freedom available to the designer and builder of machines and processes. In this context, standards of practice provide a means of mapping the universal onto the local. All one has to do is think of the great variety of local circumstances for which bridges are designed and the equally great variety of designs that result.... Local contingencies must govern the design and construction of any particular bridge within the frame of relative universals embodied in the standards.

Shapiro's observation focuses on how standards of practice allow engineers freedom to adapt their designs to local, variable circumstances. This often brings surprises, not only in design but also in regard to the adequacy of formal standards of practice. As Louis L. Bucciarelli points out, standards of practice are based on the previous experience and testing of engineers. Design operates on the edge of "the new and the untried, the unexperienced, the ahistorical."[29] Thus, as engineers come up with innovative designs (such as LeMessurier's Citicorp structure), we should expect formal standards of practice themselves sometimes to be challenged and found to be in need of change. All the more reason why courts of law are unwilling simply to equate the standard of care with current formal standards of practice.

3.10   THE RANGE OF STANDARDS OF PRACTICE

Some standards of practice are clearly only local in their scope. The New York City building code requirement that high-rise structures be tested for wind resistance at 90 degree angles applied only within a limited geographic region. Such specific code requirements are local in their origin and applicability. Of course, one would expect somewhat similar requirements to be in place in comparable locales in the US, as well as in other high-rise locales around the world. This suggests that local codes, particularly those that attempt to ensure quality and safety, reflect more general standards of safety and good engineering practice.

One test of whether we can meaningfully talk of more general standards is to ask whether the criteria for engineering competence are only local (e.g., New York City civil engineers, Chicago civil engineers). The answer seems clearly to be "no" within the boundaries of the United States, especially for graduates of accredited engineering programs at United States colleges and universities.

However, as Vivian Weil has argued, there is good reason to believe that professional standards of engineering practice can cross national boundaries.[30] She offers the example of the early twentieth century Russian engineer Peter Palchinsky. Critical of major engineering projects in Russia, Palchinsky was nevertheless regarded to be a highly competent engineer in his homeland. He also was a highly regarded consultant in Germany, France, England, the Netherlands, and Italy. Although he was regarded as politically dangerous by Russian leaders at the time, no one doubted his engineering abilities—either in Russia or elsewhere.

Weil also reminds readers of two fundamental principles of engineering that Palchinsky applied wherever he practiced:[31]

> Recall that the first principle was: gather full and reliable information about the specific situation. The second was: view engineering plans and projects in context, taking into account impacts on workers, the needs of workers, systems of transportation and communication, resources needed, resource accessibility, economic feasibility, impacts on users and on other affected parties, such as people who live downwind.

Weil goes on to point out that underlying Palchinsky's two principles are principles of common morality, particularly respect for the well-being of workers—a principle that Palchinsky argued was repeatedly violated by Lenin's favored engineering projects.

We have noted that the codes of ethics of engineering societies typically endorse principles that seem intended to apply to engineers in general rather than only to members of those particular societies. Common morality was suggested as providing the ground for basic provisions of those codes (for example, concern for the safety, health, and welfare of the public). Whether engineers who are not members of professional engineering societies actually do, either explicitly or implicitly, accept the principles articulated in a particular society's code of ethics is, of course, another matter. However, even if some do not, it could be argued that they *should*. Weil's point is that there is no reason, in principle, to believe that supportable international standards cannot be formulated and adopted. Furthermore, this need not be restricted to abstract statements of ethical principle. As technological developments and their resulting products show up across the globe, they can be expected to be accompanied by global concerns about quality, safety, efficiency, cost effectiveness, and sustainability. This, in turn, can result in uniform standards in many areas regarding acceptable and unacceptable engineering design, practice, and products. In any case, in the context of an emerging global economy, constructive discussions of these concerns should not be expected to be only local.

3.11 THE PROBLEM OF MANY HANDS

Individuals often attempt to evade personal responsibility for wrongdoing. Perhaps the most common way this is done, especially by individuals in large organizations, is by pointing out that many individuals had a hand in causing the harm. The argument here goes as follows: "So many people are responsible for the tragedy that it is irrational and unfair to pin the responsibility on any individual person, including me." Let us call this the *problem of fractured responsibility* or (preferably) the *problem of many hands.*[32] In response to this argument, philosopher Larry May has proposed the following principle to apply to the responsibility of individuals in a situation where many people are involved: "[I]f a harm has resulted from collective inaction, the degree of individual responsibility of each member of a putative group for the harm should vary based on the role each member could, counterfactually, have played in preventing the inaction."[33] Let us call this the *principle of responsibility for inaction in groups.* Our slightly modified version of this principle reads as follows: In a situation in which a harm has been produced by collective inaction, the degree of responsibility of each member of the group depends on the extent to which the member could reasonably be expected to have tried to prevent the action. The qualification "the extent to which each member could reasonably be expected to have tried to prevent the action" is necessary because there are limits to reasonable expectation here. If a person could have prevented an undesirable action only by taking his own life, sacrificing his legs, or harming someone else, then we cannot reasonably expect him to do it.

A similar principle can apply to collective action. Let us call it the *principle of responsibility for action in groups.* In a situation in which harm has been produced by collective action, the degree of responsibility of each member of the group depends on the extent to which the member caused the action by some action reasonably avoidable on his part. Again, the reason for the qualification is that if an action causing harm can only be avoided by extreme or heroic action on the individual's part (such as taking his own life, sacrificing his legs, or harming someone else), then we may find reason for not holding the person responsible, or at least holding him less responsible.

3.12   CHAPTER SUMMARY

Obligation- and role-responsibility require that engineers exercise a standard of care in their work. Engineers need to be concerned with complying with the law, adhering to standard norms and practices, and avoiding wrongful behavior. But this may not be good enough. The standard of care view insists that existing regulatory standards may be inadequate, for these standards may fail to address problems that have yet to be taken adequately into account.

We might wish for some sort of algorithm for determining what our responsibilities are in particular circumstances. But this is an idle wish. Even the most detailed codes of ethics of professional engineering societies can provide only general guidance. The determination of responsibilities in particular circumstances depends on discernment and judgment on the part of engineers. Beyond this are "good works," exemplary work that cannot be comfortably accommodated as simply obligatory.

Blame-responsibility can be applied to individuals and perhaps to organizations. If we believe organizations can be morally responsible agents, it is because we believe the analogies between undisputed moral agents (people) and organizations are stronger than the disanalogies. In any case, organizations can be criticized for the harms they cause, asked to make reparations for harm done, and assessed as needing to be reformed.

Individuals can be responsible for harm by intentionally, recklessly, or negligently causing harm. Some argue that individuals cannot be responsible for harm in situations where many individuals have contributed to the harm, but we can proportion responsibility to the degree to which an individual's action or inaction is responsible for the harm.

3.13 ENGINEERING ETHICS ON THE WEB

Check your understanding of the material in this chapter by visiting the companion website for *Engineering Ethics*. The site includes multiple choice study questions, suggested discussion topics, and sometimes additional case studies to complement your reading and study of the material in this chapter.

NOTES

1. This account is based on three sources: Columbia Accident Investigation Board, vol. 1 (Washington, DC: National Aeronautics and Space Administration, 2003); "Dogged Engineer's Effort to Assess Shuttle Damage," *The New York Times*, Sept. 26 2003, p. A1; William Langewiesche, "Columbia's Last Flight," *Atlantic Monthly*, Nov. 2003, pp. 58–87.

2. The next several paragraphs, as well as some later segments of this chapter are drawn from Michael S. Pritchard, "Professional Standards for Engineers," in Anthonie Meijers, ed., *Handbook Philosophy of Technology and Engineering Sciences*, Part V, "Normativity and Values in Technology," Ibo van de Poel, ed. (Elsevier Science, 2010).

3. The list that follows is based on interviews of engineers and managers conducted by James Jaksa and Michael S. Pritchard and reported in Michael S. Pritchard, "Responsible Engineering: The Importance of Character and Imagination," *Science and Engineering Ethics*, 7:3, 2001, pp. 394–395.

4. See, for example, the Association for Computing Machinery: ACM Code of Ethics and Professional Conduct, 2.2 Acquire and maintain professional competence.

5. This is a major theme of Stuart Shapiro's, "Degrees of Freedom: The Interaction of Standards of Practice and Engineering Judgment," *Science, Technology, & Human Values*, 22:3, Summer 1997.

6. Shapiro, p. 290.

7. Joshua B. Kardon, "The Structural Engineer's Standard of Care," presented at the OEC International Conference on Ethics in Engineering and Computer Science, March 1999. This article is available at http://www.onlineethics.org.

8. Ibid. Kardon bases this characterization on Paxton v. County of Alameda (1953) 119c.C.A. 2d 393, 398, 259P 2d 934.

9. For further discussion of this case, see Citicorp in Cases. See also Joe Morgenstern, "The Fifty-Nine Story Crisis," *The New Yorker*, May 29, 1995, pp. 49–53.

10. Columbia Accident Investigation Board, p. 6.

11. Nevertheless, the investigation eventually resulted in the displacement of no less than a dozen key people at NASA, as well as a public vindication of Rocha for doing the right thing.

12. Ibid., p. 9.

13. Ibid.

14. Ibid., p. 177.

15. For discussions of this issue see, for example, Peter French, *Collective and Corporate Responsibility* (New York: Columbia University Press, 1984); Kenneth E. Goodpaster and John B. Matthews, Jr., "Can a Corporation Have a Conscience?" *Harvard Business Review*, 60, Jan.–Feb. 1982, pp. 132–141; and Manuel Velasquez, "Why Corporations Are not Morally Responsible for Anything They Do," *Business and Professional Ethics Journal*, 2:3, Spring 1983, pp. 1–18.

16. *Black's Law Dictionary*, 6th ed. (St. Paul, MN: West 1990), p. 340.

17. See Peter French, "Corporate Moral Agency" and "What Is Hamlet to McDonnell-Douglas or McDonnell-Douglas to Hamlet: DC-10," in Joan C. Callahan, ed., *Ethical*

Issues in Professional Life (New York: Oxford University Press, 1988), pp. 265–269, 274–281. The following discussion has been suggested by French's ideas, but it diverges from them in several ways.

18. These three senses all fall on the blame-responsibility side. A less explored possibility is that corporations can be morally responsible agents in positive ways.

19. Coombs v. Beede, 89 Me. 187, 188, 36 A. 104 (1896). This is cited and discussed in Margaret N. Strand and Kevin Golden, "Consulting Scientist and Engineer Liability: A Survey of Relevant Law," *Science and Engineering Ethics*, 3:4, Oct. 1997, pp. 362–363.

20. We are indebted to Martin Curd and Larry May for outlining parallels between legal and moral notions of responsibility for harms and their possible applications to engineering. See Martin Curd and Larry May, *Professional Responsibility for Harmful Actions*, Module Series in Applied Ethics, Center for the Study of Ethics in the Professions, Illinois Institute of Technology (Dubuque, IA: Kendall/Hunt, 1984).

21. The next several paragraphs are based on Michael S. Pritchard, "Good Works," *Professional Ethics*, 1:1, Fall 1992, pp. 155–177. It should be noted that the notion of "good works" is not precise. It is meant to be suggestive, and it is best discussed through examples, not definitions. Philosopher J. O. Urmson captures what we have in mind by reminding us that there is a "vast array of actions, having moral significance, which frequently are performed by persons who are far from being moral saints or heroes but which are neither duties nor obligations…." (J. O. Urmson, "Hare on Intuitive Moral Thinking," in Douglas Seanor and N. Fotion, eds., *Hare and Critics*, Oxford, England: Clarendon Press, 1988, p. 168.)

22. Personal communication with statistician Michael Stoline at Western Michigan University.

23. This account is based on G. P. E. Meese, "The Sealed Beam Case," *Business & Professional Ethics*, 1:3, Spring 1982, pp. 1–20.

24. H. H. Magsdick, "Some Engineering Aspects of Headlighting," *Illuminating Engineering*, June 1940, p. 533, cited in Meese, p. 17.

25. For information about 3P/3M programs see: http://www.mmm.com/sustainability.

26. Information on Ford Pinto here is based on a case study prepared by Manuel Velasquez, "The Ford Motor Car," in his *Business Ethics: Concepts and Cases*, 3rd ed. (Englewood Cliffs, NJ: Prentice-Hall, 1992), pp. 110–113.

27. Shapiro, p. 290.

28. Ibid., p. 293.

29. Louis L. Bucciarelli, *Designing Engineers* (Cambridge, MA: MIT Press, 1994), p. 135.

30. Vivian Weil, "Professional Standards: Can They Shape Practice in an International Context?", *Science and Engineering Ethics*, 4:3, 1998, pp. 303–314.

31. Ibid., p. 306. Similar principles are endorsed by disaster relief specialist Frederick Cuny and his Dallas, Texas, engineering relief agency. Renowned for his relief efforts around the world, Cuny's principles of effective and responsible disaster relief are articulated in his *Disasters and Development* (New York: Oxford University Press, 1983).

32. The phrase "the problem of many hands" is suggested by Helen Nissenbaum in "Computing and Accountability" in Deborah G. Johnson and Helen Nissenbaum, *Computers, Ethics, and Social Values* (Upper Saddle River, NJ: Prentice-Hall, 1995), p. 529.

33. Larry May, *Sharing Responsibility* (Chicago: University of Chicago Press, 1992), p. 106. For a more nuanced discussion of these notions, as well as notions of responsibility in engineering, see Michael Davis, "Ain't No One Here but Us Social Forces," *Science and Engineering Ethics*, 18:1, March 2012, pp. 13–34.

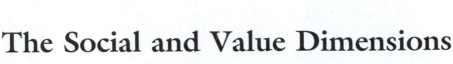

The Social and Value Dimensions of Technology

Main Ideas in This Chapter

- Many engineers and engineering students find it difficult to appreciate the social dimension of technology. The social embeddedness of technology manifests itself in the way that technology affects individuals and particular practices and the way social values can affect technology.

- Technology can also raise questions about social policy. Two examples are the effect of information technology on privacy and intellectual property.

- Technological determinism is the belief that technology has a life of its own and cannot be controlled by humans.

- Technological optimism is the belief that the effects of technology on humans are by and large good.

- Technological pessimism is the belief that technology, although beneficial, has many bad effects on society and individuals.

- Among the undesirable effects of technology identified by technological pessimists are the diminution of human freedom, the elimination of many complex relationships that make human life meaningful, and the quantification and standardization of the natural world.

- Engineers should develop a critical attitude toward technology that recognizes both technology's desirable and undesirable aspects. Engineers with this attitude can promote democratic deliberation about technology policy and better recognize the value issues that arise in design.

TROY, LISA, AND PAUL WERE engineering students in a prominent North American university. Troy and Lisa were graduate students, and Paul was an undergraduate.[1] They were chosen for a study of the attitudes of engineering students toward the social dimension of engineering because they had shown interest in topics such as the effect of technology on workers, especially with regard to occupational health and safety. Yet, even these students had difficulties integrating such concerns into their engineering studies.

Commenting on a class that focused on the humanistic aspects of technology, Troy remarked, "We've got enough to worry about [as engineers] and now we've got to worry about this."[2] On the final exam of a course in technology and society, he wrote to the teaching assistant, "My life was great until I met you."[3] Commenting on the same topic, Lisa said, "My engineering education didn't give me really a political context, and it sort of denied a political context by denoting that everything was objective and quantifiable and could be sort of foreseen. And if it couldn't be foreseen, we didn't measure it and we didn't take account of it."[4]

There was a difference in how these three students perceived the introduction of the social and humanistic elements into their thinking as engineers. Paul saw the socially oriented view as an extension of his engineering education. Lisa perceived a fundamental conflict between what she learned in engineering class and the social and humanistic orientation. Troy fluctuated between the views of Paul and Lisa. Troy and Lisa spoke of a moment when the importance of the social and humanistic dimension of engineering "just hit me" (Troy) or "sort of clicked with me" (Lisa). Before that time, they could make no sense of what their teachers and project leaders were telling them about the social context of engineering. After that moment of insight, they had a foothold on the broader perspective.[5]

4.1   TECHNOLOGY IS SOCIALLY EMBEDDED

Despite the difficulties the three students had in appreciating the social dimension of technology, the importance of this dimension is recognized by scholars. In their textbook, *Ethics in Engineering*, philosopher Mike W. Martin and engineer Roland Schinzinger develop the idea of *engineering as social experimentation* in part to express the idea that technology, and therefore engineering, is an integral part of the social order.[6] There are several interesting analogies between engineering and scientific experimentation. First, engineering works—whether consumer products, bridges, or buildings—have experimental subjects, just like scientific experiments. In engineering the subjects are members of the public who utilize the products of engineering. Second, as in any experiment, there is always an element of uncertainty about the outcome. Engineers never know for sure how well a new automobile will perform on the road, or whether a new building will withstand a hurricane. Yet there is a need to gain new knowledge that can only come by experimentation. Only by innovation can technology advance. Third, like experimenters, engineers must assume responsibility for their experiments. They must think about the possible consequences of their work, both good and bad, and attempt to eliminate as many bad consequences as possible. This concept of engineering as social experimentation fits well with a definition of technology favored by many scholars, a definition that also highlights the social dimensions of technology. Rather than define technology as the making and using of tools or as the application of science to practical problems, these scholars define technology as a "system" composed of many things, such as physical objects and tools, knowledge, inventors, operators, repair people, managers, government regulators, and others.[7] Troy, Lisa and Paul struggled to understand their engineering work as part of a larger system in which technology is *embedded* in society.

A full understanding of the embeddedness of technology in society requires that we appreciate the fact that the relationship of technology and society works two ways: technology affects society and society affects technology. We shall explore this two-way causal relationship in more detail, beginning with the causal relationship that is possibly the easiest to appreciate: the effect of technology on society. In considering these issues, we shall often use examples from information technology.

4.2 TECHNOLOGY AFFECTS SOCIETY

Technology affects our behavior in many ways. Taking an obvious example with a very simple technology, speed bumps virtually force us to drive more slowly. Historically, the invention of the printing press had an enormous impact on European civilization and was a major factor in the Protestant Reformation. Similarly, it is difficult to deny the effects of the development of the technology of warfare on the conduct of warfare itself. In our own time, technology affects the jobs we hold. Some jobs have been diminished in numbers due to technology, such as jobs for bank tellers and travel agents. Others have been created, such as computer programmers. Technology has created new health issues, such as those associated with extensive computer use.

Technology has also affected our social relationships in many ways, some of them affecting people in different generations differently. For many young people, the elapse of several hours with no cell phone call or text message prompts them to wonder whether their friends still care about them, but for many of an older generation the absence of such communications is a welcome relief. Many young people feel that they are not in a genuine romantic relationship until they are "Facebook official," but older people find this hard to understand. Regular use of social networking sites such as Facebook, MySpace, and Bebo almost certainly has an effect on human relationships. As is often the case, the technologies probably affect even our definitions of crucial terms—in this case what it means to have a "friendship" or "relationship."

Philosopher Shannon Vallor recognizes the "psychological and informational value of social networking sites for people with serious illnesses, for victims of violent crime, or those suffering and alienated in other ways."[8] However, she raises concerns about the influence of these same technologies on what she calls the "communicative virtues," especially in their early development in young people. These virtues include patience, honesty, empathy, fidelity, reciprocity, and tolerance, and they are the ones necessary, she thinks, for the development of effective and satisfying interpersonal relationships. She worries that the Internet may not be conducive to the development of such relationships. At the very least, it probably affects how these relationships develop.

Patience is an important virtue for sustaining close relationships. One must be willing to remain in communication with a friend, even when it may sometimes be boring or irritating to do so; but on the Internet, we can always say "gotta run" or just click the person off. Honesty in personal relationships is the willingness to offer one's authentic self in relationship with another, but social networking sites offer opportunities for massive misrepresentation of oneself, which is incompatible with genuine friendship.

Finally, empathy or compassion, although crucial for genuine relationships, may require an encounter with the embodied presence of another person, enabling us to see bodily expressions of pain, anger, disgust, or caring. The best expressions of sympathy and compassion may be physical touching and embrace, none of which is possible in online relationships. Whether or not Vallor's concerns are well-founded—and only empirical research can determine this—it is reasonable to suppose that social networking technology has affected interpersonal relationships in some way.

4.3   SOCIETY AFFECTS TECHNOLOGY

One of the easiest ways to appreciate the effects of society on the development of technology is through acquaintance with the rapidly growing field of Science and Technology Studies (STS), a discipline created by sociologists, historians, and philosophers. Detailed investigations of technology have shown that there are usually several workable solutions to a technical problem and that social and value factors often determine which solution is adopted. Sociologists of technology Trevor Pinch and Wiebe Bijker illustrate this theme with the early history of the bicycle.[9] The early evolution of the bicycle had two "branches": a sportsman's bike with a high front wheel that was relatively unstable and a more utilitarian version with a smaller front wheel that was more stable. The sportsman's version was designed for speed and was especially attractive to young athletic males. The utilitarian version was more appropriate for pleasure riding and ordinary transportation. Eventually, the utilitarian design came to be more widely accepted, and the high-wheeled bike disappeared. Most people evidently decided that producing a sportsman's toy was not as important as producing a useful means of transportation.[10]

On a still more subtle level of analysis, STS researchers have found that even concepts that are usually thought to have a purely technical definition often have a social and value dimension. For example, what constitutes "effective functioning" or "efficiency"—especially important terms in technology—is not determined wholly by technical considerations, but also in part by social considerations.

In engineering, the efficiency of a device is taken to be a purely quantitative ratio of energy input and energy output. However, in practice, whether a device is considered to "work well" is a product of the character and interests of a user group.[11] Child labor was in some ways more "efficient" than the use of adults, but when it was decided that the use of child labor was immoral, children were no longer taken into account as a possible source of more efficient labor. The use of child labor was no longer considered in determining "efficiency." Instead, children were redefined as learners and consumers, not laborers. These so-called technical concepts, then, have a social dimension.[12]

Another example of how social considerations help to define the concept of efficiency is found in the history of boiler explosions in the United States. Boiler explosions took the lives of many people, especially on steamboats, in the early nineteenth century. In 1837, at the request of the US Congress, the Franklin Institute undertook a rigorous examination of boiler construction. Boilermakers and steamboat owners resisted higher standards, and the US Congress did not impose the higher standards until 1852, after many more people had been killed in steamboat accidents. The accident rate decreased dramatically, however, after thicker walls and safety valves were mandated. What *constituted* or defined a proper boiler was changed by the new standards, which were issued by the American Society of Mechanical Engineers. Although it might be more "efficient" in the older sense of the term to build the boilers by the old standards, the concept of "efficiency" no longer allows this as an option.

A similar process seems to be occurring in many areas related to the environment. Standards for consumption of gasoline are changing. Even if it is more "efficient" to build automobiles by older standards or to use less environmentally friendly standards in other areas, society will almost certainly continue to change the standards in favor of the environment. Many design standards that were once controversial no longer are, and design standards already incorporate many safety and environmental considerations that probably cannot be justified economically or even by a consideration of trade-offs. Society has simply made certain decisions that are no longer in dispute. They become part of the definition of what it means to design a product, such as an automobile.

4.4 TECHNOLOGY AND SOCIAL POLICY: PRIVACY

So far we have focused on the way technology affects individuals and particular practices and how social values can affect technology. Another aspect of the embeddedness of technology is the way it raises larger questions about social policy. Two examples are policies regarding privacy and intellectual property. We turn first to the issue of privacy.

We value our privacy, by which we mean the ability to control that which we think of as belonging to us. Privacy is different from anonymity, which is being unknown by, or "invisible" to, others. With privacy, the central value is to be able to control what we think of as rightfully ours to control, whether it is information about us (hence the value of *informational privacy*), or our property (hence the value of *physical privacy*), the ability to make decisions for ourselves (hence the value of *decisional privacy*), or the ability to control our name, likeness, or other aspects of our identity (hence the value of *proprietary privacy*). Computers can violate our informational privacy by serving as the means for constructing databases about our income, purchasing habits, and perhaps even more intimate characteristics, such as political and religious affiliations and sexual orientation. They can violate our decisional privacy by gathering information that can be used to intimidate us and thus inhibit our action. They can violate our proprietary privacy when they are used in "identity theft."[13]

Probably the most important kind of privacy to be considered here is informational privacy, a value that is especially important from the respect for persons perspective. Part of our respect for our own individual autonomy and identity is tied to our ability to control how much information others have about us, thereby controlling the intimacy of our relationship with them. Yet computers assist in the wholesale invasion of our informational privacy. Computer matching can collect apparently unrelated bits of information about us from various sources and put them together into a portrait that may or may not be complimentary. The information is usually used for marketing purposes. Purchase of diapers may indicate we have a young family and extensive purchases of liquor together with a record of arrests for driving while intoxicated may indicate we have a problem with alcohol. Matching can also assist in gathering information that can identify potential wrongdoers, even before they have committed a crime and without giving them any opportunity to defend themselves. Facebook and other social networking sites can be used to collect information about us from our posts, and potential employers often look at this information. This is such an important consideration that college students have become more careful about what they post on such sites.

As with most social issues, however, there are relevant utilitarian arguments as well as respect for persons arguments. Computer matching and other computer programs enable law enforcement officers to identify actual criminals. We can use credit cards because there are credit records that distinguish good from bad credit risks. We can prevent the sale of handguns to convicted felons because computerized criminal records are easily accessible. We can cash checks because computerized records enable retailers to have information about checking accounts. Databases allow targeted marketing, which not only is more efficient for business but also protects us from being subject to irrelevant advertising. In addition to commercial uses, governmental agencies also find computerized databases useful. The proposed National Information System would be useful in eliminating welfare fraud and in identifying physicians who double bill for medical services. The FBI has proposed a national computerized criminal history system that would combine in a single database the 195 million criminal history records in the United States. The system would no doubt be of great value to the criminal justice system.

The issue of computers and privacy presents the typical moral problem as we have described it earlier: a conflict of values, or a moral "dilemma." As with most such problems, the best solution is often a creative middle way. One attempt to find such a solution is the Privacy Act, passed by the US Congress in 1974, which prohibits the executive branch from using information gathered in one program area in an entirely different and unrelated area. Operating with the assumption that one way to limit power is to divide it, the act prohibited the creation of integrated national information systems. Enforcement was left to governmental agencies, however, and the various agencies have interpreted the law to suit their own purposes. As a result, the act has lost much of its force.

An approach that mirrors some of the considerations of the Privacy Act and that appears to be an attempt to find a creative middle way solution is a set of guidelines for "fair information practices." The guidelines include provisions designed to honor the competing values of personal privacy and social utility.[14] Some of the guidelines are that data systems containing personal information should be public knowledge; that personal information should be collected for narrow, specific purposes and in ways consistent with those purposes; that personal information about individuals should be collected only with the informed consent of the individuals or their legal representatives; that personal information about individuals should be shared with third parties only with the consent of the individuals; that the information about individuals should be stored for only a limited time and should be reviewable by the individuals; and that those who collect personal data should ensure the security and integrity of personal data systems.

Critics can point out various limitations of these guidelines. Informed consent of individuals can be difficult to obtain. Since information may be stored for only a limited time, it would have to be requested repeatedly. Some individuals might use the opportunity to "correct" information about them to modify the information to their own advantage. Nevertheless, these guidelines suggest the broad outlines of a creative middle way solution to the problem of computers and privacy. Thus technology can pose significant issues for public policy, and in this way it is deeply embedded in the social, political, and legal fabric of society.

4.5 TECHNOLOGY AND PUBLIC POLICY: INTELLECTUAL PROPERTY

Information technology also raises important questions with regard to intellectual property, again suggesting the embeddedness of this technology in the political, legal, and moral fabric of society. Two such questions are the following.

Should Software Be Protected?

Computer programs are often worth a lot of money in the marketplace. Should they receive legal protection? One justification for giving them legal protection is suggested

by the US Constitution. The Constitution authorizes Congress "to promote the progress of science and the useful arts, by securing for limited times to authors and inventors the exclusive right to their respective writings and discoveries." This justification is
utilitarian, and some people believe that rates of technological innovation have been
greatest in those societies that recognize intellectual property rights. Interestingly,
there are also utilitarian arguments for *not* granting protection to protectors of software. Some people have maintained that there was more innovation and experimentation in the early days of software development when software was free.[15] Another
argument for granting legal protection is that protection tends to increase the price
and perhaps reduce the quality of software because competition is limited or reduced.
These are all utilitarian arguments, so their validity depends on which policy would in
fact be most effective in promoting the public good.

Another type of justification for giving legal protection to software is based on the
respect for persons perspective, which holds that respecting the person implies according a person the right to control his or her own body, and this in turn implies the right
to control the labor of his or her own body, and the products of that labor. To control
the products of one's labor, the ability to copyright those products may be required.

Both the utilitarian arguments and the respect for persons arguments have considerable moral force. Because of its basis in the Constitution, the utilitarian argument
is prominent in legal controversies in the United States. Because of its great intuitive
appeal, however, the argument based on respect for persons has an important place in
our thinking about ownership. Given the relative ease of free-riding on the work of
others, the considerable expense and effort involved in creative innovation, and the
force of the moral arguments, most of us would probably conclude that the creators of
software deserve protection. The question is: How much protection should be given
and how should it be implemented?

How Should Software Be Protected?

Two principal options have been proposed for protecting intellectual property: copyright and patents. The peculiar nature of software, however, makes both of these
options problematic. Software does not fit the paradigm or typical case of either something that should be copyrighted or something that should be patented. In some ways,
software is like a "work of authorship" and should be appropriate for copyright. A
program is, after all, written in a "language" and has a logical sequence like a story or
play. In other ways, software is more analogous to an invention because it is a list of
ways to react to certain conditions, much like a machine might react to conditions.
Because of these problems of classification, some people have suggested that software
should be classified as a "legal hybrid" and that special laws should be made for the
protection of software that are different from the laws applicable to either copyright or
patent.[16] Just as there should be special laws to protect some products of biotechnology, such as plant hybrids, so should there be special laws to protect software.

However, there are disadvantages to creating special laws just to protect software,
one of which is that such laws in the United States might not be recognized throughout the rest of the world. So the legal hybrid approach has not gained wide acceptance,
and we must look at what might well be called the copyright/patent controversy.
Because software partakes of characteristics that are appropriate to copyrightable material and characteristics that are appropriate to patentable material, a line-drawing problem arises that involves an application issue. Does software fit more closely the

paradigm for a patentable creation or for a copyrightable creation? We might begin by examining copyrights more closely, since copyright has been the most popular form of protection for software.

Software is appropriate for copyright only if we view programs as literary works. However, a central tenet of US law is that copyright can protect only the expression of an idea, not the idea itself. Copyright law holds that a basic idea is not copyrightable, but a particular expression of an idea might be copyrightable. One cannot copyright an idea for a novel in which boy meets girl, they fall in love, and they live happily thereafter. An author can only copyright a particular story embodying this theme, which is written or "expressed" in considerable detail. The author must describe the background of the boy and girl, the circumstances of their meeting, the events that led to their engagement and marriage, and the reasons why their lives were filled with bliss. To refer to an actual case, the idea of a jewel-encrusted lifelike bee pin cannot be copyrighted because this idea is inseparable from its expression. The expression may not be copyrighted because protecting the expression would be conferring a monopoly on the use of the idea.[17]

In determining whether an expression is copyrightable, the courts use several tests. First, the expression must be original—that is, it originated with the author. Second, the expression must be functional in the sense of having some useful purpose. Third, the expression must be nonobvious: "When an expression goes no further than the obvious, it is inseparable from the idea itself."[18] Fourth, there must be several or many different ways of expressing the idea. If there are no other ways—or few other ways—of expressing it, then the software creator cannot lay a significant claim to originality in the sense of uniqueness.

Even though the following case occurred some time ago, it is a classic case in software patent law and an excellent example for us in applying the criteria set out above. On June 28, 1990, an important decision was rendered with regard to a lawsuit between Lotus Development Corporation, the creator of the Lotus 1-2-3 Spreadsheet, and Paperback International, the creator of the VP-Planner Spreadsheet. Lotus had sued Paperback International for infringement of its copyright on Lotus 1-2-3. Paperback had copied the entire menu structure of the Lotus 1-2-3 program. The manual of the VP-Planner even contained the following statement: "VP-Planner is designed to work like Lotus 1-2-3, keystroke for keystroke…. VP-Planner's worksheet is a feature-for-feature work alike for the 1-2-3. It does micros. It has the same command tree. It allows the same kind of calculations, the same kind of numerical information. Everything 1-2-3 does, VP-Planner does."

Paperback in turn alleged that only the part of a computer program written in some computer language, such as C, is copyrightable. It argued that the more graphic parts of a program, such as the overall organization of the program, the structure of the program's command system, the menu, and the general presentation of information on the screen, are not copyrightable. Lotus countered by arguing that copyright protection extends to all elements of a computer program that embody original expression. In the end, the judge ruled that even though the idea of an electronic spreadsheet is not copyrightable, the Lotus spreadsheet was original and nonobvious enough to be copyrightable, and that VP-Planner had infringed on the copyright. Accordingly, District Judge Keaton ruled that VP-Planner had infringed on the Lotus copyright. Let us assume that Lotus 1-2-3 is distinct enough from the basic idea of a spreadsheet to be classifiable as an expression of an idea. Is it a copyrightable expression? Using the method of line-drawing, Table 4.1 gives an analysis of the issue.

TABLE 4.1   Is Lotus 1-2-3 Copyrightable?

Feature	Copyrightable	Lotus 1-2-3	Noncopyrightable
Originated with author	Yes	X———————	No
Functional	Yes	X———————	No
Nonobvious	Yes	X———————	No
Alternate expressions	Yes	X———————	No

© Cengage Learning

4.6   EVALUATING TECHNOLOGY: TECHNOLOGICAL DETERMINISM AND TECHNOLOGICAL OPTIMISM

Up to this point we have been primarily concerned with demonstrating the social embeddedness of technology by showing that technology is not only shaped in its development by social forces, but also shapes society on both an individual and social policy level. We have not attempted to resolve any of the problems raised, but rather to show how deeply technology is socially embedded. Ultimately, however, we must evaluate technology—or various technologies—especially with regard to the social effects. To begin the consideration of this evaluative process, we introduce and explain, in this section and the next, three terms: technological determinism, technological optimism, and technological pessimism.

Technological determinism holds that technological development has a life of its own, an internal logic that cannot be controlled by individual humans or even the whole society. For example, the steamship was developed from prior wind-driven vessels, and diesel-powered ships could not have been built without the steamship. Furthermore, according to technological determinism, a technology that can be developed usually will be developed, and it is likely that a technology that can be put to a given use will be put to that use.

If it were true, technological determinism would have important implications for the ethical evaluation of technology. If there is little that individuals or even a society can do to slow down, speed up, or direct the development of technology, then ethical evaluation would be pointless. There is little point in ethically evaluating technology if we cannot control it. Furthermore, if technology is going to go on its merry way regardless of what we do, why assume responsibility for it? Why take responsibility for what we cannot control? We have already given evidence, however, that technological determinism is not true. STS research has shown that technological development is influenced by social forces and that it often can develop in alternative ways. This is incompatible with technological determinism, and most scholars have concluded that the claim that humans cannot influence the development of technology is false. If technological determinism is false, as we believe it is, the way is left open for a moral evaluation of technology, or of particular examples of technology. What evaluation(s) should be made?

One answer is provided by *technological optimism*, which holds that the effects of technology on human well-being are, on balance, good. Technology enables us to provide for our basic needs and even some luxuries, and it does so without our having to spend all of our waking hours simply trying to survive. Even if technology has some negative effects, such as pollution and harm to the environment, the overall effects are overwhelmingly positive, and the problems it creates can probably be remedied by technology itself. Hence, a generally positive evaluation of technology is justified.

For many, evidence for the technological optimist's judgment that the overall effects of technology are good is overwhelming. A prime example is India.[19] The country seems finally poised to experience the kind of explosive economic development necessary if the millions who live on less than $1 a day are to escape their current condition, and signs of development are everywhere. Approximately 5 million new mobile phone connections are added each month, and hundreds of shopping malls are under construction. Much of India's prime office space has been built in the last few years. A hotel room in Bangalore, India's technology capital, can cost $299 a day. Three of India's largest companies by stock market evaluation are in information technology, an industry that barely existed in 1991. This is an industry that, according to some experts, can do for India what automobiles did for Japan and oil did for Saudi Arabia. A young software engineer who has graduated from one of India's elite institutes of technology is in high demand.

We are all familiar with India's telemarketing and call centers, but the country is also moving into areas that involve more judgment and higher levels of expertise. For example, there is a growing business in "litigation support" for American multinationals such as DuPont, in which thousands of documents and emails are examined with regard to their relevance to a particular case. With their background in the English language and the common law tradition, Indians are particularly well-suited to legal outsourcing. India has also become a favored place for outsourcing clinical trials. Manufacturing, however, is probably an essential ingredient in the rise from poverty, and India has some shining success stories here as well. Tata Steel is the world's lowest cost steel producer. India also has outstanding capacity in concrete, pharmaceuticals, and automotive parts. Its strength is generally as a high-value rather than a low-cost producer.

India's story has been repeated in many other areas of the world. China is further along the road to economic development than India, and South Korea and Japan have already achieved industrialized status. Insofar as we are considering the role of technological development in the liberation of millions of people from disease and poverty, most of us would probably consider the effects of technology to be overwhelmingly on the positive side.

On the more general and theoretical level, Francis Bacon (1561–1626), who held that knowledge is power, and nineteenth-century mathematician and philosopher Auguste Comte (1798–1857), who believed that the progress of science is related to human progress generally, are often taken as precursors of modern technological optimism. More recently, Immanuel Mesthene, the director of Harvard University's Program on Technology and Society (which has been discontinued), has argued for a thesis that seems to underlie the thinking of many scientists and engineers, namely that science and technology have made everything in principle understandable and controllable and that there is nothing to stop virtually unlimited technological development. This development, Mesthene believes, promotes democracy in some ways, by assisting in such things as instant voting and better communication of information, but it also requires increasing reliance on expert knowledge. As the gap between the knowledge of experts and that of ordinary citizens continues to increase, ordinary citizens must recognize the priority of expert opinion in some areas and cede ever more control of social institutions to experts—a trend that obviously poses a threat to democracy.

Controlling such effects of technology as pollution does in fact require expert knowledge, but experts can show us how to charge these effects to their producers. As is so often the case, technology increases our options, just like putting new items on the menu increases our options at a restaurant.[20] Overall, the benefits of technology and technological progress far outweigh the disadvantages.

4.7   EVALUATING TECHNOLOGY: TECHNOLOGICAL PESSIMISM

Some version of technological optimism, perhaps with some of the qualifications that Mesthene suggests, is embraced by large numbers of people in our society, including many engineers. But technological pessimists want to enter a cautionary note. Technological pessimists, even though they do not oppose all technological development, are much more likely to point out its undesirable effects. Appreciating this point of view is important if we are to have a balanced view of technology. On a practical level, the insights of technological pessimism may help engineers make better decisions about the technologies they design and develop.

In thinking about the negative effects of technology, the first thing that comes to mind is its frequently deleterious effect on the environment. However, we postpone this issue for another chapter. Instead we focus on two claims often made by technological pessimists: that technology can threaten human freedom, and that it can diminish the meaningfulness of our lives. To be sure, technology can also promote freedom and meaning in many ways. As the example of India illustrates, technological development can liberate humans from dawn-to-dusk toil. This gives them the freedom to participate in political life or to pursue other activities that make their lives more meaningful. Nevertheless, pessimists can point out other ways in which technology has very different effects.

Technology as a Threat to Freedom

Critics of technology maintain that it can be an instrument of oppression of the socially disadvantaged and in other ways limit people's freedom. In his important essay, "Do Artifacts Have Politics?" Langdon Winner holds that many technological artifacts have political or social effects, and that many of these effects harm the lower socioeconomic classes.[21] In an often-cited example, Winner tells the story of how Robert Moses, the late master-builder of public works in New York City, used his power to limit the freedom of economically disadvantaged citizens to travel to Jones Beach, a desirable recreational area. Moses ordered the clearances on the bridges over the access roads to Jones Beach to be abnormally low. This had the effect of excluding buses, which in turn made it difficult for the economically disadvantaged, who had to use public transportation, to get to the beach. Thus, what looked like a simple design decision disproportionally limited the freedom of a social class. Although the factual accuracy of this story has been disputed, it illustrates the way engineering works can have political consequences.

In another of Winner's examples, the industrialist Cyrus McCormick had machines in his factories designed so that they required only unskilled workers, enabling him to eliminate the skilled workers in his factory in Chicago who had formed a union, and to destroy the union itself. In another of his examples, a mechanical tomato harvester, developed by researchers at the University of California, enabled farmers to reduce the number of farm workers needed to harvest tomatoes. The land-owners were able to increase their profits, but many farm workers lost their jobs.

Not only has technology been used in ways that harm the economically disadvantaged, but Winner believes that some technologies support or even require authoritarian power structures that may threaten democratic policies. In his study of modern business, Alfred Chandler gives evidence that technologically sophisticated business enterprises—railroads, manufacture, electricity, and chemicals, to name a few—require authoritarian power structures.[22] Similarly, while solar power is compatible with decentralization, nuclear power plants and nuclear weapons require tightly organized management structures. Winner appears to believe that these authoritarian structures may exert an undesirable influence on democratic institutions.

For many technological pessimists, the most worrisome way that technology can be used to limit freedom is in the area of surveillance. These technologies have special importance in promoting repressive measures in authoritarian regimes, but they can also implement repression even in democratic countries. We have already seen how technology can threaten individual privacy and produce challenging moral problems for social policy. It can also empower authoritarian social policies. One of the most dramatic examples of the alliance of information technology with authoritarian regimes is the story of Google's abortive attempt to cooperate with censorship in China.[23] Google.cn went live in 2006, but its decision to create a search engine on the .cn domain almost immediately produced problems with the Chinese government. To avoid a demand by the Chinese government for personal information, Google stored the information outside China. It also did not offer Gmail, Picasa, blogging, and other services, and YouTube was blocked entirely. In 2008, when China hosted the Olympics, the government demanded still further restrictions. While other search engines, such as Microsoft's, complied, Google stalled. Then a major hacking operation resulted not only in the loss of some of Google's most precious intellectual property, but also the exposure of the emails of Chinese dissidents and human rights activists. In 2010, Google gave up attempting to reconcile its ethical principles with doing business in China and decided to leave China.

In the United States, the government has thousands of databases containing vast amounts of information about US citizens. The FBI's controversial "Carnivore" program can filter through all traffic on any Internet service provider to which it is attached. While this capability is supposed to be used to track the communications of particular individuals, only government-created software instructions prevent it from trolling through all of the Internet traffic that goes through the provider. Under the Patriot Act, the FBI can force anyone to turn over records on their customers or clients, enabling the government to examine such items as the Internet correspondence, financial records, and medical histories of any individual. In the name of protecting national security, the "TIPS" program encourages citizens to spy on each other. Many other such programs are a potential threat to the freedom of citizens, especially to those associated with political dissent.[24]

Technology and Decline of Meaning

Living a meaningful life requires being enmeshed in a web of relationships that connects us with other human beings and with the natural world. Technological pessimists sometimes maintain that technology breaks some of these relationships. We can begin with the connections of humans with each other.[25] We have already seen that Vallor raises the question of whether social networking promotes social disengagement by cutting off some of the normal dimensions of interpersonal relationships. Emails do not convey the unique features of another person as well as a handwritten letter, to say nothing of face-to-face encounters. In an attempt to overcome the difficulties in communicating feeling and mood in emails, we put an emoticon at the end of a sentence.

However, other technologies can also weaken the ties of human relationships. In a well-known example, Albert Borgman illustrates the loss of a complex nexus of relationships by contrasting a fireplace with a modern furnace.[26] The fireplace was once a focal point for family life. The family gathered there for conversation and storytelling. Often the mother built the fire, the children brought in the wood, and the father cut the wood. Contrast the hearth with the modern furnace, from which heat appears without effort and without the involvement of family members.

Similar considerations apply to the traditional family meal, as contrasted with the microwave meal. The traditional meal is enmeshed in a complex web of relationships, associations, and memories. The mother prepared the food which might have been raised in a family garden in which even the children worked. Mealtime was a time for grace and then discussion of experiences of the day, thus linking the family members with each other and the transcendent. This web of relationships cannot be reproduced in the practice of "grabbing a bite" on the run, using food from a preprepared dish, heated in a microwave and consumed in solitude.

Technology can also disrupt a web of relationships that connects us with the natural world. To develop this theme, philosopher Martin Heidegger came up with the concept of "enframing."[27] We can think of enframing as the attitude of looking at things in the natural world from a certain perspective, to the exclusion of other perspectives. In economics, for example, one can take the perspective of cost-benefit analysis, eliminating all other perspectives. Everything is looked at from the standpoint of its cost, relative to its benefit—all measured in economic terms. In evaluating a hydroelectric project in terms of cost-benefit analysis, all noneconomic considerations are eliminated, including such considerations as beauty and aesthetic value. For Heidegger, technological enframing sees natural objects as a "standing reserve." From this perspective, trees are a resource for wood, which will be used for construction or other human purposes. Rivers are a standing reserve for the production of hydroelectric power. Minerals from the earth are resources for manufacturing processes. Ultimately, Heidegger believes, this attitude encourages us to see ourselves and other humans as "human resources" to be utilized for human purposes.

A major mechanism for efficient exploitation of nature as a standing reserve is standardization and quantification, which are of central importance in both science and engineering. Standardizing features of the natural world in quantifiable units eliminates many aspects of our experiences that are meaningful, but it facilitates the purposes of science and engineering. The standardization of time is an interesting example. Biological rhythms speed up and slow down, and our most intimate experience of time is similar. Sometimes (as in pleasant experiences), time "flies," whereas at other times (as in painful experiences) time drags on exceedingly slowly. Uniformity in the form of standardized units of time must be imposed upon, not read out of, our experience of time. Clocks—those paradigmatic technological artifacts—produce an artificial experience of time. For "clock time," minutes and hours are of uniform duration. Units of clock time are not affected by our experience of the world, and looking at our experience through the lens of clock time can lead us to be insensitive to the way our lives are actually experienced. Uniform measurement of time did not exist in the same way before the invention of the clock, although uniformity has always been loosely tied to astronomical events. Thinking of our time in quantitative terms, as a collection of hours and minutes rather than as a sequence of experiences, is a modern invention. Prior to the fourteenth century, the day was divided into hours of light and darkness, generally of 12 hours each. This meant that in London the hour varied from 38 to 82 minutes.

Quantification and standardization of units of spatial measure shows a similar history. In eighteenth-century France, a séterée of land was larger or smaller, depending on the quality of the soil.[28] Until the nineteenth century in Europe, many measures of commodities and objects varied, depending both on the local traditions and on the qualities of what was measured.[29] Measurements of space in terms of a "stone's throw" or a "day's walk" were common in earlier cultures, but they have generally been replaced by standardized and objective measures. The concepts of "objective" and "subjective" have been reversed. Instead of "objective" referring to what is most immediately present in our experience, it now refers to what is measured by abstract and uniform measures. Immediate experience is relegated to the realm of subjectivity.

As technology evolves, nature changes from that which surrounds and encloses or transcends us to that which we control and manage. The idea of nature as something that transcends us and that we cannot control recedes into the background. Think of the difference in our relationship to the natural world when we are driving on a highway in a comfortable car, as opposed to struggling to climb a mountain on a hike, or camping by ourselves in a lonely place in the middle of the night. In the former experiences we feel in control, whereas in the latter we feel surrounded by and even overwhelmed by the natural world. To be sure, highways and automobiles can be of great value in promoting comfort and efficiency and even in relieving various types of human suffering, but something has been lost, namely the transcendence of the world to human concerns.

4.8   A CRITICAL ATTITUDE TOWARD TECHNOLOGY

The controversy between technological optimism and technological pessimism is not one that we must resolve one way or the other; indeed, finding a middle ground is more ideal. Insofar as possible, technology should be utilized to promote human well-being, and the undesirable aspects should be eliminated. Perhaps we can say that technological optimism should motivate the development of technology and that technological pessimism should be involved in determining the direction of that development. For example, as we develop computerized communication because of its speed and efficiency, we should take precautions to preserve important "human" dimensions of communication. This frame of mind—being aware of the advantages as well as the possible ill effects of technology—is *the critical attitude toward technology*. It can be encouraged and implemented in any number of ways.

Democratic Deliberation on Technology

One way to encourage the critical attitude toward technology is to assist in intelligent and informed democratic deliberation on science policy. In a democracy, debates about public policy regarding science and technology face a dilemma. Let us call it the *democratic dilemma*. On the one hand, the public has the prerogative of making or at least influencing decisions about science and technology. On the other hand, the public often has insufficient understanding of the scientific and technological issues—and the simplifications necessary to get understandable information across to the public may produce serious distortions. This conflict between democracy and scientific and technological elitism is present in Vannevar Bush's *Science—The Endless Frontier*, which is commonly acclaimed as the most important single document in science policy.[30] The document focuses on science policy rather than technology policy, but the issues are fundamentally the same. For Bush, the problem for public policy is a conflict between the desire of scientists to appeal for public support by showing the benefits that science can confer on society and the equally strong desire of scientists to protect science from interference by citizens whose understanding of science is minimal.

What are the responsibilities of engineers with regard to the democratic dilemma as it affects technology policy? These responsibilities can be summarized in three words: alert, inform, and advise. First, as the primary creators of technology, engineers have a special responsibility to alert the public to issues raised by technology. In particular, engineers have a responsibility to alert the public to potential dangers from technology. The public may have some general awareness of the issues of privacy and ownership of intellectual property as these issues affect public policy. For many other problems, however, this is not the case. Short of being alerted to the problem by experts, the public may not know the dangers of a new automobile design or the hazards to the environment posed by a new chemical process. This responsibility to alert the public to threats to public safety and health may sometimes involve whistle-blowing, but an engineer should always first try to work through organizational means to alert the public. Second, engineers also have a responsibility to inform the public of the issues on both sides of a debate. A new technology may pose dangers, but it may also have great potential benefits. Apart from tutoring by experts, the public has little chance of gaining even a minimal insight into such issues. Finally, engineers should in some instances offer advice and guidance on an issue, especially when there is some degree of consensus in the engineering community.

An obvious objection to these proposals is: "It is unfair to impose these heavy responsibilities on individual engineers." For the most part, we agree. Often, it is only individual engineers who are close enough to a technology to be aware of the issues it raises, but more often the responsibility to alert, inform, and advise should fall on engineering organizations, especially the professional societies. Unfortunately, with few exceptions, engineering societies have not adequately taken up these responsibilities. One notable exception is the involvement of the American Society of Mechanical Engineers in establishing specifications for pressure vessels in the United States. After a series of tragic explosions, the US Congress decided it was time to write specifications for safe boiler construction into federal law. The professional expertise of mechanical engineers was essential in establishing these criteria.

One of the reasons for the reluctance of engineering societies to enter into public debate over technology policy is that the membership may be divided about the issue. But we offer two responses. First, at the very least professional societies could offer a balanced presentation of the relevant issues. Second, such activities could increase the visibility of the engineering profession and enhance its status.

The Critical Attitude in Design

Richard Sclove argues that "technologies should … structurally support the social and institutional conditions necessary to establish and maintain strong democracy" and that this criterion should govern design.[31] While this criterion may not be sufficiently broad, engineers must identify and responsibly consider value issues in the design process. A study by two researchers from the Netherlands, Ibo van de Poel and A. C. van Gorp, illustrates how issues for ethical reflection can arise in the design process.[32] Following another scholar, W. G. Vincinti, they identify two types of design challenges.[33] Without going into the elaborate classification they propose, we present some of their examples of design projects that raise value issues.

In one project, the challenge was to design a sustainable car, where sustainability was closely associated with light weight. Light weight tended to make the car less safe, however, so the values of safety and sustainability had to be discussed and their relative moral weight determined. Even with respect to sustainability, ethical considerations surfaced. Is the value of sustainability derived from an obligation to respect nature for its own sake or from an obligation to allow future generations to fulfill their needs?

In another example, the challenge was to develop a coolant that did not contribute to ozone depletion like the traditional chlorofluorocarbons, such as CFC 12. It turns out, however, that there is a trade-off between flammability and environmental harm. The more environmentally friendly coolants tend to be more flammable. Although one might think that flammability poses a safety issue, some challenged even this assumption. Thus, the nature of these two values and their relative importance had to be discussed.

In a third example, the challenge was to create a housing system for laying hens. Important ethical issues were the environmental emissions of the chickens, the labor circumstances for farmers, and the health and welfare of the laying hens. These design problems raised significant issues regarding safety, sustainability, the environment, animal welfare and health, labor conditions, and so forth. As STS studies have demonstrated, there is no single correct way to resolve a design problem. So a critical attitude toward the design issues is required. It is not too much to ask engineers to think about these issues, as many engineers are currently doing. Such thought can lead to more creative designs and a more humanly satisfying life.

4.9   CHAPTER SUMMARY

Engineers and engineering students sometimes have trouble appreciating the social dimensions of technology. The concept of engineering as social experimentation expresses the idea that engineering is an integral part of the social order, that it is embedded in the social order. This embeddedness expresses itself in the ways technology affects society and the ways in which technology is affected by social values. A particularly valuable source of insight into the social shaping of technology is studied in the academic field of Science and Technology Studies, which is composed of sociologists, historians, and philosophers.

One of the ways technology affects society is by raising issues in social policy. Two areas that illustrate this effect are privacy and intellectual property. To what extent should individual privacy be abridged in the name of certain larger social goods? How should the rights of individuals to control and profit from their own intellectual property be balanced against the social value of free and open access to technology for technological advancement? These issues illustrate typical conflicts between utilitarian and respect for persons ways of thinking.

Technological determinists hold that technological development has a life of its own, an internal logic that cannot be controlled by individual humans or even the whole society. The evidence from STS, however, is that social values do shape the evolution of technology. Technological optimists hold that the effects of technology on human welfare are for the most part good, and there is strong evidence for this claim, especially if one looks at the ability of technology to raise millions of people out of poverty and hunger. However, technological pessimists hold that technology can have undesirable effects. Some technological pessimists argue that technology can be a threat to individual freedom, that it can diminish the quality of human relationships, that it can contribute to an exploitative attitude toward the natural world, and that it can interfere with the appreciation of the world as transcending human concerns.

The answer to the problems posed by technological pessimism is a critical attitude toward technology, which appreciates both the beneficial and harmful effects of technology. The critical attitude can manifest itself in engineers' helping the public to correctly understand technology so that they may better participate in the formulation of technology policy, and in designing technology so as to avoid some of its harmful effects.

4.10 ENGINEERING ETHICS ON THE WEB

Check your understanding of the material in this chapter by visiting the companion website for *Engineering Ethics.* The site includes multiple choice study questions, suggested discussion topics, and sometimes additional case studies to complement your reading and study of the material in this chapter.

NOTES

1. Sarah Kuhn, "When Worlds Collide: Engineering Students Encounter Social Aspects of Production," *Science and Engineering Ethics*, 1998, pp. 457–472.
2. Ibid., p. 461.
3. Ibid., p. 465.
4. Ibid., p. 466.
5. Ibid., p. 467.
6. Mike W. Martin and Roland Schinzinger, *Ethics in Engineering*, 4th ed. (Boston: McGraw-Hill, 2005), pp. 88–100.
7. Val Dusek, *Philosophy of Technology: An Introduction* (Malden, MA: Blackwell, 2006), pp. 32–36.
8. Shannon Vallor, "Social Networking Technology and the Virtues," *Ethics and Information Technology*, 2010, vol. 12, pp. 157–170.
9. Trevor J. Pinch and Wiebe E. Bijker, "The Social Construction of Facts and Artifacts: Or How the Sociology of Science and the Sociology of Technology Might Benefit Each Other," in W. E. Bijker, T. P. Hughes, and T. Pinch, eds., *The Social Construction of Technological Systems: New Directions in the Sociology and History of Technology* (Cambridge, MA: MIT Press, 1987), pp. 17–50.
10. Andrew Feenberg, "Democratic Rationalization: Technology, Power, and Freedom," in R. C. Scharff and V. Dusek, *Philosophy of Technology* (Malden, MA: Blackwell, 2003), pp. 554–655.
11. Val Dusek, *Philosophy of Technology: An Introduction*, p. 205.
12. See Feenberg, op. cit., pp. 659–660.
13. For the distinction between these four types of privacy, see Anita L. Allen, "Genetic Privacy: Emerging Concepts and Values," in Mark Rothstein, ed. *Genetic Secrets* (New Haven, CT: Yale University Press, 1997), p. 33.

14. For the list of standards from which this list is taken, see Anita L. Allen, "Privacy." In Hugh LaFollette, ed., *The Oxford Handbook of Practical Ethics* (Oxford: Oxford University Press, 2003), p. 500.

15. Richard Stallman, "Why Software Should Be Free," in D. G. Johnson and Helen Nissenbaum, *Computer Ethics and Social Policy* (Upper Saddle River, NJ: Prentice-Hall, 1995), pp. 190–200.

16. Office of Technology Assessment, "Evolution of Case Law on Copyrights and Computer Software," in Johnson and Nissenbaum, p. 165.

17. Herbert Rosenthan Jewelry Corp. v. Kalpakian, 446 F.2d 738, 742 (9th Cir. 1971). Cited in Lotus Development Corporation v. Paperback Software International and Stephenson Software, Limited, Civ. A., No. 87-76-K. United States District Court. D. Massachusetts. June 28, 1990. Reprinted in Johnson and Nissenbaum, pp. 236–252.

18. Lotus Development Corporation v. Paperback Software International and Stephenson Software, Limited, p. 242.

19. This account is taken mostly from "Now for the Hard Part: A Survey of Business in India," *The Economist*, June 3–9, 2006, special insert, pp. 3–18. For a somewhat more negative account, see "The Myth of the New India," *New York Times*, July 6, 2006, p. A23.

20. Emmanuel G. Mesthene, "The Social Impact of Technological Change" in *Philosophy of Technology*, edited by Robert C. Scharff and Val Dusek (Malden, MA: Blackwell, 2003), pp. 617–637. These selections are taken from "Technology and Wisdom" in *Technology and Social Change*, edited by Emmanuel G. Mesthene (Indianapolis: Bobbs-Merril Inc., 1967), pp. 109–115.

21. Langdon Winner, *The Whale and the Reactor* (Chicago: University of Chicago Press, 1986), pp. 19–39. Reprinted in David M. Kaplan, ed., *Readings in the Philosophy of Technology* (Lanham, MD: Rowman & Littlefield, 2009), pp. 251–263.

22. Alfred D. Chandler, Jr., *The Visible Hand: The Managerial Revolution in American Business* (Cambridge: Belknap, 1977), p. 244.

23. Http://tech.fortune.cnn.com/2011/04/15/googles-ordeal-in-china/.

24. "Bigger Monster, Weaker Chains" by Jay Stanley and Barry Steinhard, January 2003. American Civil Liberties Union Technology and Liberty Program. Reprinted Davod M. Kaplan, op. cit., pp. 293–308.

25. For this and the following paragraphs, we have found Andrew Feenberg's "Technology and Meaning" in his *Questioning Technology* (New York: Routledge, 1999) to be useful.

26. "Focal Things and Practices," in David M. Kaplan, ed., *Readings in the Philosophy of Technology* (New York: Rowman & Littlefield, 2004), pp. 115–136. Taken from Albert Borgman, *Technology and the Character of Contemporary Life: A Philosophical Inquiry* (Chicago: University of Chicago Press, 1984).

27. Martin Heidegger, *The Question Concerning Technology and Other Essays*, translated by William Lovitt (New York: Harper Colophon Books, 1977), p. 19.

28. Witold Kula, *Measures and Men*, R. Szreter, trans. (Princeton, NJ: Princeton University Press, 1986), pp. 30–31.

29. Sergio Sismondo, *An Introduction to Science and Technology Studies* (Malden, MA: Blackwell, 2004), pp. 32–36.

30. Vannevar Bush, *Science—The Endless Frontier: A Report to the President on a Program for Postwar Scientific Research* (Washington, DC: National Science Foundation, 1980)

31. Richard E. Sclove, *Democracy and Technology* (New York: Guilford Press, 2000).

32. Ibo van de Poel and A. C. van Gorp, "The Need for Ethical Reflection in Engineering Design," *Science, Technology, and Human Values*, 31:3, 2006, pp. 333–360.

33. W. G. Vincinti, "Engineering Knowledge, Type of Design, and Level of Hierarchy: Further Thoughts about What Engineers Know," in P. Kroes and M. Bakker, eds., *Technical Development and Science in the Industrial Age* (Dordrecht, The Netherlands: Kluwer, 1992), pp. 17–34.

CHAPTER FIVE

Trust and Reliability

Main Ideas in This Chapter

- This chapter focuses on issues regarding the importance of trustworthiness in engineers: honesty, confidentiality, intellectual property, expert witnessing, public communication, and conflicts of interest.
- Forms of dishonesty include lying, deliberate deception, withholding information, and failure to seek out the truth.
- Dishonesty in engineering research and testing includes plagiarism and the falsification and fabrication of data.
- Engineers are expected to respect professional confidentiality in their work.
- Integrity in expert testimony requires not only truthfulness but also adequate background and preparation in the areas requiring expertise.
- Conflicts of interest are especially problematic because they threaten to compromise professional judgment.

JOHN IS A CO-OP STUDENT who has a summer job with Oil Exploration, Inc., a company that does exploratory contract work for large oil firms.[1] The company drills, tests, and writes advisory reports to clients based on the test results. As an upper-level undergraduate student in petroleum engineering, John is placed in charge of a field team of roustabouts and technicians who test drill at various sites specified by the customer. John has the responsibility of transforming rough field data into succinct reports for the customer. Paul, an old high school friend of John's, is the foreperson of John's team. In fact, Paul was instrumental in getting this high-paying summer job for John.

While reviewing the field data for the last drilling report, John notices that a crucial step was omitted, one that would be impossible to correct without returning to the site and repeating the entire test at great expense to the company. The omitted step involves the foreperson's adding a certain test chemical to the lubricant being pumped into the test drill site. The test is important because it provides the data for deciding whether the drill site is worth developing for natural gas protection. Unfortunately, Paul forgot to add the test chemical at the last drill site.

John believes that Paul is likely to lose his job if his mistake comes to light. Paul cannot afford to lose his job at a time when the oil business is slow and his wife is expecting a child. John learns from past company data files that the chemical additive indicates the presence of natural gas in approximately 1 percent of the tests.

Should John withhold the information that the test for natural gas was not performed from his superiors? Should the information be withheld from the customer?

5.1 INTRODUCTION

Earlier we noted William F. May's observation that as society has become increasingly professionalized, it has also become more dependent on the services of professionals whose knowledge and expertise are not widely shared or understood. What this means is that, in its ignorance, the public must place its trust in the reliable performance of engineers, both as individuals and as members of teams of engineers who work together. This chapter focuses on areas of moral concern that are especially relevant to the trustworthiness of engineers: honesty and dishonesty, confidentiality, intellectual property, expert witnessing, informing the public, and conflicts of interest.

5.2 HONESTY

In light of the enduring emphasis on honesty in our moral traditions, it is not surprising that engineering codes contain many references to honesty. The third canon of the code of ethics of the Institute of Electrical and Electronics Engineers (IEEE) encourages all members "to be honest and realistic in stating claims or estimates based on available data." Canon 7 requires engineers "to seek, accept, and offer honest criticism of technical work." The American Society of Mechanical Engineers (ASME) code of ethics is equally straightforward. Fundamental Principle II states that engineers must practice the profession by "being honest and impartial." The seventh Fundamental Canon states, "Engineers shall issue public statements only in an objective and truthful manner." A subsection enjoins engineers not to "participate in the dissemination of untrue, unfair, or exaggerated statements regarding engineering."

The importance of honesty in engineering practice is a major focus of this chapter. However, in addition to issues of honesty, we also explore other important aspects of professional judgment and communication. For example, the second canon of the IEEE code requires members to avoid conflicts of interest because they can distort professional judgment. A subsection of Canon 3 of the ASCE code requires members not to issue statements on engineering matters "which are inspired or paid for by interested parties, unless they indicate on whose behalf the statements are made." Here again, the emphasis is on full disclosure. A subsection of Canon 4 of the same code speaks to the matter of confidentiality, an area in which withholding information is justified. It enjoins engineers to avoid conflicts of interest and forbids them from using "confidential information coming to them in the course of their assignments as a means of making personal profit if such action is adverse to the interests of their clients, employers, or the public."

The more detailed National Society for Professional Engineers (NSPE) code admonishes engineers "to participate in none but honest enterprise." The preamble states that "the services provided by engineers require honesty, impartiality, fairness, and equity." The third Fundamental Canon (1.3) requires engineers to "avoid deceptive acts in the solicitation of professional employment." In the Rules of Practice, there are several references to honesty. In item II.1.d, the code states the following: "Engineers shall not permit the use of their name or firm name nor associate in business ventures with any person or firm which they have reasons to believe is engaging in fraudulent or dishonest business or professional practices." Items II.2.a–II.2.c and II.3.a–II.3.c in the Rules of Practice give more detailed direction for the practice of the profession. Item II.3 states that "engineers shall issue public statements only in an objective and truthful manner." Item II.5 states that "engineers shall avoid deceptive ads in the solicitation of professional employment." Items II.5.a and II.5.b give more detailed explanations regarding how to implement this statement. In Section III, "Professional Obligations," the code refers to the obligation for engineers to be honest and truthful and not to misrepresent facts—and does so in six different locations (III.1.a, III.1.d, III.2.c, III.3.a, III.7, and III.8). In a statement that speaks directly to John's situation, part (a) of the third Rule of Practice states, "Engineers shall be objective and truthful in professional reports, statements, or testimony. They shall include all relevant and pertinent information in such reports, statements, or testimony."

5.3 FORMS OF DISHONESTY

Lying

When we think of dishonesty, we usually think of lying. Ethicists have long struggled over the definition of lying. One reason for the difficulty is that not every falsehood is a lie. If an engineer mistakenly conveys incorrect test results on soil samples, she is not lying even though she may not be telling the truth. To lie, a person must intentionally or at least knowingly convey false or misleading information. But even here complications arise. A person may give information that she believes to be false, even though it is actually true. In this case, we may be perplexed as to whether we should describe her action as lying. Her intention is to lie, but what she says is actually true.

To make matters more complicated, a person may give others false information by means other than making false statements. Gestures and nods, as well as indirect statements, can give a false impression in a conversation, even though the person has not told an outright lie. Despite these complications, most people believe that lies—or at least paradigm cases of lies—have three elements: First, a lie ordinarily involves something that is believed to be false or seriously misleading. Second, a lie is ordinarily stated in words. Third, a lie is made with the intention to deceive. So perhaps we can offer the following working definition: "A lie is a statement believed to be false or seriously misleading, made with the intention to deceive." Of course, this definition leaves the phrase "seriously misleading" open for interpretation, but the open-ended nature of this working definition is deliberate. We call some misleading statements lies and others not.

Deliberate Deception

If Andrew discusses technical matters in a manner that implies knowledge that he does not have to impress an employer or potential customer, then he is certainly engaging in deliberate deception, even if he is not lying. In addition to misrepresenting one's own expertise, one can misrepresent the value of certain products or designs by praising their advantages inordinately. Such deception can sometimes have more disastrous consequences than outright lying.

Withholding Information

Omitting or withholding information can be another type of deceptive behavior. If Jane deliberately fails to discuss some of the negative aspects of a project she is promoting to her superior, she engages in serious deception even though she is not lying.

Failing to report that you own stock in a company whose product you are recommending is a form of dishonesty. Perhaps we can say in more general terms that one is practicing a form of dishonesty by omission (1) if one fails to convey information that the audience would reasonably expect would not be omitted and (2) if the intent of the omission is to deceive.

Failure to Seek Out the Truth

The honest engineer is one who is committed to finding the truth, not simply avoiding dishonesty. Suppose engineer Mary suspects that some of the data she has received from the test lab are inaccurate. In using the results as they are, she is neither lying nor concealing the truth. But she may be irresponsible in using the results without inquiring further into their accuracy. Honesty in this positive sense is part of what is involved in being a responsible engineer.

It would not be correct to assume that lying is always more serious than deliberate deception, withholding information, failing to adequately promote the dissemination of information, or failing to seek out the truth. Sometimes the consequences of lying may not be as serious as the consequences of some of these other actions. The order of these first four types of misusing the truth reflects primarily the degree to which one is actively distorting the truth rather than the seriousness of the consequences of the actions.

5.4 WHY IS DISHONESTY WRONG?

The term "honest" has such a positive connotation and the term "dishonest" such a negative one that we may forget that telling the full truth may sometimes be wrong and concealing the truth may sometimes be the right thing to do. A society in which people are totally candid with each other would be difficult to tolerate. The requirement of total candor would mean that people would be brutally frank about their opinions of each other and unable to exercise the sort of tact and reticence that we associate with polite and civilized society. In regard to professionals, the requirement never to conceal truth would mean that engineers, physicians, lawyers, and other professionals could not protect confidentiality or proprietary information. Doctors could never misrepresent the truth to their patients, even when there is strong evidence that this is what the patients prefer and that the truth could be devastating.

Despite possible exceptions, however, dishonesty and the various other ways of misusing the truth are generally wrong. A helpful way to see this is to consider dishonesty from the standpoints of the ethics of respect for persons and utilitarian thinking; each can provide valuable suggestions for thinking about moral issues related to honesty.

Let us review some of the major components of the respect for persons perspective. As discussed in Chapter 2, actions are wrong if they violate the moral agency of individuals. Moral agents are human beings capable of formulating and pursuing goals and purposes of their own—they are autonomous. The word "autonomy" comes from two Greek terms: "autos," meaning "self," and "nomos," meaning "rule" or "law". A moral agent is autonomous in the sense of being self-governing.

Thus, to respect the moral agency of patients, physicians have three responsibilities. First, they must ensure that their patients make decisions about their medical treatment with informed consent. They must see to it that their patients understand the consequences of their decisions and rationally make decisions that have some relationship to their life plans. Second, they have some responsibility to ensure that patients make decisions without undue coercive influences such as stress, illness, and family pressures. Finally, physicians must ensure that patients are sufficiently informed about options for treatment and the consequences of the options.

Engineers have some degree of responsibility to ensure that employers, clients, and the general public make autonomous decisions, but their responsibilities are more limited than those of physicians. Their responsibilities probably extend only to the third of these three conditions of autonomy, ensuring that employers, clients, and the general public make decisions regarding technology with understanding, particularly understanding of their consequences. We have seen, for example, that the IEEE code requires members to "disclose promptly factors that might endanger the public or the environment" and that when the safety, health, and welfare of the public are endangered ASCE members must "inform their clients or employers of the possible consequences." In engineering, this applies to such issues as product safety and the provision of professional advice and information. If customers do not know that a car has an unusual safety problem, then they cannot make an informed decision regarding whether to purchase it. If a customer is paying for professional engineering advice and is given misinformation, then he again cannot make a free and informed decision.

The astronauts on the *Challenger* were informed on the morning of the flight about the ice buildup on the launching pad and were given the option of postponing the launch. They chose not to exercise that option. However, no one presented them with the information about O-ring behavior at low temperatures. Therefore, they did not give their fully informed consent to launch despite the O-ring risk because they were unaware of the risk. The *Challenger* incident is a tragic example of the violation of the engineer's obligation to protect informed consent. The fault, however, was not primarily with the engineers but with the managers who supported the launch and did not inform the astronauts of the danger.

Many situations are more complex. To be informed, decision makers must not only have the relevant information but also understand it. Furthermore, nobody has all of the relevant information or has complete understanding of it, so being informed in both of these senses is a matter of degree. Therefore, the extent of the engineer's obligation regarding informed consent will sometimes be controversial, and whether or not the obligation has been fulfilled will also sometimes be controversial. We return to these considerations later, but what we have said here is enough to show that even withholding information or failing to adequately disseminate it can be serious violations of professional responsibilities.

Now let us turn to the utilitarian perspective on honesty. The utilitarian perspective requires that our actions promote human happiness and well-being. The profession of engineering contributes to this utilitarian goal by providing designs for the creation of buildings, bridges, chemicals, electronic devices, automobiles, and many other things on which our society depends. It also provides information about technology that is important in decision making at the individual, corporate, and public policy levels.

Dishonesty in engineering research can undermine these functions. If engineers report data falsely or omit crucial data, then other researchers cannot reliably depend on their results. This can undermine the relations of trust on which a scientific community is founded. Just as a designer who is untruthful about the strength of materials she specifies for a building threatens the collapse of the building, a researcher who falsifies the data reported in a professional journal threatens the collapse of the infrastructure of engineering.

Dishonesty can also undermine informed decision making. Managers in both business and government, as well as legislators, depend on the knowledge and judgments provided by engineers to make decisions. If these are unreliable, then the ability of those who depend on engineers to make good decisions regarding technology is undermined. To the extent that this happens, engineers have failed in their obligation to promote the public welfare.

From both the respect for persons and utilitarian perspectives, then, outright dishonesty as well as other forms of misusing the truth with regard to technical information and judgment are usually wrong. These actions undermine the moral agency of individuals by preventing them from making decisions with free and informed consent. They also prevent engineers from promoting the public welfare.

5.5   DISHONESTY ON CAMPUS

Three students were working on a senior capstone engineering design project. The project was to design, build, and test an inexpensive meter that would be mounted on the dashboard of automobiles and would measure the distance a car could travel on a gallon of gasoline. Even though personal computers, microchip calculators, and "smart instruments" were not available at the time, the students came up with a clever approach that had a good chance of success. They devised a scheme to instantaneously measure voltage equivalents of both gasoline flow to the engine and speedometer readings on the odometer while keeping a cumulative record of the quotient of the two. In other words, miles per hour divided by gallons per hour would give the figure for the miles the automobile is traveling per gallon of gasoline. The students even devised a way to filter and smooth out instantaneous fluctuations in either signal to ensure time-averaged data. Finally, they devised a benchtop experiment to prove the feasibility of their concept. The only thing missing was a flow meter that would measure the flow of gasoline to the engine in gallons per hour and produce a proportional voltage signal. Today, customers can order this feature as an option on some automobiles, but at the time the design was remarkably innovative. The professor directing the project was so impressed that he found a source of funds to buy the flow meter. He also encouraged the three students to draft an article describing their design for a technical journal.

Several weeks later, the professor was surprised to receive a letter from the editor of a prominent journal accepting for publication the "excellent article" that, according to the letter, he had "coauthored" with his three senior design students. The professor knew that the flow meter had not yet arrived, nor had he seen any draft version of the paper, so he asked the three students for an explanation. They explained that they had followed the professor's advice and prepared an article about their design. They had put the professor's name on the paper as senior author because, after all, it was his idea to write the paper and he was the faculty advisor. They did not want to bother the professor with the early draft. Furthermore, they really could not wait for the flow-measuring instrument to arrive because they were all graduating in a few weeks and planned to begin new jobs. Finally, because they were sure the data would give the predicted results, they simulated some time-varying voltages on a power supply unit to replicate what they thought the flow-measuring voltages would be. They had every intention, they said, of checking the flow voltage and the overall system behavior after the flow meter arrived and, if necessary, making minor modifications in the paper.

As a matter of fact, the students incorrectly assumed that the flow and voltages would be related linearly. They also made false assumptions about the response of the professor to their actions. The result was that the paper was withdrawn from the journal, and the students sent letters of apology to the journal. Copies of the letter were placed in their files, the students received an F in the senior design course, and their graduation was delayed 6 months. Despite this, one of them requested that the professor write a letter of recommendation for a summer job he was seeking!

A student's experience in engineering school is a training period for his or her professional career. If dishonesty is as detrimental to engineering professionalism as we have suggested, then part of this training should be in professional honesty. Furthermore, the pressures that students experience in the academic setting are not that different from (and perhaps less than) those they will experience in their jobs. If it is morally permissible to cheat on exams and misrepresent data on laboratory reports and design projects, then why isn't it permissible to misrepresent data to please the boss, get a promotion, or keep a job?

As we shall see in the next section, there are exact counterparts in the scientific and engineering communities to the types of dishonesty exhibited by students. Smoothing data points on the graph of a freshman physics laboratory report to get an A on the report, selecting the research data that support the desired conclusion, entirely inventing the data, and plagiarism of the words and ideas of others all have obvious parallels in nonacademic settings.

5.6   DISHONESTY IN RESEARCH AND TESTING

Dishonesty in science and engineering takes several forms: falsification of data, fabrication of data, and plagiarism. Falsification involves distorting data by smoothing out irregularities or presenting only those data which fit one's favored theory and discarding the rest. Fabrication involves inventing data and even reporting results of experiments that were never conducted. Plagiarism is the use of the intellectual property of others without proper permission or credit. It takes many different forms. Plagiarism is really a type of theft. Drawing the line between legitimate and illegitimate use of the intellectual property of others is often difficult, and the method of line drawing is useful in helping us discriminate between the two. Some cases are undeniable examples of plagiarism, such as when the extended passages involving the exact words or the data of another are used without proper permission or attribution. On the other side of the spectrum, the quotation of short statements by others with proper attribution is clearly permissible. Between these two extremes are many cases in which drawing the line is more difficult.

Multiple authorship of papers can often raise particularly vexing issues with regard to honesty in scientific and technological work. Sometimes, as many as 40 to 50 researchers are listed as the authors of a scientific paper. One can think of several justifications for this practice. First, often a large number of scientists participate in some forms of research, and they all make genuine contributions. For example, large numbers of people are sometimes involved in medical research or research with a particle accelerator. Second, the distinction between whether someone is the author of a paper or merely deserves to be cited may indeed be tenuous in some circumstances. The fairest or at least the most generous thing to do in such circumstances is to cite such people as authors.

However, there are less honest motives for the practice, the most obvious one being the desire of most scientists for as many publications as possible. This is true of both academic and nonacademic scientists. In addition, many graduate and postdoctoral students need to be published to secure jobs. Sometimes, more senior scientists are tempted to list graduate students as authors, even though their contribution to the publication was minimal, to make the student's research record appear as impressive as possible.

From a moral standpoint, there are at least two potential problems with multiple authorship. First, it is fraudulent to claim significant credit for scientific research when, in fact, a contribution is relatively insignificant. If claims to authorship are indeed fraudulent, then those who are evaluating the scientist or engineer are not able to make informed decisions in their evaluations. Second, fraudulent claims to authorship give one an unfair advantage in the competition for jobs, promotions, and recognition in the scientific community. From the standpoint of fairness alone, unsubstantiated claims to authorship should be avoided.

5.7 CONFIDENTIALITY

One can misuse the truth, not only by dishonesty through lying or otherwise distorting or withholding the truth, but also by disclosing it in inappropriate circumstances. Engineers in private practice might be tempted to disclose confidential information without the consent of the client. Information may be confidential if it is either given to the engineer by the client or discovered by the engineer in the process of work done for the client.

Given that most engineers are employees, a more common problem involving the improper use of information is the violation of proprietary information of a former employer. Using designs and other proprietary information of a former employer can be dishonest and may even result in litigation. Even using ideas one developed while working for a former employer can be questionable, particularly if those ideas involve trade secrets, patents, or licensing arrangements.

Most engineers are employees of large corporations, but some, especially civil engineers, subcontract for design firms that have clients. For these engineers, there is an obligation to protect the confidentiality of the client–professional relationship, just as with lawyers and physicians. Confidentiality would ordinarily cover both sensitive information given by the client and information gained by the professional in work paid for by the client.

An engineer can mishandle client–professional confidentiality in two ways. First, she may break confidentiality when it is not warranted. Second, she may refuse to break confidentiality when the higher obligation to the public requires it. The following is an example of the first type of mishandling.[2] Jane, a civil engineer, is contracted to do a preliminary study for a new shopping mall for Greenville, California. The town already has a mall that is 20 years old. The owner of the existing mall is trying to decide whether to renovate or close the old mall. He has done a lot of business with Jane and asks her detailed questions about the new mall. Jane answers the questions.

The following is another example in the first category. Suppose Engineer A inspects a residence for a homeowner for a fee. He finds the residence in generally good condition, although it is in need of several minor repairs. Engineer A sends a copy of his one-page report to the homeowner, showing that a carbon copy was sent to the real estate firm handling the sale of the residence.

This case was considered by the NSPE Board of Ethical Review, which ruled that "Engineer A acted unethically in submitting a copy of the home inspection to the real estate firm representing the owners." It cites section II.1.c of the NSPE code, which states, "Engineers shall not reveal facts, data, or information obtained in a professional capacity without the prior consent of the client or employer except as authorized by law or this Code."[3]

This opinion seems correct. The clients paid for the information and therefore could lay claim to its exclusive possession. The residence was fundamentally sound, and there was no reason to believe that the welfare of the public was at stake. The case would have been more difficult if there had been a fundamental structural flaw. Even here, however, we can argue that there was no fundamental threat to life. Prospective buyers are always free to pay for an inspection themselves.

The following hypothetical case raises more serious questions regarding whether confidentially should be overridden. Suppose engineer James inspects a building for a client before the client puts the building up for sale. James discovers fundamental structural defects that could pose a threat to public safety. James informs the client of these defects in the building and recommends its evacuation and repair before it is put up for sale. The client replies:

> James, I am not going to evacuate the building, and I am certainly not going to spend a lot of money on the building before I put it up for sale. Furthermore, if you reveal the information to the authorities or to any potential buyer, I am going to take whatever legal action I can against you. Not only that, but I have a lot of friends. If I pass the word around, you will lose a lot of business. The information is mine. I paid for it, and you have no right to reveal it to anyone else without my permission.

James's obligation to his client is clearly at odds with his obligation to the public. Although he may have an obligation to potential buyers, his more immediate and pressing one is to protect the safety of the current occupants of the building. Note that the section of the NSPE code quoted previously requires engineers to keep the confidentiality of their clients in all cases, except where exceptions are authorized "by law or this Code." This is probably a case in which part of the code (specifically, the part emphasizing the higher obligation to the safety of the public) should override the requirement of confidentiality.

Even here, however, James should probably try to find a creative middle way that allows him to honor his obligations to his client, the occupants of the building, and potential buyers. He might attempt to persuade the client that his intention to refuse to correct the structural defects is morally wrong and probably not even in his long-term self-interest. He might argue that the client may find himself entangled in lawsuits and that surely he would find it difficult to live with himself if a catastrophe occurred.

Unfortunately, such an approach might not work. James's client might refuse to change his mind. Then James must rank his competing obligations. Most engineering codes, including the NSPE code, are clear that the engineer's first obligation is to the safety of the public, so James must make public the information about the structural defects of the building, at least according to the NSPE code as we interpret it.

Still, not all cases involving confidentiality will be as clear-cut as the one James faces. In fact, his situation might serve as one extreme on a spectrum of cases. The other extreme might be a case in which an engineer breaks confidentiality to promote his own financial interests. Between these two extremes are many other possible situations in which the decision might be difficult. Again, in such cases, it is appropriate to use the line-drawing method.

5.8 INTELLECTUAL PROPERTY

Intellectual property is property that results from mental labor. It can be protected in several ways, including as trade secrets, patents, trademarks, and copyrights.

Trade secrets are formulas, patterns, devices, or compilations of information that are used in business to gain an advantage over competitors who do not possess the trade secrets. The formula for Coca-Cola is an example of a trade secret. Trade secrets must not be in the public domain and the secrecy must be protected by the firm because trade secrets are not protected by patents.

Patents are documents issued by the government that allow the owner of the patent to exclude others from making use of the patented information for 20 years from the date of filing. To obtain a patent, the invention must be new, useful, and nonobvious. As an example, the puncture-proof tire is patented.

Trademarks are words, phrases, designs, sounds, or symbols associated with goods or services. "Coca-Cola" is a registered trademark.

Copyrights are rights to creative products such as books, pictures, graphics, sculptures, music, movies, and computer programs. Copyrights protect the expression of the ideas but not the ideas themselves. The script of *Star Wars*, for example, is copyrighted.

Many companies require their employees to sign a patent assignment whereby all patents and inventions of the employee become the property of the company, often in exchange for a token fee of $1. Sometimes, employees find themselves caught between two employers with respect to such issues. Consider the case of Bill, a senior engineering production manager of a tire manufacturing company, Roadrubber, Inc. Bill has been so successful in decreasing production costs for his company by developing innovative manufacturing techniques that he has captured the attention of the competition. One competing firm, Slippery Tire, Inc., offers Bill a senior management position at a greatly increased salary. Bill warns Slippery Tire that he has signed a standard agreement with Roadrubber not to use or divulge any of the ideas he developed or learned at Roadrubber for 2 years following any change of employment.

Slippery Tire's managers assure Bill that they understand and will not try to get him to reveal any secrets and also that they want him as an employee because of his demonstrated managerial skills. After a few months on the job at Slippery Tire, someone who was not a part of the earlier negotiations with Bill asks him to reveal some of the secret processes that he developed while at Roadrubber. When Bill refuses, he is told, "Come on, Bill, you know this is the reason you were hired at the inflated salary. If you don't tell us what we want to know, you're out of here." This is a clear case of an attempt to steal information. If the managers who attracted Bill to Slippery Tire were engineers, then they also violated the NSPE code.

"Professional Obligations," item III.1.d of the NSPE code, says, "Engineers shall not attempt to attract an engineer from another employer by false or misleading pretenses." Some cases are not as clear. Sometimes an employee develops ideas at Company A and later finds that those same ideas can be useful—although perhaps in an entirely different application—to her new employer, Company B.

Suppose Betty's new employer is not a competing tire company but one that manufactures rubber boats. A few months after being hired by Rubberboat, Betty comes up with a new process for Rubberboat. It is only later that she realizes that she probably thought of the idea because of her earlier work with Roadrubber. The processes are different in many ways, and Rubberboat is not a competitor of Roadrubber, but she still wonders whether it is right to offer her idea to Rubberboat.

Let's examine what the NSPE code of ethics has to say about such situations. As already noted, under Rules of Practice, item II.1.c states, "Engineers shall not reveal facts, data, or information obtained in a professional capacity without the prior consent of the client or employer except as authorized or required by law or this Code." Item III.4 states,

> Engineers shall not disclose confidential information concerning the business affairs or technical processes of any present or former client or employer without his consent. (a) Engineers in the employ of others shall not without the consent of all interested parties enter promotional efforts or negotiations for work or make arrangements for other employment as a principal or to practice in connection with a specific project for which the engineer has gained particular and specialized knowledge. (b) Engineers shall not, without the consent of all interested parties, participate in or represent an adversary interest in connection with a specific project or proceedings in which the engineer has gained particular specialized knowledge on behalf of a former client or employer.

Similarly, the Model Rules of Professional Conduct for the National Council of Examiners for Engineering and Surveying (NCEES) require engineers to "not reveal facts, data, or information obtained in a professional capacity without the prior consent of the client or employer as authorized by law" (I.1.d).

These code statements strongly suggest that even in the second case Betty should tell the management at Rubberboat that it must enter into licensing negotiations with Roadrubber. In other words, she must be honest in fulfilling all of her still existing obligations to Roadrubber.

Other cases can be even less clear, however. Suppose the ideas Betty developed while at Roadrubber were never used by Roadrubber. She realized they would be of no use and never even mentioned them to management at Roadrubber. Thus, they might not be considered a part of any agreement between her and Roadrubber. Still, the ideas were developed using Roadrubber's computers and laboratory facilities. Or suppose Betty's ideas occurred to her at home while she was still an employee of Roadrubber, although the ideas probably would never have occurred to her if she had not been working on somewhat related problems at Roadrubber.

We can best deal with these problems by employing the line-drawing method. As we have seen, the method involves pointing out similarities and dissimilarities between the cases whose moral status is clear and the cases whose moral status is less clear. Additional features may come to light in analyzing a particular case. There can also be other intermediate cases between the ones presented here. The particular case of interest must be compared with the spectrum of cases to determine where the line between permissible and impermissible action should be drawn.

5.9 EXPERT WITNESSING

Engineers are sometimes hired as expert witnesses in cases that involve accidents, defective products, structural defects, and patent infringements, as well as in other areas where competent technical knowledge is required. Calling upon an expert witness is one of the most important moves a lawyer can make in such cases, and engineers are usually well compensated for their testimony. However, being an expert witness is time-consuming and often stressful.

Expert witnesses face certain ethical pitfalls. The most obvious is perjury on the witness stand. A more likely temptation is to withhold information that would be unfavorable to the client's case. In addition to being ethically questionable, such withholding can be an embarrassment to the engineer because cross-examination often exposes it. To avoid problems of this sort, an expert should follow several rules.

First, she should not take a case if she does not have adequate time for a thorough investigation. Rushed preparation can be disastrous for the reputation of the expert witness as well as for her client. Being prepared requires not only general technical knowledge but also detailed knowledge of the particular case and the process of the court before which the witness will testify.

Second, she should not accept a case if she cannot do so with good conscience. This means that she should be able to testify honestly and not feel the need to withhold information to make an adequate case for her client.

Third, the engineer should consult extensively with the lawyer so that the lawyer is as familiar as possible with the technical details of the case and can prepare the expert witness for cross-examination.

Fourth, the witness should maintain an objective and unbiased demeanor on the witness stand. This includes sticking to the questions asked and keeping an even temper, especially under cross-examination.

Fifth, the witness should always be open to new information, even during the course of the trial. The following example does not involve an expert witness, but it does show how important new information gained during a trial can be. During a trial of an accident case in Kansas, the defendant discovered in his basement an old document that conclusively showed that his company was culpable in the accident. He introduced this new evidence in court proceedings, even though it cost his company millions of dollars and resulted in the largest accident court judgment in the history of Kansas.[4]

One position a potential expert witness can take with respect to a client is to say something like the following:

> I will have only one opinion, not a "real" opinion and a story I will tell for you on the witness stand. My opinion will be as unbiased and objective as I can possibly make it. I will form my opinion after looking at the case, and you should pay me to investigate the facts of the case. I will tell the truth and the whole truth as I see it on the witness stand, and I will tell you what I will say beforehand. If you can use my testimony, I will serve as an expert witness for you. If not, you can dismiss me.

This approach may not solve all the problems. If an expert witness is dismissed by a lawyer because he has damaging evidence, then is it ethically permissible to simply walk away, without revealing the evidence, even when public safety is involved? Should the witness testify for the other side if asked?

5.10   INFORMING THE PUBLIC

Some types of professional irresponsibility in handling technical information may be best described as a failure to inform those whose decisions are impaired by the absence of the information. From the standpoint of the ethics of respect for persons, this is a serious impairment of moral agency. The failure of engineers to ensure that technical information is available to those who need it is especially wrong where disasters can be avoided.

Dan Applegate was Convair's senior engineer directing a subcontract with McDonnell Douglas in 1972.[5] The contract was for designing and building a cargo hatch door for the DC-10. The design for the cargo door's latch was known to be faulty. When the first DC-10 was pressure tested on the assembly line, the cargo hatch door blew out and the passenger cabin floor buckled, resulting in the destruction of several hydraulic and electrical power lines. Modifications in the design did not solve the problem. Later, a DC-10 flight over Windsor, Ontario, had to make an emergency landing in Detroit after the cargo hatch door flew open and the cabin floor again buckled. Fortunately, no one was injured.

In light of these problems, Applegate wrote a memo to the vice president of Convair, itemizing the dangers of the design. However, Convair managers decided not to pass this information on to McDonnell Douglas because of the possibility of financial penalties and litigation if accidents occurred. Applegate's memorandum was prophetic. Two years later, in 1974, a fully loaded DC-10 crashed just outside Orly Field in Paris, killing all 346 passengers. The crash happened for the reasons that Applegate had outlined in his memorandum. There were genuine legal impediments to disclosing the dangers in the DC-10 design to the federal government or to the general public, but this story emphasizes the fact that failure to disclose information can have catastrophic consequences.

In this case, most of us would probably say that Dan Applegate's professional responsibility to protect the safety of the public required that he do something to make his professional concerns about the DC-10 known. In requiring engineers to notify employers "or such other authority as may be appropriate" if their "professional judgment is overruled under circumstances where the safety, health, property, or welfare of the public are endangered," the NSPE code seems to imply this (II.1.a). Using almost identical language, the NCEES Model Rules of Professional Conduct require registrants to "notify their employer or client and such other authority as may be appropriate when their professional judgment is overruled under circumstances where the life, health, property, and welfare of the public is endangered" (I.c). Applegate's memo was a step in the right direction. Unfortunately, his superiors did not pass his concerns on to the client (McDonnell Douglas). Who bears responsibility for the client never receiving this information is another matter. However, the failure to alert others to the danger resulted in massive expense and loss of life and denied passengers the ability to make an informed decision in accepting an unusual risk in flying in the aircraft.

Similar issues are raised in another well-known case involving the Ford Pinto gas tank in the early 1970s. At the time the Pinto was introduced, Ford was making every effort to compete with the new compact Japanese imports by producing a car in less than 2 years that weighed less than 2000 pounds and cost less than $2000.[6] The project engineer, Lee Iacocca, and his management team believed that the American public wanted the product they were designing. They also believed that the American public would not be willing to pay the extra $11 to eliminate the risk of a rupturing gas tank. The engineers who were responsible for the rear-end crash tests of early prototype models of the Pinto knew that the Pinto met the current regulations for safety requirements in rear-end collisions; however, they also knew that the car failed the new higher standards that were to go into effect in just 2 years. In fact, the car failed 11 of 12 rear-end collisions at the newly prescribed 20-miles-per-hour crash tests. In the new crashes, the gas tanks ruptured and the vehicles caught fire. Thus, many engineers at Ford knew that the drivers of the Pinto were subject to unusual risks of which they were unaware. They also knew that management was not sympathetic to their safety concerns. One of the engineers working on the Pinto test program found that the ignorance of potential drivers about the car's dangers was unacceptable and decided to resign and make the information public. The engineer thus gave car buyers the knowledge they needed to purchase the Pinto with informed consent.

There is evidence that Ford management did not necessarily have a callous disregard for safety. Only a few years earlier, Ford management voluntarily reported that some line employees, in a misguided show of company loyalty, had falsified EPA emissions data on new engines to bring Ford into compliance with EPA regulations on a new model. As a result of this honest disclosure, Ford was required to pay a stiff fine and had to substitute an older model engine on the new car at even greater expense.

The obligation of engineers to protect the health and safety of the public requires more than refraining from telling lies or simply refusing to withhold information. It sometimes requires that engineers aggressively do what they can to ensure that the consumers of technology are not forced to make uninformed decisions regarding the use of that technology. This is especially true when the use of technology involves unusual and unperceived risks. This obligation may require engineers to do what is necessary to either eliminate the unusual risks or, at the very least, inform those who use the technology of its dangers. Otherwise, their moral agency is seriously eroded. Placing yourself in the position of the seven *Challenger* astronauts, you probably would have wanted to hear all of the relevant engineering facts about the risky effects of low temperatures on the rocket booster O-ring seals before giving permission for liftoff. Similar considerations apply to those who flew the DC-10 or drove Pintos.

5.11   CONFLICTS OF INTEREST

John is employed as a design engineer at a small company that uses valves. In recommending product designs for his company's clients, he usually specifies valves made by a relative, even when valves made by other companies might be more appropriate. Should his company's clients discover this, they might well complain that John is involved in a conflict of interest. What does this mean?

Michael Davis has provided one of the most useful discussions of conflicts of interest. Using a modified version of Davis's definition, we shall say that a conflict of interest exists for a professional when, acting in a professional role, he or she has interests that tend to make a professional's judgment less likely to benefit the customer or client than the customer or client is justified in expecting.[7] In the preceding example, John has allowed his interest in maintaining a good relationship with his relative to unduly influence his professional judgment. He has betrayed the trust that his clients have placed in his professional judgment by serving his personal interest in his relative rather than the interests of his clients as he is paid to do.

Conflicts of interest can strike at the heart of professionalism. This is because professionals are paid for their expertise and unbiased professional judgment in pursuing their professional duties, and conflicts of interest threaten to undermine the trust that clients, employers, and the public place in that expertise or judgment. When a conflict of interest is present, there is an inherent conflict between a professional actively pursuing certain interests and carrying out his or her professional duties as one should.

Engineering codes of ethics usually have something to say about conflicts of interest. Cases involving conflicts of interest are the most common kinds of cases brought before the NSPE's Board of Ethical Review. Fundamental Canon 4 of the NSPE code addresses the idea that engineers should act as "faithful agents or trustees" in performing their professional duties. The first entry under the heading is that engineers should disclose all "known" or "potential" conflicts of interest to their employers or clients. Section III on professional obligations specifies some specific prohibitions:

5. Engineers shall not be influenced in their professional duties by conflicting interests.

   a. Engineers shall not accept financial or other considerations, including free engineering designs, from material suppliers for specifying their product.

   b. Engineers shall not accept commissions or allowances, directly or indirectly, from contractors or other parties dealing with clients or employers for the Engineer in connection with work for which the Engineer is responsible.

In considering these prohibitions and conflicts of interest more generally, however, several important points must be kept in mind. First, a conflict of interest is not just any set of conflicting interests. An engineer may like tennis and swimming and cannot decide which interest is more important to her. This is not a conflict of interest in the special sense in which this term is used in professional ethics because it does not involve a conflict that is likely to influence professional judgment.

Second, simply having more commitments than one can satisfy in a given period of time is not a conflict of interest. Overcommitment can best be characterized as a conflict of commitment. This, too, should be avoided. However, a conflict of interest involves an inherent conflict between a particular duty and a particular interest, regardless of how much time one has on one's hands. For example, serving on a review panel for awarding research grants and at the same time submitting a grant proposal to that review panel creates an inherent conflict between one's interest in being awarded a grant and one's responsibility to exercise impartial judgment of proposal submissions.

Third, the interests of the client, employer, or public that the engineer must protect are restricted to those that are morally legitimate. An employer or client might have an interest that can be served or protected only through illegal activity (e.g., fraud, theft, embezzlement, and murder). An engineer has no professional duty to serve or protect such interests. On the contrary, the engineer may have a duty to expose such interests to external authorities.

Fourth, a distinction is sometimes made between *actual* and *potential* conflicts of interest. The following are examples: Actual. John has to recommend parts for one of his company's products. One of the vendors is Ajax Suppliers, a company in which John has heavily invested. Potential. Roger will have a conflict of interest if he agrees to serve on a committee to review proposals if he has already submitted his own proposal to be reviewed.

The first hypothetical case illustrates something very important about conflicts of interest. Having a conflict of interest need not, in itself, be unethical. John has a conflict of interest, but he has not necessarily done anything wrong—yet. What he does about his conflict of interest is what matters. If he tries to conceal from others that he has the conflict of interest and then recommends Ajax, he will have engaged in ethically questionable behavior. But he could acknowledge the conflict of interest and refrain from recommending in this case. Thus, his conflict of interest would not result in his judgment being compromised.

Fifth, even though it is best to avoid conflicts of interest, sometimes this cannot reasonably be done. Even then, the professional should reveal the existence of the conflict rather than wait for the customer or the public to find out about it on their own. In line with this, Fundamental Canon 4 of the NSPE code states:

> a. Engineers shall disclose all known or potential conflicts of interest to their employers or clients by promptly informing them of any business association, interest, or other circumstances which could influence or appear to influence their judgment or the quality.

After disclosure, clients and employers can decide whether they are willing to risk the possible corruption of the professional's judgment that such a conflict of interest might cause. Thus, the free and informed consent of clients and employers is preserved.

What if an engineer is convinced that he or she does not have a conflict of interest even though others may think otherwise? Two comments should be stated regarding this issue. First, self-deception is always possible. In a case in which there actually is a conflict of interest, one may have some motivation not to acknowledge this to oneself. Second, it is important to realize that even the appearance of a conflict of interest decreases the confidence of the public in the objectivity and trustworthiness of professional services and thus harms both the profession and the public. Therefore, it is best for engineers to use caution regarding even the appearance of a conflict of interest.

An important part of any professional service is professional judgment. Allowing this to be corrupted or unduly influenced by conflicts of interest or other extraneous considerations can lead to another type of misusing the truth. Suppose engineer Joe is designing a chemical plant and specifies several large pieces of equipment manufactured by a company whose salesperson he has known for many years. The equipment is of good quality, but newer and more innovative lines may actually be better. In specifying his friend's equipment, Joe is not giving his employer or client the benefit of his best and most unbiased professional judgment. In some cases, this may be a form of dishonesty, but in any case Joe's judgment is unreliable.

5.12 CHAPTER SUMMARY

Recognizing the importance of trust and reliability in engineering practice, codes of ethics require engineers to be honest and impartial in their professional judgments. Forms of dishonesty include not only lying and deliberate deception but also withholding the truth and failing to seek out the truth. From the standpoint of the ethics of respect for persons, dishonesty is wrong because it violates the moral agency of individuals by causing them to make decisions without informed consent. From the utilitarian perspective, dishonesty is wrong because it can undermine the relations of trust on which a scientific community is founded, as well as informed decision making, thus impeding the development of technology.

Dishonesty on campus accustoms a student to dishonesty, which can carry over into his or her professional life. There are, in fact, exact counterparts in the scientific research and engineering communities to the types of dishonesty exhibited by students on campus.

An engineer should respect professional confidentiality. The limits of confidentiality are controversial and often difficult to determine in engineering as in most professions. Decisions to the proper use of intellectual property with regard to trade secrets, patents, and copyrighted material are often difficult to make because they may involve varying degrees of use of intellectual property. The line-drawing method is useful in resolving these problems.

Integrity in expert testimony requires engineers to take cases only when they have adequate time for preparation, to refuse to take cases when they cannot testify in good conscience on behalf of their client, to consult extensively with the lawyer regarding the technical and legal details of the case, to maintain an objective and unbiased demeanor, and always to be open to new information. Engineers also misuse the truth when they fail to seek out or inform employers, clients, or the public of relevant information, especially when this information concerns the health, safety, and welfare of the public.

A conflict of interest exists for professionals when, acting in their professional roles, they have other interests that, if actively pursued, threaten to compromise their professional judgment and interfere with satisfactorily fulfilling their professional duties.

5.13   ENGINEERING ETHICS ON THE WEB

Check your understanding of the material in this chapter by visiting the companion website for *Engineering Ethics*. The site includes multiple choice study questions, suggested discussion topics, and sometimes additional case studies to complement your reading and study of the material in this chapter.

NOTES

1. We are indebted to our student, Ray Flumerfelt, Jr., for this case. Names have been changed to protect those involved.
2. We are indebted to Mark Holtzapple for this example.
3. *Opinions of the Board of Ethical Review*, vol. VI (Alexandria, VA: National Society of Professional Engineers, 1989), p. 15.
4. See "Plaintiffs to Get $15.4 Million," *Miami County Republic* [Paola, Kansas], April 27, 1992, p. 1.
5. Paul Eddy, *Destination Disaster: From the Tri-Motor to the DC-10* (New York: Quadrangle/New York Times Book Company, 1976), pp. 175–188. Reprinted in Robert Baum, *Ethical Problems in Engineering*, vol. 2 (Troy, NY: Center for the Study of the Human Dimensions of Science and Technology, 1980), pp. 175–185.
6. Grimshaw v. Ford Motor Co., App., 174 Cal. Rptr. 348, p. 360.
7. Michael Davis, "Conflict of Interest," in Deborah Johnson, ed., *Ethical Issues in Engineering* (Englewood Cliffs, NJ: Prentice Hall, 1991), p. 234. For further discussion of conflicts of interest, see Michael Davis and Andrew Stark, eds., *Conflicts of Interest in the Professions* (New York: Oxford University Press, 2001); and Michael S. Pritchard, *Professional Integrity: Thinking Ethically* (Lawrence: University Press of Kansas, 2006), pp. 60–66.

CHAPTER SIX

Risk and Liability in Engineering

Main Ideas in This Chapter

- For engineers and risk experts, risk is the product of the likelihood and magnitude of harm.

- Engineers and risk experts have traditionally identified harms and benefits with factors that are relatively easily quantified, such as economic losses or the number of human lives lost.

- In a new version of the way engineers and risk experts deal with risk, the "capabilities" approach focuses on the effects of risks and disasters on the capabilities of people to live the kinds of lives they value.

- The public conceptualizes risk in a different way from engineers and risk experts, taking account of such factors as free and informed consent to risk and whether risk is justly distributed.

- Government regulators have a still different approach to risk because they place more weight on avoiding harm to the public than producing good.

- Engineers have techniques for estimating the causes and likelihood of harm, but their effectiveness is limited.

- Engineers must protect themselves, their clients, and their employers from unjust liability for harm while also protecting the public from risk.

ON THE FOGGY SATURDAY MORNING of July 28, 1945, a twin-engine US Army Air Corps B-25 bomber lost in the fog crashed into the Empire State Building 914 feet above street level. It tore an 18-by-20-foot hole in the north face of the building and scattered flaming fuel into the building. New York firemen put out the blaze in 40 minutes. The crew members and 10 persons at work perished.[1] The building was repaired and still stands.

Just 10 years later, in 1955, the leaders of the New York City banking and real estate industries got together to initiate plans for the New York City World Trade Center (WTC), which would later become known as the Twin Towers, the world's tallest buildings at the time.[2] However, as the plans emerged, it became clear that the buildings required new construction techniques.

On September 11, 2001, terrorists attacked the Twin Towers by flying two hijacked Boeing 727 passenger jets into them, each jet smashing approximately two-thirds of the way up its respective tower. A significant consequence of the attack was the fire that started over several floors due to high-octane aviation fuel. The fires isolated more than 2000 workers in the floors above them. Only 18 of the more than 2000 were able to descend the flaming stairwells to safety. Most of the 2000 perished in the later collapse of the buildings. By comparison, almost all of the workers in the floors below the fire were able to make it down to safety before the towers collapsed. Differences in high-rise building construction techniques as well as the difference in the quantity of fuel involved are factors in the very different performance of these newer structures compared to the Empire State Building. As reported in the *New York Times*, the present plans for the 9/11 ground-zero memorial building call for high-rise stairwell designs that would diminish the likelihood of this kind of tragedy.

In the hour following the plane crashes that destroyed or damaged many exterior columns and removed the fire protection from others, the intense heat of the flames (more than 1000 degrees Fahrenheit) caused the structural steel members to lose strength, resulting in beams sagging and an inward deflection of the remaining exterior columns. As a result, the floor structures broke away from the exterior columns. As the top floors fell, they created impact loads on the lower floors that the exterior columns could not support, and both buildings progressively collapsed.[3]

For an engineer, 9/11 raises questions of how this structural failure could have happened, why the building codes did not better protect the public, and how such a disaster can be prevented in the future. There are even larger questions about acceptable risk and the proper approach to risk as an issue of public policy.

6.1   INTRODUCTION

The concern for safety is ever-present in engineering. How should engineers deal with issues of safety and risk, especially when they involve possible liability for harm? Changes in building technology from the time of the Empire State Building, which withstood the impact and fire caused by the B-25 aircraft, until the time of the design and construction of the World Trade Center, have been speculated on as factors in the very different performance of the two towers under similar events. The Empire State Building involved much heavier construction, with significant masonry cladding compared to the lighter glass cladding of the WTC towers. The lighter construction techniques reduce construction costs for taller buildings, and lighter buildings require less massive columns for comparable heights. The lighter columns were certainly an important difference in increasing the vulnerability (risk) to both impact and fire damage, compared to the Empire State Building. This illustrates an important fact: engineering necessarily involves risk, and risk changes as technology changes. One cannot avoid risk simply by remaining with tried and true designs, but new technologies involve risks that may not be as well understood, potentially increasing the chance of failure or even introducing a previously unknown mode of failure. Without new technology, there is no progress. A bridge or building is constructed with new materials or with a new design. New machines are created and new compounds synthesized, always without full knowledge of their long-term effects on humans or the environment. Even new hazards can be found in products, processes, and chemicals that were once thought to be safe. Thus, risk is inherent and dynamic in engineering.

Virtually all engineering codes of ethics give a prominent place to safety, stating that engineers must hold paramount the safety, health, and welfare of the public. The first Fundamental Canon of the National Society of Professional Engineers Code requires members to "hold paramount the safety, health, and welfare of the public." Section III.2.b instructs engineers not to "complete, sign, or seal plans and/or specifications that are not in conformity with applicable engineering standards." Section II.1.a instructs engineers that if their professional judgment is overruled in circumstances that endanger life or property, they shall notify their employer or client and such other authority as may be appropriate. Although "such other authority as may be appropriate" is left undefined, it probably includes those who enforce local building codes and regulatory agencies.

Safety and risk obviously are related ideas; engineers work to make their designs safe. However, no activity or system is perfectly risk free, and making any engineered system safer generally means increasing the costs of that system. Engineered systems that are too expensive are not affordable to the taxpaying public or to the purchasing consumer, which means cost constraints are very real. Engineers must try to achieve designs that meet cost constraints so they will be affordable and must work to design and operate engineered systems in ways that are acceptably safe, which is to say in ways that do not introduce unacceptable risks. To determine acceptable levels of safety in engineering systems, we instead try to identify the risks of harm and find ways to quantify those risks. When the level of risk is determined to be acceptable, we can conclude the design in question is acceptably safe. Generally acceptable levels of safety are codified in the specific design codes for the product or system in question, and the designing engineer only has to adhere to accepted practice, but when the proposed design deviates from accepted practice in some important parameter, it may be that the proposed design may introduce previously unidentified risks.

We begin this chapter by considering three different approaches to risk and safety, all of which are important in determining public policy regarding risk. Then we examine more directly the issues of risk communication and public policy concerning risk, including one example of public policy regarding risk—building codes. Next, we consider the difficulties in both estimating and preventing risk from the engineering perspective, including the problem of self-deception. Finally, we discuss some of the legal issues surrounding risk, including protecting engineers from undue liability and the differing approaches of tort law and criminal law to risk.

Risk is managed in different ways in different engineering tasks. Risk is managed in engineering design by developing design codes, rules for design proven to produce designs consistent with accepted engineering practice (and with acceptable risks). These design rules involve some basic engineering principles, such as redundancy and the design for failure modes that give visible warning (e.g., large deflections before collapse).

Risk is also managed in operation of engineering systems by careful design and continuous review of engineering systems and processes. Consider the engineering process that is a part of every engineering design office intended to prevent the release of construction drawings for bidding or construction before final review, approval, and sealing by the responsible professional engineer (PE). One failure mode of that engineering system is the premature release of construction drawings because of human error. A procedure is in place to ensure proper review and approval, but unless that procedure is followed by all personnel involved, this failure mode can occur. And as personnel involved in the process change, training and process review are required to keep the system operating as planned. Operation of a nuclear power plant offers the same challenges, but with the potential for greater problems. Continuous training and review of published processes are critical. Operations engineers should always be watchful for potential weaknesses in the systems they operate. Suppose an operations engineer, thinking broadly about safety, had noticed the vulnerability to tsunami flooding of the backup generators at the Fukushima Nuclear Plant and initiated improvements—then one of the greatest disasters of our time might have been averted.

Risk is generally increased by innovation. Engineering educators encourage innovative solutions to engineering design problems, but sometimes fail to emphasize the relationship between innovation and risk. Innovation, by definition, involves design features or details that are somehow outside the envelope of current practice. Design standards may not anticipate the issues raised by a particular innovative solution. Thus, many more questions must be addressed by the engineer proposing an innovative solution to be sure newly introduced risks are identified. The design of the Citicorp building is recognized as a significantly innovative structural engineering solution to a difficult design constraint, and the story of that building is an important illustration of how an engineer is expected to respond when a new risk is identified. But the new risk arose because the designer did not anticipate all the risks introduced by his innovative framing method, which was also not anticipated in the design codes and standard practice. The structural engineer who chooses to employ truly innovative framing systems or details must realize he has a greater responsibility to identify new risks of failure introduced by the new framing system.

Innovation can also increase the risk of another type of failure. If an engineered system proves to be too expensive to construct or manufacture, or for some other reason is not acceptable to the public, or if it does not provide the intended benefit to the public so that the costs exceed the benefit, then it represents an engineering failure, and some or all of the investment that has been expended to develop the design is lost. This risk is generally increased with innovative engineering designs.

6.2 THE ENGINEER'S APPROACH TO RISK

Risk as the Product of the Probability and Magnitude of Harm

To assess a risk, an engineer must identify it and quantify it. Engineers define risk as the product of the likelihood of an event and the magnitude of the resulting harm.[4] A relatively slight harm that is highly likely might then constitute a greater risk than a more serious harm that is far less likely. When engineers quantify risk in this way, they must observe that the units of this quantity will depend on the exact harm being considered, so they must be cautious not to quantitatively compare or add risk quantities that have different units. For example, it is possible to compute the risk of death by electrocution for a utility lineman performing a specific operation, and it is possible to compute the risk of bridge collapse due to a ship impact with the bridge pier, but it is not possible to quantitatively compare these two different risk calculations because they have different harms, or units. But the risk of death because of bridge collapse resulting from ship impact could be compared with, or added to, the first example cited.

We can define a harm as an invasion or limitation of a person's freedom or wellbeing. Engineers have traditionally thought of harms in terms of things that can be relatively easily quantified, namely, as impairments of our physical and economic wellbeing or the public health, safety, or welfare. Faulty design of a building can cause it to collapse, resulting in economic loss to the owner and perhaps death for the inhabitants. Faulty design of a chemical plant can cause accidents and economic disaster.

These harms are then measured in terms of the numbers of lives lost, the cost of rebuilding or repairing buildings and highways, and so forth.

Engineers and other experts on risk often believe that the public is confused about risk, sometimes because the public does not have the correct factual information about the likelihood of certain harms. A 1992 National Public Radio story on the Environmental Protection Agency (EPA) began with a quote from EPA official Linda Fisher that illustrated the risk expert's criticism of public understanding of risk:

> A lot of our priorities are set by public opinion, and the public quite often is more worried about things that they perceive to cause greater risks than things that really cause risks. Our priorities often times are set through Congress ... and those [decisions] may or may not reflect real risk. They may reflect people's opinions of risk or the Congressmen's opinions of risk.[5]

Every time Fisher refers to "risk" or "real risk," we can substitute "probability of death or injury." Fisher believes that whereas both members of the US Congress and ordinary laypeople may be confused about risk, the experts know what it is. Risk is something that can be objectively measured—namely, the product of the likelihood and the magnitude of harm.

One Engineering Approach to Defining Acceptable Risk

The engineering concept of risk focuses on the factual issues of the probability and magnitude of harm and contains no implicit evaluation of whether a risk is morally acceptable. In order to determine whether a risk is acceptable, engineers and risk experts considering engineering solutions often use a cost-benefit analysis that is fundamentally a utilitarian approach. The cost-benefit approach compares the costs, including the quantified costs of the imposed risks of the engineering actions under consideration, with the benefits of the actions. Then the engineering solution that maximizes net benefits (benefits minus costs) consistent with economic and other constraints is typically selected. For simplest comparison in a cost-benefit analysis, both the costs and benefits are expressed in equivalent monetary values. This cost-benefit approach to comparing alternative engineering actions has much in common with the utilitarian approach to choices between alternative actions in moral issues. The utilitarian approach to moral issues involves a qualitative, if not quantitative, comparison of the utility (benefits) with the harms (costs), allowing the selection of the alternative that results in the greatest good for the greatest number. Given the earlier definition of risk as the product of the probability and the consequences of harm, we can state the engineer's criterion of acceptable risk in the following way: an acceptable risk is one in which the product of the probability and magnitude of the harm is equaled or exceeded by the product of the probability and magnitude of the benefit.

Consider a case in which a manufacturing process produces bad-smelling fumes that might be a threat to public health. From the cost-benefit standpoint, is the risk to the workers from the fumes acceptable? To determine whether this is an acceptable risk from the cost-benefit perspective, one would have to compare the cost associated with the risk to the cost of preventing or drastically reducing it. To calculate the cost of preventing the harms, we would have to include the costs of modifying the process that produces the fumes, the cost of providing protective masks, the cost of providing better ventilation systems, and the cost of any other safety measures necessary to mitigate the risk. Then we must calculate the cost of not preventing the deaths caused by the fumes. Here, we must include such factors as the cost of additional health care, the cost of possible lawsuits because of the deaths, the cost of bad publicity, the loss of income to the families of the workers, and other costs associated with the loss of life. If the total cost of preventing the loss of life is greater than the total cost of not preventing the deaths, then the current level of risk is acceptable. If the total cost of not preventing the loss of life is greater than the total cost of preventing the loss, then the current level of risk is unacceptable.

The utilitarian approach to risk embodied in cost-benefit analysis has undoubted advantages in terms of clarity, elegance, and susceptibility to numerical interpretation. Nevertheless, there are some limitations that must be kept in mind.

First, it may not be possible to anticipate all of the effects associated with each option. Insofar as this cannot be done, the cost-benefit method will yield an unreliable result.

Second, it is not always easy to translate all of the risks and benefits into monetary terms. How do we assess the risks associated with a new technology, with eliminating a wetland, or with eliminating a species of bird in a Brazilian rain forest? Apart from doing this, however, a cost-benefit analysis is incomplete.

The most controversial issue in this regard is, perhaps, the monetary value that should be placed on human life. One way of doing this is to estimate the value of future earnings, but this implies that the lives of retired people and others who do not work commercially, such as housewives, are worthless. So a more reasonable approach is to attempt to place the same value on people's lives that they themselves place on their lives. For example, people often demand a compensating wage to take a job that involves more risk. By calculating the increased risk and the increased pay that people demand for more risky jobs, some economists say, we can derive an estimate of the monetary value people place on their own lives. Alternatively, we can calculate how much more people would pay for safety in an automobile or other things they use by observing how much more they are willing to pay for a safer car. Unfortunately, there are various problems with this approach. In a country in which there are few jobs, a person might be willing to take a risky job he or she would not be willing to take if more jobs were available. Furthermore, wealthy people are probably willing to pay more for safety than are poorer people.

Third, cost-benefit analysis in its usual applications makes no allowance for the distribution of costs and benefits. Suppose more overall utility could be produced by exposing workers in a plant to serious risk of sickness and death. As long as the good of the majority outweighs the costs associated with the suffering and death of the workers, the risk is justified. Yet most of us would probably find that an unacceptable account of acceptable risk.

Fourth, the cost-benefit analysis gives no place for informed consent to the risks imposed by technology. We shall see in our discussion of the lay approach to risk that most people think informed consent is one of the most important features of justified risk. As a result, the layperson sometimes disagrees with risk experts (engineers) in assessment of acceptable risks. The case of the Ford Pinto is instructive as an example where a cost-benefit analysis of the risks proved unacceptable to the public. Ford compared the costs and benefits of various upgrades to the fuel tank of the Pinto to reduce the risk of fire resulting from rear end collisions. Analysis of the risks included assignment of costs for medical treatment of burn victims and a cost of $200,000 for each resulting death. Numbers of accidents, burn victims, and deaths were inferred from the estimated production numbers of the vehicle, vehicle life, and vehicular accident rates. These costs were compared to the costs of an improved fuel tank and filler line system intended to reduce the chance of fuel spills, and the cost-benefit calculations favored production of the Pinto without the improvements. While it may seem as if Ford's estimate of the value of human life ($200,000) was far too low, it should be pointed out that in 1970 one of the authors, then a recent engineering graduate with an annual salary of about $10,000, carried only a $5,000 life insurance policy (and drove a Ford Pinto). So it probably was not that particular valuation of human life that so frustrated the juries who heard initial wrongful death product liability lawsuits. Rather, it was the fact that being burned alive in an otherwise survivable automobile accident probably ranks high on jurors' list of unacceptable rights violations.

Despite these limitations, cost-benefit analysis has a legitimate place in risk evaluation and may be decisive when no serious threats to individual rights are involved. Cost-benefit analysis is systematic, offers a degree of objectivity, and provides a way of comparing risks and benefits by the use of a common measure—namely, monetary cost. But the Pinto case teaches us that an engineer using the utilitarian approach (cost-benefit analysis) to risk assessment in design decisions should always, at the conclusion, ask him- or herself if a respect-for-persons approach should trump or limit the outcome of the cost-benefit analysis.

Expanding the Engineering Account of Risk: The Capabilities Approach to Identifying Harm and Benefit

As we have pointed out, engineers, in identifying risks and assessing acceptable risk, have traditionally identified harm with factors that are relatively easily quantified, such as economic losses and the number of lives lost.[6] However, four main limitations exist with this rather narrow way of identifying harm. First, often only the immediately apparent or focal consequences of a hazard are included, such as the number of fatalities or the number of homes without electricity. However, hazards can have auxiliary consequences, or broader and more indirect harms to society. Second, both natural and engineering hazards might create opportunities, which should be accounted for in the aftermath of a disaster. Focusing solely on the negative impacts and not including these benefits may lead to overestimating the negative societal consequences of a hazard. Third, there remains a need for an accurate, uniform, and consistent metric to quantify the consequences (harms or benefits) from a hazard. For example, there is no satisfactory method for quantifying the nonfatal physical or psychological harms to individuals or the indirect impact of hazards on society. The challenge of quantification is difficult and complex, especially when auxiliary consequences and opportunities are included in the assessment. Fourth, current techniques do not demonstrate the connection between specific harms or losses, such as the loss of one's home and the diminishment of individual or societal well-being and quality of life. Yet it is surely the larger question of effect on quality of life that is ultimately at issue when considering risk.

In their work on economic development, economist Amartya Sen and philosopher Martha Nussbaum have derived a notion of "capabilities" that the two scholars believe may be the basis of a more adequate way of measuring the harms (and sometimes the benefits) of disasters, including engineering disasters.[7] Philosopher Colleen Murphy and engineer Paolo Gardoni have developed a capabilities-based approach to risk analysis, which focuses on the effect of disasters on overall human well-being. Well-being is defined in terms of individual capabilities, or "the ability of people to lead the kind of life they have reason to value." Specific capabilities are defined in terms of functionings, or what an individual can do or become in his or her life that is of value. Examples of functionings are being alive, being healthy, and being sheltered. A capability is the real freedom of individuals to achieve a functioning, and it refers to the real options he or she has available. Capabilities are constituent elements of individual well-being.

Capabilities are distinct from utilities, which refer to the mental satisfaction, pleasure, or happiness of a particular individual. Often, people's preferences or choices are used to measure satisfaction. Utilities are assigned to represent a preference function. In other words, if an individual chooses A over B, then A has more utility than B. Using utilities to measure the well-being of individuals, however, is problematic because happiness or preference satisfaction is not a sufficient indicator of an individual's well-being. For example, a person with limited resources might learn to take pleasure in small things, which are only minimally satisfying to a person with more ample means. The individual in a poverty-stricken situation might have all of his or her severely limited desires satisfied. From the utilitarian standpoint, the person would be described as happy and be said to enjoy a high standard of living. Yet this individual might still be objectively deprived. The problem here is that utilitarianism does not take into account the number and quality of options that are available to individuals, which is precisely what capabilities capture.

From the capabilities standpoint, a risk is the probability that individuals' capabilities might be reduced due to some hazard. In determining a risk, the first step is to identify the important capabilities that might be damaged by a disaster. Then, to quantify the ways in which the capabilities might be damaged, we must find some "indicators" that are correlated with the capabilities. For example, an indicator of the impairment of the capability for play might be the loss of parks or gym facilities. Next, the indicators must be scaled onto a common metric so that the normalized values of the indicators can be compared. Then, a summary index is constructed by combining the information provided by each normalized indicator, creating a hazard index (HI). Finally, to put the HI into the relevant context, its value is divided by the population affected by the hazard, creating the hazard impact index, which measures the hazard impact per person.

According to its advocates, there are four primary benefits of using the capabilities-based approach in identifying the societal impact of a hazard. First, capabilities capture the adverse effects and opportunities of hazards beyond the consequences traditionally considered. Second, since capabilities are constitutive aspects of individual well-being, this approach focuses our attention on what should be our primary concern in assessing the societal impact of a hazard. Third, the capabilities-based approach offers a more accurate way to measure the actual impact of a hazard on individuals' well-being. Fourth, rather than considering diverse consequences, which increases the difficulty of quantification, the capabilities-based approach requires considering a few properly selected capabilities.[8]

In addition to identifying more accurately and completely the impact of a hazard, its advocates believe the capabilities-based approach provides a principled foundation for judging the acceptability and tolerability of risks.[9] Judgments of the acceptability of risks are made in terms of the impact of potential hazards on the capabilities of individuals. Thus, according to the capabilities approach, a risk is acceptable if the probability is sufficiently small that the adverse effect of a hazard will fall below a threshold of the minimum level of capabilities attainment that is acceptable in principle. The "in principle" qualification captures the idea that, ideally, we do not want individuals to fall below a certain level. We might not be able to ensure this, however, especially immediately after a devastating disaster. In practice, then, it can be tolerable for individuals to temporarily fall below the acceptable threshold after a disaster, as long as this situation is reversible and temporary and the probability that capabilities will fall below a tolerability threshold is sufficiently small. Capabilities can be a little lower, temporarily, as long as no permanent damage is caused and people do not fall below an absolute minimum.

6.3   THE PUBLIC'S APPROACH TO RISK

Expert and Layperson: Differences in Factual Beliefs

The capabilities approach may give a more adequate account of the harms and benefits that should be measured. However, when one encounters the lay public's approach to risk, one still seems to be entering a different universe. The profound differences between the engineering and public approach to risk have been the sources of miscommunication and even acrimony. Two questions then arise: Why does an engineer need to understand these differences? And what are the grounds for these profound differences in outlook on risk?

With respect to the first question, the answer is that the engineer, when quantifying risks and benefits, must remember to think about the public's understanding and acceptance of the risks that the engineer's work will impose and know that it may be very different from the way engineers assess risks. If the engineer makes decisions about the acceptability of a certain risk and somehow miscalculates the public's perception, and if harms should occur from risks considered acceptable in an engineering assessment, the public may view the engineer's actions from a different perspective and unsympathetically. The public, we should remember, sometimes is manifested in groups of twelve serving as juries and charged with evaluating whether engineers have made these decisions about risk in an acceptable manner.

With respect to the second question, the first difference is that engineers and risk experts believe that the public is sometimes mistaken in estimating the probability of death and injury from various activities or technologies. Recall EPA official Linda Fisher's reference to "real risk," by which she meant the actual calculations of probability of harm. Risk expert Chauncey Starr has a similarly low opinion of the public's knowledge of probabilities of harm. He notes that people tend to overestimate the likelihood of low-probability risks associated with causes of death and to underestimate the likelihood of high-probability risks associated with causes of death. The latter tendency can lead to overconfident biasing, or *anchoring*. In anchoring, an original estimate of risk is made—an estimate that may be substantially erroneous. Even though the estimate is corrected, it is not sufficiently modified from the original estimate. The original estimate anchors all future estimates and precludes sufficient adjustment in the face of new evidence.[10]

Other scholars have reported similar findings. A study by Slovic, Fischhoff, and Lichtenstein shows that although even experts can be mistaken in their estimations of various risks, they are not as seriously mistaken as laypeople.[11] The study contrasts actual versus perceived deaths per year.[12] Experts and laypeople were asked their perception of the number of deaths per year for such activities as smoking, driving a car, driving a motorcycle, riding in a train, skiing, and so on. On a graph that plots perceived deaths (on the vertical axis) against actual deaths (on the horizontal axis) for each of several different risks, if the perception (by either laypeople or experts) of deaths were accurate, then the result would be a 45-degree line. In other words, actual and perceived deaths would be the same for the plots of the perceptions of either laypersons or experts. Instead, the experts were consistently approximately one order of magnitude (i.e., approximately 10 times) low in their perceptions of the perceived risk, and the lay public was still another order of magnitude (i.e., approximately 100 times) too low, resulting in lines of less than 45 degrees for experts and even less for laypersons.

"Risky" Situations and Acceptable Risk

It does appear to be true that the engineer and risk expert, on the one hand, and the public on the other hand, differ regarding the probabilities of certain events. The major difference, however, is in the conception of risk itself and in beliefs about acceptable risk. One of the differences here is that the public often combines the concepts of risk and acceptable risk—concepts that engineers and risk experts separate sharply. Furthermore, public discussion is probably more likely to use the adjective "risky" than the noun "risk."

We can begin with the concepts of "risk" and "risky." In public discussion, the use of the term "risky," rather than referring to the probability of certain events, more often than not has the function of a warning sign, a signal that special care should be taken in a certain area.[13] One reason for classifying something as risky is that it is new and unfamiliar. For example, the public may think of the risk of food poisoning from microbes as being relatively low, whereas eating irradiated food is "risky." In fact, in terms of probability of harm, there may be more danger from microbes than radiation, but the dangers posed by microbes are familiar and commonplace, whereas the dangers from irradiated foods are unfamiliar and new. Another reason for classifying something as risky is that the information about it might come from a questionable source. We might say that buying a car from a trusted friend who testifies that the car is in good shape is not risky, whereas buying a car from a used car salesman whom we do not know is risky.

Laypeople do not evaluate risk strictly in terms of expected deaths or injury. They consider other factors as well. For example, they are generally willing to take voluntary risks that are 1000 times (three orders of magnitude) as uncertain as involuntary risks. Thus, voluntarily assumed risks are more acceptable than risks not voluntarily assumed. The amount of risk people are willing to accept in the workplace is generally proportional to the cube of the increase in the wages offered in compensation for the additional risk. For example, doubling wages would tend to convince a worker to take eight times the risk. But laypeople may also separate by three orders of magnitude the risk perceived to be involved in involuntary exposure to danger (e.g., when a corporation places a toxic waste dump next door to one's house) and the risk involved in voluntary exposure (e.g., smoking). Here, voluntarily assumed risks are viewed as inherently less risky, not simply more acceptable. Laypeople also seem to be content with spending different amounts of money in different areas to save a life. In his study of 57 risk-abatement programs at five different government agencies in Washington, DC, including the EPA and the Occupational Safety and Health Administration

(OSHA), Starr shows that such programs vary greatly in the amount of money they spend to save a life. Some programs spend $170,000 per life, whereas others spend $3 million per life.[14]

Another researcher, D. Litai, has separated risk into 26 risk factors, each having a dichotomous scale associated with it.[15] For example, a risk may have a natural or a human origin. If the risk has a human origin, Litai concludes from an analysis of statistical data from insurance companies that the perceived risk is 20 times greater than a risk with a natural origin. An involuntarily assumed risk, whether of natural or human origin, is perceived as being 100 times greater than a voluntarily assumed risk. An immediate risk is perceived as being 30 times greater than an ordinary one. By contrast, a regular risk is perceived as being just as great as an occasional one, and necessary risk is just as great as a luxury-induced one. Here again, there is evidence of the amalgamation of the concepts of risk and acceptable risk.

Two issues in the public's conception of risk and acceptable risk have special moral importance: free and informed consent and equity or justice. These two concepts follow more closely the ethics of respect for persons than utilitarianism. According to this ethical perspective, as we have seen, it is wrong to deny the moral agency of individuals. Moral agents are beings capable of formulating and pursuing purposes of their own. We deny the moral agency of individuals when we deny their ability to formulate and pursue their own goals or when we treat them in an inequitable manner with respect to other moral agents. Let us examine each of these concepts in more detail.

Free and Informed Consent

To give free and informed consent to the risks imposed by technology, three things are necessary. First, a person must not be coerced. Second, a person must have the relevant information. Third, a person must be rational and competent enough to evaluate the information. Unfortunately, determining when meaningful and informed consent has been given is not always easy, for several reasons.

First, it is difficult to know when consent is free. Have workers given their free consent when they continue to work at a plant with known safety hazards? Perhaps they have no alternative form of employment.

Second, people are often not adequately informed of dangers or do not evaluate them correctly. As we have seen, sometimes laypeople err in estimating risk. They underestimate the probability of events that have not occurred before or that do not get their attention, whereas they overestimate the probability of events that are dramatic or catastrophic.

Third, it is often not possible to obtain meaningful informed consent from individuals who are subject to risks from technology. How would a plant manager obtain consent from local residents for his plant to emit a substance into the atmosphere that causes mild respiratory problems in a small percentage of the population? Is the fact that the residents do not protest sufficient evidence that they have consented? What if they do not know about the substance, do not know what it does, do not understand its effects correctly, or are simply too distracted by other things?

In light of the problems in getting free and informed consent, we could compensate individuals after the fact for actual harms done to them through technology. For example, people could be compensated for harms resulting from a defective design in an automobile or a release of a poisonous gas from a chemical plant. This approach has the advantage that consent does not have to be obtained, but it also has several disadvantages. First, it does not tell us how to determine adequate compensation. Second, it limits the freedom of individuals because some people would never have consented. Third, sometimes there is no adequate compensation for a harm, as in the case of serious injury or death.

There are problems with both informed consent and compensation as ways of dealing with the ethical requirement to respect the moral agency of those exposed to risk because of technology. Nevertheless, some effort must be made to honor this requirement. Now let us return to the second requirement of the respect-for-persons morality with regard to risk.

Equity or Justice

The ethics of respect for persons places great emphasis on respecting the moral agency of individuals, regardless of the cost to the larger society. Philosopher John Rawls expresses this concern:[16] "[E]ach member of society is thought to have an inviolability founded upon justice … which even the welfare of everyone else cannot override." As an example of the requirement for justice derived from the ethics of respect for persons, consider the following example from Cranor,[17] quoting a woman describing how her husband's health had been severely damaged by byssinosis caused by cotton dust:

> My husband worked in the cotton mill since 1937 to 1973. His breath was so short he couldn't walk from the parking lot to the gate the last two weeks he worked.
>
> He was a big man, liked fishing, hunting, swimming, playing ball, and loved to camp. We liked to go to the mountains and watch the bears. He got so he could not breathe and walk any distance, so we had to stop going anywhere. So we sold our camper, boat, and his truck as his doctor, hospital, and medicine bills were so high. We don't go anywhere now. The doctor said his lungs were as bad as they could get to still be alive. At first he used tank oxygen about two or three times a week, then it got so bad he used more and more. So now he has an oxygen concentrator, he has to stay on it 24 hours a day. When he goes to the doctor or hospital he has a little portable tank.
>
> He is bedridden now. It's a shame the mill company doesn't want to pay compensation for brown lung. If they would just come and see him as he is now, and only 61 years old.

A utilitarian might be willing to trade off the great harm to Mr. Talbert that resulted from a failure to force cotton mills to protect their workers from the risk of byssinosis for the smaller advantages to an enormous number of people. After all, such protection is often highly expensive, and these expenses must eventually be passed on to consumers in the form of higher prices for cotton products. Higher prices also make US cotton products more expensive and thus less competitive in world markets, thereby depriving US workers of jobs. Regulations that protect workers might even force many (perhaps all) US cotton mills to close. Such disutilities might well out-weigh the disutilities to the Mr. Talberts of the world.

From the standpoint of the ethics of respect for persons, however, such considerations must not be allowed to obscure the fact that Mr. Talbert has been treated unjustly. Although many people enjoy the benefits of the plant, only Mr. Talbert and a few others suffer the consequences of unhealthy working conditions. The benefits and harms have been inequitably distributed. His rights to bodily integrity and life were unjustly violated. From the standpoint of the Golden Rule, probably few, if any, observers would want to be in Mr. Talbert's position.

Of course, it is not possible to distribute all risks and benefits equally. Sometimes those who endure the risks imposed by technology may not share the benefits to the same degree. For example, several years ago a proposal was made to build a port for unloading liquefied natural gas in the Gulf of Mexico off the coast of Texas. The natural gas would be shipped to many parts of the United States, so most citizens of the country would benefit from this project. Only those residents close to the port, however, would share the risks of the ships or storage tanks exploding.[18] Because there is no way to equalize the risk, informed consent and compensation should be important considerations in planning the project. Thus, informed consent, compensation, and equity are closely related considerations in moral evaluation.

Even though laypeople often combine the concept of risk with the concept of acceptable risk, we shall formulate a lay criterion of acceptable risk in the following way:

> An acceptable risk is one in which (1) risk is assumed by free and informed consent, or properly compensated, and in which (2) risk is justly distributed, or properly compensated.

We have seen that there are often great difficulties in implementing the requirements of free and informed consent, compensation, and justice. Nevertheless, they are crucial considerations from the layperson's perspective—and from the moral perspective.

6.4 COMMUNICATING RISK AND PUBLIC POLICY

Communicating Risk to the Public

The preceding sections show that different groups have somewhat different agendas regarding risk. Engineers are most likely to adopt the risk expert's approach to risk. They define risk as the product of the magnitude and likelihood of harm and are sympathetic with the utilitarian way of assessing acceptable risk. The professional codes require engineers to hold paramount the safety, health, and welfare of the public, so engineers have an obligation to minimize risk. However, in determining an acceptable level of risk for engineering works, they are likely to use, or at least be sympathetic with, the cost-benefit approach.

The lay public comes to issues of risk from a very different approach. Although citizens sometimes have inaccurate views about the probabilities of harms from certain types of technological risks, their different approach cannot be discounted in terms of simple factual inaccuracies. Part of the difference in approach results from the tendency to combine judgments of the likelihood and acceptability of risk. (The term "risky" seems to include both concepts.) For example, use of a technology is more risky if the technology is relatively new, and if information about it comes from a source (either expert or nonexpert) that the public has come to regard as unreliable. More important, the lay public considers free and informed consent and equitable distribution of risk (or appropriate compensation) to be important in the determination of acceptable risk.

In addition, government regulators, with their special obligation to protect the public from undue technological risks, are more concerned with preventing harm to the public than with avoiding claims for harm that turn out to be false. This bias contrasts to some extent with the agendas of both the engineer and the layperson. Although, as government regulators, they may often use cost-benefit analysis as a part of their method of determining acceptable risk, they have a special obligation to prevent harm to the public, and this may go beyond what cost-benefit considerations require. On the other hand, considerations of free and informed consent and equity, while important, may be balanced by cost-benefit considerations.

In light of these three different agendas, it is clear that social policy regarding risk must take into consideration wider perspectives than the risk expert approach would indicate. At least two reasons exist for this claim. First, the public and government regulators will probably continue to insist on introducing their own agendas into the public debate about technological risk. In a democracy, this probably means that these considerations will be a part of public policy regarding technological risk, whether or not engineers and risk experts approve. This is simply a fact to which engineers and risk experts must adjust. Second, we believe the two alternative approaches to risk each have a genuine moral foundation. Free and informed consent, equity, protecting the public from harm—these are morally legitimate considerations. Therefore, public policy regarding risk should probably be a mix of the considerations we have put forth here as well as, no doubt, many others we have not discussed.

What, then, is the professional obligation of engineers regarding risk? One answer is that engineers should continue to follow the risk expert's approach to risk and let public debate take care of the wider considerations. We believe there is some validity to this claim, and in the next section we return to a consideration of issues in typical engineering approaches to risk. However, as we have argued in Chapter 4 and elsewhere, we believe engineers have a wider professional obligation. Engineers have a professional obligation to participate in democratic deliberation regarding risk by contributing their expertise to this debate. In doing so, they must be aware of alternative approaches and agendas to avoid serious confusion and undue dogmatism. In light of this, we propose the following guidelines for engineers in risk communication:[19]

1. Engineers, in communicating risk to the public, should be aware that the public's approach to risk is not the same as that of the risk expert. In particular, "risky" cannot be identified with a measure of the probability of harm. Thus, engineers should not say "risk" when they mean "probability of harm." They should use the two terms independently.

2. Engineers should be wary of saying, "There is no such thing as zero risk." The public often uses "zero risk" to indicate not that something involves no probability of harm but that it is a familiar risk that requires no further deliberation.

3. Engineers should be aware that the public does not always trust experts and believes that experts have sometimes been wrong in the past. Therefore, engineers, in presenting risks to the public, should be careful to acknowledge the possible limitations in their position. They should also be aware that laypeople may rely on their own values in deciding whether or not to base action on an expert's prediction of probable outcomes.

4. Engineers should be aware that government regulators have a special obligation to protect the public, and that this obligation may require them to take into account considerations other than a strict cost-benefit approach. Although public policy should take into account cost-benefit considerations, it should take into account the special obligations of government regulators.

5. Professional engineering organizations, such as the professional societies, have a special obligation to present information regarding technological risk. They must present information that is as objective as possible regarding probabilities of harm.

They should also acknowledge that the public, in thinking about public policy regarding technological risk in controversial areas (e.g., nuclear power), may take into consideration factors other than the probabilities of harm.

A major theme in these guidelines is that engineers should adopt a critical attitude toward the assessment of risk. This means that they should be aware of the existence of perspectives other than their own. The critical attitude also implies that they should be aware of the limitations in their own abilities to assess the probabilities and magnitude of harms. In the next section, we consider an example of these limitations and the consequent need for the critical attitude even in looking at the mode of risk assessment characteristic of engineering.

An Example of Public Policy: Building Codes

One of the most immediate ways in which public policy must rely on engineering expertise and engineering is in turn affected by public policy is through local building codes. The local building codes specify factors of safety and construction steps (e.g., fireproofing or material requirements) that are required in the area. Building codes have the status of law and may not be changed without public hearings and legislative action. The legislature will often appoint a committee of experts to propose a new building code or necessary changes in an existing one. For example, following the collapse of the World Trade Center's Twin Towers, there was a major multiagency investigative effort to identify the causes of the collapses and to propose changes in New York City's building codes that would improve egress and otherwise reduce risks of death.

One of the more important ways professional engineers show a concern for the general public (and their safety) is in carrying out the local building code requirements in designing such things as buildings, elevators, escalators, bridges, walkways, roads, and overpasses. When a responsible engineer recognizes a violation of a building code in a design and does not object to it, the engineer bears some responsibility for any injuries or deaths that result. Similarly, when an engineer learns of a proposed change in a building code that he or she is convinced creates danger for the public and does nothing to prevent this change, the engineer bears some responsibility for any harm done.

The Twin Towers case illustrates these issues.[20] The New York City building codes in place in 1945 required that all stairwells be surrounded with heavy masonry and concrete structure. As a consequence, in 1945, the firemen were able to get to the area inside the Empire State Building immediately through the stairwells and put out the fire in 40 minutes. In the intervening years between the design of the Empire State Building and the World Trade Center Towers, building codes underwent a general change nationwide, with the "prescriptive" code requirements tending to be replaced by "performance" code requirements. One example is the way fireproofing coatings for steel structural members were specified in the early codes. Then, a certain thickness of concrete was specified, but as improved materials for fireproofing evolved that resulted in lower dead loads and more economical application methods, codes were changed to specify instead a certain level of performance. Similar changes in high-rise construction materials and methods, such as the use of lightweight concrete floor slabs and lighter floor joist systems, helped make taller structures more affordable. Some of these more economical and lighter weight building components may have been factors in the very different performance of the two newer towers compared to the much heavier Empire State Building, and some critics have suggested we should revert to the older technology for tomorrow's buildings.

But reverting to 50-year-old practices is not the answer, nor is it even feasible. Rather it is up to today's engineers to help maintain performance standards in model building codes that will produce structures that are affordable without introducing unacceptable risk to the public they will serve. The Federal Emergency Management Agency (FEMA) and the Structural Engineering Institute of the American Society of Civil Engineers studied building code issues related to the WTC collapses and loss of life and concluded that the structures performed well in response to the crash impact loadings, and continued standing even after the resulting severe damage, which is a testament to their design, but the resulting fire started by the approximately 10,000 gallons of burning jet fuel was further fed by building furnishings and materials of construction causing temperatures too high for the structural steel members. While the fire protection features of the design and construction were found to meet or exceed minimum code requirements, the study recommends more detailed evaluation of several features for future building code requirements, including floor truss systems and their robustness, impact resistant enclosures around egress paths, resistance of fire protection to physical damage, and location of egress paths. But the authors of the study did not recommend specific requirements to harden structures against aircraft impact, concluding that "it may not be technically feasible to develop design provisions that would enable all structures to be designed and constructed to resist the effects of impacts by rapidly moving aircraft, and the ensuing fires, without collapse."

As another example of a serious shortcoming of the New York City building codes, see the Citicorp building case in the appendix. In this case, William LeMessurier designed the building's main load-carrying steel structure to a code-specified worst-case wind condition that was incorrect. Fortunately, LeMessurier recognized the error in the code and modified the already built structure to correct for it. The codes were subsequently corrected.

Building codes are one of the aspects of public policy that both directly affect engineers and most clearly require information from engineers in their formulation. They illustrate one of the most concrete and specific ways in which engineering expertise is needed in the formulation of public policy and in which public policy in turn vitally affects engineering design.

6.5 DIFFICULTIES IN DETERMINING THE CAUSES AND LIKELIHOOD OF HARM: THE CRITICAL ATTITUDE

Estimating risk, no doubt defined in terms of the probabilities and magnitudes of harm, has been described by one writer as looking "through a glass darkly."[21] It would be highly desirable, of course, to be able to accurately predict the harm resulting from engineering work. Instead, engineers can only estimate the magnitude and probability of harm. To make matters worse, often engineers cannot even make estimates satisfactorily. In actual practice, therefore, estimating risk (or "risk assessment") involves an uncertain prediction of the probability of harm. In this section, we consider some of the methods of estimating risk, the uncertainties in these methods, and the value judgments that these uncertainties necessitate.

Limitations in Identifying Failure Modes

With respect to new technologies, engineers and scientists must have some way of estimating the risks that they impose on those affected by them. One of the methods for assessing risk involves the use of a fault tree. In a fault tree analysis, we begin with an undesirable event, such as the loss of cooling water to a nuclear power plant's reactor core. Figure 6.1a outlines the problem, illustrating that there is a triply redundant system, with cooling water from pump 1, pump 2, or the emergency supply sufficient to maintain a safe core temperature. Figure 6.1b shows a fault tree analysis that identifies all anticipated reasons for an interruption in cooling water supply. Fault trees are often used to anticipate hazards for which there is little or no direct experience, such as nuclear meltdowns. They enable an engineer to analyze systematically different events or failure modes that could produce the undesirable end result. A failure mode is a way in which a structure, mechanism, system, or process can malfunction. For example, a structural member can fail in tension, crush or buckle in compression, crack or rupture in bending, suffer loss of section and strength because of corrosion or abrasion, burst because of excessive internal pressure, or lose strength or even burn because of excessive temperature.

Fault tree analysis has been criticized as offering too optimistic a perspective, most significantly because the fault tree analysis is the estimation of the aggregate probability of identified failure modes. It is sometimes the case that failure modes causing harm are not identified during these analyses. As a result, their risks are not estimated. In such a case, the analysis can be misleading, implying a lower risk than actually exists.

Example Cooling Water System

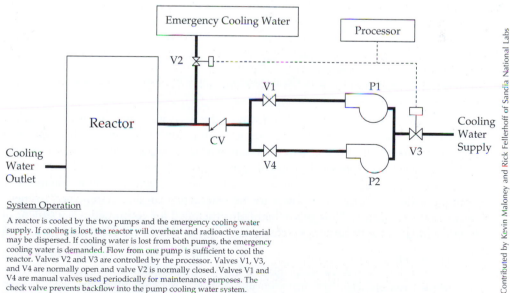

System Operation

A reactor is cooled by the two pumps and the emergency cooling water supply. If cooling is lost, the reactor will overheat and radioactive material may be dispersed. If cooling water is lost from both pumps, the emergency cooling water is demanded. Flow from one pump is sufficient to cool the reactor. Valves V2 and V3 are controlled by the processor. Valves V1, V3, and V4 are normally open and valve V2 is normally closed. Valves V1 and V4 are manual valves used periodically for maintenance purposes. The check valve prevents backflow into the pump cooling water system.

FIGURE 6.1a Example Cooling Water System for Nuclear Reactor

Contributed by Kevin Maloney and Rick Fellerhoff of Sandia National Labs

Cooling System Fault Tree

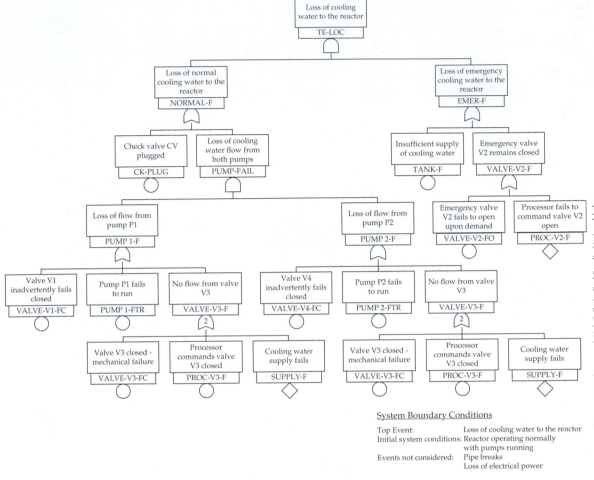

FIGURE 6.1b Fault Tree Analysis of Loss of Cooling Water Supply to Nuclear Reactor Core

The March 2011 failure and meltdown of the reactors at the Fukushima Nuclear Power Plant is a case in point. The disaster was caused by a tsunami closely following a significant earthquake. The reactors shut down automatically following the earthquake, according to the usual protocol, but the consequent tsunami destroyed the backup electrical generators providing power for the emergency cooling systems. The subsequent delay in providing power to the emergency cooling systems led to meltdowns in three reactors. This failure highlights the need for continued reassessment of design standards for operational plants. According to the World Nuclear Association,

> The tsunami countermeasures taken when Fukushima Daiichi was designed and sited in the 1960s were considered acceptable in relation to the scientific knowledge then, with low recorded run-up heights for that particular coastline. But through to the 2011 disaster, new scientific knowledge emerged about the likelihood of a large earthquake and resulting major tsunami. However, this did not lead to any major action by either the plant operator, Tepco, or government regulators, notably the Nuclear & Industrial Safety Agency (NISA).

The tsunami countermeasures could also have been reviewed in accordance with IAEA [International Atomic Energy Agency] guidelines which required taking into account high tsunami levels, but NISA continued to allow the Fukushima plant to operate without sufficient countermeasures, despite clear warnings.[22]

A different approach to a systematic examination of failure modes is the event tree analysis. Here, we reason forward from a hypothetical event to determine what consequences this hypothetical event might have and the probabilities of these consequences. Figure 6.2 illustrates in schematic form an event tree analysis. This simplified event tree for an accident involving a loss of coolant in a typical nuclear power plant begins with a failure and enumerates the various events to which this failure could lead. This event tree shows the logical relationships between the possible ways that a pipe break can affect the safety systems in a nuclear plant. If both a pipe and on-site power fail simultaneously, then the outcome will be an enormous release of radioactive coolant. If these two systems are independent, then the probability of this happening is the product of the two probabilities taken separately. For example, if there is one chance in 10^4 ($P1 = 0.0001 = 10^{-4}$) that the pipe will break and one chance in 10^5 ($P2 = 0.00001 = 10^{-5}$) that the on-site power will simultaneously fail, then the chance of a loss of a large release is $P = P1 \times P2 = 10^{-9}$, or 1 in 1 billion.

Although engineers rightly believe that it is necessary to go through such analyses to ensure that they have taken into account as many failure modes as possible, the analyses have severe limitations. First, it is not possible to anticipate all of the mechanical, physical, electrical, and chemical problems that might lead to failure. For example, the possibility of terrorist attacks has added a new dimension to risk analysis and estimation.

Second, it is never possible to anticipate all of the types of human error that could lead to failure. Third, the probabilities assigned to the failure modes are often

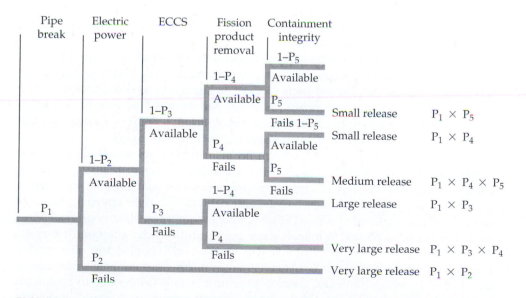

FIGURE 6.2 An Event Tree Analysis of a Pipe Break in a Nuclear Plant

Source: Reproduced, with permission, from the *Annual Review of Energy*, vol. 6. © 1981 by Annual Reviews, Inc. Courtesy N. C. Rasmussen.

highly conjectural and not always based on solid experimental testing. We are not, for example, going to melt down a nuclear reactor to determine the probability of such an occurrence leading to a chain reaction fission explosion. In many cases, we do not know the probability of the behavior of materials at extremely elevated temperatures.

Limitations due to Tight Coupling and Complex Interactions

Sociologist Charles Perrow[23] confirms some of these problems by arguing that there are two characteristics of high-risk technologies that make them especially susceptible to accidents and allow us to speak of "normal accidents." These two features are the "tight coupling" and "complex interactions" of the parts of a technological system. These two factors make accidents not only more likely but also more difficult to predict and control. This, in turn, makes risk more difficult to estimate.

In tight coupling, the temporal element is crucial. Processes are tightly coupled if they are connected in such a way that one process is known to affect another and will usually do so within a short time. In tight coupling, there is usually little time to correct a failure and little likelihood of confining a failure to one part of the system. As a result, the whole system is damaged. A chemical plant is tightly coupled because a failure in one part of the plant can quickly affect other parts of the plant. A university, by contrast, is loosely coupled because if one department ceases to function, then the operation of the whole university is usually not threatened.

In complex interaction, the inability to predict consequences is crucial. Processes can be complexly interactive in that the parts of the system can interact in unanticipated ways. No one dreamed that when X failed, it would affect Y. Chemical plants are complexly interactive in that parts affect one another in feedback patterns that cannot always be anticipated. A post office, by contrast, is not so complexly interactive. The parts of the system are related to one another for the most part in a linear way that is well understood and the parts do not usually interact in unanticipated ways that cause the post office to cease functioning. If a post office ceases to function, it is usually because of a well-understood failure.

Examples of complexly interactive and tightly coupled technical systems include not only chemical plants but also nuclear power plants, electric power grid networks, space missions, and nuclear weapons systems. Being tightly coupled and complexly interactive, they can have unanticipated failures, and there is little time to correct the problems or keep them from affecting the entire system. This makes accidents difficult to predict and disasters difficult to avoid once a malfunction appears.

Unfortunately, it is difficult to change tightly coupled and complexly interactive systems to make accidents less likely or to make them easier to predict. To reduce complexity, decentralization is required to give operators the ability to react independently and creatively to unanticipated events. To deal with tight coupling, however, centralization is required. To avoid failures, operators need to have command of the total system and to be able to follow orders quickly and without question. It may not be possible, furthermore, to make a system both loosely coupled and noncomplex. Engineers know that they can sometimes overcome this dilemma by including localized and autonomous automatic controls to protect against failures due to complexity and couple them with manual overrides to protect against tight coupling failures. Nevertheless, according to Perrow, some accidents in complex, tightly coupled systems are probably inevitable and, in this sense, "normal."

The following is an example of an accident in a system that was complexly interactive and tightly coupled. In the summer of 1962, the New York Telephone Company completed heating system additions to a new accounting building in Yonkers, New York. The three-story, square-block building was a paradigm of safe design, using the latest technology.

In October 1962, after the building was occupied and the workers were in place, final adjustments were being made on the building's new, expanded heating system located in the basement. This system consisted of three side-by-side, oil-fired boilers. The boilers were designed for low pressures of less than 6.0 psi and so were not covered by the boiler and pressure vessel codes of the American Society of Mechanical Engineers. Each boiler was equipped with a spring-loaded safety relief valve that had been designed to open and release steam into the atmosphere if the boiler pressure got too high. Each boiler was also equipped with a pressure-actuated cutoff valve that would cut off oil flow to the boiler burners in the event of excessive boiler pressure. The steam pressure from the boilers was delivered to steam radiators, each of which had its own local relief valve. Finally, in the event that all else failed, a 1-foot-diameter pressure gauge with a red "Danger Zone" marked on the scale and painted on the face sat on the top of each boiler. If the pressure got too high, the gauge was supposed to alert a custodian who operated the boilers so he could turn off the burners.

On October 2, 1962, the following events transpired:[24]

1. The building custodian decided to fire up boiler 1 in the heating system for the first time that fall. The electricians had just wired the control system for the new companion boiler (boiler 3) and successfully tested the electrical signal flows.

2. The custodian did not know that the electricians had left the fuel cutoff control system disconnected. The electricians had disconnected the system because they were planning to do additional work on boiler 3 the following week. They intended to wire the fuel cutoffs for the three boilers in series (i.e., high pressure in any one would stop all of them).

3. The custodian mechanically closed the header valve because it was a warm Indian summer day and he did not want to send steam into the radiators on the floors above. Thus, the boiler was delivering steam pressure against a blocked valve, and the individual steam radiator valves were out of the control loop.

4. As subsequent testing showed, the relief valve had rusted shut after some tests the previous spring in which the boilers had last been fired. (Later, laws were enacted in New York State that require relief valves for low-pressure boiler systems to be operated by hand once every 24 hours to ensure that they are not rusted shut. At the time, low-pressure boiler systems were not subject to this requirement.)

5. This was on Thursday, the day before payday, and the custodian made a short walk to his bank at lunch hour to cash a check soon after turning on boiler 1.

6. The cafeteria was on the other side of the wall against which the boiler end abutted. Employees were in line against the wall awaiting their turn at the cafeteria serving tables. There were more people in line than there would have been on Friday because on payday many workers went out to cash their paychecks and eat their lunches at local restaurants.

7. Boiler 1 exploded. The end of the boiler that was the most removed from the wall next to the cafeteria blew off, turning the boiler into a rocket-like projectile. The

boiler lifted off its stanchions and crashed into the cafeteria, after which it continued to rise at great velocity through all three stories of the building. Twenty-five people were killed and almost 100 seriously injured.

The events that led to this disaster were complexly interrelated. There is no possible way that fault tree or event tree analyses could have predicted this chain of events. If the outside temperature had been cooler, the custodian would not have closed the header valve and the individual steam radiator valves in each upstairs room would have opened. If the relief valve had been hand operated every day, its malfunction would have been discovered and probably corrected. If the time had not been noon and the day before payday, the custodian might have stayed in the basement and seen the high-pressure reading and turned off the burners. If it had not been lunch time, the unfortunate victims would not have been in the cafeteria line on the other side of the wall from the boiler.

The events were also tightly coupled. There was not much time to correct the problem once the pressure started to rise, and there was no way to isolate the boiler failure from a catastrophe in the rest of the building. There was one engineering design change that, if adopted, could have broken the chain of events and prevented the accident. It would have been a simple matter to include a fuel flow cutoff if the fuel cutoff system were in any way disabled. However, in complex interconnected systems such as this one, hindsight is always easier than foresight.

Normalizing Deviance and Self-Deception

Still another factor that increases risk and also decreases our ability to anticipate harm is increasing the allowable deviations from proper standards of safety and acceptable risk. Sociologist Diane Vaughn refers to this phenomenon as the "normalization of deviance."[25]

Every design carries with it certain predictions about how the designed object should perform in use. Sometimes these predictions are not fulfilled, producing what are commonly referred to as anomalies. Rather than correcting the design or the operating conditions that led to anomalies, engineers or managers too often do something less desirable. They may simply accept the anomaly or even increase the boundaries of acceptable risk. Sometimes this process can lead to disaster.

This process is dramatically and tragically illustrated by the events that led to the *Challenger* disaster.[26] Neither the contractor, Morton Thiokol, nor NASA expected the rubber O-rings that sealed the joints in the solid rocket booster (SRB) to be touched by the hot gases of motor ignition, much less to be partially burned. However, because previous shuttle flights showed damage to the sealing rings, the reaction by both NASA and Thiokol was to accept the anomalies without attempting to remedy the problems that caused the anomalies.

The following are examples of how deviance was normalized before the disaster:

1. In 1977, test results showed that the SRB joints would rotate open at ignition, creating a larger gap between the tang and clevis. According to NASA engineers, the gap was large enough to prevent the secondary seal from sealing if the primary O-ring failed late in the ignition cycle. Nevertheless, after some modifications, such as adding sealing putty behind the O-rings, the joint was officially certified as an acceptable risk, even though the joint's behavior deviated from design predictions.[27]

2. Another anomaly was discovered in November 1981 after flight STS-2, which showed "impingement erosion" of the primary O-ring in the right SRB's aft field joint.[28] The hot propellant gases had moved through the "blow holes" in the zinc chromate putty in the joints. The blow holes were caused by entrapped air introduced at the time the putty was installed. Even though this troubling phenomenon was not predicted, the joints were again certified as an acceptable risk.

3. A third anomaly occurred in 1984 with the launch of STS-41-B when, for the first time, two primary O-rings on two different joints were eroded.[29] Again, the erosion on two joints was termed an acceptable risk.[30]

4. Another anomaly occurred in 1985 when "blow-by" of hot gases had reached the secondary seal on a nozzle joint. The nozzle joints were considered safe because, unlike the field joints, they contained a different and quite safe secondary "face seal." The problem was that a similar malfunction could happen with the field joint with the danger much more serious, and these problems were not dealt with.

5. Perhaps the most dramatic example of expanding the boundaries of acceptable risk was in the area of the acceptable temperature for launch. Before the *Challenger* launch, the lowest temperature of the seals at launch time was 53°F. (At that time, the ambient temperature was in the high 60s.) On the night before the launch of the *Challenger*, however, the temperature of the seals was expected to be 29° and its ambient temperature below freezing. Thus, the boundaries for acceptable risk were expanded by 24°.

The result of (1) accepting these anomalies without making any adequate attempt to remedy the basic problem (poor seal design) and (2) lowering the temperature considered acceptable for launch was the tragic destruction of the *Challenger* and the loss of its crew. Vaughn argues that these kinds of problems cannot be eliminated from technological systems and that, as a result, accidents are inevitable. Whether or not this is the case, there is no question that technology imposes risk on the public and that these risks are often difficult to detect and eliminate.

The case also illustrates how the self-deception involved in normalizing deviance can limit the ability of engineers to correctly anticipate risk. Some of the engineers, and especially engineering managers, repeatedly convinced themselves that allowing still one more deviation from design expectations would not increase the chance of failure or was at least an acceptable risk. The result was a tragic disaster.

6.6   THE ENGINEER'S LIABILITY FOR RISK

We have seen that risk is difficult to estimate and that engineers are often tempted to allow anomalies to accumulate without taking remedial action, and even to expand the scope of acceptable risk to accommodate them. We have also seen that there are different and sometimes incompatible approaches to the definition of acceptable risk as exhibited by risk experts, laypeople, and government regulators.

Another issue that raises ethical and professional concerns for engineers regards legal liability for risk. There are at least two issues here. One is that the standards of proof in tort law and science are different, and this produces an interesting ethical conflict. Another issue is that in protecting the public from unnecessary risk, engineers may themselves incur legal liabilities. Let us consider each of these issues.

The Standards of Tort Law

Litigation that seeks redress from harm most commonly appeals to the law of torts, which deals with injuries to one person caused by another, usually as a result of fault or negligence of the injuring party. Many of the most famous legal cases involving claims of harm from technology have been brought under the law of torts. The litigation involving harm from asbestos is one example. In 1973, the estate of Clarence Borel,[31] who began working as an industrial insulation worker in 1936, brought suit against Fiberboard Paper Products Corporation:

> During his career he was employed at numerous places usually in Texas, until disabled from the disease of asbestosis in 1969. Borel's employment necessarily exposed him to heavy concentrations of asbestos generated by insulation materials. In a pretrial deposition Borel testified that at the end of the day working with insulation materials containing asbestos his clothes were usually so dusty that he could barely pick them up without shaking them. Borel stated, "You just move them a little bit and there is going to be dust and I blowed this dust out of my nostrils by the handfuls at the end of the day. I even used Mentholatum in my nostrils to keep some of the dust from going down my throat, but it is impossible to get rid of all of it. Even your clothes just stay dusty continuously, unless you blow it off with an air hose." In 1964, doctors examined Borel in connection with an insurance policy and informed him that x-rays of his lungs were cloudy. The doctors told Borel that the cause could be his occupation as an installation worker and advised him to avoid asbestos dust as much as he possibly could. On January 19, 1969, Borel was hospitalized and a lung biopsy was performed. Borel's condition was diagnosed as pulmonary asbestosis. Since the disease was considered irreversible Borel was sent home.... [His] condition gradually worsened during the remainder of 1969. On February 11, 1970, he underwent surgery for the removal of his right lung. The examining doctors determined that Borel had a form of lung cancer known as mesothelioma, which had been caused by asbestos. As a result of these diseases, Borel later died before the district case reached the trial stage.[32]

The federal district court in Texas decided in favor of the estate of Mr. Borel and the Fifth Circuit Court of Appeals upheld the decision.

The standard of proof in tort law is the preponderance of evidence, meaning that there is more and better evidence in favor of the plaintiff than the defendant. The plaintiff must show

> (1) that the defendant violated a legal duty imposed by the tort law, (2) that the plaintiff suffered injuries compensable in the tort law, (3) that the defendant's violation of legal duty caused the plaintiff's injuries, and (4) that the defendant's violation of legal duty was the proximate cause of the plaintiff's injuries.[33]

The standard of proof that a given substance was the proximate cause of a harm is less stringent than that which would be demanded by a scientist, who might well call for 95 percent certainty. It is also less stringent than the standard of evidence in criminal proceedings, which calls for proof beyond reasonable doubt.

As an illustration of this lower standard of evidence, consider the case of Rubanick v. Witco Chemical Corporation and Monsanto Co. The plaintiff's sole expert witness, a retired cancer researcher at New York's Sloan-Kettering Cancer Center, testified that the deceased person's cancer was caused by exposure to polychlorinated biphenyls (PCBs). He based his opinion on

> (1) the low incidence of cancer in males under 30 (the deceased person was 29), (2) the decedent's good dietary and nonsmoking habits and the absence of familial genetic

predisposition to cancer, (3) 5 of 105 other Witco workers who developed some kind of cancer during the same period, (4) a large body of evidence showing that PCBs cause cancer in laboratory animals, and (5) support in the scientific literature that PCBs cause cancer in human beings.[34]

The court did not require the expert to support his opinion by epidemiological studies, merely that he demonstrate the appropriate education, knowledge, training, and experience in the specific field of science and an appropriate factual basis for his opinion.[35]

Other better known cases, such as that of Richard Ferebee, who alleged that he suffered lung damage as a result of spraying the herbicide paraquat, also accepted standards of evidence for causal claims that would not have been acceptable for research purposes.[36]

Some courts, however, have begun to impose higher standards of evidence for recovery of damages through tort standards that are similar to those used in science. In the Agent Orange cases, Judge Jack B. Weinstein argued that epidemiological studies were the only useful studies having any bearing on causation, and that by this standard no plaintiff had been able to make a case. Bert Black,[37] a legal commentator, has taken a similar view. He believes that the courts (i.e., judges) should actively scrutinize the arguments of expert witnesses, demanding that they be supported by peer-reviewed scientific studies or at least have solid scientific backing. In some cases, he believes, they should even overrule juries who have made judgments not based on scientific standards of evidence.[38]

Even though this view represents a departure from the normal rules of evidence in tort law, it might in some cases be fairer to the defendants because some decisions in favor of plaintiffs may not be based on valid proof of responsibility for harm. The disadvantage is also equally obvious. By requiring higher standards of proof, the courts place burdens of evidence on plaintiffs that they often cannot meet. In many cases, scientific knowledge is simply not adequate to determine causal relationships, and this would work to the disadvantage of the plaintiffs. There are also problems with encouraging judges to take such an activist role in legal proceedings. The major ethical question, however, is whether we should be more concerned with protecting the rights of plaintiffs who may have been unjustly harmed or with promoting economic efficiency and protecting defendants against unjust charges of harm. This is the ethical issue at the heart of the debate.

Protecting Engineers from Liability

The apparent ease with which proximate cause can be established in tort law may suggest that the courts should impose a more stringent standard of acceptable risk. But other aspects of the law afford the public less protection than it deserves. For example, the threat of legal liability can inhibit engineers from adequately protecting the public from risk. Engineers in private practice may face especially difficult considerations regarding liability and risk, and in some cases, they may need increased protection from liability.

Consider, for example, the safety issues in excavating for foundations, pipelines, and sewers.[39] A deep, steep-sided trench is inherently unstable. Sooner or later, the sidewalls will collapse. The length of time that trench walls will stand before collapsing depends on several factors, including the length and width of the cut, weather conditions, moisture in the soil, composition of the soil, and how the trench was excavated. People who work in deep trenches are subjected to considerable risk, and hundreds of laborers are injured or killed each year when the walls collapse.

To reduce the risk, construction engineers can specify the use of trench boxes in their designs. A trench box is a long box with an upside-down U-shaped cross section that is inserted inside the trench to protect the laborers. As long as workers remain inside the trench boxes, their risk of death or injury is greatly reduced.

Unfortunately, the use of trench boxes considerably increases the expense and time involved in construction projects. The boxes must be purchased or rented, and then they must be moved as excavation proceeds, slowing construction work and adding further expense. In addition, the handling of trench boxes introduces another risk of injury to workers involved. Engineers are placed in an awkward position with regard to the use of trench boxes, especially where the boxes are not required by building codes. If they do not specify the use of the boxes, then they may be contributing to a situation that subjects workers to a high risk of death and injury. If they do specify the use of boxes, then they may be incurring liability in case of an accident because of the use of trench boxes. With situations such as this in mind, the National Society of Professional Engineers has been actively lobbying the US Congress to pass a law that specifically excludes engineers from liability for accidents where construction safety measures are specified by engineers but then are either not used or used improperly by others. This would enable engineers more effectively to protect the safety of workers. Unfortunately, the proposals have never become law.

The problem with trench boxes illustrates a more general issue. If engineers were free to specify safety measures without being held liable for their neglect or improper use, they could more easily fulfill one aspect of their responsibility to protect the safety of the public.

6.7 BECOMING A RESPONSIBLE ENGINEER REGARDING RISK

The development of new technology is intimately connected with risk. The obligation of engineers is to be ethically responsible with regard to risk. The first step in the process of becoming ethically responsible about risk is to be aware of the fact that risk is often difficult to estimate and can be increased in ways that may be subtle and treacherous. The second step is to be aware that there are different approaches to the determination of acceptable risk. In particular, engineers have a strong bias toward quantification in their approach to risk, which may make them insufficiently sensitive to the concerns of the lay public and even the government regulators. The third step is to assume their responsibility, as the experts in technology, to communicate issues regarding risk to the public, with the full awareness that both the public and government regulators have a somewhat different agenda with regard to risk.

We conclude with an attempt to formulate a principle of acceptable risk. To formulate this principle, let us consider further some of the legal debate about risk.

The law seems to be of two minds about risk and benefits. On the one hand, some laws make no attempt to balance the two. The Chemical Food Additives Amendments to the Food, Drug and Cosmetics Act, enacted in 1958, require that a chemical "deemed to be unsafe" not be added to food unless it can be "safely used."[40] Safe use was defined by the Senate Committee on Labor and Public Welfare as meaning that "no harm will result" from its addition to food.[41] The well-known Delaney Amendment also prohibits the addition to food of any chemical known to cause cancer when ingested by animals.[42]

On the other hand, there is often an attempt to strike a balance between the welfare of the public and the rights of individuals. The Toxic Substances Control Act of 1976 authorized the EPA to regulate any chemical upon a finding of "unreasonable risk of injury to health or the environment."[43] But it is only "unreasonable risk" that triggers regulation, so some degree of risk is clearly tolerated. The report of the House Commerce Committee describes this balancing process as follows:

> Balancing the probabilities that harm will occur and the magnitude and severity of that harm against the effect of proposed regulatory action on the availability to society of the benefits of the substance or mixture, taking into account the availability of substitutes for the substance or mixture which do not require regulation, and other adverse effect which such proposed action may have on society.

Having said this, the report goes on to say that "a formal benefit-cost analysis under which monetary value is assigned to the risks ... and to the costs of society" is not required.[44]

The Atomic Energy Act of 1954 continually refers to the "health and safety of the public" but makes little attempt to define these terms. The Nuclear Regulatory Commission's rules, however, use the expression "without undue risk" and seem to suggest again a balancing of risks and benefits.[45] In the words of one legal commentator, in practice, especially in the earlier years, "the acceptability of risk was measured largely in terms of the extent to which industry was capable of reducing the risk without jeopardizing an economic and financial environment conducive to continuing development of the technology."[46] Again, we have an attempt to balance protection of individuals and promotion of the public welfare.

Sometimes the conflict between these two approaches is evident in a single debate. In a Supreme Court case involving exposure to benzene in the workplace, OSHA took an essentially respect for persons standpoint, arguing that the burden of proof should be on industry to prove that a given level of exposure to benzene was not carcinogenic. In its rebuke of OSHA, the Supreme Court argued that in light of the evidence that current standards did not lead to harm to workers, risk must be balanced against benefits in evaluating more stringent standards and that the burden of proof was on OSHA to show that the more stringent standards were justified.[47]

Given these considerations, we can construct a more general principle of acceptable risk, which may provide some guidance in determining when a risk is within the bounds of moral permissibility:

> People should be protected from the harmful effects of technology, especially when the harms are not consented to or when they are unjustly distributed, except that this protection must sometimes be balanced against (1) the need to preserve great and irreplaceable benefits, and (2) the limitation on our ability to obtain informed consent.

The principle does not offer an algorithm that can be applied mechanically to situations involving risk. Many issues arise in its use; each use must be considered on its own merits. We can enumerate some of the issues that arise in applying the principle.

First, we must define what we mean by "protecting" people from harm. This cannot mean that people are assured that a form of technology is free from risk. At best, "protection" can only be formulated in terms of probabilities of harm, and we have seen that even these are subject to considerable error.

Second, many disputes can arise as to what constitutes a harm. Is having to breathe a foul odor all day long harm? What about workers in a brewery or a sewage disposal plant? Here the foul odors cannot be eliminated, so the question of what harms should be eliminated cannot be divorced from the question of whether the harms can be eliminated without at the same time eliminating other goods.

Third, the determination of what constitutes a great and irreplaceable benefit must be made in the context of particular situations. A food additive that makes the color of frozen vegetables more intense is not a great and irreplaceable benefit. If such an additive were found to be a powerful carcinogen, then it should be eliminated. On the other hand, most people value automobiles highly, and they would probably not want them to be eliminated, despite the possibility of death or injury from automobile accidents.

Fourth, we have already pointed out the problems that arise in determining informed consent and the limitations in obtaining informed consent in many situations. From the standpoint of the ethics of respect for persons, informed consent is a consideration of great importance. However, it is often difficult to interpret and apply.

Fifth, the criterion of unjust distribution of harm is also difficult to apply. Some harms associated with risk are probably unjustly distributed. For example, the risks associated with proximity to a toxic waste disposal area that is not well constructed or monitored are unjustly distributed. The risks associated with coal mining might also be conceded to be unjustly distributed, but the energy provided by coal may also be considered a great and irreplaceable benefit. So the requirement to reduce risk in the coal industry might be that the risks of coal mining should be reduced as much as possible without destroying the coal industry. This might require raising the price of coal enough to make coal mining safe and more economically rewarding.

Sixth, an acceptable risk at a given point in time may not be an acceptable risk at another point in time. Engineers with operational responsibilities as well as those with design responsibilities have an obligation to protect the health and safety of the public. This obligation requires engineers to reduce risk when new risks emerge or when risk awareness changes or even when technological innovation allows further reduction of known risks. This obligation was not recognized or discharged by operators or regulators at the Fukushima nuclear power plant, where the improved predictions of tsunami risks should have triggered countermeasures.

6.8 CHAPTER SUMMARY

Risk is a part of engineering and especially of technological progress. The concept of "factors of safety" is important in engineering. Virtually all engineering codes give a prominent place to safety. Engineers and risk experts look at risk in a somewhat different way from others in society. For engineers, risk is the product of the likelihood and magnitude of harm. An acceptable risk is one in which the product of the probability and magnitude of the harm is equaled or exceeded by the product of the probability and magnitude of the benefit, and no other option exists where the product of the probability and magnitude of the benefit is substantially greater. In calculating harms and benefits, engineers have traditionally identified harm with factors that are relatively easily quantified, such as economic losses and loss of life. The "capabilities" approach attempts to make these calculations more sophisticated by developing a more adequate way of measuring the harms and benefits from disasters to overall well-being, which it defines in terms of the capabilities of people to live the kind of life they value. A risk is acceptable if the probability is sufficiently small that the adverse effect of a hazard will fall below a threshold of the minimum level of capabilities attainment that is acceptable in principle.

The public does not conceptualize risk simply in terms of expected deaths or injury but, rather, considers other factors as well, such as whether the harm in question is unacceptably severe, whether a risk is assumed with free and informed consent, or whether the risk is imposed justly. Government regulators take a still different approach to risk because they have a special obligation to protect the public from harm. Consequently, they place greater weight on protecting the public than on benefiting the public. In light of these different agendas, social policy must take into account a wider perspective than that of the risk expert.

Engineers, and especially professional engineering societies, have an obligation to contribute to public debate on risk by supplying expert information and by recognizing that the perspectives in the public debate will comprise more than the perspective of the risk expert. Debates over building codes illustrate some aspects of this public debate over risk.

Estimating the causes and likelihood of harm poses many difficulties. Engineers use various techniques, such as fault trees and event trees. However, the phenomena of "tight coupling" and "complex interactions" limit our ability to anticipate disasters. The tendency to accept increasing deviations from expected performance can also lead to disasters.

Engineers need to protect themselves from undue liability for risk, but this need sometimes raises important issues for social policy. One issue is the conflict between the standards of science and tort law. The standard of proof in tort law for whether something causes a harm is the preponderance of evidence, but the standard of evidence in science is much higher. The lower standard of tort law tends to protect the rights of plaintiffs who may have been unjustly harmed, and the higher standard of science tends to protect defendants and perhaps promote economic efficiency. The problems engineers have in protecting themselves from unjust liabilities while protecting the public from harm are illustrated by the use of trench boxes. Finally, a principle of acceptable risk provides some guidance in determining when a risk is within the bounds of moral permissibility.

6.9 ENGINEERING ETHICS ON THE WEB

Check your understanding of the material in this chapter by visiting the companion website for *Engineering Ethics*. The site includes multiple choice study questions, suggested discussion topics, and sometimes additional case studies to complement your reading and study of the material in this chapter.

NOTES

1. "B-25 Crashes in Fog," *New York Times*, July 29, 1945, p. 1.

2. Peter Glantz and Eric Lipton, "The Height of Ambition," *New York Times Sunday Magazine*, Sept. 8, 2002, p. 32.

3. Bazant, Z. and Verdure, M., "Mechanics of Progressive Collapse: Learning from World Trade Center and Building Demolitions," *J. Engineering Mechanics*, ASCE, March 2007, pp. 308–319.

4. William W. Lowrance, "The Nature of Risk," in Richard C. Schwing and Walter A. Albers, Jr., eds., "Societal Risk Assessment Safe Enough?" *Plenum*, 1980, p. 6.

5. The National Public Radio story was aired on "Morning Edition," Dec. 3, 1992. This account is taken from the Newsletter of the Center for Biotechnology Policy and Ethics, Texas A & M University, 2:1, Jan. 1, 1993, p. 1.

6. For further discussion of the concept of capabilities and description of this approach to measuring harm in this section, see Amartya Sen, *Development as Freedom* (New York: Anchor Books, 1999); Martha Nussbaum, *Women and Human Development: The Capabilities Approach* (New York: Cambridge University Press, 2000); Colleen Murphy and Paolo Gardoni, "The Role of Society in Engineering Risk Analysis: A Capabilities-Based Approach," *Risk Analysis*, 26:4, pp. 1073–1083; and Colleen Murphy and Paolo Gardoni, "The Acceptability and the Tolerability of Societal Risks: A Capabilities-based Approach," *Science and Engineering Ethics*, 14:1, 2008, pp. 77–92. We are indebted to Professors Murphy and Gardoni for supplying the basis of this section.

7. S. Anand and Amartya Sen, "The Income Component of the Human Development Index," *Journal of Human Development*, 1:1, 2000, 83–106.

8. Colleen Murphy and Paolo Gardoni, "Determining Public Policy and Resource Allocation Priorities for Mitigating Natural Hazards; A Capabilities-based Approach," *Science & Engineering Ethics*, 13:4, 2007, pp. 489–504.

9. Colleen Murphy and Paolo Gardoni, "The Acceptability and the Tolerability of Societal Risks: A Capabilities-Based Approach," *Science and Engineering Ethics*, 14:1, 2008, pp. 77–92.

10. Chauncey Starr, "Social Benefits versus Technological Risk," *Science*, 165, Sept. 19, 1969, pp. 1232–1238. Reprinted in Theodore S. Glickman and Michael Gough, *Readings in Risk* (Washington, DC: Resources for the Future), pp. 183–193.

11. Paul Slovic, Baruch Fischhoff, and Sarah Lichtenstein, "Rating the Risks," *Environment*, 21:3, April 1969, pp. 14–20, 36–39. Reprinted in Glickman and Gough, pp. 61–74.

12. Starr, pp. 183–193.

13. For this and several of the following points, see Paul B. Thompson, "The Ethics of Truth-Telling and the Problem of Risk," *Science and Engineering Ethics*, 5, 1999, pp. 489–510.

14. Starr, op. cit., pp. 183–193.

15. D. Litai, "A Risk Comparison Methodology for the Assessment of Acceptable Risk," PhD dissertation, Massachusetts Institute of Technology, Cambridge, MA, 1980.

16. John Rawls, A Theory of Justice (Cambridge, MA: Harvard University Press, 1971), p. 3.

17. Carl F. Cranor, *Regulating Toxic Substances: A Philosophy of Science and the Law* (New York: Oxford University Press, 1993), p. 152.

18. Ralph L. Kenny, Ram B. Kulkarni, and Keshavan Nair, "Assessing the Risks of an LGN Terminal," in Glickman and Gough, pp. 207–217.

19. This list was suggested by the four "dicta for risk communication" proposed by Paul Thompson, in Thompson, op. cit., pp. 507–508. Although some items in this list are the same as Thompson's, we have modified and expanded his list.

20. *World Trade Center Building Performance Study: Data Collections, Preliminary Observations and Recommendations*, FEMA 403, Federal Emergency Management Agency, Federal Insurance and Mitigation Administration, Washington, DC, September 2002.

21. Cranor, *Regulating Toxic Substances*, p. 11.

22. World Nuclear Association Web page on Fukushima Accident 2011, updated April 14, 2012, found at http://www.world-nuclear.org/info/fukushima_accident_inf129.html.

23. Charles Perrow, *Normal Accidents: Living with High-Risk Technologies* (New York: Basic Books, 1984), p. 3.

24. See *New York Times*, Oct. 15, 1962, for an account of this tragic event. The engineering details are cited from an unpublished report by R. C. King, H. Margolin, and M. J. Rabins to the City of New York Building Commission on the causes of the accident.

25. Diane Vaughn, *The Challenger Launch Decision* (Chicago: University of Chicago Press, 1996), pp. 409–422.

26. See the Presidential Commission on the Space Shuttle *Challenger* Accident, "Report to the President by the Presidential Commission on the Space Shuttle *Challenger* Accident."

27. See Vaughn, pp. 110–111. The following account is taken from Vaughn and from personal conversations with Roger Boisjoly. This account should be attributed to the authors, however, rather than to Diane Vaughn or Roger Boisjoly.

28. Ibid., pp. 121 ff.

29. Ibid., pp. 141 ff.

30. Ibid., pp. 153 ff.

31. Borel v. Fiberboard Paper Products Corp. et al., 493 F.2d (1973) at 1076, 1083. Quoted in Cranor, *Regulating Toxic Substances*, p. 52.

32. Cranor, *Regulating Toxic Substances*, p. 58.

33. 576 A.2d4 (N.J. Sup. Ct. A.D.1990) at 15 (concurring opinion).

34. Cranor, *Regulating Toxic Substances*, p. 81. Summarized from "New Jersey Supreme Court Applies Broader Test for Admitting Expert Testimony in Toxic Case," *Environmental Health Letter*, Aug. 27, 1991, p. 176.

35. "New Jersey Supreme Court Applies Broader Test," p. 176.

36. Ferebee v. Chevron Chemical Co., 736 F.2d 11529 (D.C. Cir 1984).

37. Bert Black, "Evolving Legal Standards for the Admissibility of Scientific Evidence," *Science*, 239, 1987, pp. 1510–1512.

38. Bert Black, "A Unified Theory of Scientific Evidence," *Fordham Law Review*, 55, 1987, pp. 595–692.

39. See R. W. Flumerfelt, C. E. Harris, Jr., M. J. Rabins, and C. H. Samson, Jr., *Introducing Ethics Case Studies into Required Undergraduate Engineering Courses, Final Report to the NSF on Grant DIR-9012252*, Nov. 1992, pp. 262–285.

40. Public Law No. 85-929, 72 Stat. 784 (1958).

41. Senate Report No. 85-2422, 85th Congress, 2nd Session (1958).

42. c21 United States Code, sect. 348 (A) (1976).

43. Public Law No. 94-469, 90 Stat. 2003 (1976). The same criterion of "unreasonable risk" is found in the Flammable Fabrics Act. See Public Law No. 90-189, Stat. 568 (1967).

44. Public Law No. 83-703, 68 Stat. 919 (1954), 42 United States Code 2011 et. seq. (1976).

45. 10 CFR 50.35 (a) (4).

46. Harold P. Green, "The Role of Law in Determining Acceptability of Risk," in *Societal Risk Assessment: How Safe Is Safe Enough?* (New York: Plenum, 1980), p. 265.

47. Industrial Union Department, AFL-CIO v. American Petroleum Institute et al., 448 U.S. 607 (1980).

CHAPTER SEVEN

Engineers in Organizations

Main Ideas in This Chapter

- Communication and culture are vital components within the organization. Employees should understand communication channels and cultural norms within the organization.

- Value emphasizes what others get from our efforts and values emphasize who we are. Value can be created and developed through organizational innovation and hard work.

- Employees should take advantage of organizational resources in order to enhance their own integrity and independence.

- Organizational and management practices may be unchanged for years, which can result in blind spots, or obstacles to ethical decision making. Understanding the obstacles and remedies for these obstacles can improve the organization's communication and ethical decision making.

- Many organizations hire an ethics and compliance officer to study inappropriate policies and procedures and to assist employees in appropriate communication and daily ethical choices at work.

- Engineers and managers have different perspectives, both legitimate, and it is useful to distinguish between decisions that should be made by managers, or from a management perspective, and decisions that should be made by engineers, or from an engineering perspective.

- There will be differences of opinion within the organization between engineers themselves and between engineers and management. Careful verbal and written communication needs to be utilized to work through disagreements.

- Whistleblowing sometimes becomes a necessary option for an employee when other avenues of communication fail. An employee should explore numerous ways of solving an organizational problem before whistleblowing. However, new federal regulations are in place to assist employees who believe they have exhausted all other means of solving the workplace problem.

IN 2012 *FORBES* MAGAZINE NAMED JEFF BEZOS one of "America's Best Leaders."[1] Bezos, Founder and CEO of Amazon.com, Inc., says one of his secrets to success is understanding what the customer needs and wants. Proud of two of Amazon's new projects, the Kindle tablets and E-book readers, Bezos says these creations have been "defined by customers' desires rather than engineers' tastes."[2] Engineers working for Bezos who don't understand the importance of this maxim could quickly find themselves out of work at Amazon. These two projects had to suit customers who wanted "an e-book reader that could download any book in 60 seconds or less."[3] Bezos explained he didn't want to be pinned down by technical arguments; rather Amazon's engineers were free to solve technical challenges in the ways they chose.[4] As a CEO who likes to cut costs, he didn't cut costs on the Kindle tablets or E-book readers. Finance and time weren't issues. The best possible product for the customer was his main goal. Bezos prefers teamwork and experiments are "hatched and managed by the smallest teams possible."[5] Engineers wanting to work for Amazon in software and other web engineering areas will likely find work interesting at Amazon. Quick changes through small innovation teams are credited with many of the recent successes at the company.[6]

7.1 INTRODUCTION

Jeff Bezos' organizational leadership style is similar to that which is advocated by University of Michigan Business Professor David Ulrich. Ulrich supports an ethics template centered on "the value of values" to guide employees and leaders in organizations. His template begins with the individual's personal life, then branches to workers and leaders in organizational settings. Central to his view is that individuals have obligations to themselves, their co-workers and their communities. "Informed ethical choices must constantly be made in all of these areas," and for Ulrich this includes the community.[7] By understanding the community's values, individuals will better understand customers.

Within "the value of values," Ulrich emphasizes that *value* focuses outside the organizations; and *values* come from within the employee.[8] He holds that *value* emphasizes what *others* get from our efforts and that *values* emphasize who we are. He stresses that value can be created and developed through organizational innovation and hard work; however, he finds that values are often inherited and may be honed through self-awareness and experience.[9] He explains, "Value can be measured by impact; values are measured by the strength of our character. Value derives from the worth of our work to stakeholders; values reflect the worth of our work to us. Both value and values matter to communities, organizations and individuals."[10]

Ulrich believes that unless organizations create value for those who use their products or services, the organization loses its right to exist.[11] Amazon's Bezos leads the same way. He explains that every day an employee will have the opportunity to serve the customer better. Amazon employees know they won't have fancy offices or first class airline flights, but they will be given numerous opportunities to show how they value the customers. Bezos says his ethic is delivering the product the customer wants. Ulrich holds that organizational values are defined by the customers, investors, and communities in which organizations choose to operate. He comments:

> Traditionally, an organization's culture is defined as the norms, expectations, patterns, unwritten rules, and rituals inside a company. These internal patterns shape our experience and determine if we are inside or outside the company. When we talk about culture, we would rather explore it from the outside/in.[12]

Exploring a culture from the outside/in is a first step for Ulrich. For example, as an employee an engineer should strive to understand the culture every day at work.

"The value of an organization's culture is not the identity of those inside the organization looking out, but how that identity captures the mind, feet, and heart of the customers we serve."[13] Ulrich finds that for a rich working life the following is the value of values:

> Within the organizations where we work, learn, worship, and play, we need to recognize and deliver value to the customers and investors who give us the right to exist as a company, and we need to make sure that our personal values ensure a legacy of goodness.[14]

Ray Anderson and Interface

Valuing the customer enabled Ray C. Anderson to change his successful business into an even more successful model of business values. Anderson's firm, Interface Carpets Global is in the business of manufacturing modular carpet tiles. Anderson was the founder and 38 year CEO of Interface Carpets. (Anderson died in 2011 still holding those titles.) He had an engineering background as an honors graduate from Georgia Institute of Technology's School of Industrial and Systems Engineering and founded Interface Carpets in 1973. Twenty years later, Anderson's personal and professional attitude toward the customer was changed when engineer Jim Hartzfield, from the research division, relayed a question from a sales associate: "Some customers want to know what Interface is doing for the environment. How should we answer?"[15]

Anderson explained that he wasn't as worried about the harms to the environment as he was concerned about his client. He commented, "I wasn't about to ignore any customer's concerns or to turn my back on any piece of business. If we didn't answer the question Jim had relayed, I knew we stood to lose other sales."[16]

As both Ulrich and Bezos could agree, Anderson needed to focus on his customers' needs. Anderson began by reading Paul Hawken's *The Ecology of Commerce*. The book transformed Anderson's customer driven goals into a series of environmentally friendly business practices. "Mission Zero," was a promise initiated by Anderson and Interface to eliminate any negative impact the company might have on the environment by the year 2020. In 2009, Anderson estimated Interface was half-way to its goal of redesign of processes and products, the pioneering of new technologies, and efforts to reduce or eliminate waste and harmful emissions while increasing the use of renewable materials and sources of energy.[17]

The Anderson case can serve as encouragement that upper level management may change its values when supplied with information that is ethically and financially convincing.

7.2 AVOIDING BLIND SPOTS

Prior to the prodding of engineer Jim Hartzfield, Ray Anderson was seemingly unaware of his customers' environmental concerns and unconcerned about the environmental impact of producing his company's product. This can be seen as an instance of correcting a "blind spot." Applying this term to organizational and business arenas, Dennis Moberg draws an analogy between business blind spots and blind spots we experience when driving an automobile.[18] Once regular attention is given to the deficit area, driving habits can be developed to help compensate for this perceptual deficit. In the case of driving, such adaptations are welcomed by all. However, in the business arena, blind spots often protect us from having to face unwelcome information.

Max H. Bazerman and Ann E. Tenbrunsel, authors of *Blind Spots*, contend that, although nearly all of us want to think of ourselves as ethically decent, our blind spots result in a tendency to overestimate how ethical we actually are.[19] This blindness should not be confused with unethical intent. We are capable of this, too, of course. But Bazerman and Tenbrunsel are more interested in explaining how otherwise decent, well-intentioned people can, without consciously intending to do so, lend support to ethically unacceptable outcomes.

Self-deception is a key to much of this. Although we might well be sincerely opposed to wrongdoing and not want to be complicit in it, we may also be highly motivated, perhaps through fear or lack of courage, to turn the other way. Taking action against wrongdoing may risk unpopularity, censorship, or even retaliation (e.g., demotion or job loss). But we cannot take action against that which we do not notice. Not noticing may in many instances be what we might call *willful blindness*.[20]

Ignorance of vital information is an obvious barrier to responsible action. If an engineer does not realize that a design poses a safety problem, for example, then he or she will not be in a position to do anything about it. Sometimes such a lack of awareness is willful avoidance—a turning away from information in order to have to deal with the challenges it may pose. However, often it results from a lack of imagination, from not looking in the right places for necessary information, from a failure to persist, or from the pressure of deadlines. Although there are limits to what engineers can be expected to know, these examples suggest that ignorance is not always a good excuse.

In the case of the *Columbia* disaster, Rodney Rocha accused NASA managers of "acting like an ostrich with its head in the sand."[21] NASA managers seemed to him to have convinced themselves that past successes are an indication that a known defect would not cause problems, instead of deciding the issue on the basis of testing and sound engineering analysis. Often, instead of attempting to remedy the problem, they simply engaged in the practice of normalizing deviance, discussed in Chapter 6. There we saw how the boundaries of acceptable risk can be enlarged without a sound engineering basis. Instead of attempting to eliminate foam strikes or do extensive testing to determine whether the strikes posed a safety-of-flight issue, managers "increasingly accepted less-than- specification performance of various components and systems, on the grounds that such deviations had not interfered with the success of previous flights."[22] Enlarging on the issue, the *Columbia* Accident Investigation Board observed: "With each successful landing, it appears that NASA engineers and managers increasingly regarded the foam-shredding as inevitable, and as either unlikely to jeopardize safety or simply an acceptable risk."[23]

Finally, there was a subtle shift in the burden of proof with respect to the shuttle. Instead of requiring engineers to show that the shuttle was safe to fly or that the foam strike did not pose a safety-of-flight issue, was the appropriate position. "The engineers found themselves in the unusual position of having to prove that the situation was unsafe—a reversal of the usual requirement to prove that a situation is safe." As the Board observed, "Imagine the difference if any Shuttle manager had simply asked, 'Prove to me that Columbia has not been harmed.'"[24]

An important lesson is that organizations need continually to determine whether important factors are being underestimated, or even overlooked, and whether this is the result of time pressures, viewing matters only in the short term, or some other shortcoming. In any case, once an organization has identified such problems, possible remedies need aggressively to be sought. Key questions here are: First, what role might engineers play in *identifying* serious problems? Second, how might they best *communicate* these problems to managers who have responsibilities in these areas? Third, what promising ways of *resolving*, or at least minimizing, these problems can they suggest?

In the case of the *Columbia*, it seems that NASA managers were often ignorant of serious problems associated with the shuttle. One of the reasons for this is that as information made its way up the organizational hierarchy, more and more of the dissenting viewpoints were filtered out, resulting in an excessively sanitized version of the facts. According to the *Columbia* Accident Investigation Board, there was a kind of "cultural fence" between engineers and managers. This resulted in high-level managerial decisions that were based on insufficient knowledge of the facts.[25]

A common feature of human experience is that we tend to interpret situations from very limited perspectives and it takes special efforts to acquire a more objective viewpoint. In regard to ethics, Bazerman and Tenbrunsel refer to this as *bounded ethicality*.[26] Although these limited perspectives can sometimes be narrowly self-interested, they need not be. It is not just self-interest that interferes with our ability to understand things from larger perspectives. For example, we may have good intentions for others but fail to realize that their perspectives are different from ours in important ways. For example, some people may not want to hear bad news about their health. They may also assume that others are like them in this respect. So, if they withhold bad news from others, this is done with the best of intentions—even if others would prefer hearing the bad news. Similarly, an engineer may want to design a useful product but fail to realize how different the average consumer's understanding of how to use it is from those who design it. This is why test runs with typical consumers are needed.

Insofar as NASA managers may have made decisions from an exclusively management perspective, concentrating on such factors as schedule, political ramifications, and cost, they were thinking too narrowly. This does not mean that their thinking was narrowly self-interested. Most likely they had the well-being of the organization and the astronauts at heart. Nevertheless, making decisions from this exclusively management perspective led to many mistakes.

Michael Davis warns of the danger of what he calls *microscopic vision*. Precise and accurate as it may be, microscopic vision greatly limits our field of vision. When we look into a microscope, we see things that we could not see before—but only in the narrow field of resolution on which the microscope focuses. We gain accurate, detailed knowledge—at a microscopic level. At the same time, we cease to see things at the more ordinary level. This is the price of seeing things microscopically. Only when we lift our eyes from the microscope will we see what is obvious at the everyday level. Every skill, says Davis, involves microscopic vision to some extent:

> A shoemaker, for example, can tell more about a shoe in a few seconds than I could tell if I had a week to examine it. He can see that the shoe is well or poorly made, that the materials are good or bad, and so on. I can't see any of that. But the shoemaker's insight has its price. While he is paying attention to people's shoes, he may be missing what the people in them are saying or doing.[27]

Just as shoemakers need to raise their eyes and listen to their customers, engineers sometimes need to raise their eyes from their world of scientific and technical expertise and look around them in order to understand the larger implications of what they are doing.

Large organizations tend to foster microscopic thinking. Each person has his or her own specialized job to do, and he or she is not responsible, from the organizational standpoint, for the work of others. This was evidently generally true of the NASA organizational structure. It may also have been a contributing factor to the *Columbia* accident.

7.3   AUTONOMY AND AUTHORITY

Engineering codes of ethics emphasize the importance of engineers exercising independent, objective judgment in performing their functions. This is sometimes called professional autonomy. At the same time, the codes of ethics insist that engineers have a duty of fidelity to their employers and clients. Independent consulting engineers may have an easier time maintaining professional autonomy than the vast majority of engineers, who work in large, hierarchical organizations. Most engineers are not their own bosses, and they are expected to defer to authority in their organizations.

An important finding of the research of social psychologist Stanley Milgram is that a surprisingly high percentage of people are inclined to defer uncritically to authority.[28] In his famous obedience experiments during the 1960s, Milgram asked volunteers to administer electric shocks to "learners" whenever they made a mistake in repeating word pairs (e.g., nice/day and rich/food) that volunteers presented to them earlier. He told volunteers that this was an experiment designed to determine the effects of punishment on learning. No shocks were actually administered, however. Milgram was really testing to determine the extent to which volunteers would continue to follow the orders of the experimenter to administer what they believed were increasingly painful shocks. Surprisingly (even to Milgram), nearly two-thirds of the volunteers continued to follow orders all the way up to what they thought were 450-volt shocks—even when shouts and screams of agony were heard from the adjacent room of the "learner." The experiment was replicated many times to make sure that the original volunteers were a good representation of ordinary people rather than especially cruel or insensitive people.[29]

There is little reason to think that engineers are different from others in regard to obeying authority. In the Milgram experiments, the volunteers were told that the "learners" would experience pain but no permanent harm or injury. Perhaps engineers would have had doubts about this as the apparent shock level moved toward the 450-volt level. This would mean only that the numbers need to be altered for engineers, not that they would be unwilling to administer what they thought were extremely painful shocks.

One of the interesting variables in the Milgram experiments was the respective locations of volunteers and "learners." The greatest compliance occurred when "learners" were not in the same room with the volunteers. Volunteers tended to accept the authority figure's reassurances that he would take all the responsibility for any unfortunate consequences. However, when volunteers and "learners" were in the same room and in full view of one another, volunteers found it much more difficult to divest themselves of responsibility.

Milgram's studies seem to have special implications for engineers. As previously noted, engineers tend to work in large organizations in which the division of labor often makes it difficult to trace responsibility to specific individuals. The combination of the hierarchical structure of large organizations and the division of work into specialized tasks contributes to the sort of "distancing" of an engineer's work from its consequences for the public. This tends to decrease the engineer's sense of personal accountability for those consequences. However, even though such distancing might make it easier psychologically to be indifferent to the ultimate consequences of one's work, this does not really relieve one from at least partial responsibility for those consequences.

One further interesting feature of Milgram's experiments is that volunteers were less likely to continue to administer what they took to be shocks when they were in the presence of other volunteers. Apparently, they reinforced each other's discomfort at continuing, and this made it easier to disobey the experiment. However, as discussed in the next section, group dynamics do not always support critical response. Often quite the opposite occurs, and only concerted effort can overcome the kind of uncritical conformity that so often characterizes cohesive groups.

7.4 GROUPTHINK

A noteworthy feature of the organizational settings within which engineers work is that individuals tend to work and deliberate in groups. This means that an engineer will often participate in group decision making rather than function as an individual decision maker. Although this may contribute to better decisions ("two heads are better than one"), it also creates well-known but commonly overlooked tendencies to engage in what Irving Janis calls *groupthink*—situations in which groups come to agreement at the expense of critical thinking.[30] Janis documents instances of groupthink in a variety of settings, including a number of historical fiascos (e.g., the bombing of Pearl Harbor, the Bay of Pigs invasion, and the decision to cross the 38th parallel in the Korean War).[31] Concentrating on groups that are characterized by high cohesiveness, solidarity, and loyalty (all of which are prized in organizations), Janis identifies eight symptoms of groupthink:

- an *illusion of invulnerability* of the group to failure;
- a strong "we-feeling" that views outsiders as adversaries or enemies and encourages *shared stereotypes* of others;
- *rationalizations* that tend to shift responsibility to others;
- an *illusion of morality* that assumes the inherent morality of the group and thereby discourages careful examination of the moral implications of what the group is doing;
- a tendency of individual members toward *self-censorship*, resulting from a desire not to "rock the boat";
- an *illusion of unanimity*, construing silence of a group member as consent;
- an application of *direct pressure* on those who show signs of disagreement, often exercised by the group leader who intervenes in an effort to keep the group unified; and
- *mindguarding*, or protecting the group from dissenting views by preventing their introduction (by, for example, outsiders who wish to present their views to the group).[32]

Traditionally, engineers have prided themselves on being good team players, which compounds the potential difficulties with groupthink. How can the problem of groupthink be minimized for engineers? Much depends on the attitudes of group leaders, whether they are managers or engineers (or both). Janis suggests that leaders need to be aware of the tendency of groups toward groupthink and take constructive steps to resist it. He notes that after the ill-advised Bay of Pigs invasion of Cuba, President John F. Kennedy began to assign each member of his advisory group the role of critic. He also invited outsiders to some of the meetings, and he often absented himself from meetings to avoid influencing unduly its deliberations.

NASA engineers and managers apparently were often affected with the group-think mentality. Commenting on management's decision not to seek clearer images of the leading edge of the left wing of the shuttle in order to determine whether the foam strike had caused damage, one employee said, "I'm not going to be Chicken Little about this."[33] The *Columbia* Accident Investigation Board described an orga-nizational culture in which "people find it intimidating to contradict a leader's strategy or a group consensus," evidently finding this characteristic of the NASA organiza-tion.[34] The general absence of a culture of dissent that the board found at NASA would have encouraged the groupthink mentality.

To overcome the problems associated with the uncritical acceptance of authority, organizations must establish a culture in which dissent is accepted and even encour-aged. The *Columbia* Accident Investigation Board cites organizations in which dissent is encouraged, including the US Navy Submarine Flooding Prevention and Recovery program and the Naval Nuclear Propulsion programs. In these programs, managers have the responsibility, not only of encouraging dissent, but also of coming up with dissenting opinions themselves if such opinions are not offered by their subordinates. According to the Board, "program managers [at NASA] created huge barriers against dissenting opinions by stating preconceived conclusions based on subjective knowl-edge and experience, rather than on solid data." Toleration and encouragement of dissent, then, was noticeably absent in the NASA organization. If dissent is absent, then critical thinking is absent.

Another widely discussed instance in which groupthink may have been operative involves the production of General Motors' Corvair automobile in the early 1960's. Safety differences were heatedly discussed among engineers and management. The car was released for public sale even though some engineers insisted the Corvair had stabilizing problems.[35] The first models (1960–1963) had a swing-axle suspension design which was prone to "tuck under" in certain circumstances. An anti-roll bar was needed to stabilize the vehicle.[36] Yet, it was decided to solve the problem by requiring higher tire pressure at a level that was outside the tire manufacturer's recom-mended tolerances. Additionally, according to Ralph Nader, a strong critic of the car, the tire pressure changes were not clearly stated to Chevrolet salespeople and Corvair owners.[37] There was a failure to recognize the seriousness of the engineering problems with the car. Nader claimed that rather than making the necessary stabilizing change, the General Motors team added styling features to the dashboard. These shiny dash-board features caused a visual impediment in the form of windshield glare, allegedly triggering crashes because of flashes obstructing the driver's vision. These styling changes cost $700. It was estimated that the safety changes needed would have only cost about 23 cents.[38] John DeLorean was an engineer and vice president with General Motors at the time. He believed that individually the executives were "moral men." However, thinking as a group, he concluded that they made immoral decisions.[39]

7.5 ENGINEERS AND MANAGERS

Management theorist Joseph Raelin, says, "There is a natural conflict between management and professionals because of their differences in educational background, socialization, values, vocational interests, work habits, and outlook."[40] We can be somewhat more precise about the areas of conflict between engineers and managers.

First, although engineers may not always maintain as much identity with their wider professional community as some other professionals (e.g., research scientists), engineers do often experience a conflict between loyalty to their employer and loyalty to their profession.[41] Most engineers want to be loyal employees who are concerned about the financial well-being of their firms and who carry out instructions from their superiors without protest. In the words of many engineering codes, they want to be "faithful agents" of their employers. At the same time, as engineers they are also obligated to hold paramount the health, safety, and welfare of the public. This obligation requires engineers to insist on high standards of quality and (especially) safety.[42]

Second, most managers are not engineers and do not have engineering expertise, so communication is often difficult. Engineers sometimes complain that they have to use oversimplified language in explaining technical matters to managers and that their managers do not really understand the engineering issues.

Third, many engineers who are not managers aspire to the management role in the future, where the financial rewards and prestige are perceived to be greater. Thus, many engineers who do not yet occupy the dual roles of engineer and manager probably expect to do so at some time in their careers. This conflict can be internalized within the same person because many engineers have roles as both engineers and managers. For example, Robert Lund, vice president for engineering at Morton Thiokol at the time of the *Challenger* disaster, was both an engineer and a manager. Before the disaster, Lund was even directed by his superior to take the managerial rather than the engineering perspective.

This account of the differences between the perspectives of engineers and managers suggests the possibility of frequent conflicts. This prediction is confirmed by a well-known study by sociologist Robert Jackall. Although his study focuses only infrequently on the relationship between managers and professionals, his occasional references to the relationship of managers to engineers and other professionals make it clear that he believes his general description of the manager–employee relationship applies to the relationship of managers to professionals, including engineers. In his study of managers in several large US corporations, Jackall found that large organizations place a premium on "functional rationality," which is a "pragmatic habit of mind that seeks specific goals." Jackall found that the managers and firms he studied had several characteristics that were not conducive to respecting the moral commitments of conscientious professionals.[43]

First, the organizational ethos does not allow genuine moral commitments to play a part in the decisions of corporate managers, especially highly placed ones. A person may have whatever private moral beliefs she chooses, as long as these beliefs do not influence behavior in the workplace. She must learn to separate individual conscience from corporate action. Managers, according to Jackall, prefer to think in terms of trade-offs between moral principles, on the one hand, and expediency, on the other hand. What we might think of as genuine moral considerations play little part in managerial decisions, according to Jackall. Faulty products are bad because they will ultimately harm the company's public image, and environmental damage is bad for business or will ultimately affect managers in their private role as consumers.

This attitude is in contrast to that of White, an employee who, according to Jackall, was concerned with a problem of excessive sound in his plant. White defined the issue of possible harm to employees as a moral concern instead of approaching it pragmatically. In another example, Jackall recounted the story of Brady, an accountant who found financial irregularities that were traced to the CEO. Whereas Brady saw the issue as a moral one, managers did not. In discussing the case, they held that Brady should have kept his mouth shut and dropped the matter. After all, the violations were small relative to the size of the corporation.[44]

Second, loyalty to one's peers and superiors is the primary virtue for managers. The successful manager is the team player, the person who can accept a challenge and get the job done in a way that reflects favorably upon himself and others.[45] Third, lines of responsibility are deliberately blurred to protect oneself, one's peers, and one's superiors. Details are pushed down and credit is pushed up. Actions are separated from consequences insofar as this is possible so that responsibility can be avoided. In making difficult and controversial decisions, a successful manager will always get as many people involved as possible so he can point his finger at others if things go wrong. He should also avoid putting things in writing to avoid being held responsible. Protecting and covering for one's boss, one's peers, and oneself supersedes all other considerations.

According to this account of managerial decision making, the moral scruples of professionals have no place. In such an atmosphere, a principled professional would often appear to have no alternative to organizational disobedience. Such was the case with Joe Wilson, an engineer who found a problem with a crane that he believed involved public health and safety. Wilson wrote a memo to his boss, who replied that he did not need such a memo from Wilson and that the memo was not constructive. After Wilson was fired and went public, a *New York Times* investigation cited a corporate official's comment that Wilson was someone who "was not a team player."[46]

If engineers typically work in an organizational environment like the one Jackall describes, their professional and ethical concerns will have little chance of being accorded respect. There is, however, a more constructive aspect of Jackall's study. He does suggest some characteristics of managerial decision making that are useful in analyzing the manager–engineer relationship:

1. Jackall's study implies that managers have a strong and probably overriding concern for the well-being of the organization. Well-being is measured primarily in financial terms, but it also includes a good public image and relatively conflict free operation.

2. Managers have few, if any, loyalties that transcend their perceived obligations to the organization. They do not, for example, have professional obligations that they might consider to override or even counterbalance their obligations to the organization.

3. The managerial decision-making process involves making trade-offs among the relevant considerations. Ethical considerations are only one type of consideration. Furthermore, if we are to believe Jackall, managers tend not to take ethical considerations seriously, unless they can be translated into factors affecting the well-being (e.g., the public image) of the firm.

Jackall presents a very pessimistic picture of the place of a morally committed professional in an organization. In the next section, we suggest ways in which engineers can have a much more positive and productive relationship between them and their organizations.

7.6   BEING MORALLY RESPONSIBLE IN AN ORGANIZATION

The Importance of Organizational Culture

Our earlier example of Ray Anderson demonstrates engineering having a positive, direct effect on the top leader. Both CEO Anderson and the engineers seem to be concerned about values in ways that conflict with the perspectives of typical managers, as depicted by Raelin. Anderson's global company remains committed to its 2020 goal of eliminating any negative impact it may have on the environment, with the engineers participating in the goal in areas such as factory design, materials for carpets and pads, glues and even natural carpet dyes.[47]

In similar ways CEO Bezos pushes Amazon software engineers and other employees. In 1997 he proclaimed, "This is day 1 for the internet. We still have so much to learn." He still describes the internet as an "uncharted world, imperfectly understood, and yielding new surprises all the time."[48]

Bezos listens to the three sources David Ulrich suggests – himself, his customers and the community which purchases 20 million products sold through Amazon. Amazon's managers constantly evaluate about 500 measurable goals with 80 percent of these focused on customer objectives. Engineers constantly discuss better methods of customer evaluation. Amazon has 154 million customers and 56,000 employees. Bezos' net worth is estimated at $19 billion.[49] Besides salary, most employees have stock options. At Amazon the Bezos leadership isn't merely "trickle down." He demands that discussion and innovation move from the employee upward through management.

Three Types of Organizational Culture

Not all organizations are guided in the progressive ways of Interface Carpets or Amazon.com. In order to be morally responsible in an organization without suffering the fate of the employees in Jackall's study, engineers must first have some understanding of the organization in which they are employed. This knowledge helps engineers to understand (1) how they and their managers tend to frame issues under the influence of the organization and (2) how one can act in the organization effectively, safely, and in a morally responsible way.

The qualities of the organization we have in mind here often fall into the category of "organizational culture." It is generally agreed that organizational culture is set at the top of an organization—by high-level managers, by the president or chief executive officer of the organization, by directors, and sometimes by owners. If the organization values success and productivity over integrity and ethical principles, these values will powerfully influence the decisions of members of the organization. The values become, in the words of one writer, "a mindset, a filter through which participants view their world."[50] If this filter is strongly rooted in an organizational culture of which one is a part, it is an even more powerful influence on behavior.

Some writers use the term "organizational scripts" or "schemas" to refer to the way an organization conditions its members to view the world in a certain way, seeing some things and not seeing others. Dennis Gioia was a manager at Ford. He made the recommendation not to recall the Pinto, even though the car had been involved in the tragic deaths of passengers after relatively minor accidents. He describes his experience at Ford as follows:

> My own schematized … knowledge influenced me to perceive recall issues in terms of the prevailing decision environment and to unconsciously overlook key features of the Pinto case, mainly because they did not fit an existing script. Although the outcomes of the case carry retrospectively obvious ethical overtones, the schemas driving my perceptions and actions precluded considerations of the issues in ethical terms because the scripts did not include ethical dimensions.[51]

We have to be careful here not to allow an appreciation of the influence of organizational culture to completely override a belief in individual moral responsibility. Nevertheless, employees, including professional employees, do make decisions in the context of the organization in which they are employed, and one needs to understand the forces that bear upon his or her decision making.

With funding from the Hitachi Corporation, Michael Davis and his associates studied the positions of engineers in engineering firms. Their published study, often called the Hitachi report, found that companies fall, roughly, into one of three categories: engineer-oriented companies, customer-oriented companies, and finance-oriented companies. Understanding these three types of firms helps us understand the organizational cultures in which engineers work.

Engineer-Oriented Companies

In these firms, there is general agreement that quality takes priority over other considerations, except safety. In the words of one manager, "We have overdesigned our products and would rather lose money than diminish our reputation."[52] Engineers often described their relationship to managers in these kinds of firms as one in which negotiation or arriving at consensus was prominent. Engineers often said that managers would rarely overrule them when there was a significant engineering issue, although they might make the final decision when primarily such issues as cost or marketing are involved. Managers in such companies said that they never withhold information from engineers, although they suspect engineers sometimes withhold information in order to cover up a mistake.

Customer-Oriented Companies

Decision making is similar to that of engineer oriented firms, but with four significant differences. First, managers think of engineers as advocates of a point of view different from their own. Whereas managers must focus on such business factors as timing and cost, engineers should focus on quality and safety. Second, more emphasis is placed on business considerations than in engineer-oriented companies. Third, as with engineer-oriented companies, safety outranks quality. Sometimes quality can be sacrificed to get the product out the door. Finally, communication between engineers and managers may be somewhat more difficult than in engineer-oriented firms. Managers are more concerned about engineers' withholding information, even though consensus is highly valued.

Finance-Oriented Companies

Although possessing far less information about this category of firms, Davis conjectures, based on the information available, that these firms are more centralized and that this has important consequences. For example, engineers may receive less information for making decisions and consequently their decisions are given less weight by managers. Managers are less inclined to try to reach consensus, and engineers are seen as having a "staff" and advisory function.

Acting Ethically without Having to Make Difficult Choices

Acting in an ethical manner and with little harm to oneself is generally easier in engineer-oriented and customer-oriented companies than in finance-oriented companies. In the first two types of firms, more respect is given to the types of values with which engineers are typically concerned, especially safety and quality. Communication is better, and there is more emphasis on arriving at decisions by consensus rather than by the authority of the managers. All of this makes it much easier for an engineer to act in a professional and ethical manner. However, there are some additional suggestions that should make acting ethically easier and less harmful to the employee.

First, engineers and other employees should be encouraged to report bad news. Sometimes there are formal procedures for lodging complaints and warnings about impending trouble. If possible, there should be formal procedures for lodging complaints. One of the best known procedures is the Differing Professional Views and Differing Professional Opinions of the Nuclear Regulatory Commission.[53] Another procedure is the Amoco Chemical Hazard and Operability program.[54] In addition, many large corporations have "ombudsmen" and "ethics officers," who can promote ethical behavior as well as serve as a conduit for complaints. Some have suggested, however, that in-house ethics officers are too much the creatures of the organizations in which they work; instead, they contend, outside ethics consultants should be hired to handle complaints and internal disagreements. The argument is that in-house ethics officers have been nurtured in the organizational culture and are dependent on the organizations for their salaries, so they are not able to adopt a genuinely objective perspective.[55]

Second, companies and their employees should adopt a position of *critical* loyalty rather than uncritical or blind loyalty. Uncritical loyalty to the employer is placing the interests of the employer, as the employer defines those interests, above every other consideration. By contrast, critical loyalty is giving due regard to the interests of the employer but only insofar as this is possible within the constraints of the employee's personal and professional ethics. We can think of the concept of critical loyalty as a creative middle way that seeks to honor the legitimate demands of the organization but also to honor the obligation to protect the public.

Third, when making criticisms and suggestions, employees should focus on issues rather than personalities. This helps avoid excessive emotionalism and personality clashes.

Fourth, written records should be kept of suggestions and especially of complaints. This is important if court proceedings are eventually involved. It also serves to "keep the record straight" about what was said and when it was said.

Fifth, complaints should be kept as confidential as possible for the protection of both the individuals involved and the firm.

Sixth, provisions should be made for neutral participants from outside the organization when the dispute requires it. Sometimes, employees within the organization are too emotionally involved in the dispute or have too many personal ties to make a dispassionate evaluation of the issues.

Seventh, explicit provision for protection from retaliation should be made, with mechanisms for complaint if an employee believes he or she has experienced retaliation. Next to the fear of immediate dismissal, probably the greatest fear of an employee who is in disagreement with a superior is that he or she will suffer discrimination in promotion and job assignment, even long after the controversy is resolved. Protection from this fear is one of the most important of employee rights, although it is one of the most difficult to provide.

Eighth, the process for handling organizational disobedience should proceed as quickly as possible. Delaying resolution of such issues can be a method of punishing dissent. Sufficient delay often allows management to perform the actions against which the protest was made. Prolonging the suspense and cloud of suspicion that accompanies an investigative process also serves to punish a protesting employee, even if his or her actions were completely justifiable.

7.7 PROPER ENGINEERING AND MANAGEMENT DECISIONS

Functions of Engineers and Managers

How should we understand the boundary between decisions that should be made by engineers and those that should be made by managers? An answer to this question must begin with a delineation of the proper functions of engineers and managers in an organization and of the contrasting points of view associated with these differing functions.

The primary function of engineers within an organization is to use their technical knowledge and training to create structures, products, and processes that are of value to the organization and its customers. But engineers are also professionals, and they must uphold the standards that their profession has decided should guide the use of their technical knowledge. Thus, engineers have a dual loyalty—to the organization and to their profession. Their professional loyalties go beyond their immediate employer.[56]

These obligations include meeting the standards usually associated with good design and accepted engineering practice. The criteria embedded in these standards include such considerations as efficiency and economy of design, the degree of invulnerability to improper manufacturing and operation, and the extent to which state of-the-art technology is used.[57] We summarize these considerations by saying that engineers have a special concern for quality.

Engineers also ascribe preeminent importance to safety. Moreover, they are inclined to be cautious in this regard, preferring to err on the conservative side in safety considerations. In the *Challenger* case, for example, the engineers did not have firm data on the behavior of the O-rings at low temperatures, even though their extrapolations indicated that there might be severe problems. So they recommended against the launch.

The function and consequent perspective of managers is different. Their function is to direct the activities of the organization, including the activities of engineers. Rather than being oriented toward standards that transcend their organization, they are more likely to be governed by the standards that prevail within the organization and, in some cases, perhaps by their own personal moral beliefs. Both Jackall and the Hitachi report imply that managers view themselves as custodians of the organization and are primarily concerned with its current and future well-being. This well-being is measured for the most part in economic terms, but it also includes such considerations as public image and employee morale.

This perspective differs from that of engineers. Rather than thinking in terms of professional practices and standards, managers tend to enumerate all of the relevant considerations ("get everything on the table," as they sometimes say) and then balance them against one another to come to a conclusion. Managers feel strong pressure to keep costs down and may believe engineers sometimes go too far in pursuing safety, often to the detriment of such considerations as cost and marketability. By contrast, engineers tend to assign a serial ordering to the various considerations relevant to design so that minimal standards of safety and quality must be met before any other considerations are relevant.[58] Although they may also be willing to balance safety and quality against other factors to some extent, engineers are more likely to believe that they have a special obligation to uphold safety and quality standards in negotiations with managers. They will usually insist that a product or process must never violate accepted engineering standards and that changes be made incrementally. These considerations suggest a distinction between what we call a proper engineering decision (PED), a decision that should be made by engineers or from an engineering perspective, and what we call a proper management decision (PMD), a decision that should be made by managers or from the management perspective. While not claiming to give a full definition of either PED or PMD in the sense of necessary and sufficient conditions, we can formulate some of the features that should ordinarily characterize these two types of decision procedures. We refer to the following descriptions as "characterizations" of proper engineering and management decisions. They are as follows:

PED: a decision that should be made by engineers or at least governed by professional engineering standards because it either (1) involves technical matters that require engineering expertise or (2) falls within the ethical standards embodied in engineering codes, especially those that require engineers to protect the health and safety of the public.

PMD: a decision that should be made by managers or at least governed by management considerations because (1) it involves factors relating to the well-being of the organization, such as cost, scheduling, and marketing, and employee morale or welfare; and (2) the decision does not force engineers (or other professionals) to make unacceptable compromises with their own technical or ethical standards.

We make three preliminary remarks about these characterizations of engineering and management decisions. First, the characterizations of the PED and PMD show that the distinction between management and engineering decisions is made in terms of the standards and practices that should predominate in the decision-making process. Furthermore, the PMD makes it clear that management standards should never override engineering standards when the two are in substantial conflict, especially with regard to safety and perhaps even quality. However, what is considered a "substantial conflict" may often be controversial. If engineers want much more than acceptable safety or quality, then it is not clear that the judgment of engineers should prevail. Second, the PMD specifies that a legitimate management decision not only must not force engineers to violate their professional practices and standards but also must not force other professionals to do so either. Even though the primary contrast here is the difference between engineering and management decisions, the specification of a legitimate management decision must also include this wider prohibition against the violation of other professional standards. A complete characterization of a legitimate management decision should also include prohibitions against violating the rights of nonprofessional employees, but this would make the characterization even more complicated and is not relevant for our purposes.

Third, engineers should be expected to give advice, even in decisions properly made by managers. Management decisions can often benefit from the advice of engineers. Even if there are no fundamental problems with safety, engineers may have important contributions with respect to such issues as improvements in design, alternative designs, and ways to make a product more attractive. Furthermore, engineers may be in the best position to anticipate the sorts of problems products could that pose down the road—problems regarding how well the product functions and in regard to making repairs or improvements when necessary. As best they can, they need to forewarn managers of the problems that may lie ahead and advise them of available alternatives. This requires both the exercise of engineering imagination and the employment of good communication skills with those who do not have their engineering expertise.

Paradigmatic and Nonparadigmatic Examples

Several terms in both characterizations are purposely left undefined. The characterization of the PED does not define "technical matters," and it certainly does not define "health" and "safety." PMD does not fully specify the kinds of considerations that are typical management considerations, citing only "factors relating to the wellbeing of the company, such as cost, scheduling, marketing, and employee morale or welfare." The characterization of the PMD requires that management decisions not force engineers to make "unacceptable compromises with their own professional standards," but it does not define unacceptable. We do not believe that it is useful to attempt to give any general definition of these terms. The application of these terms will be relatively uncontroversial in some examples, and no attempts at definition can furnish a definitive clarification in all of the controversial cases.

It will be useful to employ the line-drawing technique in handling moral issues that arise in this area. We refer to the relatively uncontroversial examples of PEDs and PMDs as paradigmatic.[59] The characterizations of PED and PMD provided earlier are intended to describe such paradigms. These two paradigms can be thought of as marking the two ends in a spectrum of cases.

We can easily imagine a paradigmatic PED. Suppose engineer Jane is participating in the design of a chemical plant that her firm will build for itself. She must choose between valve A and valve B. Valve B is sold by a friend of Jane's manager, but it fails to meet minimum specifications for the job. It has, in fact, been responsible for several disasters involving loss of life, and Jane is surprised that it is still on the market. Valve A, by contrast, is a state-of-the-art product. Among other things, it has a quicker shutoff mechanism and is also much less prone to malfunctions in emergencies. Although it is 5 percent more expensive, the expense is one that Jane's firm can well afford. Valve A, therefore, is the clear and unequivocal choice in terms of both quality and safety. Table 7.1 illustrates this.

Here, the decision should be made by Jane or other engineers, or at least in accordance with engineering considerations. This is because (1) the decision involves issues related to accepted technical standards and (2) the decision relates in important

TABLE 7.1 A Paradigmatic PED

Feature	PMD	Test	PED
Technical expertise	Not needed	———————— X	Needed
Safety	Not important	———————— X	Important
Cost	Important	———————— X	Not important
Scheduling	Important	———————— X	Not important
Marketing	Important	———————— X	Not important

© Cengage Learning

ways to the safety of the public and therefore to the ethical standards of engineers. The choice between valves A and B is a paradigmatic PED.

We can modify the example to make it a paradigmatic PMD. Suppose valves A and B are equal in quality and safety, but valve B can be supplied much faster than valve A, is 15 percent cheaper, and is manufactured by a firm that is a potential customer for some of the products of Jane's firm. Valve A, however, is made by a firm that is potentially an even bigger customer for some of the products of Jane's firm, although cultivating a relationship with this firm will require a long-term commitment and be more expensive. If there are no other relevant considerations, the decision as to whether to purchase valve A or valve B should be made by managers, or at least made in accordance with management considerations. Comparing the decision by the two criteria in the PMD, we can say that (1) management considerations (e.g., speed of delivery, cost, and the decision as to which customers should be cultivated) are important, and (2) no violation of engineering considerations would result from either decision. Table 7.2 illustrates this case.

Many cases will lie between the two extremes of paradigmatic PEDs and paradigmatic PMDs. Some cases may lie so near the center of the imaginary spectrum of cases that they might be classified as either PED or PMD. Consider another version of the same case in which valve A has a slightly better record of long-term reliability (and is therefore somewhat safer), but valve B is 10 percent cheaper and can be both delivered and marketed more quickly. In this case, rational and responsible people might well differ on whether the final decision on which valve to buy should be made by engineers or managers. Considerations of reliability and safety are engineering considerations, but considerations of cost, scheduling, and marketing are typical management

TABLE 7.2 A Paradigmatic PMD

Feature	PMD	Test	PED
Technical expertise	Not needed	X ————————	Needed
Safety	Not important	X ————————	Important
Cost	Important	X ————————	Not important
Scheduling	Important	X ————————	Not important
Marketing	Important	X ————————	Not important

© Cengage Learning

TABLE 7.3   PED/PMD: A Nonparadigmatic Case

Feature	PMD	Test	PED
Technical expertise	Not needed	—————————X———	Needed
Safety	Not important	——————————X———	Important
Cost	Important	—X———————————	Not important
Scheduling	Important	——————X———————	Not important
Marketing	Important	——————X———————	Not important

© Cengage Learning

considerations. Table 7.3 illustrates this situation. Would ordering valve B be an "unacceptable" compromise of engineering standards of safety and quality? Are the cost, scheduling, and marketing problems significant enough to overbalance the engineering considerations? Here, rational people of good will might differ in their judgments. In considering a case such as this, it is important to remember that, as in all line-drawing cases, the importance or moral "weight" of the feature must be considered. One cannot simply count the number of features that fall on the PMD or PED side or where the "X" should be placed on the line.

Many issues regarding pollution also illustrate the problematic situations that can arise in the interface between proper engineering and proper management decisions. Suppose process A is so much more costly than process B that the use of process A might threaten the survival of the company. Suppose, furthermore, that process B is more polluting, but it is not clear whether the pollution poses any substantial threat to human health. Here again, rational people of good will might differ on whether management or engineering considerations should prevail.

7.8 RESPONSIBLE ORGANIZATIONAL DISOBEDIENCE

Sometimes engineers encounter difficulties attempting to be both loyal employees and responsible professionals. The engineer finds herself in a position of having to oppose her managers or her organization. Jim Otten finds the expression "organizational disobedience" appropriate as a generic term to cover all types of actions taken by an employee that are contrary to the wishes of her employer. Given the similarities between this kind of action and civil disobedience, the term seems appropriate.[60] We do not follow Otten's definition exactly, but we use his expression and define *organizational disobedience* as a protest of, or refusal to follow, an organizational policy or action.

It is helpful to keep the following two points about organizational disobedience in mind. First, the policy that a professional employee disobeys or protests may be either specific or general. It may be a specific directive of a superior or a general organizational policy, either a single act or a continuing series of actions.

Second, the employer may not intend to do anything morally wrong. For example, when an engineer objects to the production of a faulty type of steel pipe, he is not necessarily claiming that his firm intends to manufacture a shoddy product. Rather, he is objecting to a series of actions that would probably result in unfortunate consequences, however unintended.

There are at least three distinct areas in which responsible engineers might be involved in organizational disobedience:

1. Disobedience by contrary action, which is engaging in activities contrary to the interests of the company, as perceived by management.
2. Disobedience by nonparticipation, which is refusing to carry out an assignment because of moral or professional objections.
3. Disobedience by protest, which is actively and openly protesting a policy or action of an organization.

What guidelines should the responsible engineer use in deciding when to engage in organizational disobedience in these areas, and how should he or she carry out this disobedience? We consider the first two types of organizational disobedience in this section and the third type in the next.

Disobedience by Contrary Action

Engineers may sometimes find that their actions outside the workplace are objectionable to managers. Objections by managers are usually in one of two areas. First, managers may believe that a particular action or perhaps the general lifestyle of an employee reflects unfavorably on the organization. For example, an engineer might be a member of a political group that is generally held in low esteem by the community. Second, managers may believe that some activities of employees are contrary to the interests of the organization in a more direct way. For example, an engineer may be a member of a local environmental group that is pressuring his or her company to install antipollution equipment that is not required by law or is lobbying to keep the company from purchasing some wetland area that it intends to drain and use for plant expansion. How should an engineer handle such delicate situations?

Although we cannot investigate all of the issues fully here, a few observations are essential. Disobedience by contrary action is not a paradigm case of harm to the organization (compared, for example, with theft or fraud), and its restriction by the organization is not a paradigm case of restriction of individual freedom (compared, for example, with a direction to do something the employee thinks is seriously immoral). Nevertheless, they are examples of harm to the individual and the organization. Let us consider some of the arguments that might be offered to confirm this claim.

On the one hand, there is no doubt that an organization can be harmed in some sense by the actions of employees outside the workplace. A company that has a reputation for hiring people whose lifestyles are offensive to the local community may find hiring others difficult, and it may lose business as well. The harm that an organization may suffer is even more obvious when employees engage in political activities that are directly contrary to the interests of the organization. A manager can argue with some persuasiveness that the simplistic assertion that nothing the employee does after 5 o'clock affects the organization does not do justice to the realities of business and community life. On these grounds, a manager might assert that the organization's right to the loyalty of its employees requires the employee not to harm the organization in these ways.

On the other hand, an employee's freedom suffers substantial curtailment if organizational restrictions force her to curtail activities to which she has a deep personal commitment. Nor can the manager persuasively argue that employees should simply resign if management finds their activities outside the workplace objectionable because the same activities might harm other organizations in the same way. Thus, consistently applying the argument that employees should never do anything that harms the organization results in the conclusion that employees should never engage in lifestyles or political activities that are controversial. This amounts to a substantial limitation of an employee's freedom.

In surveying these arguments, we believe that a good case can be made that organizations should not punish employees for disobedience by contrary action. Punishing employees for disobedience by contrary action, amounts to a considerable infringement on individual freedom. Moreover, employees may not be able to avoid this type of harm to organizations simply by changing jobs. Many organizations might be harmed by an engineer's political views or efforts on behalf of the environment. Thus, allowing this type of harm to count as justification for organizational control permits organizations to exert considerable influence over an employee's life outside the workplace. In a society that values individual freedom as much as ours does, such a substantial abridgement of individual freedom is difficult to justify.

Despite these considerations, however, many managers will act strenuously when they believe they or their organizations are threatened by actions of employees outside the workplace. Therefore, two observations may be appropriate. First, some actions by employees outside the workplace harm an organization more directly than others. An engineer's campaign for tighter restrictions on her own company's environmental pollution will probably have a more direct effect on her company than an engineer's private sexual life, for example. Employees should be more careful in areas in which the harm to their organization is more direct.

Second, there can be a major difference in the degree to which curtailment of an employee's activities outside the workplace encroaches on his freedom. Curtailment of activities closely associated with one's personal identity and with strong moral or religious beliefs is more serious than limitation of activities that are associated with more peripheral beliefs. Therefore, employees should allow themselves more freedom in areas that are closely related to their basic personal commitments than in areas more peripheral to their most important concerns.

Disobedience by Nonparticipation

In one of the most famous legal cases that falls in this category, Dr. Grace Pierce, a physician, strongly objected to some impending tests on humans of a drug for diarrhea. Dr. Pierce had not actually refused to participate in the conduct of the tests, but the firm assumed that she would refuse and transferred her to another area. She eventually resigned.[61] Engineers are most likely to engage in disobedience by nonparticipation in projects that are related to the military and in projects that may adversely affect the environment. Engineer James, a pacifist, may discover that the underwater detection system that his company has contracted to build has military applications and thereupon request to be relieved of an assignment to the project. Engineer Betty may request not to be asked to design a condominium that will be built in a wetland area.

Disobedience by nonparticipation can be based on professional ethics or personal ethics. Engineers who refuse to design a product that they believe is unsafe can base their objections on their professional codes, which require engineers to give preeminence to considerations of public safety, health, and welfare. Engineers who refuse to design a product that has military applications because of their personal objections to the use of violence must base their refusal on personal morality because the codes do not prohibit engineers from participating in military projects. The basis of objections to participating in projects that engineers believe are harmful to the environment is more controversial. Some of the engineering codes have statements about the environment and some do not; when present, the statements are usually very general and not always easy to interpret.

Several things should be kept in mind about disobedience by nonparticipation. First, it is possible (although perhaps unlikely) for an employee to abuse the appeal to conscience, using it as a way to avoid projects he finds boring or not challenging or as a way to avoid association with other employees with whom he has personal difficulties. An employee should be careful to avoid any behavior that would support this interpretation of his or her actions. Second, it is sometimes difficult for employers to honor a request to be removed from a work assignment. For example, there may be no alternative assignments, there may be no other engineer who is qualified to do the work, or the change may be disruptive to the organization. These problems are especially severe in small organizations.

Nevertheless, we believe an organization, when it can do so, should honor most requests for nonparticipation in a project when the requests are based on conscience or a belief that the project violates professional standards. Common morality holds that a violation of one's conscience is a serious moral matter. Employers should not force employees to make a choice between losing their job or violating personal or professional standards. Sometimes employers may not have any alternative work assignments, but many organizations have found ways to respect employees' views without undue economic sacrifice.

7.9 DISOBEDIENCE BY PROTEST

Richard Nixon v. Ernest Fitzgerald

In 1969, President Richard Nixon asked for the termination of Ernest Fitzgerald, an engineer and manager for the US Air Force. In 1965, Fitzgerald was Deputy for Management Systems at the Pentagon. Early in his work, he began warning superiors about cost overruns on defense contracts. Other employees were blindly following orders from their officers to conceal the cost overruns, but not Fitzgerald. In 1968 and 1969 he insisted on testifying before Congress about $2.3 billion in concealed cost overruns in the Lockheed C-5A transport plane. Because of his testimony before Congress, he was fired by order of President Nixon for allegedly revealing classified information.[62] Fitzgerald was fired by Secretary of Defense Melvin Laird. In an appeal he was reinstated.[63] Fitzgerald was involved in several legal cases that defined government employees' rights, including the US Supreme Court case *Nixon v. Fitzgerald*. He was influential in the passage the Civil Reform Act of 1978, which was the forerunner to the Whistleblower Protection Act of 1989.[64]

We have saved this third type of organizational protest for a separate section because it is the best known and most extensively discussed form of organizational disobedience. In some situations, engineers find the actions of the employer to be so objectionable that they believe mere nonparticipation in the objectionable activity is insufficient. Rather, some form of protest, or "whistleblowing," is required. We begin by making some general comments about whistleblowing and then consider two important theories of whistleblowing.

What Is Whistleblowing?

The origin and exact meaning of the metaphor of whistleblowing are uncertain. According to Michael Davis, there are three possible sources of the metaphor: a train sounding a whistle to warn people to get off the track, a referee blowing a whistle to indicate a foul, or a police officer blowing a whistle to stop wrongdoing.[65] One problem with all of these metaphors, as Davis points out, is that they depict whistleblowers as outsiders, whereas a whistleblower is more like a team player who calls a foul play on his own team. This suggests two characteristics of whistleblowing: (1) One reveals information that the organization does not want revealed to the public or some authority and (2) one does this out of approved channels. An important distinction is between internal and external whistleblowing. In internal whistleblowing, the alarm about wrongdoing stays within the organization, although the whistleblower may bypass his immediate superiors, especially if they are involved in the wrongdoing. In external whistleblowing, the whistleblower goes outside the organization, alerting a regulatory organization or the press. Another important distinction is between open and anonymous whistleblowing. In open whistleblowing, the whistleblower reveals his identity, whereas in anonymous whistleblowing the whistleblower attempts to keep his identity secret. Whether internal or external, open or anonymous, however, a whistleblower is usually defined as a person who is an insider, one who is a part of the organization. For this reason, the question of loyalty always arises. Therefore, whistleblowing needs a justification. Let's look at the two major approaches to the justification of whistleblowing. One uses primarily utilitarian considerations and the other employs considerations more appropriate to the standpoint of respect for persons.

Whistleblowing: A Harm-Preventing Justification

Richard DeGeorge has provided a set of criteria that he contends must be satisfied before whistleblowing can be morally justified.[66] DeGeorge believes that whistleblowing is morally *permissible* provided that

1. the harm that "will be done by the product to the public is serious and considerable";
2. the employees report their concern to their superiors, and;
3. "getting no satisfaction from their immediate superiors, they exhaust the channels available" within the organization.

DeGeorge believes that whistleblowing is morally *obligatory* provided that

1. the employee has "documented evidence that would convince a responsible, impartial observer that his view of the situation is correct and the company policy is wrong"; and
2. the employee has "strong evidence that making the information public will in fact prevent the threatened serious harm."

Within the DeGeorge model we note the potential harm to the public. This is what initiates the consideration that whistleblowing might be justified. The public will benefit if these harms are eliminated. There is also potential harm to the organization, and the prospective whistleblower must attempt to minimize this harm by first trying to use available channels within the organization. There is also potential harm to the whistleblower, and the risk of harm must only be undertaken when there is some assurance that others would be convinced of the wrong and the harm might be prevented. There is no reason, DeGeorge seems to believe, to risk one's career if there is little chance the whistleblowing will have the desired effect. Taken as general tests for justified or required whistleblowing have much to be said for them. However, there are times when DeGeorge's criteria are too demanding.[67]

1. The first criterion seems too strong. DeGeorge seems to assume that the employee must know that harm will result and that the harm must be great. Sometimes an employee is not in a position to gather evidence that is totally convincing. Perhaps just believing on the basis of the best evidence available that harm will result is sufficient.

2. It should not always be necessary for employees to report their criticisms to their superiors. Often, one's immediate superiors are the cause of the problem and cannot be trusted to give unbiased evaluation of the situation.

3. It should not always be necessary to exhaust the organizational chain of command. Sometimes there is not time to do this before a disaster will occur. Also, sometimes employees have no effective way to make their protests known to higher management except by going public.

4. It is not always possible to get documented evidence of a problem. Often, organizations deprive employees of access to the vital information needed to make a conclusive argument for their position. They deprive protesting employees of access to computers and other sources of information necessary to make their case.

5. The obligation to make the protest may not always mean there will be strong evidence that a protest will prevent the harm. Just giving those exposed to a harm the chance to give free and informed consent to the potential harm is often a sufficient justification of the protest.

6. Some have argued that if the whistleblower does not have evidence that would convince a reasonable, impartial observer that her view of the situation is correct (criterion 4), her whistleblowing could not prevent harm and would not even be morally permissible, much less obligatory. Thus, if criterion 4 is not fulfilled, whistleblowing might not even be permissible.[68]

Whistleblowing: A Complicity-Avoiding View

Michael Davis has proposed a very different theory of the justification of whistleblowing: "We might understand whistleblowing better if we understand the whistleblower's obligation to derive from the need to avoid complicity in wrongdoing rather than from the ability to prevent harm."[69] Davis formulates his "complicity theory" in the following way.

You are morally required to reveal what you know to the public (or to a suitable agent or representative of it) when

(C1) what you will reveal derives from your work for an organization;

(C2) you are a voluntary member of that organization;

(C3) you believe that the organization, though legitimate, is engaged in a serious moral wrong;

(C4) you believe that your work for that organization will contribute (more or less directly) to the wrong if (but not only if) you do not publicly reveal what you know;

(C5) you are justified in beliefs C3 and C4; and

(C6) beliefs C3 and C4 are true.[70]

According to complicity theory, the primary moral motivation for blowing the whistle is to avoid participating in an immoral action, not to prevent a harm to the public. Thus, it is more in agreement with the basic ideas of the respect for persons tradition. One blows the whistle first and foremost to avoid violating moral precepts. Preventing harm to the public is, of course, desirable; but it is not a necessary part of the justification of whistleblowing.

Davis' approach to the moral justification of whistleblowing has several distinct advantages. First, since preventing harm to the public is not necessarily a motivation for whistleblowing, one does not have to know that harm would result if he does not blow the whistle. Second, since preventing harm to the organization is not necessarily a motivation for blowing the whistle, one does not have to first work through organizational channels. Third, since preventing harm to oneself is not necessarily a motivation for whistleblowing, one does not have to be sure that blowing the whistle will prevent the harm before one risks one's career. Nevertheless, there are problems with Davis' theory as well.[71]

First, the requirement that what one reveals must derive from one's work in the organization (C1) and must contribute to the wrongdoing (C4) seems much too restrictive. Suppose engineer Joe is asked to review a design for a structure submitted to a customer by another member of the organization in which he is employed. Joe finds the design highly defective and, in fact, that it would be a serious threat to public safety if the structure were to be built. According to Davis, Joe would not have any obligation to blow the whistle because the design had nothing to do with Joe's work with the organization. Yet this seems implausible. Joe may well have an obligation to blow the whistle if the design poses a serious threat because of its potential for harm to the public regardless of his own involvement in the design.

Second, Davis also requires that a person be a voluntary member of an organization. But suppose Michael, an Army draftee, discovers a situation that poses a serious threat to his fellow soldiers. Michael has a moral obligation to blow the whistle, and the fact that he was drafted seems to have little relevance.

Third, Davis believes that one is only justified in blowing the whistle if in fact one believes that serious wrongdoing by the organization has occurred. An additional consideration is that one may be justified in blowing the whistle if one has good reason to believe that wrongdoing will occur. Even if one turned out to be mistaken, one would still be justified in blowing the whistle, especially from the standpoint of the ethics of respect for persons. Otherwise, one's moral integrity would be compromised because one would be involved in activities that at least one *believes* to be wrong. To be doing something one believes to be wrong is still a serious compromise of one's moral integrity, even if by some more objective standard one is not actually involved in wrongdoing.

Finally, Davis does not take sufficient account of what many people would consider to be a clear—and perhaps the most important—justification of whistleblowing, namely that it is undertaken to prevent harm to the organization or (more often) to the public. Although avoiding complicity in wrongdoing is a legitimate and important justification for blowing the whistle, at the very least, it need not be the only one.

Despite the criticisms of both theories, there does seem to be truth in both. For Davis, whistleblowing must be justified because otherwise the whistleblower violates the obligation of loyalty. He justifies blowing the whistle to keep himself from complicity in wrongdoing. For DeGeorge, whistleblowing must be justified because of the harm it can produce to the organization and to the whistleblower. These harms can sometimes be outweighed by the harm to the public that would otherwise occur. All of these considerations seem valid. From a practical standpoint, they are all important to consider when thinking about blowing the whistle.

Some Practical Advice on Whistleblowing

We conclude this section with some practical considerations on protesting organizational wrongdoing.

First, take advantage of any formal or informal processes your organization may have for making a protest. Your organization may have an "ethics hotline" or an ombudsman. The Nuclear Regulatory Commission has a formal process for registering what it calls "Differing Professional Opinions."[72] Many managers have an "open door" policy, and there may be other informal procedures for expressing to a superior a different assessment of a situation.

Second, determine whether it is better to keep your protest as confidential as possible or to involve others in the process. Sometimes the most effective way to work within an organization is to work confidentially and in a nonconfrontational way with superiors and colleagues. At other times, it is important to involve your peers in the process so that a manager cannot justify disregarding your protest by assuming that it is the result of one disgruntled employee.

Third, focus on issues, not personalities. People get defensive and hostile when they are personally attacked, whether these people are your superiors or your peers. Therefore, it is usually a better tactic to describe the issues in impersonal terms insofar as this is possible.

Fourth, keep written records of the process. This is important if court proceedings are eventually involved. It also serves to "keep the record straight" about what was said and when it was said.

Fifth, present positive suggestions in association with your objection. Your protest should have the form, "I have a problem that I want to bring to your attention, but I also think I have a way to solve it." This approach keeps your protest from being wholly negative and suggests a positive solution to the problem you have identified. Positive suggestions can be helpful to managers, who must deal with the problem in a practical way.

Sixth, whistleblowing has new governance areas. Both the Sarbanes-Oxley Act of 2002[73] and the Dodd-Frank Act of 2010[74] encourage and even financially reward whistleblowing. Fair warning and loyalty to the organization regarding certain legal problems may be put aside. Under Dodd-Frank provisions, employees who are whistleblowers can be awarded a percentage of the funds that are deemed fraudulent, under certain conditions.[75] For example, awards can range from 10 percent to 30 percent of the amount of monetary sanctions in cases over $1 million.[76] However, it still seems likely that most employees will work carefully with managers to correct problems before exposing organizational problems to the press or the government.

7.10 EMPLOYEE AND EMPLOYER

Paul Lorenz was a mechanical engineer employed by Martin Marietta. He was laid off on July, 25, 1975, for allegedly failing to engage in acts of deception and misrepresentation concerning the quality of materials used by Martin Marietta in designing equipment for the National Aeronautics and Space Administration (NASA). The equipment was for the external tank of the space shuttle program. Before he was laid off, Lorenz was informed that he should "start playing ball with management." After being laid off, he filed a tort claim against Martin Marietta for wrongful discharge on the grounds that he was fired for refusing to perform an illegal act. Federal law does prohibit knowingly and willingly making a false representation to a federal agency. However, lower courts rejected Lorenz's claim on the grounds that Colorado recognized no claim of wrongful discharge against employers.

In 1992, the Colorado Supreme court concluded that "Lorenz did present sufficient evidence at trial to establish a prima facie case for wrongful discharge under the public-policy exception to the at-will employment doctrine." The Court directed a new trial in accordance with its findings, but the new trials never took place, probably because of an out-of-court settlement between Mr. Lorenz and his former employer.[77]

Analysis of Lorenz Case

This is an important case in the development of the law regarding the rights of professional employees in the workplace. The crucial idea in the case was the so-called "public-policy exception" to the traditional common law doctrine of "employment at will." Common law is the tradition of case law or "judge-made law" that originated in England and is fundamental in US law. It is based on a tradition in which a judicial decision establishes a precedent, which is then used by succeeding jurists as the basis for their decisions in similar cases. Common law is distinguished from statutory law, or laws made by legislative bodies.

Traditionally, US law has been governed by the common law doctrine of "employment at will," which holds that in the absence of a contract, an employer may discharge an employee at any time and for virtually any reason. Recent court decisions, such as this one, have held that the traditional doctrine must be modified if there is an important interest at stake. Precisely how far the public policy exception extends is still being formulated by the courts, but it includes such things as a refusal to break the law (such as in the Lorenz case), performing an important public obligation (e.g., jury duty), exercising a clear legal right (e.g., exercising free speech or applying for unemployment compensation), and protecting the public from a clear threat to health and safety. In general, the public policy exception has not been invoked to protect an employee when there is a mere difference in judgment with the employer.[78] The courts have also given more weight to the codes of administrative and judicial bodies, such as state regulatory boards, than to the codes promulgated by professional societies.[79]

In addition to the judicial modification of at-will employment, dissenting employees have also received some statutory protection, primarily through whistleblower laws. The first such state law was passed in Michigan in 1981. If the employee is unfairly disciplined for reporting an alleged violation of federal, state, or local law to public authorities, the employee can be awarded back pay, reinstatement to the job, costs of litigation, and attorney's fees. The employer can also be fined up to $500.[80] New Jersey's Conscientious Employee Protection Act forbids termination for conduct undertaken for the sake of compliance with "a clear mandate of public policy concerning the public health, safety, or welfare."[81] Many cases in the area of what might very generally be called "employee rights" involve nonprofessional employees, but our special interest is professional employees, especially engineers. Many of the cases, like the Lorenz case, involve a conflict between professional employees and managers. In fact, most of the classic cases in engineering ethics involve conflicts between engineers and managers.

7.11   ROGER BOISJOLY AND THE *CHALLENGER* DISASTER

Two events in the professional life of engineer Roger Boisjoly, both related to the *Challenger* disaster, illustrate several themes in this chapter. One of these events is the teleconference between Morton Thiokol and NASA the night before the launch of the *Challenger*. This dramatic event illustrates the conflict between engineers and management in decision making. The second experience is Boisjoly's testimony before the Presidential Commission on the Space Shuttle *Challenger* Accident. Boisjoly's testimony raises the issue of whistleblowing and the extent of the legitimacy of loyalty of an engineer to the organization in which he or she is employed.

Proper Management and Engineering Decisions

Robert Lund, vice president of engineering at Morton Thiokol, was both an engineer and a manager. In the teleconference on the evening before the fateful launch, he, in concert with other engineers, had recommended against launch. The recommendation was based on a judgment that the primary and secondary O-rings might not seal properly at the low temperatures at which the vehicle would be launched. NASA officials expressed dismay at the no-launch recommendation, and Thiokol executives requested an interruption in the teleconference to reassess their decision. During the 30-minute interruption, Jerald Mason, senior vice president of Morton Thiokol, turned to Lund and told him to take off his engineering hat and put on his management hat. Afterwards, Lund reversed his no-launch recommendation.

In admonishing Lund to take off his engineering hat and put on his management hat, Mason was saying that the launch decision should be a management decision. Testifying before the Rogers Commission, which investigated the *Challenger* accident, Mason gave two reasons for this belief. First, the engineers were not unanimous: "[W]ell, at this point it was clear to me we were not going to get a unanimous decision."[82] If engineers disagreed, then there was presumably not a clear violation of the technical or ethical standards of engineers; thus, it could be argued that neither requirement of the PMD was being violated.

There are reasons to doubt the factual accuracy of Mason's claim, however. In his account of the events surrounding the *Challenger* given at the Massachusetts Institute of Technology (MIT) in 1987, Roger Boisjoly reported that Mason asked if he was "the only one who wanted to fly."[83] This would suggest that he did not have evidence at this point that other engineers wanted to fly. Whatever validity Mason could give to his argument that some engineers supported the launch (and therefore that the opposition of the engineers to the launch was not unanimous) was apparently based on conversations with individual engineers after the teleconference. So Mason probably had little justification at the time of the teleconference for believing that the nonmanagement engineers were not unanimously opposed to the launch. Nevertheless, Mason may be correct in maintaining that there was some difference of opinion among those most qualified to render judgment, even if this information was not confirmed until after the event. If engineers disagreed about the technical issues, then the engineering considerations were perhaps not as compelling as they would have been if the engineers had been unanimous. Thus, the first part of the PED criterion may not have been fully satisfied. Those who did not find a technical problem probably would not find an ethical problem either. So the second criterion of the PED may also not have been fully satisfied.

Mason's second reason was that no numbers could be assigned to the time required for the O-rings to seal at various temperatures:

Dr. Keel: Since Mr. Lund was your vice president of engineering and since he presented the charts and the recommendations not to launch outside of your experience base—that is, below a temperature of 53 degrees for the O-rings—in the previous 8:45 Eastern Standard Time teleconference, what did you have in mind when you asked him to take off his engineering hat and put on his management hat?

Mr. Mason: I had in mind the fact that we had identified that we could not quantify the movement of that, the time for movement of the primary [O-ring]. We didn't have the data to do that, and therefore it was going to take a judgment rather than a precise engineering calculation, in order to conclude what we needed to conclude.[84]

This might also be a reason for holding that the decision to launch did not violate criterion 2 of the PMD and did not clearly satisfy criterion 1 of the PED. However, the fact that no calculations could be made to determine the time it would take the O-rings to seal at various temperatures does not necessarily justify the conclusion that a management decision should be made. Surely the fact that failure of the O-rings to seal could destroy the *Challenger* implies that the engineering considerations were of paramount importance even if they could not be adequately qualified. The engineer's concern for safety is still relevant.

Nevertheless, Mason's comment may make a valid observation. Given that engineers generally prefer to make judgments on the basis of quantitative calculations, they may well have been uncomfortable with the fact that there were no precise numbers for the degree of degradation of the O-rings at lower temperatures. As a result, the engineering judgment did not have the same degree of decisiveness that it would have had otherwise. All that Roger Boisjoly could argue was that the degree of degradation seemed to be correlated with temperature, and even the data he used to back up this claim were limited.

Mason's arguments, taken together, might be seen as an attempt to meet criterion 2 of the PMD. If the decision to recommend launch is not a clear violation of engineering practice, then an engineer would not violate his technical practices by recommending launch. Thus, Mason's argument could be seen as a claim that the decision whether to launch was at the very least not a paradigm instance of a PED. A paradigm PED would be one in which (among other things) the experts clearly agree and there are quantitative measures that unambiguously point to one option rather than another. Thus, the recommendation to launch was at the very least not a paradigm case of a violation of technical engineering practices.

Mason might also have argued that criterion 1 of the PMD was satisfied. A renewed contract with NASA was not assured, and failure to recommend launch might have been the decisive factor that persuaded NASA officials not to renew the contract with Morton Thiokol. Thus, the well-being of the company might have been substantially harmed by a no-launch recommendation.

Despite these arguments, we believe that the launch decision was properly an engineering decision, even though it perhaps was not a paradigm case of such a decision.

First, criterion 1 of the PMD was not as compelling a consideration as Mason may have supposed. There was no evidence that a no-launch decision would threaten the survival of Morton Thiokol, or even that it would in any fundamental way jeopardize Thiokol's well-being. In any case, engineering considerations should have had priority.

Second, criterion 2 of the PED was relevant because the decision to launch violated the engineer's propensity to modify or change criteria only in small increments. The temperature on the launch day was more than 20 degrees below that of any previous launch day. This was an enormous change, which should have given an engineer good reason to object to the launch.

Third, criterion 1 of the PED was relevant. Even though the quantitative data were limited and clearly did not give conclusive evidence that there would be a disaster, the data did seem to point in that direction so that the engineering need for quantitative measures was satisfied to some extent. Engineers, furthermore, are alert to the fact that composites, such as the ones the O-rings are made of, are temperature sensitive and that one could reasonably expect substantially lower temperatures to produce substantially greater blow-by problems.

Fourth, criterion 2 of the PED was also relevant because life was at stake. Engineers are obligated by their codes of ethics to be unusually cautious when the health and safety of the public are involved. This should be particularly important when those at risk do not give informed consent to special dangers. This was the case with the astronauts, who did not have any knowledge of the problems with the O-rings. The importance of the safety issue was further highlighted because of the violation of the practice of requiring the burden of proof to be borne by anyone advocating a launch decision rather than a no-launch decision. In testimony before the Rogers Commission, Robert Lund recounts this all-important shift in the burden of proof:

Chairman Rogers: How do you explain the fact that you seemed to change your mind when you changed your hat?

Mr. Lund: I guess we have got to go back a little further in the conversations than that. We have dealt with Marshall for a long time and have always been in the position of defending our position to make sure that we were ready to fly, and I guess I didn't realize until after that meeting and after several days that we had absolutely changed our position from what we had before. But that evening I guess I had never had those kinds of things come from the people at Marshall that we had to prove to them that we weren't ready.... And so we got ourselves in the thought process that we were trying to find some way to prove to them it wouldn't work, and we were unable to do that. We couldn't prove absolutely that the motor wouldn't work.

Chairman Rogers: In other words, you honestly believed that you had a duty to prove that it would not work?

Mr. Lund: Well that is kind of the mode we got ourselves into that evening. It seems like we have always been in the opposite mode. I should have detected that, but I did not, but the roles kind of switched.[85]

This last-minute reversal of a long-standing policy, requiring the burden of proof to rest with anyone recommending a no-launch rather than a launch decision, was a serious threat to the integrity of the engineering obligation to protect human life.

Although hindsight no doubt benefits our judgment, it does seem that the decision whether to recommend launch was properly an engineering decision rather than a management decision, even though it may not have been a paradigm case of a proper engineering decision. There is insufficient reason to believe that the case diverged so much from the paradigm engineering decision that management considerations should have been allowed to override the engineering constraints. Engineers, not managers, should have had the final say on whether to launch. Or, if the person making the recommendation wore both an engineering hat and a management hat—as Robert Lund did—he should have kept his engineering hat on when he made the decision. The distinction between paradigmatic engineering and management decisions and the attendant methodology developed here help to confirm this conclusion.

Whistleblowing and Organizational Loyalty

Boisjoly's attempt in the teleconference to stop the launch was probably not an instance of whistleblowing. It certainly was not an instance of external whistleblowing because Boisjoly made no attempt to alert the public or officials outside Thiokol and NASA. His actions on the night before the launch were probably not even internal whistleblowing because (1) they did not involve revealing information that was not known (rather, they made arguments about the information already available) and (2) he did not go out of approved channels. His testimony before the Rogers Commission, however, might be considered a case of whistleblowing because it did fulfill these two criteria. His testimony revealed information that the general public did not know, and it used channels outside the organization, namely the Rogers Commission. Was his testimony a case of justified whistleblowing?

First, let us look at DeGeorge's criteria. Since his criteria are utilitarian in orientation and focus on preventing harm, our first response might be to say that Boisjoly's testimony before the Rogers Commission could not be an instance of whistleblowing because the tragedy had already occurred. One writer has argued, however, that Boisjoly thought his testimony might contribute to the safety of future flights. He cites as his evidence a speech Boisjoly made at MIT, during which he reminded the audience that, as professional engineers, they had a duty "to defend the truth and expose any questionable practice that may lead to an unsafe product."[86] Whether or not Boisjoly actually believed his testimony might prevent future disasters, we can ask whether his testimony is in fact justified as a possible way to prevent future disasters. Certainly the harm of future disasters is serious and considerable (criterion 1). We can probably agree that, given his past experience, Boisjoly had reason to believe that reporting his concerns to his superiors would not give satisfaction (criteria 2 and 3). If this is correct, his testimony, considered as a case of whistleblowing, would be justified. Given the facts of the *Challenger* disaster, his testimony would probably convince a responsible, impartial observer that something should be done to remedy the O-ring problems (criterion 4). Whether he had strong evidence for believing that making this information public would prevent such harms in the future (criterion 5) is probably much more doubtful.

We can probably conclude, therefore, that from the standpoint of DeGeorge's criteria, Boisjoly's whistleblowing was justified but not required. In any case, it is clear that—as one would expect from criteria that adopt a utilitarian standpoint—the major issue has to do with the legitimacy of our beliefs about the consequences of certain courses of action.

Now let us consider Boisjoly's testimony from the standpoint of Davis' criteria for justified whistleblowing. Unlike DeGeorge's criteria, where concern for preventing future harms must be the primary consideration, here we must be concerned with Boisjoly's need to preserve his own moral integrity. Was he complicit enough in the wrongdoing so that whistleblowing was necessary to preserve his own moral integrity? To review the criteria, his whistleblowing was certainly related to his work in the organization. Furthermore, he was a voluntary member of that organization. Also, he almost certainly believed that Morton Thiokol, though a legitimate organization, was engaged in a serious moral wrong. The central issue is raised by the fourth criterion, namely whether he believed that his work for Thiokol contributed (more or less directly) to the disaster so that if (but not only if) he failed to publicly reveal what he knew he would be a contributor to the disaster. Following on this are the questions of whether he was justified in a belief that continued silence would make him complicit in wrongdoing and whether in fact this belief was true.

In order to better focus on the question of what it means to say that one's work contributes to wrongdoing, A. David Kline asks us to consider the following two examples.[87] In the first example, Researcher 1 is directed by his tobacco company to provide a statistical analysis that shows that smoking is not addictive. He knows that his analysis is subject to serious criticism, but his company nevertheless uses his work to mislead the public. In the second example, Researcher 2 is directed by his tobacco company to study the issue of smoking and addiction. He concludes that there is strong evidence that smoking is addictive, but his firm ignores his work and makes public claims that smoking is not addictive. According to Kline, Researcher 1 is complicit in the deception of the public, and Researcher 2 is not complicit. However, Boisjoly's situation, according to Kline, is closer to that of Researcher 2 than that of Researcher 1. Since the claim that Boisjoly was complicit in wrongdoing is false, Kline believes that Davis cannot justify Boisjoly's blowing the whistle by his criteria. Boisjoly is not required to blow the whistle in order to preserve his own moral integrity.

However, let us modify Davis' criteria so that the question becomes whether remaining silent would make Boisjoly complicit in future wrongdoing by Thiokol. Here, there are two questions: whether blowing the whistle would prevent future wrongdoing (a factual question) and whether silence would make Boisjoly complicit in wrongdoing (an application question). If the answer to both of these questions is in the affirmative, Boisjoly should blow the whistle.

We shall leave it to the reader to more fully explore these questions, but only point out that both theories of whistleblowing add useful dimensions to the study of the moral dimensions of the issue. It is important to ask whether blowing the whistle will prevent wrongdoing and to ask whether and to what extent our own moral integrity is compromised by silence. In practical deliberation, both questions are important. A final issue raised by Boisjoly's testimony is whether he violated the obligation of loyalty to his firm. His action was probably a violation of uncritical loyalty, but it was not a violation of critical loyalty, at least if his blowing the whistle was justified. In this situation, these two questions cannot be divorced.

7.12 CHAPTER SUMMARY

Outstanding organizational leaders such as Amazon's Jeff Bezos and Interface Carpets' Ray Anderson have set high standards for organizational behavior and communication. Both leaders expect ethical employees who value the customer and the communities where they operate. With thorough communication, small work teams and other strategies, the culture within an organization can be agreeable.

Conflicts between employees, including engineers, and managers often occur in the workplace. Sociologist Robert Jackall gives a negative account of the moral integrity of managers, implying that it may be difficult for an employee to preserve his integrity in the workplace. Other writers, however, have contradicted this account, implying that employees can usually be morally responsible without sacrificing their careers. In order to preserve their careers and their integrity, employees should educate themselves in the "culture" of their organization. They should also adopt some common-sense techniques for minimizing the threats to their careers when making a legitimate protest.

Given that engineers and managers have different perspectives, problems can be avoided if organizations make a distinction between decisions that should be made by managers and decisions that should be made by engineers. In general, engineers should make the decision when technical matters or issues of professional ethics are involved. Managers should make the decision when considerations related to the wellbeing of the organization are involved and the technical and ethical standards of engineers are not compromised. Many decisions do not neatly fall into either category, and the line-drawing method can be useful in deciding who should make a decision.

Sometimes organizational disobedience is necessary. One type of organizational disobedience is engaging in activities (typically outside the workplace) contrary to the interest of the organization, as these interests are defined by managers. Another type of organizational disobedience is refusing to participate, or asking to be relieved of an obligation to participate, in some task in the organization. A third type of organizational disobedience is protesting a policy or action of an organization. The most widely discussed example of this third type of disobedience is whistleblowing. Richard DeGeorge's theory of justified whistleblowing focuses on the weighing of the relevant harms and benefits. Michael Davis' theory of justified whistleblowing focuses on the question whether whistleblowing is required in order to relieve one of complicity in wrongdoing. The Sarbanes-Oxley and Dodd-Frank acts have guidelines that reward whistleblowing by employees. Employers are hopeful, that problems within the organization can be solved when recognized before the information is taken public. Common law on the rights of employees in the workplace has been governed by the common law doctrine of employment at will, which holds that in the absence of a contract, an employer may discharge an employee at any time and virtually for any reason. Some recent court decisions have modified this doctrine by an appeal to "public policy," which gives protection to some actions by employees. Some statutory law also accords employees some rights against their employers.

7.13   ENGINEERING ETHICS ON THE WEB

Check your understanding of the material in this chapter by visiting the companion website for *Engineering Ethics*. The site includes multiple choice study questions, suggested discussion topics, and sometimes additional case studies to complement your reading and study of the material in this chapter.

NOTES

1. George Anders, "Jeff Bezos Gets It," *Forbes*, April 23, 2012, p. 76.
2. Ibid, p. 81.
3. Ibid.
4. Ibid, p. 82.
5. Ibid.
6. Ibid, p. 82, 84.
7. David Ulrich, "The Value of Values," Talk at Utah Valley University, March 1, 2010, p. 1.
8. Ibid., p. 2.
9. Ibid.
10. Ibid.
11. Ibid., p. 11.
12. Anders, "Jeff Bezos Gets It," p. 82.
13. Ulrich, "The Value of Values," p. 4.
14. Ibid.
15. Ray C. Anderson and Robin White, *Confessions of a Radical Industrialist: Profits, People, Purpose—Doing Business by Respecting the Earth* (New York: St. Martin's Griffin, 2009), p. 17.
16. Ibid.
17. Ibid
18. Dennis Moberg, "Ethics Blind Spots in Organizations: How Systematic Errors in Person Perception Undermine Moral Agency," *Organizational Studies*, 27, no. 3, 2006, p. 414.
19. Max H. Bazerman, and Ann E. Tenbrunsel, *Blind Spots: Why We Fail to Do What's Right and What to Do about It* (Princeton: Princeton University Press, 2011), p. 29.
20. For an excellent discussion of various forms this can take, see Margaret Heffernan, *Willful Blindness* (Princeton, NJ: Walker and Company, 2011).
21. "Dogged Engineer's Effort to Assess Shuttle Damage," p. A1.
22. *Columbia* Accident Investigation Board, p. 24.
23. Ibid, p. 122
24. Ibid, p. 198
25. Ibid, pp., 168, 170, 198.
26. Bazerman and Tenbrunsel, p. 5
27. This expression was introduced into engineering ethics literature by Michael Davis. See his "Explaining Wrongdoing," Journal of Social Philosophy, XX, now 1 & 2, Spring-Fall 1989, pp. 74–90. Davis applies this notion to the *Challenger* disaster, especially when Robert Lund was asked to take off his engineer's hat and put on his manager's hat.
28. Stanley Milgram, *Obedience to Authority* (New York: Harper & Row, 1974).
29. It might be thought that, after a series of unpopular wars and a variety of social protest movements, Milgram's results could not be replicated today—we are less likely to defer, uncritically to authority. However, a recent replication of much of the Milgram experiment suggests that this is not so. See Jerry Bulger, "Replicating Milgram: Would People Obey Today?" *American Psychologist*, 2009, vol. 64, no. 1, pp. 1–11.
30. Irving Janis, *Groupthink*, 2nd ed. (Boston: Houghton Mifflin, 1982).
31. The most recent edition of the McGraw-Hill video *Groupthink* features the *Challenger* disaster as illustrating Janis's symptoms of groupthink.
32. Ibid, pp. 174–175.
33. "Dogged Engineer's Effort to Assess Shuttle Damage," p. A1.
34. *Columbia* Accident Investigation Board, p. 203.
35. J. Patrick Wright, *On a Clear Day You Can See General Motors*, (Detroit, MI: Wright Enterprises, 1979), p. 237.
36. Ibid.
37. Ralph Nader, *Unsafe at Any Speed*, New York: Grossman Publishers, 1965, p. 14.

38. Ibid.
39. Wright, *On a Clear Day*, p. 237.
40. Joseph A. Raelin, *The Clash of Cultures: Managers and Professionals* (Boston: Harvard Business School Press, 1985), p. xiv.
41. Ibid., p. 12.
42. Ibid., p. 270.
43. Robert Jackall, *Moral Mazes: The World of Corporate Managers* (New York: Oxford University Press, 1988), p. 5.
44. Ibid., pp. 105–7.
45. Ibid., p. 69.
46. Ibid., p. 112.
47. Anderson and White, *Confessions*, p. 28.
48. Anders, "Jeff Bezos Gets It," p. 82.
49. Ibid., p. 76.
50. Christopher Meyers, "Institutional Culture and Individual Behavior: Creating the Ethical Environment," *Science and Engineering Ethics*, 10, 2004, p. 271.
51. Patricia Werhane, *Moral Imagination and Management Decision Making* (New York: Oxford University Press, 1999), p. 56 (Quoted in Raelin, *Clash of Cultures*, p. 271.).
52. Michael Davis, "Better Communication between Engineers and Managers: Some Ways to Prevent Many Ethically Hard Choices," *Science and Engineering Ethics*, 3, 1997, p. 185; see also pp. 184–193 for the ensuing discussion.
53. Stephen H. Unger, *Controlling Technology: Ethics and the Responsible Engineer*, 2nd ed. (New York: Wiley, 1994), pp. 122–23.
54. See the discussion in Davis, op. cit., p. 207.
55. Meyers, op. cit., p. 257.
56. Raelin also points out the importance of professional loyalties that transcend the organization, contrasting the "local" orientation of managers with the "cosmopolitan" orientation of most professionals. While describing engineers as more locally oriented than most professionals, he does not deny that engineers have loyalties to professional norms that transcend loyalties to their own organization. See Raelin, pp. 115–18, for a description of the local–cosmopolitan distinction.
57. State-of-the-art technology may not always be appropriate. If an engineer is designing a plow for use in a less industrialized country, then simplicity, ease of repair, and availability of repair parts may be more important than the use of the most advanced technology.
58. We are indebted to Michael Davis for this and several other insights in this section. Davis uses John Rawls's term lexical ordering to describe the assigning of priorities. Rawls, however, seems to equate serial ordering with lexical ordering. He defines a lexical order as "an order which requires us to satisfy the first principle in the ordering before we can move on to the second, the second before we consider the third, and so on. A principle does not come into play until those previous to it are either fully met or do not apply. A serial ordering avoids, then, having to balance principles at all; those earlier in the ordering have an absolute weight, so to speak, with respect to the later ones, and hold without exception." See John Rawls, *A Theory of Justice* (Cambridge, MA: Harvard University Press, 1971), p. 43; see also Michael Davis, "Explaining Wrongdoing," *Journal of Social Philosophy*, 20, Spring–Fall 1988, pp. 74–90.
59. For purposes of this analysis, we are assuming that all decisions are either PEDs or PMDs— that is, they should be made by either managers or engineers rather than by anyone else.
60. Jim Otten, "Organizational Disobedience," in Albert Flores, ed., *Ethical Problems in Engineering* (Troy, NY: Center for the Study of the Human Dimensions of Science and Technology, 1980), pp. 182–86.
61. *Pierce v. Ortho Pharmaceutical* 319 A.2d, p. 178. This case occurred in 1982.

62. Alison Ross Wimsatt, "The Struggles of Being Ernest: A. Ernest Fitzgerald, Management Systems Deputy in the Office of the Asst. Sec of the Air Force," *Industrial Management*, July 2005, p. 28.

63. Ibid.

64. Ibid.

65. Michael Davis, "Whistleblowing," in Hugh LaFollette, ed., *The Oxford Handbook of Practical Ethics* (New York: Oxford University Press, 2003), p. 540.

66. Richard T. DeGeorge, *Business Ethics* (New York: Macmillan, 1982), p. 161. This account is taken directly from Richard T. DeGeorge, "Ethical Responsibilities of Engineers in Large Organizations," *Business and Professional Ethics Journal*, 1, no. 1, Fall 1981, pp. 1–14.

67. Several of these criticisms are suggested by Gene G. James, "Whistle-Blowing: Its Moral Justification," reprinted in Deborah G. Johnson, ed., *Ethical Issues in Engineering* (Englewood Cliffs, NJ: Prentice Hall, 1991), pp. 263–78.

68. Ibid

69. Michael Davis, "Whistleblowing," p. 549.

70. Ibid, pp. 549–50.

71. Several of these criticisms are taken from A. David Kline, "On Complicity Theory," *Science and Engineering Ethics*, 12, 2006, pp. 257–64.

72. See Unger, *Controlling Technology*, pp. 122–23.

73. Sarbanes-Oxley Act 2002. "The Sarbanes-Oxley Act." Last modified 2006. Accessed April 7, 2012. http://www.soxlaw.com.

74. Dodd-Frank Wall Street Reform and Consumer Protection Act of 2010, Pub. L. No. 111-203, 124 Stat. 1376 (2012), (http://www.sec.gov/about/laws/wallstreetreform-cpa.pdf).

75. Allen B. Roberts, "Dodd-Frank Bounty Awards and Protections Change: Whistleblower Stakes—Will Opportunity for Personal Gain Frustrate Corporate Compliance?" *Bloomberg Finance L. P.*, 5, no. 23, 2011.

76. Ibid.

77. Justice Quinn, "The Opinion of the Court in *Lorenz v. Martin Marietta Corp., Inc.*" 802 P.2d 1146 (Colo. App. 1990).

78. See "Protecting Employees at Will against Wrongful Discharge: The Public Policy Exception," *Harvard Law Review*, 96, no. 8, June 1983, pp. 1931–51.

79. Genna H. Rosten, "Wrongful Discharge Based on Public Policy Derived from Professional Ethics Codes," *52 American Law Reports*, 5, p. 405.

80. *Wall Street Journal*, April 13, 1981.

81. NJ Stat Ann at 34:19-1 to 19-8.

82. *Report of the Presidential Commission on the Space Shuttle Challenger Accident*, vol. IV, Feb. 26, 1986 to May 2, 1986, p. 764.

83. Roger Boisjoly, "The *Challenger* Disaster: Moral Responsibility and the Working Engineer," in Deborah Johnson, *Ethical Issues in Engineering* (Englewood Cliffs, NJ: Prentice Hall, 1991), p. 6.

84. *Presidential Commission on the Space Shuttle Challenger Accident*, pp. 772–773.

85. Ibid, p. 811.

86. Roger Boisjoly, "The Challenger Disaster: Moral Responsibility and the Working Engineer," op. cit., p. 14. Quoted in A David Kline, "On Complicity Theory," Science and Engineering Ethics, 12, 2006, p. 259.

87. Kline, op. cit., p. 262.

CHAPTER EIGHT

Engineers and the Environment

Main Ideas in This Chapter

- Engineering codes and environmental laws mandate a concern for the environment, but there is still considerable controversy about the nature and extent of professional or legal obligations to the environment.
- Several environmental writers were important in initiating the concern for the environment, and their ideas are still influential.
- Central to environmental philosophy are concepts such as anthropocentrism, nonanthropocentrism, obligations to future generations, and environmental justice.
- Business responses to environmental regulations vary from subminimal to progressive. Business responses can go beyond the law in several ways, one example being the CERES Principles.
- A major aspect of the engineering response to the environmental challenge is the pursuit of sustainability, especially by way of Life Cycle Analysis.
- The philosophy of environmental stewardship provides a basis for professional obligation to the environment. To implement it effectively, engineers should have the right of professional dissent from organizational actions that oppose environmentalism.

MARK HOLTZAPPLE, PROFESSOR OF CHEMICAL engineering at Texas A&M University, is a paragon of an environmentally conscious engineer. Early in his career, Holtzapple decided to devote his research agenda to developing energy-efficient and environmentally friendly technologies. To this end, he is pursuing several areas of research, including:

- *Biomass conversion.* He is developing a process that converts biological material into useful fuels and chemicals. Feedstocks to the process include municipal solid waste, sewage sludge, agricultural residues (e.g., sugarcane bagasse, corn stover, or manure), and energy crops (energy cane or sweet sorghum). He has a pilot plant near his university that will generate data needed to help commercialize the process. The process is sustainable and reduces greenhouse gas emissions.
- *A water-based air conditioner.* This air conditioner does not employ environmentally destructive refrigerants, and it promises to be substantially more energy-efficient than are conventional air conditioners.
- *StarRotor engine.* This rotary engine is highly efficient and emits virtually no pollution. It can use a wide variety of fuels, including gasoline, diesel, methane,

alcohol, and even vegetable oil. Holtzapple believes the engine should last for as long as 1 million miles when used in automobiles.

- *Water desalinization.* He is currently working on a water-desalinization process that he believes will cost-effectively convert seawater into freshwater suitable for human consumption.

Among his numerous awards, Professor Holtzapple won the 1996 Green Chemistry Challenge Award given by the President and Vice-President of the United States.

8.1 INTRODUCTION

Engineers have a complex relationship to the environment. On the one hand, they have helped to produce some of the environmental problems that plague human society. Air and water pollution, flooding of farm land, draining of wetlands—all of these can be attributed in part to engineering. On the other hand, engineers like Dr. Holtzapple can design projects, products, and processes that reduce or eliminate the same threats to environmental integrity. If engineers have contributed to environmental problems, they are also an essential part of their solution.

What obligations does the engineering profession have toward the environment and how should those obligations be fulfilled? This chapter will address this question. We begin by pointing out that engineers' own codes are beginning to impose environmental obligations on engineers. We continue by pointing out that the law also sets up parameters regarding the environment within which engineers must practice. Then we consider ethical issues raised by environmental concerns and some positions that can be taken regarding them. Finally, we suggest that engineers should practice good environmental stewardship.

8.2 ENVIRONMENTAL IMPERATIVES IN ENGINEERING CODES AND THE LAW

Many engineering codes now make reference to the environment, although most of the provisions are stated in relatively weak terms. The National Society of Professional Engineers (NSPE) code, for example, only "encourages" (not requires) engineers to "adhere to the principles of sustainable development in order to protect the environment for future generations" (iii.2.d). The American Society of Civil Engineers (ASCE) code says that engineers "should be committed to improving the environment by adherence to the principles of sustainable development so as to enhance the quality of life of the general public" (1.e). The same code uses the word "shall" in other guidelines that are mandatory. Requirements in other engineering codes are often even less detailed.

Federal environmental laws, which began to be enacted during the 1960s, impose restrictions on engineering to protect the environment. In 1969 Congress passed the National Environmental Policy Act (NEPA), which may well be the most important and influential environmental law in history. It has served as a model for legislation not only in the particular states in the United States but also in many other countries. The act declared "a national policy which will encourage productive and enjoyable harmony between man and his environment." The act attempts to "assure for all Americans safe, healthful, productive and aesthetically and culturally pleasing surroundings."[1] One of its best-known mandates is the environmental impact statement, which is now required of federal agencies when their decisions affect the environment. Congress then created the Environmental Protection Agency (EPA) to enforce its mandates.

Many statutes, such as the Clean Air Act (1970), the Resource Conservation and Recovery Act (RCRA) (1976), and others, expanded the jurisdiction of the federal government in environmental areas. One other environmental law merits special attention. The Pollution Prevention Act of 1990 established pollution prevention as a national objective. The act requires the EPA to develop and implement a strategy to promote reduction of the pollutant's source. This policy is in sharp contrast to most environmental protection laws, which simply attempt to manage pollutants once they have been created. This act established pollution prevention as the most desirable practice, followed by recycling, treatment, and disposal, in descending order of preference.

Faced with the challenge of interpreting environmental laws, the courts have usually adopted a middle path between extremes. On the one hand, as the famous Supreme Court decision regarding allowable levels of benzene in the workplace shows, "safe" does not mean "risk free."[2] On the other hand, as the 1986 decision of the Circuit Court in the District of Columbia shows, some costs to industry can be tolerated for the sake of environmental protection as long as they are not "grossly disproportionate" to the level of safety achieved.[3]

Most environmental laws focus on making the environment "clean"—that is, free from various pollutants, but there is considerable controversy about the proper criterion for "clean." It is not easy, however, to formulate the precise criterion for "clean" that the courts would endorse or that would seem to be justifiable. Here are several possibilities for consideration: (1) According to the *comparative criterion*, the environment is "clean" if it imposes no greater threat to human life or health than do other risks. (2) According to the *normalcy criterion*, the environment is "clean" if the pollutants present in it are normally present in nature to the same degree. (3) According to the *optimal pollution reduction criterion*, the environment is "clean" if funds required to reduce pollution further could be used in other ways that would produce more overall human well-being. (4) According to the *maximum protection criterion*, the environment is "clean" only if any identifiable risk from pollution that poses a threat to human health has been eliminated, up to the limits of technology and legal enforcement. (5) According to the *demonstrable harm criterion*, the environment is "clean" if every pollutant that is demonstrably harmful to human health has been eliminated. (6) According to the *degree of harm criterion*, the environment is "clean" if cost is not a factor in removing clear and pressing threats to human health, but when the degree of harm is uncertain, economic factors are considered.

The first two criteria impose rather weak standards. The third criterion, which is clearly utilitarian, is a form of cost-benefit analysis. The fourth criterion disregards considerations of cost. The fifth criterion requires proof of harm to human health, which is sometimes very difficult to obtain. The sixth seems to the authors to provide the best balance of cost and health considerations and may be closest to the positions taken in many court decisions.

8.3   THE ENVIRONMENTAL CHALLENGE

Both the environmental laws passed in the last few decades in the United States and elsewhere and the environmental statements in engineering codes reflect a widespread and increasing belief that the human effect on the environment is a cause for concern. This belief has many different sources. Two of these are the writings of influential environmental thinkers and philosophical discussions of environmentalism. In the next two sections we discuss these sources. These sources challenge the traditional neglect of the environment.

Three Influential Writers

Aldo Leopold was an American author and scientist. In 1949 he published one of the most important books in the environmental movement, *A Sand County Almanac*, a series of essays on environmental topics, some of them describing the land around his home in Sauk County, Wisconsin. Leopold used the expression "biotic community" to refer to the living and nonliving aspects of the natural world. Leopold's view is that nature is something to which we belong rather than something that belongs to us:

> We abuse land because we regard it as a commodity belonging to us. When we see land as a community to which we belong we may begin to use it with love and respect.... Perhaps such a shift in values can be achieved by reappraising things unnatural, tame, and confined in terms of things natural, wild, and free.[4]

Viewing nature as an interdependent biotic community, Leopold believed, elicits an ethical response. He called the ethical response the "land ethic" and stated its moral standard in these words: "A thing is right when it tends to preserve the integrity, stability, and beauty of the biotic community. It is wrong when it tends otherwise."[5]

Rachel Carson was a marine biologist with the US Fish and Wildlife Service who had a deep love of the natural world. In her time, DDT had become recognized as the most powerful pesticide available, but whose application resulted in massive insect kills. In *Silent Spring*, which was published in 1962 and took four years to complete, she described how DDT entered the food chain and accumulated in the fatty tissue of humans and animals. In one chapter she described a fictional scene in which there was a silent spring because all of the birds, as well as many other forms of life, had been killed by DDT exposure.

In 1968 Garrett Hardin published "The Tragedy of the Commons" in the journal *Science*. In this famous and influential essay, Hardin depicts a problem that can be described in the following way.[6] Suppose there is a plot of land that can support a number of animals indefinitely. Call this the *carrying capacity* of the plot of land, which we shall assume to be 100 animals. The land is jointly owned by 10 farmers, each of whom owns 10 animals, bringing the land to carrying capacity. Suppose each animal is worth $1, so that each farmer's animals are worth $10. One farmer, Greedy Farmer, decides to add one animal to his flock, so that all of the animals, using the land at above its carrying capacity, become leaner and are worth only $.95 each. Although the other farmers' flocks are now worth less, Greedy Farmer has 11 animals and a flock worth $10.45. Greedy Farmer thus reaps a benefit at the expense of the other farmers. Ultimately, everyone will probably suffer, because the overused land may continue to decline in productivity, but in the short run Greedy Farmer benefits at the expense of his neighbors. The point of our account of Hardin's simple story is that people can be driven by self-interest to abuse the environment in ways that ultimately harm everyone. Such policies are especially harmful to future generations, and Hardin's story has often been used as an argument for sustainability.

Key Environmental Concepts

These and other "environmental prophets," as they might be called, have highlighted the need to formulate the ethical demands that environmental considerations impose on us.

This formulation has been controversial, however, because our ethical systems, at least in the West, have been oriented primarily towards the responsibilities that humans have for each another. We are not used to thinking about our ethical obligations to the nonhuman world. It is easy to see why this is the case by considering the two moral models we have used before. From the utilitarian standpoint, our primary or even exclusive obligation is to promote human happiness or well-being. From the respect for persons standpoint, only humans are understood as moral agents, so only humans have rights that command our respect. In this section we can only enumerate some of the most significant philosophical issues that can arise when we think about the environment.

Given this human-centered or anthropocentric orientation of traditional Western ethics, it is not surprising that a common form of environmental ethics is *anthropocentrism*, which holds that nonhuman natural objects, including other animals, have value only as they contribute to human well-being. Natural objects, we can say, have only *instrumental value*—that is, value only insofar as they are used or appreciated by human beings. Destruction of forests can affect the supply of wood and the availability of recreational opportunities. Flooding farmlands or destroying the ecosystem can diminish the food supply for humans. Draining wetlands can damage the ecosystem in ways that ultimately harm human beings. The beauty of the natural world can have value because it gives pleasure to humans.

Garrett Hardin's argument for environmental concerns appears to be primarily anthropocentric in orientation: violating the carrying capacity of a plot of land can ultimately harm us or at least harm future generations. Rachel Carson's argument may also be anthropocentric, but this is not clear. Engineering codes appear to give an anthropocentric—and broadly utilitarian—justification for protecting the environment. Most codes commit engineers to holding paramount the safety, health, and welfare of the public. Insofar as protecting the environment is necessary to protect human safety, health, and welfare, the codes implicitly require environmental protection, whether or not they explicitly mention the environment. However, as we have seen, many engineering codes now have explicit environmental provisions, most or all of which appear to be anthropocentric in orientation.

Some environmentalists believe exclusively human-oriented ethical thinking is inadequate to justify a proper concern for the environment. They propose instead a *nonanthropocentric ethics*, which holds that at least some natural objects other than human beings have value in themselves, apart from their usefulness to human beings. To say that nonhuman entities can have value in themselves is to say that they have *intrinsic value* and not simply instrumental value. Nonanthropocentrists differ with regard to the nonhuman entities to which they ascribe intrinsic value. These differences are related to the criteria for *moral status*, or the ability to command moral obligation because of intrinsic value, which nonanthropocentrists adopt.[7] Some utilitarians find the criterion in the ability to experience pleasure, pain, and other conscious mental states. This criterion extends the scope of moral status from humans to most vertebrate animals (mammals, birds, fish, reptiles, and amphibians) and perhaps even to some complex invertebrates. Others argue that anything that strives to maintain its existence and reproduce its kind has moral status, thus extending the area of ethical concern to all organic life. Still others argue that organic life cannot exist without the supportive ecosystem, so that the entire ecosystem has moral status. Aldo Leopold's "land ethic" belongs in this category.

It is possible to combine elements of both an anthropocentric and nonanthropocentric ethics. A possible construction of a moral standard that has a stronger anthropocentric element than Leopold's, for example, but also a clear nonanthropocentric component:

> An action is right if it preserves and protects the natural world, even if it is not necessary to promote human welfare, but it is justifiable to take actions that harm the environment if the production of a human good is sufficiently great.

Consider the following case. Blind salamanders live in the aquifers beneath the city of Austin, Texas. They serve no human purpose, but the citizens of the city believe they should be protected. However, if destroying the salamanders is the only way to save large numbers of people in Austin, the destruction is justified by the above criterion. There is probably no way to define the term "sufficiently" in the above criterion in a general way. One must determine in particular situations what the term means.

We do not get very far into a discussion of environmental issues—and especially sustainability—until another question appears: what ethical obligations, if any, do we have to future generations of human beings? The anthropocentric orientation is the most widely accepted basis of an argument for the obligation to consider the well-being of future generations. When asked why they think we have an obligation to protect the environment, many people will reply, "Because we have an obligation to pass on to our children an environment that is in as good a shape as we found it." The reasons for this obligation and how extensive these obligations are turn out to be a matter of considerable controversy. Some who are skeptical of any obligation to future generations point out that moral obligations are ordinarily based on reciprocity. For example, if I have a right to life, you have a duty not to kill me. No such reciprocity exists between the present and future generations, since future generations cannot reciprocate to us in any way. Another objection is that we cannot know what future generations would demand of us. Despite these and other difficulties, most people probably believe we have obligations to future generations. Furthermore, regardless of how much the desires and needs of future generations might differ from our own, they would need certain basic things, such as clean air, clean water, and some natural resources.

One final problem raised by environmentalism deserves mention. *Environmental justice* refers to questions about the equitable distribution of environmental goods and harms, especially with regard to pollution and resource depletion. For example, in the 1980s, studies showed that the city of Houston, Texas, had placed all of its landfills and 75 percent of its waste incinerators in African-American communities, even though African-Americans made up only 25 percent of its population. Other research showed that the environmentally dirtiest zip codes in California were in those areas heavily populated by Latinos and African-Americans.[8] The issue of environmental justice arises in many engineering disasters, such as those in Bhopal, India, and Chernobyl, Russia, and it can pose serious problems for engineering responsibility.

8.4 RESPONDING TO THE ENVIRONMENTAL CHALLENGE: THE BUSINESS RESPONSE

Three Attitudes toward the Environment

Industry attitudes toward the environment fall into roughly three groups.[9] The first attitude is what we can call the *subminimal attitude*. Industries in this group do as little as possible—and sometimes less than is required—in meeting environmental regulations. They often have no full-time personnel assigned to environmental issues, devote minimal financial resources to environmental matters, and fight environmental regulations. If it is cheaper to pay the fines than make the mandated changes, this is what they will do. Managers in this group generally believe that the primary goal of business is to make money and that environmental regulations are merely an impediment go this goal.

The second attitude is what we call the *minimalist* or *compliance attitude*. Firms adopting this orientation accept governmental regulation as a cost of doing business, but their compliance is often without enthusiasm or commitment. Managers often have a great deal of skepticism about the value of environmental regulation. Nevertheless, these companies usually have established policies that regulate environmental matters and have established separate units devoted to them.

A third attitude is what we call the *progressive attitude*. In these companies, being responsive to environmental concerns has the complete support of the CEO. The companies have well-staffed environmental divisions, use state-of-the-art equipment, and generally have good relationships with governmental regulators. The companies generally view themselves as good neighbors and believe that it is probably in their long-term interests to go beyond legal requirements because doing so generates good will in the community and avoids lawsuits. More than this, however, they may be genuinely committed to environmental protection and even environmental enhancement.

An Example of the Progressive Attitude: The CERES Principles

After the oil spill from the *Exxon Valdez*, a number of oil companies voluntarily adopted a set of principles that embody a progressive attitude toward the environment. Originally called the Valdez Principles, the principles were renamed after Ceres, the Roman goddess of agriculture and fertility. We strongly suggest that the reader review this admirable set of principles for protecting the environment in their complete form at http://www.iisd.org/educate/learn/ceres.htm. The following is our summary, in abbreviated form, of the ten principles:

1. *Protection of the biosphere.* Reduce and make progress toward the elimination of any environmentally damaging substance, safeguard habitats, and protect open spaces and wilderness, while preserving biodiversity.
2. *Sustainable use of natural resources.* Make sustainable use of renewable natural sources, such as water, soils, and forests, and make careful use of nonrenewable resources.
3. *Reduction and disposal of wastes.* Reduce and, if possible, eliminate waste, and handle and dispose of waste through safe and responsible methods.
4. *Energy conservation.* Conserve energy and improve the energy efficiency of all operations, and attempt to use environmentally safe and sustainable energy sources.
5. *Risk reduction.* Strive to minimize environmental damage and health and safety risks to employees and surrounding communities, and be prepared for emergencies.
6. *Safe products and services.* Reduce and, if possible, eliminate the use, manufacture, or sale of products and services that cause environmental damage or health or safety hazards, and inform customers of the environmental impacts of products or services.

7. *Environmental restoration.* Promptly and responsibly correct conditions the company has caused that endanger health, safety, or the environment, redress injuries, and restore the environment when it has been damaged.

8. *Informing the public.* Inform in a timely manner everyone who may be affected by the actions of the company that affect health, safety, or the environment, and refrain from taking reprisals against employees who report dangerous incidents to management or appropriate authorities.

9. *Management commitment.* Implement these principles in a process that ensures that the board of directors and chief executive officer are fully informed about environmental issues and fully responsible for environmental policy, and make demonstrated environmental commitment a factor in selecting members of the board of directors.

10. *Audits and reports.* Conduct an annual self-evaluation of progress in implementing these principles, and complete and make public an annual CERES report.

Corporate self-interest no doubt plays a prominent role in motivating firms to adopt such policies. Many firms and industry groups have adopted progressive policies only after legal problems or strong and persistent public criticism. Probably one of the motivations for these policies is the desire to regain the trust of the public and avoid still more bad publicity. Progressive environmental policies also can keep firms out of trouble in the first place. Finally, progressive environmental policies may result in the creation of new products and processes, which can become profitable in the marketplace as environmental regulations become stricter.

8.5 RESPONDING TO THE ENVIRONMENTAL CHALLENGE: SUSTAINABILITY

What Is Sustainability?

A major element in the contemporary environmental movement, especially as it affects engineering, is the emphasis on sustainability. What does the term mean? According to the *American Heritage Dictionary*, it means "to keep in existence, maintain; prolong." As applied to the environment, sustainability implies not only keeping something in existence but also maintaining it at approximately the same level of quality or functioning. Thus, sustainable agriculture is not only maintaining the ability of the land to produce food but also maintaining its ability to produce food of approximately the same quality and quantity.

The best-known definition of sustainability is in the report of the World Commission on Environment and Development (WCED), commonly referred to as the Brundtland Report (G. H. Brundtland, prime minister of Norway, was the chairman of the commission). This document did not define sustainability but rather "sustainable development" as "development that meets the needs of the present without compromising the ability of future generations to meet their own needs."[10] The report identified five goals for sustainable development: economic growth, a fair distribution of resources to sustain economic development, more democratic political systems, adoption of lifestyles (a goal especially aimed at the more developed countries) that are more compatible with living within the planet's ecological means, and population levels (a goal especially aimed at the developing countries) that are more compatible with the planet's ecological means.

The report was an attempt to combine the need of the developing world for continued economic development in order to raise the standard of living, with the need for sustainability with regard to the limited resources of the earth and the needs of future generations. By combining the ideas of sustainability and development, the WCED implied that it is possible to have both sustainability and continued economic development. Some have denied this possibility, even maintaining that the term "sustainable development" combines two incompatible ideas, since the planet has limited resources.

How can we formulate a realistic concept of sustainability? First, consider the ideas of the following two writers. Economist Robert Solow says that sustainability is the obligation to conduct ourselves in such a way that we leave to posterity the ability to be as well off as we are: "What we are transmitting to our heirs is a *generalized* capacity to be as well off as we ourselves are."[11] Solow does not distinguish between renewable resources such as forests and nonrenewable resources such as hydrocarbons. He also assumes in his analysis that there is no difference between natural capital (water, hydrocarbons, etc.) and human capital (the products generated by human activity). Another assumption is the interchangeability of resources so that substitutes or replacements can always be found for every resource and ecosystem that our technology requires. For example, perhaps we can replace fossil fuels with solar energy. Engineer and environmental thinker John Ehrenfeld defines sustainability as "the possibility that human and other life will flourish on the planet forever."[12] Ehrenfeld's definition also assumes that replacements can be found for any and all resources needed by humans. It nevertheless makes the point that sustainability should be considered a goal or limit towards which humans, including engineers, should strive.

We can take these definitions as pointing towards a goal of *realistic sustainability*, which includes the following elements: (1) minimizing the use of nonrenewable resources and replacing them with renewable substitutes, (2) utilizing renewable resources only at the rate at which they can be replaced, (3) designing products and processes that are recyclable and minimize the production of waste, and (4) promoting the equitable distribution of the earth's resources and the benefits of economic development worldwide. Although the fourth criterion might seem to be beyond the scope of professional engineering, it is an important practical consideration in sustainability, since social stability may not be possible without it. For practical purposes, the first three are the most important for most engineers. How can these goals be realized?

Life Cycle Analysis

A considerable amount of funding for engineering projects comes through the National Science Foundation (NSF), which emphasizes sustainability in its Emerging Frontiers in Research and Innovation grants. Private enterprise is also finding "green" projects to be increasingly profitable. One of the most important techniques in developing environmentally friendly products is Life Cycle Assessment (LCA).[13] LCA is a "cradle-to-grave" analysis of the environmental impact of a product or a process—from the derivation of the raw materials from the earth to manufacture and use, to its final disposal. LCA does not measure many considerations that are important to industry, such as cost, availability of products, and marketability, so it does not provide an assessment of all the relevant considerations. However, it can be useful in industry in many ways: in making decisions regarding environmental impact, in reporting environmental impact to government agencies, and in marketing products as "environmentally friendly."

The LCA method has four parts: (1) In the *goal and scope definition*, the product or process is defined, as well as the context of the assessment, the boundaries of the analysis, and the environmental effects to be considered. The boundaries of the analysis include the geographical area considered, the temporal boundaries of the study, and the boundaries between the current life cycle and the related life cycles of other technical systems. (2) In the *inventory analysis*, a listing of the relevant inputs and outputs of a product is made, and the energy, water, materials used, and environmental releases are identified and quantified. Included here is the release of carbon dioxide and other greenhouse gases. The data collection forms must be properly designed, and of course the data must be accurate. Data collection is the most resource-consuming part of the LCA. (3) In the *impact assessment*, the most significant environmental impacts associated with the product are identified and quantified, including the resource use, human health and ecological consequences, and greenhouse gas emissions. In this phase, the potential human and ecological effects of the energy, water, and materials used that were identified in the inventory analysis are the focus of the analysis. (4) In the *interpretation* phase, the results of the first three phases are evaluated, along with the assumptions that are made and the degree of uncertainty that was assumed. The preferred product or process is then selected.

Here are some examples of how LCA can be used. A life cycle assessment has been done on diesel engines used on a bus fleet driven under urban conditions and a truck fleet driven mainly on highways. The main goal of this LCA was to determine whether it is beneficial from the environmental standpoint to use E-diesel fuels that contain ethanol rather than traditional fuels.[14] In another LCA, steel and plastic packaging were compared to determine which packaging has less environmental impact, what happens to the packaging after delivery to the end user, and what the differences are between packaging in Sweden and the rest of the world.[15]

8.6 ENVIRONMENTAL STEWARDSHIP AND ENGINEERING PROFESSIONALISM AND ETHICS

The emergence and increasing importance of environmental issues exhibits a recurring theme—the importance of an attitude of care or stewardship toward the natural world. In this section we consider this theme and its implication for engineering professionalism and ethics.

A Philosophy of Environmental Stewardship

A steward is a person charged with caring for property, often the property of another person, such as a king. Two aspects of stewardship are paramount. First, the steward has a duty of care for the property for which he has responsibility. Second, the property for which the steward has responsibility has value, usually great value. The concept of stewardship has been applied to the relationship of humans to the natural world, implying both that humans have a responsibility of care for the natural world and that the natural world has great value.

Stewardship ethics can be justified on either anthropocentric or non-anthropocentric grounds. A person taking the anthropocentric position will say that care for the natural world is necessary to protect the health and well-being of humans. Environmental degradation and a wasteful use of natural resources can produce health issues, decrease the production of food, limit the ability of present and future generations to provide for their material well-being, and give rise to many other undesirable consequences. A person taking the nonanthropocentric position will say that the natural world has intrinsic value apart from its usefulness to humans. One of the advantages of stewardship ethics from the practical standpoint of the engineer is that one need not resolve the anthropocentric/nonanthropocentric controversy. The important thing is that engineers, because of their special working relationship with the environment, have a special duty of care for the natural world.

The ethics of stewardship and care for the natural world has not been emphasized in traditional Western ethics, although some believe there is a basis for it in respect for persons and utilitarian thinking. First consider the standpoint of respect for persons ethics. This position has traditionally focused on our duty to respect human beings as moral agents. It is fundamentally anthropocentric. Nonhuman entities, to say nothing of inanimate objects, have no moral status. Therefore many Western ethicists believe that the only way to apply respect for persons ethics to environmental issues is by way of anthropocentrism: we should value and care for the natural world because of its importance to moral agents. Moral agents are dependent on the natural world for the resources necessary to achieve their purposes, and even for life itself. On these grounds, environmental stewardship is warranted.

With utilitarianism, the situation is somewhat more complex. Since the beginning of the utilitarian movement in the nineteenth century, utilitarians have believed that any being capable of experiencing pleasure and especially pain deserves moral consideration, thereby including many animal species in the realm of beings having moral status. The inclusion of animals not able to experience pleasure and pain, and of plants and inanimate objects, can be justified only because they are important to human well-being. The utilitarian can agree, then, that plants, the earth, air, and water have value, but this value can only be instrumental. While not exclusively anthropocentric or human-centered, utilitarianism cannot attribute intrinsic value to some aspects of nature. If we want to say that all of the natural world has intrinsic value and is deserving of our stewardship, we must go beyond the respect for persons and the utilitarian perspectives. Developing this new ethics is an important part of contemporary environmental ethics.

Environmental Stewardship and Professional Obligations

Because engineers create much of the technology that is involved in both environmental degradation and environmental improvement, they have a special professional obligation to the environment. Thus, engineers should share in the responsibility for environmental concerns because they are often causal agents in projects and activities that affect the environment for good or ill. Engineers design dams that flood farmlands and wild rivers. They design chemical plants that pollute the air and water. They also design solar energy systems that make hydroelectric projects unnecessary and pollution-control systems that eliminate the discharge of pollutants into the air and water. Furthermore, they usually are (or should be) aware of the effects of their work on the environment. If engineers are morally responsible agents in issues that affect the environment, they should also be required as professionals to be good environmental stewards.

Some critics object to imposing responsibilities on engineers regarding the environment. One objection is that many judgments regarding the environment fall outside of the professional expertise of engineering, often finding their basis in the biological sciences. If Engineer Mary objects to designing a plant on a drained wetland because she believes it will cause unacceptable damage to the ecology of the area, she is making a judgment outside the area of her professional competence. However, Mary may be objecting on the basis of testimony of experts in the area, or the knowledge may be so common and generally accepted that it is no longer the exclusive property of the expert.

Another objection is that imposing substantial environmental obligations on engineers may cause problems for individual engineers with their employers. If engineers agree with the environmental obligations but their employers do not, they may in extreme cases face dismissal. This objection suggests that engineering codes should offer protection for professional dissent from organizational directives. An addition to professional codes that embodies this right might be stated in the following way:

> Engineers shall have the right to voice responsible objections to organizational directives with which they disagree. Where possible, organizations shall not compel engineers to participate in projects that violate their professional obligations or personal conscience.

The nature and extent of engineering environmental obligations continues to be under discussion. These obligations will almost certainly continue to increase.

8.7 CHAPTER SUMMARY

Many engineering codes have statements regarding the environment, but the statements are very general and the wording makes it clear that the codes are recommending rather than requiring actions that protect the environment. Federal environmental laws, most of which were enacted during the 1960s or later, have been interpreted by the courts as taking a middle ground that balances obligations to the environment against cost and other considerations. Criteria for what constitutes a "clean" environment also show great variation.

Among the writers who could be considered "prophets" of the environmental movement are Aldo Leopold, Rachel Carson, and Garret Hardin. Their writings were important in initiating the contemporary environmental movement. Several concepts and issues are also significant in the emerging environmental philosophy: anthropocentrism, nonanthropocentrism, environmental justice, and the nature of our obligations to future generations.

The attitudes of business firms to the increasing concern for environmental protection show considerable variation. These attitudes can be classified into three groups: subminimal, minimalist or compliance, and progressive. An example of the progressive attitude of some business groups is the CERES Principles.

One of the responses of the engineering community to environmentalism is the pursuit of sustainability, whose definition is controversial. The most widely known definition is given by the Brundtland Commission, which defines sustainable development (not sustainability) as "development that meets the needs of the present without compromising the ability of future generations to meet their own needs." This definition is controversial, as are other proposed definitions. LCA is one way to implement sustainability, a method for assessing the "cradle-to-grave" environmental impact of a product or process. It does not address some considerations that are important to business, such as cost and marketability.

The philosophy of environmental stewardship provides an appropriate way to focus the environmental challenge for engineers, because it avoids the controversial conflict between anthropocentrism and nonanthropocentrism. Environmental obligations may, however, place engineers in a difficult position with respect to their employers. For this reason, engineering codes should have a provision that advocates the right of professional employees to dissent from employer policies with which they responsibly disagree. The provision should also endorse the desirability of allowing engineers to avoid participation in projects that they find contrary to their professional obligations, if it is practically possible to do this.

8.8 ENGINEERING ETHICS ON THE WEB

Check your understanding of the material in this chapter by visiting the companion website for *Engineering Ethics*. The site includes multiple choice study questions, suggested discussion topics, and sometimes additional case studies to complement your reading and study of the material in this chapter.

NOTES

1. 42 United States Code [USC] sect. 4331 (1982), note 20.
2. Industrial Union Dept. AFL-CIO v. American Petroleum Institute, 448 US 607, 642 (1980)
3. Natural Resource Defense Council v. EPA, 804 F.2d 719 (DC Cir. 1986).
4. Aldo Leopold, *A Sand County Almanac* (New York: Oxford University Press. 1994), pp. vii, ix.
5. Ibid., pp. 224–225.
6. For this description of the problem, see David Schmidtz and Elizabeth Willott, "The Tragedy of the Commons" in R.G. Frey and Christopher Heath Wellman, eds. *A Companion to Applied Ethics* (Malden, MA: Blackwell, 2003), pp. 662–684.
7. This discussion is indebted to Mary Ann Warren's "Moral Status" in R. G. Frey and Christopher Heath Wellman, eds., *A Companion to Applied Ethics* (Malden, MA: Blackwell, 2003), pp. 439–450.
8. Kristin Shrader-Frechette, "Environmental Ethics" in Hugh LaFollette, ed., *The Oxford Handbook of Practical Ethics* (Oxford: Oxford University Press, 2003), p. 201.
9. Joseph M. Petulla, "Environmental Management in Industry," *Journal of Professional Issues in Engineering*, 113:2, April 1987, pp. 167–183. Although this survey is now somewhat dated, an engineering colleague in environmental engineering confirms that industry responses still fall into roughly these three groups. Fortunately, more industries appear to have moved to the progressive category.
10. World Commission on Environment and Development, *Our Common Future* (Oxford: Oxford University Press, 1987), Cited in Stanley R. Carpenter, "Sustainability" in *Encyclopedia of Applied Ethics*, Ed. Ruth Chadwick (San Diego, CA: Academic Press, 1998), pp. 275–293.
11. Robert Solow, *Sustainability: An Economist's Perspective*. In Dorfman, R. and Dorfman, N. (eds.), *Economics of the Environment* (New York: W. W. Norton & Co., 1991), pp. 179–187.
12. John R. Ehrenfeld, *Sustainabililty by Design* (New Haven, CN: Yale University Press, 2008), p. 6. Italics the author's.

13. For this account of the LCA we are indebted to Professor Robin Autenrieth, professor of civil engineering, Texas A&M University.
14. http://www.dantes.info/Publications/Publications-info/proj_info_publ_Ediesel.html.
15. http://www.dantes.info/Publications/Publications-info/proj_info_publ_Packaging.html.

CHAPTER NINE

Engineering in the Global Context

Main Ideas in This Chapter

- Some progress has been made in establishing international technical standards. Creating a universal concept of professionalism would facilitate progress in developing international standards of conduct.

- Economic, cultural, and social differences between countries sometimes produce "boundary-crossing problems" for engineers. Solutions to these problems must avoid absolutism and relativism and should find a way between moral rigorism and moral laxism.

- Applying the standards of one's own country without modification or uncritically adopting the standards of the host country in which one is working are rarely satisfactory solutions to the moral dilemmas that arise in international engineering.

- Adaptations of the methods and standards for resolving ethical problems discussed in Chapter 2 can make them more applicable to problems encountered in the international arena. Solutions involving creative middle ways are often particularly useful.

- Engineering work in the international arena can raise many ethical issues, including exploitation, bribery, extortion, grease payments, nepotism, excessive gifts, paternalism, and paying taxes in a country where taxes are negotiable.

WALMART IS THE LARGEST RETAILER in the world.[1] Outside of the United States, its biggest success story is in Mexico. One out of five Walmart stores is now in Mexico. A story in the *New York Times* in April of 2012, however, revealed that widespread bribery played an important role in the firm's phenomenal growth in Mexico. From approximately 2005 until the present, Walmart officials paid more than $24 million in bribes to accelerate the processing of building permits, reduce environmental regulations, and eliminate any other obstacles to rapid expansion. Envelopes of cash were often delivered to government officials, including mayors, city council members, urban planners, and low-level bureaucrats who issued permits. Some of the bribes were conveyed by middlemen, who charged 6 percent for their services. Walmart had indeed perfected the art of bribery and then concealed it with fraudulent accounting.

One of the chief promoters of bribery was Eduardo Castro-Wright, former chief executive of Walmart de Mexico. He and other executives took steps to conceal the payments from Walmart headquarters in Bentonville, Arkansas. When headquarters finally got wind of the extensive bribery, they first sent investigators, but later shut down the investigation. None of the executives who were involved in the bribery were disciplined, and some were promoted, including Castro-Wright, who became vice chairman of Walmart in 2008.

9.1   INTRODUCTION

Although this story as presented did not directly involve engineers, it illustrates perhaps the most common ethical issue faced by US engineers when they work in other countries, and often in the United States as well, namely bribery. As we shall see, however, it is far from the only problem engineers face in the international arena. Engineering is becoming a globalized profession. Engineers from the United States and other countries now have employment in various parts of the world. Engineers have also established several regional and even worldwide engineering organizations and agreements. Most of these organizations are devoted to the standardization of criteria for engineering education and licensure, but some organizations have also suggested ethical and professional standards for their members. Establishing global professional standards is an important aspect of the internationalization of engineering.

This chapter focuses on the ethical and professional issues raised by the globalization of the engineering profession. We begin with a consideration of the attempt to standardize technical qualifications for engineering education and licensure and then turn to the question whether there can be an international concept of professionalism. We then enumerate some of the ethical and professional issues engineers face in the international arena.

9.2   THE EMERGENCE OF INTERNATIONAL ENGINEERING STANDARDS

Probably the most important single attempt to standardize criteria for engineering education is the Washington Accord. Established in 1989, the accord is an agreement among bodies that have the authority to accredit engineering programs in their respective countries or jurisdictions. The Accreditation Board for Engineering and Technology (ABET), which has the responsibility for accrediting engineering programs in the United States, signed the accord for the United States. The accord recognizes "substantial agreement" among the signatories in the requirements for engineering education, so that signatory countries or jurisdictions should recognize the qualifications of engineers graduating from accredited institutions in other signatory countries or jurisdictions. The engineers in the accredited jurisdictions are expected not only to meet minimal technical standards in their education but also to maintain their competency and abide by a code of conduct, although little is said about what these codes of conduct should contain. The original signatories were the United Kingdom, Ireland, the United States, Canada, Australia, and New Zealand. Later signatories include Hong Kong, South Africa, Japan, Singapore, Chinese Taipei, Malaysia, and Turkey.

Other agreements have promoted similar mutual recognition in related areas. The Sydney Accord, initiated in 2001, recognized substantial equivalence in accreditation qualifications in engineering technology, and the Dublin Accord, initiated in 2002, recognized substantial equivalence in the qualifications for engineering technicians.[2]

A much older organization, the Fédération Européenne d'Associations Nationales d'Ingénieurs (FEANI), or the European Federation of National Engineering Associations, has established common standards in Europe for licensing individual engineers. Rather than accrediting engineering schools, which was the focus of the Washington Accord, it awards the EUR ING professional title to engineers in an effort to "facilitate the mutual recognition of engineering qualifications in Europe and to strengthen the position, role and responsibility of engineers in society." The EUR ING title is much like the PE in the United States. The organization celebrated its sixtieth anniversary in 2012.[3]

Some international organizations give prominence to the promotion of ethical ideals for the engineering profession, rather than to education and licensure. The Federation of Engineering Institutions of Asia and the Pacific (FEIAP) has as its goal "to encourage the application of technical progress to economic and social advancement throughout the world; to advance engineering as a profession in the interest of all people; and to foster peace throughout the world."[4] The Commonwealth Engineers Council (CEC), which has members in 44 countries, seeks to "advance the science, art and practice of engineering for the benefit of mankind." The organization goes on to state: "Engineering is at the heart of social and economic development. As engineers we recognize our responsibility and the importance of working closely with other professions and with the engineering community at large." The CEC also is committed to development that is sustainable.[5]

These international organizations, taken as a group, show a commitment to both preventive and aspirational ethics. The concern for preventive ethics is evident in the promotion of high standards for the accreditation of engineering schools and for the licensing of individual engineers. These standards provide protection against professional incompetence, a key aspect of preventive ethics. The recognition of the importance of engineering in economic development and quality of life reflects the orientation of aspirational ethics.

9.3 AN INTERNATIONAL CONCEPT OF ENGINEERING PROFESSIONALISM?

While globalized standards for engineering education and licensure appear to be on the horizon, progress in establishing worldwide standards for professional conduct is less evident. One prerequisite for the development of worldwide standards of professional conduct may well be agreement on the concept of professionalism itself, since professional ethics is usually thought to be based on the concept of professionalism. Some ethicists anticipate difficulties, however, in achieving this goal. Japanese scholar Tetsuji Iseda, for example, holds that the concept of "professionalism" is a Western idea which is not universally applicable. Iseda argues that the concept of "profession" has no historical roots in Japanese culture, for example. Iseda points out that the concept of professionalism in the West is closely tied to the idea of an implicit social contract between professionals and the larger society, according to which professionals agree to provide expert service and self-regulation, in exchange for high pay and social prestige. Japanese engineers do not enjoy these advantages. They earn less pay than social scientists, and they do not have the high prestige associated with many other occupational groups. It is doubtful, Iseda believes, that appeal to the concept of being a "professional" has much plausibility for Japanese engineers or that it is sufficient to motivate engineers' compliance with the high standards of conduct associated with professionalism. In place of the concept of professionalism, Iseda proposes that Japanese engineers should be encouraged to comply with high standards of conduct by an appeal to an intrinsic pride in their work itself, regardless of its social recognition.[6]

In the light of these and other problems, can an international concept of professionalism be developed? One possible way to answer this question is to appeal to the notion of a profession as a particular instance of a social role. As Iseda recognizes, social recognition is an important part of the traditional notion of professionalism, so a socially recognized role is fundamental to the concept of professionalism. What is a social role? Let us say that a *social role* is a relationship among humans defined by a set of duties, prerogatives, and virtues that are determined by the relationship itself. Fortunately, people in virtually every culture have some understanding of social roles, with their attendant duties, prerogatives, and virtues. Probably the most universally recognized role is the role of parent. Parents have the duty to provide for the physical and emotional welfare of their children; they have certain prerogatives such as training children in their early religious and moral beliefs; and they should also have certain virtues appropriate to their role as parents, such as the virtue of care. Children, on the other hand, have the duty to follow the guidance of parents and the right to expect to be taken care of physically and emotionally during their early years. They should also have certain virtues appropriate to their role as children, such as respect and obedience.

Parenthood is not the only widely recognized social role. Most cultures have many highly visible and institutionalized social roles: parents, children, military officers, priests or other religious figures, government ministers, and many others. In India, the traditional caste system, still influential in Indian society, assigns special role responsibilities and prerogatives to various castes, including workers, warriors, and priests. Confucian culture is especially known for its emphasis on the importance of compliance with the requirements of social roles. Here is a statement of Confucius about proper behavior in social roles (or *li*):

> What I have learned is this, that of all things that people live by, *li* is the greatest. Without *li* we do not know how to conduct a proper worship of the spirits of the universe; or how to establish the proper status of the king and the ministers, the ruler and the ruled, and the elders and the juniors; or how to establish the moral relationships between the sexes; between parents and children, and between brothers; or how to distinguish the different degrees of relationships in the family. That is why a gentleman holds *li* in such high regard.[7]

For many Confucians, there are five great social roles and associated virtues: kindness in the father, filial piety in the son; gentility in the eldest brother, humility and respect in the younger; religious behavior in the husband, obedience in the wife; humane consideration in elders, deference in juniors; benevolence in rulers, and loyalty in ministers and subjects.[8]

Social roles have the following characteristics, among others: (1) A social role supports a social good that is generally approved in a society. Most people in a society approve of the relationship of parents and children as promoting the proper raising of children, for example. (2) A social role is usually connected with formal or informal social institutions. The home might be considered a more informal institution, but government ministers are connected with more formal institutions. (3) A social role is usually connected with a "role morality" that consists of duties, prerogatives, and virtues that are connected to the function of the role in society. The example of parenthood has already been mentioned. (4) Social roles can conflict with each other. Most people occupy several social roles, and these roles may be associated with different obligations. In some cases, simple time requirements for performing various roles may produce conflict problems. A person's role as parent can conflict with his or her role as an employee due to conflicting time demands and perhaps for other reasons. (5) A person's social role can conflict with other aspects of his or her life. A child's desires to pursue his or her career in a distant city may conflict with his or her obligations to care for aging parents.

The parallels between social roles as they are understood in most cultures with the traditional Western notion of professionalism, including engineering professionalism, are obvious. (1) The professions, including engineering, perform functions that are perceived as a social good in most cultures. In engineering, this function is the development, operation, and distribution of technology. (2) Like other social roles, the professions, including engineering, are connected with social institutions. These include government institutions, businesses of various sorts, and professional societies. (3) The professions, including engineering, have role moralities in the form of codes of ethics and other standards of conduct that govern their behavior and are closely connected with their functions. For example, requirements of high educational standards and the prohibitions of conflicts of interest and of practicing outside the professional's area of expertise are important aspects of professional ethics in most professions, including engineering. The requirements are justified because they are important in insuring the quality of the services professionals render to clients and employers. (4) The role of professional, including the role of an engineer, can conflict with other social roles an individual may occupy. For example, one's role as an engineer may conflict with his or her role as an employee. If the employer asks the engineer to do something incompatible with his or her professional status, such as make misrepresentations in public statements about technical issues, the engineer can face a conflict between his or her role as an engineer and his or her role as an employee. (5) The role obligations of professionals, including engineers, can on occasion conflict with personal beliefs. For example, an engineer's beliefs about the environment may conflict with professional requirements. The engineer may not be sympathetic with environmental protection, even though the engineering codes require it.

Virtually all cultures have social roles that play a central part in their functioning, and a case can be made that the professions, including engineering, are another type of social role. If this is the case, developing a worldwide appreciation of the notion of a "profession" with its attendant prerogatives, obligations, and virtues, and of engineering as a profession might be possible. How can the acceptance of engineering understood as a new social role be encouraged? First, engineers must attempt to persuade people in their society of the importance and value of engineering. They should publicize engineering projects and the importance of new products and technological devices that are the results of engineering work. Especially valuable might be the promotion and publicizing of projects that improve the material standard of living of their citizens, such as provisions for clean water, sanitation, better housing, and greater food production. Second, engineers should attempt to establish in their countries the social institutions that are ordinarily associated with professions, such as professional societies and professional regulatory agencies. As we have seen, some institutions have already been created. Third, engineers should promote and demand high standards of professional education and professional practice. These standards would include standards of conduct, such as those in the standard engineering codes of ethics. Once engineering is established as a highly regarded social role, motivation to comply with the standards associated with that role might be expected to follow.

9.4   TOWARD GLOBAL STANDARDS OF CONDUCT FOR ENGINEERS

The goal of the Washington Accord is to achieve "substantial agreement" in criteria for engineering degrees. In the realm of professionalism and conduct, some believe that the ultimate goal of the engineering profession should be to achieve a similar "substantial agreement" on global ethical standards for engineers. Differing cultural and ethical traditions, however, make this goal difficult to achieve. Encountering different ethical traditions often produces dilemmas that are difficult to resolve, especially when these dilemmas are compounded by problems caused by economic underdevelopment.

Two groups of engineers face these problems in a special way. One group is US and other Western engineers whose employment takes them to non-US and particularly non-Western countries with different ethical traditions, where they must decide how and to what extent to accommodate their own ethical standards to the new environment. The other group is non-Western engineers who are attempting to establish standards of conduct for themselves and other engineers in their country, in the light of Western and other standards that may differ. For the sake of simplicity, we focus in this chapter primarily on the problems encountered by US engineers when they enter a different culture, sometimes as working engineers and sometimes as managers. Let us call the problems such engineers face *boundary crossing* problems. We can refer to the country in which they originally lived—in this case, the United States—as the *home country* and the country that they enter as the *host country*.

Simple solutions to boundary crossing problems are attractive but often unacceptable. One simple solution is to hold to home country values and ways of doing things, no matter how different from host country values. Call this the *absolutist solution* or the *imperialist solution*, because it requires importing values from the home country into a different society. Home country standards, however, may pose serious, if not insurmountable, problems if applied in host countries. For example, customs regarding such practices as grease payments may be so pervasive and deeply entrenched in a host country that it may not be possible to do business in these countries without following the customs. Also, host country values and standards might be just as defensible as home country values and standards, just different.

The other extreme is the *relativist solution*, which follows the rule, "When in Rome, do as the Romans do." Using this approach, home country citizens always follow host country laws, customs, and values even if they are contrary to home country standards. This solution can also produce severe problems. It might even lead to illegal actions. For example, the Foreign Corrupt Practices Act (FCPA), passed by the US Congress in 1977, makes it illegal for US citizens to engage in practices such as paying some kinds of bribes and making some kinds of extortion payments, although these may be common practices in the host country. Another problem is that certain practices in the host country might be so repugnant that a home country engineer would have trouble following them. For example, the health and safety standards might be so low that they are clearly endangering the health and safety of workers and perhaps the engineers themselves.

Another and related issue has to do not with what standards to adopt, but with how they should be applied. One extreme is *moral laxism*, which holds that in some situations moral principles appear so far removed from the situations at hand that they cannot be applied with any precision, so that almost any action is permissible.[9] Thus, the moral laxist allows solutions to moral problems that may involve serious violations of moral standards—either of home or host country. The solutions arrived at by the moral laxist, furthermore, may in practice be those that conform to the self-interest of the individual or the firm. The other extreme is *moral rigorism*, which holds that moral principles, whether they are those of the home country or host country, must be strictly applied in every situation.[10] The moral rigorist is unwilling to accept the fact that, although a given course of action is not ideal, it may be the best that one can do in the situation. Few moral solutions follow extreme forms of either rigorism or laxism, but the distinction is important in understanding the nature of many moral solutions, such as creative middle way solutions, which typically fall between these two extremes.

9.5 ETHICAL RESOURCES FOR GLOBALIZED ENGINEERING

The following account of resources should be considered a partial list of tools in a tool kit for thinking about how US engineers can deal with issues encountered in other cultures and how non-US engineers can construct standards appropriate for their professional work. In using the tool kit, one chooses the resources needed for resolving a particular problem. In other words, one chooses the tool that is most appropriate for a particular task.

Creative Middle Ways

Laura's firm operates a plant in Country X and produces fertilizer in an area where farmers live at subsistence levels. The plant produces relatively inexpensive fertilizer that the farmers can afford, but it also produces a considerable amount of pollution—far more than would be allowed in the United States, for example. The pollution does not violate the environmental standards in Country X. Remedying the pollution problem would require raising the price of fertilizer so much that the farmers could not afford it, probably resulting in the deaths of many people in the area. Should a US engineer be involved in the plant's operation?

A creative middle way might be participating in the operation of the plant, but with an energetic effort to find a more economical remedy to the pollution problem. Notice this is not an extreme moral rigorist solution from the perspective of US laws and standards, because considerable pollution will be allowed, even pollution that may damage individuals and the environment. Neither is the solution extreme moral laxism, since it does not require a wholesale abandonment of concern for the environment or a simple resort to self-interested considerations.

The Golden Rule

Using the Golden Rule, an engineer can ask, "Would I be willing to accept the effects of this practice?" This question is especially difficult to answer when it requires putting oneself in the position of a person in another country, where the culture, economic conditions, living conditions, and values may be different from one's own. This classic problem in applying the Golden Rule is thus especially acute when the Golden Rule is used by engineers in a host country, but it may pose difficulties even for engineers attempting to construct standards for their own country. Nevertheless, it is difficult to imagine that anyone would want to be exploited, or be forced to violate deeply held moral or religious beliefs, or have their physical person violated. In contrast, one can imagine that one might well agree to relatively high levels of pollution from a fertilizer plant in one's country, if the only other option is inability to buy fertilizer at all, with the consequent risk of starvation.

Universal Human Rights

People in many countries, including non-Western countries, now appeal to human rights in making a case for everything from minimal standards of living to protection from torture or political oppression. We have already seen that rights can be justified by the ethics of respect for persons because rights help protect the moral agency of individuals. Utilitarians also often argue that respecting the rights of individuals promotes human happiness and well-being. People live happier lives when their fundamental rights are protected. Rights from the utilitarian perspective are means to utilitarian ends, not values in and of themselves.

"Rights talk" has become a near-universal vocabulary for ethical discourse. One measure of the cross-cultural nature of rights talk is the United Nation's International Bill of Human Rights, adopted in 1948, and two later documents—the International Covenant on Economic, Social, and Cultural Rights and the International Covenant on Civil and Political Rights.[11] These documents ascribe to all human beings the rights to

- life,
- liberty,
- security of person,
- recognition before the law,
- an impartial trial,
- marriage,
- property ownership,
- freedom of thought,
- peaceful assembly and participation in government,
- social security and work,
- education,
- participation in and forming trade unions,
- nondiscrimination, and
- a minimal standard of living.

They also affirm the rights to freedom from slavery, torture, inhuman or degrading punishment, and forced marriages.

Notice that some of the rights are what we have called "positive rights." That is, they are not simply negative rights to noninterference from others, such as the rights not to be held in slavery or tortured, but rights to certain advantages, such as education, social security, and work. The positive rights require not only a negative duty to noninterference, but also a positive duty to help others achieve such rights. Most of us would consider all of these rights highly desirable. The question is whether they should be considered as rights or simply desirable things to have.

James Nickel has proposed three criteria for determining when a right is what we shall call an *international right*—that is, a right that every country should, if resources and conditions permit, grant to its citizens. In terms of generality and abstraction, an international right falls between the very abstract rights derived from respect for persons theory and the more specific rights guaranteed by laws and constitutions of individual governments. Nickel's conditions that are most relevant to our discussion are the following:

1. The right must protect something of very general importance.
2. The right must be subject to substantial and recurrent threats.
3. The obligations or burdens imposed by the right must be affordable in relation to the resources of the country, the other obligations the country must fulfill, and fairness in the distribution of burdens among its citizens.[12]

Judged by these criteria, some of the United Nations' list of rights might not be applicable. Some countries may not have the economic resources to support the claims to a minimal education and subsistence, however desirable these may be. Perhaps we should say that these rights are desirable, insofar as a country is able to provide them.

Promoting Basic Human Well-Being

Another moral consideration for determining whether ethical solutions are satisfactory is whether a solution promotes the well-being of those affected. If a solution does not promote well-being, this is a strong argument against it. One of the most important ways in which engineering can promote well-being is through economic development. However, simple economic advancement may not be an adequate criterion. As noted in the chapter on risk, economist Amartya Sen and philosopher Martha Nussbaum have addressed this issue. In particular, Nussbaum has proposed a set of "basic human functional capabilities"—that is, basic capabilities that a person needs to be able to satisfy to enjoy a reasonable quality of life:[13]

1. Being able to live a human life of normal length.
2. Being able to enjoy good health, nourishment, shelter, sexual satisfaction, and physical movement.
3. Being able to avoid unnecessary and nonbeneficial pain and to have pleasurable experiences.
4. Being able to use the senses, imagine, think, and reason.
5. Being able to form loving attachments to things and persons.
6. Being able to form a conception of the good and to engage in critical reflection about the planning of one's life.
7. Being able to show concern for others and to engage in social interaction.
8. Being able to live with concern for and in relation to animals, plants, and the world of nature.
9. Being able to laugh, play, and enjoy recreational activities.
10. Being able to live one's own life and nobody else's.

Engineering is involved, either directly or indirectly, in all of these capabilities which, according to Nussbaum, contribute to human well-being. By providing clean water and sanitation, engineering makes an important contribution to health and longevity. Production of fertilizer and other aids to agriculture increases the ability of people to feed themselves. Technological development promotes greater wealth, which is important for the other capabilities mentioned by Nussbaum.

Codes of Engineering Societies

Typical Western engineering codes provide guidance for individual engineers visiting host countries and for host-country engineers formulating guidelines for themselves and their fellow nationals. Some US engineering codes are clearly intended to apply to their members wherever they live. The Institute of Electrical and Electronics Engineers (IEEE) is explicitly an international organization. Its code opens with an acknowledgement of "the importance of our technologies in affecting the quality of life throughout the world." The code of the former American Society of Mechanical Engineers, now ASME-International, makes similar references to the international environment. A 1996 decision (Case 96-5) by the Board of Ethical Review of the National Society of Professional Engineers (NSPE) held that a member of the NSPE is bound by its code of ethics, even in another country. In this case, the issue was whether a US engineer could ethically retain a host country engineer who would then offer bribes to a host country official to get a contract. The board held that the practice would violate the NSPE code and that it would be unethical for a US engineer to be a party to such a practice.

Established professional codes give important guidance for individual engineers as they face ethical dilemmas in the international arena. They are also a source of guidance for engineers in host countries who are attempting to formulate their own codes and for engineers who are considering the possibility of an international engineering code. In the following sections, we consider some of the more specific issues that such engineers may encounter.

9.6   ECONOMIC UNDERDEVELOPMENT: THE PROBLEM OF EXPLOITATION

Exploitation, especially of the weak and vulnerable, is a serious moral problem, and it is particularly likely to occur in economically underdeveloped countries, where workers have few options for jobs. According to Robert E. Goodin, the risk of exploitation arises when the following five conditions are present.[14]

- There is an imbalance of (usually economic) power between the dominant and subordinate or exploited party.
- The subordinate party needs the resources by the dominant party to protect his or her vital interests.
- For the subordinate party, the exploitative relationship is the only source of such resources.
- The dominant party in the relationship exercises discretionary control over the needed resources.
- The resources of the subordinate party (natural resources, labor, etc.) are used without adequate compensation.

Consider the following case:

Engineer Joe's firm, Coppergiant, is the most powerful copper mining and copper smelting company in the world. It controls world prices and keeps competitors away from the most lucrative sources of copper. Joe works for Coppergiant in Country X, the firm's most lucrative source of copper. In Country X, Coppergiant buys copper at prices that are considerably below the world market and pays the workers the lowest wages for mining and smelting in the world. As a result, Coppergiant makes enormous profits. Because the company pays off government officials and has so much control over the world market in copper, no other mining and smelting company is allowed into the country. Country X is desperately poor, and copper is the major source of foreign currency.

This case meets all five of Goodin's criteria for exploitation. There is an asymmetrical balance of power between the Coppergiant's employees (and even Country X) and Joe's firm. The workers in Country X desperately need jobs and Country X needs the foreign currency. Joe's firm is the only (or major) source of jobs and foreign currency for Country X. Joe's firm, through its control of the market, exercises discretionary control over the jobs and currency. Finally, the natural and labor resource of Country X are used without adequate compensation. This is a paradigmatic case of exploitation of Country X and its workers.

Exploitation is usually wrong because it violates several of the moral standards and tests we have mentioned. It violates the Golden Rule because it is doubtful that anyone in any culture in the world would, under normal circumstances, want to be the victim of exploitation. It violates utilitarian considerations because it denies the citizens of Country X a minimal standard of living, and it keeps the citizens of Country X from realizing many of the capabilities mentioned by Nussbaum. While it is possible to argue on utilitarian grounds that the exploitation is justified because it is the only way that Country X can undergo the economic development that will ultimately benefit all of its citizens, this argument is implausible because economic development could almost certainly occur without this kind of exploitation.

Since the exploitation described in this case cannot be justified, we must conclude that the situation it describes should be changed. It may be that raising wages and copper prices to market levels would still not provide the employees of Coppergiant with adequate compensation. At this point, a creative middle way perspective might justify this condition because any further increase in wages might result in the economic collapse of Coppergiant or its exit from the county. This might leave workers and the economy of Country X in worse shape than before.

Most real-world cases are not paradigmatic cases of exploitation, because they do not satisfy all of the criteria for exploitation. In particular, a firm may not exercise discretionary control over resources, because raising prices to fund higher wages, for example, might make the firm noncompetitive in the marketplace. Whether a given level of compensation is "adequate" may raise difficult conceptual, application, and factual issues. Wages might be low by US standards and yet adequate to provide a minimum standard of living by the standards of the host country. These are issues that no code or general statement can resolve, but the fundamental issue of exploitation is one that individual engineers must often face and that may deserve attention in an international engineering code.

9.7 PAYING FOR SPECIAL TREATMENT: THE PROBLEM OF BRIBERY

Bribery is one of the most common issues faced by US engineers when they practice in host countries. In response to this problem, the US Congress passed the FCPA Act in 1977. The act is limited in its scope. It only prohibits bribery of government officials, and it allows some extortion payments to protect in-place property. Typically, a bribe is made to a government official in exchange for violating some official duty or responsibility. The payment might result, for example, in an official not making a decision to buy a product on its merits. The following is a typical or paradigmatic case of bribery:

> An executive of Company A hopes to sell 25 airplanes to the national airline of Country X. The deal requires the approval of the head of the ministry of transportation in Country X. The executive knows that the official, who has a reputation for honesty, can make a better deal elsewhere, but he is also experiencing personal financial difficulties. So the executive offers the official $300,000 to authorize the purchase of the planes from Company A. The official accepts the bribe and orders the planes to be purchased.[15]

On the basis of this paradigm case of bribery, we can give the following definition of a bribe: "A bribe is a payment of money (or something of value) to another person in exchange for his giving special consideration that is incompatible with the duties of his office, position, or role." [16]

A bribe also induces one person (the person given the bribe) to give to another person (the person giving the bribe) something that he does not deserve. Keep in mind that bribes presuppose an agreement that the bribe must be in exchange for a certain kind of conduct. If this agreement is not present, then it is difficult to distinguish bribes from gifts or rewards.

Both giving and receiving bribes are forbidden by professional engineering codes. There are several good reasons for this. First, if an engineer takes a bribe, she is creating a situation that will most likely corrupt her professional judgment and tarnish the reputation of the engineering profession. Second, if she offers a bribe, she engages in activity that will also tarnish the reputation of her profession if discovered and probably violate her obligation to promote the well-being of the public. The person who takes the bribe, such as a government official, will also be guilty of wrongdoing by violating the obligation to act in the best interests of the citizens or clients. Third, bribery can undermine the efficiency of the market by inducing someone to buy products that are not the best for the price. Fourth, bribery can give someone an unfair advantage over his or her competitors, thus violating the standards of justice and fair play.

John T. Noonan, jurist and authority on the history of morality, argues that the opposition to bribery is becoming stronger throughout the world.[17] There is massive popular discontent with bribery in Japan, Italy, and other countries. The antibribery ethic is increasingly embodied in law. Even campaign contributions, which have many similarities with bribery, are becoming increasingly suspect. Although there are many points of dissimilarity between bribery and slavery, there is some basis for saying that just as slavery was once accepted and is now universally condemned, so too bribery is increasingly held to be morally unacceptable, even if still often practiced. Bribery, then, is something that should be avoided. In most cases, at least, no creative middle way is acceptable.

9.8 PAYING FOR DESERVED SERVICES: THE PROBLEM OF EXTORTION AND GREASE PAYMENTS

Extortion

Many actions that might appear to be bribery are actually cases of extortion. Consider a variation on the case of the executive of Company A described previously. Suppose he knows he is offering the best deal on airplanes to the official of Country X who has the authority to authorize purchases for his national airlines. The executive knows, however, that his bid will not even be considered unless he offers the official a large cash payment. The payment will not guarantee that Company A will get the contract, only that his bid will at least be considered. If the executive makes the cash payment, he will be paying extortion, not a bribe.

It is more difficult to construct a definition of extortion than bribery. Here is a proposed, but inadequate, definition: "extortion is the act of threatening someone with harm (that the extorter is not entitled to inflict) to obtain benefits to which the extorter has no prior right."[18] This definition is inadequate because some actions not covered by the definition are still extortion. For example, it would be extortion if one threatened to expose the official misconduct of a government official unless he pays a large sum of money—even though exposing the official would be both morally and legally permissible. We find it impossible, however, to give a completely adequate definition of extortion. All we can say is that the definition offered previously gives a sufficient, although not a necessary, condition of extortion.

Sometimes it is difficult to know whether one is paying bribery or extortion. A customs inspector who demands a payoff from a businessperson to authorize a shipment of a product into his or her country may claim that the product does not meet the country's standards. Because the law is so complex, it may be difficult to know whether the customs official is lying and too expensive to find out. In this case, if the businessperson decides to make the payoff, she may not know whether she is paying a bribe or extortion. Of course, it may be irresponsible for the company to make no effort to find the truth.[19]

Many of the most famous cases of corruption seem to lie on the border between bribery and extortion. Between 1966 and 1970, for example, the Gulf Oil Corporation paid $4 million to the ruling Democratic Republican Party of South Korea. Gulf was led to believe that its continued flourishing in South Korea depended on these payments. If the payments gave Gulf special advantages over its competitors, the payments were bribes. If they would have been required of any competitor as a condition of operating without undeserved reprisals or restrictions, the payments were extortion.[20]

The moral status of paying extortion is different from the moral status of paying and accepting bribes for the following reasons. First, paying extortion will not usually corrupt professional judgment, while bribery often does. Second, although paying extortion can tarnish one's professional reputation, it will probably not do so as much as paying a bribe. The professional can argue that he had to pay the extortion to stay in business—that he was a victim rather than a criminal. Third, paying extortion will not cause one to act contrary to the best interests of one's employer or client by, for example, selecting an inferior product. It may, however, involve the use of a client's or employer's money in a way that is inefficient. Fourth, paying extortion does not undermine the efficiency of the market by promoting the selection of inferior or more expensive products, although it does divert funds from their most efficient use. Fifth, paying extortion does not give one an unfair advantage over others, except insofar as others do not or cannot pay the extortion. Paying extortion is sometimes a condition of doing business in a country. Assuming the business activity is good for the home and host countries and there are no serious violations of other moral standards, it may be justifiable.

Grease Payments

Grease payments are typically offered to facilitate routine bureaucratic decisions, such as hastening the passage of goods through customs or getting faster processing of permits. Grease payments usually involve relatively small amounts of money compared to many bribery or extortion payments. Some of the payments by Walmart officials in the case at the beginning of the chapter may have been grease payments, although some were so large that they are better classified as bribes. If a grease payment is required to get legitimate goods through customs or to prevent excessive or virtually permanent delays in the processing of a permit, they are forms of petty extortion. If they are payments to allow the passage of illegal goods or to enable one to get "to the head of the line" in a way that treats others unfairly, they are small bribes. Grease payments are sometimes tacitly condoned by governments. For example, in many countries government officials are poorly paid, and the government may assume that officials will receive grease payments to supplement their salary, just as employers assume that waiters will supplement their salary with tips.

Again, a moral rigorist might hold that making grease payments is impermissible, and it would surely be better if they were eliminated and replaced by more adequate salaries. Payment of salaries would be open and public rather than clandestine, as most grease payments are. Furthermore, as we have seen, grease payments are sometimes more like bribes because they enable the payer to get special considerations that he or she does not deserve. If one is not a moral rigorist, he or she may sometimes find that, if other moral tests are not seriously violated, making grease payments is sometimes acceptable.

9.9   THE EXTENDED FAMILY UNIT: THE PROBLEM OF NEPOTISM

In many areas of the world, the primary unit of society is not the individual, as it is in the modern West, but some larger group. The larger group may be an extended family, which includes brothers and sisters and their families, aunts, uncles, cousins, and so forth. The group might even be a larger unit, such as a tribe. The relationship of the members of the group is one of mutual support. If a member of the group has fallen on bad times, the other members have an obligation to care for him or her. Similarly, if a member of the group has good fortune, he or she has an obligation to find jobs for his or her relatives—perhaps a brother or sister, or their spouses or children. This custom, however, may produce problems for firms. Consider the following example, which is modeled on a real case.[21]

You work for a steel company in India, which has the policy of partially compensating its employees with a promise to hire one of the employee's children. This policy is extremely popular with employees in a country where there is a tradition of providing jobs for one's children and the members of one's extended family. But to you, the policy is nepotism and in conflict with the more desirable policy of hiring the most qualified applicant. What should you do?

If one is not a moral rigorist, he or she may hold that this is an acceptable creative middle way solution to the problem. The policy of hiring the most qualified applicant in every case is surely the most desirable one, so it is clearly an option. Hiring many members of an employee's family, regardless of qualifications, would be unacceptable, because it would seriously harm economic efficiency. This policy would also be too severe a violation of considerations of justice and the right of other applicants to non-discrimination. The policy of hiring one, but only one, family member, by contrast, seems like an acceptable creative middle way solution. It makes a concession to the deeply held convictions of many people in a tradition-oriented culture, and it promotes harmony in the workplace (and perhaps economic efficiency in this way). This solution again shows the need to take a middle way between moral rigorism and laxism.

9.10   BUSINESS AND FRIENDSHIP: THE PROBLEM OF EXCESSIVE GIFTS

For people in many cultures, business relationships are built on personal relationships. Two people first become friends, and then they do business together. The rule "Don't mix business with pleasure," often accepted in the West, seems cold and inhuman. Friendships are often cemented with gifts: the way to show affection and trust is to give a gift.

For many in the West, large personal gifts look too much like bribes. Is there a creative middle way solution to this problem? Jeffrey Fadiman has suggested an answer: give the gifts to the community, not to individuals. In one of his examples, a firm planted a large number of trees in a barren area as a gift to a community. In another example, a firm gave vehicles and spare parts to a country that was having trouble enforcing its laws against killing animals in national parks. These gifts created good will, without being bribes to individuals. To some, of course, these gifts still have too much in common with bribes, even though they are certainly not paradigmatic bribes. Like bribes, they curry influence by bestowing favors. Unlike bribes, however, they are public rather than secret, and they are not given to individuals. Unless one is a moral rigorist who says anything that looks like a bribe in any sense is wrong, such solutions may be minimally acceptable in some circumstances. They are creative middle ways between the moral requirement to avoid bribery and the desirable goal of doing business in the host country. Since the option has some features in common with bribery, however, we would not consider it a completely satisfactory solution.

In contrast to the above situations, sometimes gifts are given to individuals that are of substantial size, at least by US standards. A "normal" gift in a host country might be "excessive" by US standards. Suppose affluent members of Country X routinely give gifts of substantial size to one another as tokens of friendship and esteem. Because the gifts are routinely given and received by everyone, they do not command any special favors. Is this practice acceptable for an engineer doing business in Country X?

The following considerations are relevant. First, we must examine the gift-giving practices in the host country and determine whether the gift would be "excessive" by host country standards. If a gift is routine by host country standard, it would probably not command any special favors. Second, we must keep in mind the intent of the prohibition against excessive gifts: to prevent currying special favor and thus create unfairness in business competition. If this intent is not violated, this is an important consideration. Texas Instruments (TI) has set a policy on gift-giving in non-US countries that seems to embody these two considerations.

TI generally follows conservative rules governing the giving and receiving of gifts. However, what we consider to be an excessive gift in the United States may differ from what local customs dictate in other parts of the world. We used to define gift limits in terms of US dollars, but this is impractical when dealing internationally. Instead, we emphasize following the directive that gift-giving should not be used in a way that exerts undue pressure to win business or implies a quid pro quo.[22]

We consider this policy to be morally acceptable. It is a creative middle way between on the one hand merely rejecting the practices of the host country and perhaps not being able to do business there and on the other hand engaging in clear cases of bribery.

9.11   THE ABSENCE OF TECHNICAL-SCIENTIFIC SOPHISTICATION: THE PROBLEM OF PATERNALISM

Because of lower educational levels and the general absence of exposure to technology in their daily lives, citizens in less-industrialized countries can easily misunderstand many issues related to technology, especially those having to do with risk, health, safety, and the environment. This situation can give rise to either exploitation or paternalism. Exploitation occurs when individuals (including engineers), governments, or corporations take advantage of this ignorance to advance their own self-interest. For example, they can adopt policies that expose workers to unnecessary health and safety issues when the workers are not aware of the dangers.

Paternalism occurs when individuals (including engineers), governments, or corporations override the ability of others to decide what they should (or should not) do in the interests of those others. Because overriding the decisions of others is for their own good, this is paternalism, not exploitation. Paternalistic action has a very different motivation from exploitation: concern for the other rather than self-interest. Nevertheless, paternalistic action can give rise to serious moral concerns, because it requires overriding the decisions—or at least the ability to make decisions—of others.

Let us call the one who decides for another the *paternalist* and the person who is the object of paternalistic action the *recipient*. Here is an example of paternalism: Robin's firm operates a large pineapple plantation in Country X. The firm has been having excessive problems with maintaining the health of its workers. Robin has determined that a major reason for the health problems of its workers is the unsanitary conditions of the traditional villages in which they live. To remedy this problem, Robin has required the workers to leave their traditional villages and live in small, uniform houses on uniformly laid-out streets. He believes that the workers can be "educated" to understand the relationship of their unsanitary traditional villages to the high incidence of disease and thus to appreciate the advantages of the new living conditions. The workers, however, are strongly objecting, because the new living conditions are boring and have destroyed much of their traditional way of life.

To discuss the moral status of Robin's action, we must distinguish between weak and strong paternalism. In *weak paternalism*, the paternalist overrides the decision-making powers of the recipient when there is reason to believe the recipient is not able to exercise her moral agency effectively. In *strong paternalism*, the paternalist overrides the decision-making powers of the recipient, even when there is no reason to believe the recipient is not exercising his or her moral agency effectively. This is usually because the paternalist believes the recipient is making "bad" decisions. Of course the paternalist interprets what is "good" or "bad" according to his or her own values.

In both cases, the paternalist is overriding the recipient for his or her own good, as the paternalist sees it.

From both utilitarian and respect for persons perspectives, weak paternalism can sometimes be justified. From the respect for persons perspective, weak paternalistic action safeguards the moral agency of the recipient. In exercising paternalistic control over the recipient, the paternalist is really protecting the moral agency of the recipient, not destroying it. From the utilitarian perspective, paternalistic action can better produce well-being for the recipient and perhaps others as well, since the recipient would presumably act irrationally.

If any one of the following conditions is present, a person may not be able to exercise his or her moral agency effectively, so any one of them is sufficient to justify weak paternalism:

- A person may be under undue emotional pressure, so he or she is unable to make a rational decision.
- A person may be ignorant of the consequences of his or her action, so he or she is unable to make a genuinely informed decision.
- A person may be too young to comprehend the factors relevant to his or her decision, so he or she is unable to make a rational and informed decision.
- Time may be necessary for the paternalist to determine whether the recipient is making a free and informed decision, so the paternalist may be justified in intervening to keep the recipient from making any decision until it is clear that the recipient is making a decision that is truly free and informed.

In strong paternalism, we assume that the recipient is making a free and informed decision, but the presumption is that the recipient is not making the "right" decision, from the standpoint of the paternalist. Strong paternalism probably cannot be justified from the respect for persons perspective, but it can sometimes be justified from a utilitarian standpoint. The argument is that the recipient is not making a decision that will maximize his or her own good (or overall good), even though he or she may think that he or she is making the correct decision.

Now we can return to the example. From the short description given, it is not clear whether Robin is exercising weak or strong paternalism. If the workers do not fully understand the health risks associated with their traditional village life, Robin is exercising weak paternalism in forcing them to move into the more sanitary villages. If the workers do understand the consequences but still prefer more disease and perhaps even less health care to preserve their traditional way of life, Robin is exercising strong paternalism. Since strong paternalism is more difficult to justify than weak paternalism from the moral standpoint (because it overrides the decision-making powers of moral agents), the burden of proof to show Robin's action was justified is much greater.

Citizens of less-industrialized countries are particularly likely to experience the conditions that might justify weak paternalism, or even strong paternalism in some cases. A lower level of education and technological sophistication can render citizens in less-industrialized countries less able to make responsible decisions about their own well-being. In such cases, a rational person might consent to being treated paternalistically, and in a few cases the overall good of recipients or even of many others might justify strong paternalistic action.

Here is an example in which weak paternalism is probably justified: John is employed by a large firm that sells infant formula in Country X. The firm is the only one that markets infant formula in Country X. Many mothers mix the formula with contaminated water because they do not understand the health dangers to their infants. In order to save money, they dilute the formula too much, unaware that this leads to malnutrition in their babies. John recommends that his firm stop selling the product in Country X. Management agrees and stops the sale of the product in Country X.

In this case, at least one of the conditions sufficient to justify weak paternalism (ignorance of the consequences of action) is satisfied, so terminating the sales of the infant formula, thereby depriving the mothers in Country X of the option of using infant formula, is justified. Sufficient evidence existed that the mothers were not able to exercise their moral agency in a free and informed way.

9.12 DIFFERING BUSINESS PRACTICES: THE PROBLEM OF NEGOTIATING TAXES

Sometimes the business practices in host countries cause dilemmas for US engineers, and perhaps for engineers in the host countries as well. Consider the following case, which illustrates the practices in a number of countries: James works for a US firm in Country X, where it is customary for the government to assess taxes at an exorbitant rate because it expects firms to report only half their actual earnings. If a firm reported its actual earnings, the taxes would force it out of business. James's firm is considering whether it should adopt the local practice of dishonestly reporting its profits to Country X, even though it would be illegal to do this in the United States. Whatever its decision, it will continue to report its profits honestly to the US government.

The practice in Country X is probably not the best way to collect taxes. It opens the way to bribery in the negotiating process and unfairness in the assessment of taxes since some firms may negotiate lower taxes (especially if they bribe the officials) than others. Nevertheless, it would probably be morally permissible for James's firm to report only half of its profits to the government of Country X, as long as the practice does not violate internal policies of the firm and the firm does not report its profit inaccurately to the US government.[23] The practice does not appear to violate the Golden Rule since the firm would be willing for other firms to do the same thing. The practice does not seriously violate the rights of anyone, and it may produce more overall good than any alternative, assuming the firm's work in Country X benefits its employees and the citizens of Country X. Furthermore, although this way of collecting taxes may not be the most desirable, it finances the legitimate activities of the government of Country X. Finally, the practice is not secret since it is generally known that every firm that survives in Country X follows the same practice.

9.13 CHAPTER SUMMARY

In its move toward globalization, the engineering profession is attempting to establish international standards for technical education. The Washington Accord, established in 1989, is an attempt to establish "substantial agreement" among the signatories in the requirements for engineering education. A much older organization, the FEANI, has established common standards in Europe for licensing individual engineers. Other international organizations have emphasized the social responsibilities of engineers.

Progress in establishing worldwide standards for professional conduct, however, has been slower. To establish such standards, it would be useful to have an internationally recognized concept of what it means to be a professional. Even though the concept of "professional" is a Western concept, it is possible that the concept can be internationalized, because professional morality is role morality and all cultures appear to recognize roles (such as parent) with attendant special duties and obligations.

The problems faced by engineers when they cross cultural borders can be called *boundary crossing problems*. They are not readily solved by simply importing one's own values into another culture or by accepting the standards of the other culture without evaluation. The ethical resources developed in Chapter 2, however, can be useful in resolving boundary crossing problems, especially if they are adapted to the culture in a careful manner. Creative middle ways are especially useful in resolving boundary crossing problems, but appeal to the Golden Rule, universal human rights, conditions necessary for human well-being developed by Nussbaum, and engineering codes can also be useful.

Among the problems faced by engineers in the international environment is exploitation of vulnerable people. Bribery, which is making payments for special consideration that is incompatible with the duties of one's office, position, or role, is perhaps the most widespread problem. Paying extortion, which is giving money for something that one deserves anyhow, is perhaps less morally serious than bribery. Grease payments, which are smaller exchanges of money or something of value, may be either bribery or extortion, depending on the circumstances.

Practices and traditions in many countries require that family members secure jobs for other family members, even when the family members may not be the most qualified. Such problems of nepotism can sometimes be addressed with creative middle way solutions. The practice of giving large gifts, common in many cultures, may not necessarily involve bribery or extortion. Adapting to this practice may require giving larger gifts than would be acceptable in the United States, but the gifts must not be used as bribes. The absence of technical-scientific sophistication can lead to paternalistic behavior that is often problematic. Generally weak paternalism is easier to justify than strong paternalism. Finally, the practice of negotiating taxes can lead to bribery and other abuses, but the practice need not be rejected altogether.

9.14   ENGINEERING ETHICS ON THE WEB

Check your understanding of the material in this chapter by visiting the companion website for *Engineering Ethics*. The site includes multiple choice study questions, suggested discussion topics, and sometimes additional case studies to complement your reading and study of the material in this chapter.

NOTES

1. http://www.nytimes.com/2012/04/22/business/at-Walmart-in-mexico-a-bribe-inquiry-silenced.html?pagewanted=all.
2. http://www.washingtonaccord.org.
3. http://www.feani.org/scte/.
4. http://www.feiap.org/.
5. http://cec.ice.org.uk/.

6. Tetsuji Iseda, "How Should We Foster the Professional Integrity of Engineers in Japan? A Pride-Based Approach," *Science and Engineering Ethics* (2008), 14: 165–176.

7. Lin Yutang, *The Wisdom of Confucius*, (The Modern Library, Random House, 1938), p. 216. Quoted in John B. Noss, *Man's Religions* (New York: Macmillan, 1956), p. 348.

8. Ibid., p. 351.

9. James F. Childress and John Macquarrie, eds., *The Westminster Dictionary of the Christian Church* (Philadelphia: Westminster Press, 1986), p. 499.

10. Ibid., p. 633.

11. *The International Bill of Human Rights*, with forward by Jimmy Carter (Glen Ellen, CA: Entwhistle Books, 1981). No author.

12. James W. Nickel, *Making Sense of Human Rights: Philosophical Reflections on the Universal Declaration of Human Rights* (Berkeley: University of California Press, 1987), pp. 108–109.

13. Martha Nussbaum and Jonathan Glover, eds., *Women, Culture, and Development* (Oxford: Clarendon Press, 1995), pp. 83–85.

14. Robert E. Goodin, *Protecting the Vulnerable: A Reanalysis of Our Social Responsibilities* (Chicago: University of Chicago Press, 1985), pp. 195–196.

15. This scenario is a modification of one presented by Michael Philips titled "Bribery" in Patricia Werhane and Kendall D'Andrate, eds., *Profit and Responsibility* (New York: Edwin Mellon Press, 1985), pp. 197–220.

16. Thomas L. Carson, "Bribery, Extortion, and the 'Foreign Corrupt Practices Act,'" *Philosophy and Public Affairs*, 14:1, 1985, pp. 55–90.

17. John T. Noonan, *Bribery* (New York: Macmillan, 1984).

18. Carson, "Bribery," p. 73.

19. Ibid., p. 79.

20. Ibid., p. 75.

21. For this case and related discussion, see Thomas Donaldson and Thomas W. Dunfee, "Toward a Unified Conception of Business Ethics: Integrated Social Contract Theory," *Academy of Management Review*, 19:2, 1994, pp. 152–284.

22. http://actrav-english/telearn/global/ilo/texas.htmll

23. For a similar case with a similar conclusion, see Thomas Donaldson and Thomas W. Dunfee, *Ties that Bind: A Social Contracts Approach to Business Ethics* (Boston: Harvard Business School Press, 1999), pp. 198–207.

CASES

THE CASES LISTED HERE are presented for use in conjunction with materials in Chapters 1-9. They vary in length, complexity, and purpose. Some present factual events and circumstances. Others are fictional but realistic. Some present ethical problems for individual engineers. Others focus primarily on the corporate or institutional settings within which engineers work. Some, such as Case 44, "Where Are the Women?" focus on general problems within engineering as a profession. Others focus on large-scale issues such as global warming and the challenges and opportunities these issues pose for engineers, both individually and collectively. Some cases focus on wrongdoing and irresponsibility. Others illustrate exemplary engineering practice. A topical taxonomy of our cases appears next.

Many cases presented in previous editions of our book are not included here. However, most of them, and many others, are readily available on the Internet. Both the Online Ethics Center (www.onlineethics.org) and Texas A & M's Engineering Ethics website (www.ethics.tamu.edu) include Michael S. Pritchard, ed., *Engineering Ethics: A Case Study Approach,* a product of a National Science Foundation (NSF)-sponsored project. More than 30 cases and commentaries are presented. The Texas A & M website presents these cases in their original form, along with a taxonomy of the cases in accordance with their leading topical focus (e.g., safety and health, conflicts of interest, and honesty). (The cases are accessed under "1992 NSF Sponsored Engineering Ethics Cases.") Also included is an introductory essay by Pritchard. The Online Ethics Center presents the same cases with different individual titles, along with brief statements about each listed case. Cases and essays from two NSF-supported projects directed by Charles E. Harris and Michael J. Rabins are available at the Texas A & M website. These are also accessible at the Online Ethics Center (*Numerical and Design Problems* and *Engineering Ethics Cases from Texas A & M*). These appear under the heading "Professional Practice" and the subheading "Cases." The Online Ethics Center contains a wealth of other cases and essays that can be used in conjunction with our book. Of special interest is *Professional Ethics in Engineering Practice: Discussion Cases Based on NSPE BER Cases,* which provides access to cases and commentaries prepared by the National Society for Professional Engineer's Board of Ethical Review. These appear under the heading "Professional Practice" and the subheading "Cases" (*Discussion Cases from NSPE*).

ENGINEERING ETHICS ON THE WEB

Check your understanding of the material in this chapter by visiting the companion website for Engineering Ethics. The site includes multiple choice study questions, suggested discussion topics, and sometimes additional case studies to complement your reading and study of the material in this chapter.

Confidentiality

Conflicts of Interest

Dissent and Whistleblowing

Environmental Concerns

Ethics in Design

Exemplary Practice

CASE 1

Aberdeen Three

The Aberdeen Proving Ground is a U.S. Army facility where, among other things, chemical weapons are developed. The U.S. Army has used the facility to develop, test, store, and dispose of chemical weapons since World War II. Periodic inspections between 1983 and 1986 revealed serious problems with a part of the facility known as the Pilot Plant, including the following:

- Flammable and cancer-causing substances were left in the open.
- Chemicals that would become lethal if mixed were kept in the same room.
- Drums of toxic substances were leaking.

There were chemicals everywhere—misplaced, unlabeled, or poorly contained. When part of the roof collapsed, smashing several chemical drums stored below, no one cleaned up or moved the spilled substance and broken containers for weeks.[1]

When an external sulfuric acid tank leaked 200 gallons of acid into a nearby river, state and federal investigators were summoned to investigate. They discovered that the chemical retaining dikes were in a state of disrepair and that the system designed to contain and treat hazardous chemicals was corroded, resulting in chemicals leaking into the ground.[2]

On June 28, 1988, after 2 years of investigation, three chemical engineers—Carl Gepp, William Dee, and Robert Lentz, now know as the "Aberdeen Three"—were criminally indicted for illegally handling, sorting, and disposing of hazardous wastes in violation of the Resource Conservation and Recovery Act (RCRA). Although the three engineers did not actually handle the chemicals, they were the managers with ultimate responsibility for the violations. Investigators for the Department of Justice concluded that no one above them was sufficiently aware of the problems at the Pilot Plant to be assigned responsibility for the violations. The three engineers were competent professionals who played important roles in the development of chemical weapons for the United States. William Dee, the developer of the binary chemical weapon, headed the chemical weapons development team. Robert Lentz was in charge of developing the processes that would be used to manufacture the weapons. Carl Gepp, manager of the Pilot Plant, reported to Dee and Lentz.

Six months after the indictment, the Department of Justice took the three defendants to court. Each defendant was charged with four counts of illegally storing and disposing of waste. William Dee was found guilty of one count, and Lentz and Gepp were found guilty on three counts each of violating the RCRA. Although each faced up to 15 years in prison and $750,000 in fines, they received sentences of 1,000 hours of community service and 3 years' probation. The judge justified the relatively light sentences on the grounds of the high standing of the defendants in the community and the fact that they had already incurred enormous court costs. Because the three engineers were criminally indicted, the U.S. Army could not assist them in their legal defense. This was the first criminal conviction of federal employees under RCRA.

CASE 2

Big Dig Collapse[3]

On July 10, 2006, a husband and wife were traveling through a connector tunnel in the Big Dig tunnel system in Boston. This system runs Interstate 93 beneath downtown Boston and extends the Massachusetts Turnpike to Logan Airport. As the car passed through, at least 26 tons of concrete collapsed onto it when a suspended concrete ceiling panel fell from above. The wife was killed instantly and the husband sustained minor injuries. The Massachusetts attorney general's office issued subpoenas next day to those involved in the Big Dig project. Soon, a federal investigation ensued.

The National Transportation Safety Board (NTSB) released its findings a year after the incident. The focus of the report was the anchor epoxy used to fasten the concrete panels and hardware to the tunnel ceiling. This product was marketed and distributed by Powers Fasteners, Inc., a company that specializes in the manufacturing and marketing of anchoring and fastening materials for concrete, masonry, and steel.

Investigators found that Powers distributed two kinds of epoxy: Standard Set and Fast Set. The latter type of epoxy, the one used in the collapsed ceiling tile, was susceptible to "creep," a process by which the epoxy deforms, allowing support anchors to pull free. The investigators concluded that this process allowed a ceiling tile to give way on July 10, 2006.

According to the NTSB report, Powers knew that Fast Set epoxy was susceptible to creep and useful for short-term load bearing only. Powers did not make this distinction clear in its marketing materials— the same materials distributed to tunnel project managers and engineers. Powers, the report continued, "failed to provide the Central Artery/Tunnel project with sufficiently complete, accurate, and detailed information about the suitability of the company's Fast Set epoxy for sustaining long-term tensile-loads." The report also noted that Powers failed to identify anchor displacement discovered in 1999 in portions of the Big Dig system as related to creep due to the use of Fast Set epoxy.

On the basis of the NTSB report, Powers was issued an involuntary manslaughter indictment by the Massachusetts attorney general's office just days after the release of the report. The indictment charged that "Powers had the necessary knowledge and the opportunity to prevent the fatal ceiling collapse but failed to do so."

The NTSB also targeted several other sources for blame in the incident (although no additional indictments were made). It concluded that construction contractors Gannett Fleming, Inc. and Bechtel/Parsons Brinkerhoff failed to account for the possibility of creep under long-term load conditions. The report indicated that these parties should have required that load tests be performed on adhesives before allowing their use and that the Massachusetts Turnpike Authority should have regularly inspected the portal tunnels. It asserted that if the Authority had conducted such inspections, the creep may have been detected early enough to prevent catastrophe.

The report provided recommendations to parties interested in the Big Dig incident. To the American Society of Civil Engineers, it advised the following:

> Use the circumstances of the July 10, 2006, accident in Boston, Massachusetts, to emphasize to your members through your publications, website, and conferences, as appropriate, the need to assess the creep characteristics of adhesive anchors before those anchors are used in sustained tensile-load applications.

To what extent must engineers educate themselves on the various materials being used and processes being employed in a project in order to ensure safety? If lack of knowledge played a part in causing the collapse, how might such understanding specifically help engineers to prevent an event like this in the future? How else might engineers work to avoid a similar catastrophe?

REFERENCES

1. National Transportation Safety Board, Public Meeting of July 10, 2007, "Highway Accident Report Ceiling Collapse in the Interstate 90 Connector Tunnel, Boston, Massachusetts," July 10, 2006. This document can be accessed online at www.ntsb.gov/Publictn/2007/HAR-07-02.htm.

2. The Commonwealth of Massachusetts Office of the Attorney General, "Powers Fasteners Indicted for Manslaughter in Connection with Big Dig Tunnel Ceiling Collapse." This document can be accessed online at www.mass.gov.

CASE 3

Bridges[4]

On August 1, 2007, the I-35W bridge over the Mississippi River in Minneapolis, Minnesota, collapsed during rush hour, resulting in 13 deaths and a multitude of injuries. The bridge was inspected annually dating from 1993 and every 2 years before that since its opening in 1967. The most recent inspection, conducted on May 2, 2007, cited only minor structural concerns related to welding details. At that time, the bridge received a rating of 4 on a scale from 0 to 9 (0 - shut down, 9 - perfect). The rating of 4, although signifying a bridge with components in poor condition, meant that the state was allowed to operate the bridge without any load restrictions.

A bridge rated 4 or less is considered to be "structurally deficient." According to the U.S. Department of Transportation, this label means that "there are elements of the bridge that need to be monitored and/or repaired. The fact that a bridge is 'deficient' does not imply that it is likely to collapse or that it is unsafe. It means it must be monitored, inspected, and maintained." In some cases, load restrictions are placed on structurally deficient bridges.

Although the cause of the I-35W collapse is still under investigation, the incident raises important questions about the state of U.S. bridges. In Minnesota, there are 1,907 bridges that are structurally deficient, which means they have also received a rating of 4 or lower on inspection. Bridges may also be considered "functionally obsolete," a label that the American Society of Civil Engineers (ASCE) Report Card for America's Infrastructure defines as a bridge that has "older design features and, while it is not unsafe for all vehicles, it cannot safely accommodate current traffic volumes, and vehicle sizes and weights." In 2003, 27.1 percent of bridges in the United States were deemed either structurally deficient or functionally obsolete.

The ASCE urges that "America must change its transportation behavior, increase transportation investment at all levels of government, and make use of the latest technology" to help alleviate the infrastructure problem involving the bridge system. In order for Americans to answer this charge, they must be aware of the problem. What role should engineers and engineering societies play in informing the public about the state of U.S. bridges? Should engineers lobby for congressional support and appropriate amounts of federal spending to be allocated to bridge repairs and reconstruction?

REFERENCES

1. ASCE, "Report Card for America's Infrastructure," 2005. This document can be accessed online at http://www.asce.org/reportcard/2005/index.cfm.
2. Minnesota Department of Transportation, "Interstate 35W Bridge Collapse," 2007. This document can be accessed online at http://www.dot.state.mn.us/i35wbridge/index.html.
3. U.S. Department of Transportation, Federal Highway Administration, "I-35 Bridge Collapse, Minneapolis, MN." This document can be accessed online at http://www.fhwa.dot.gov/pressroom/fsi35.htm.

CASE 4

Cadillac Chips[5]

Charged with installing computer chips that resulted in emitting excessive amounts of carbon dioxide from their Cadillacs, General Motors (GM) agreed in December 1995 to recall nearly 500,000 late-model Cadillacs and pay nearly $45 million in fines and recall costs. Lawyers for the Environmental Protection Agency (EPA) and the Justice Department contended that GM knew that the design change would result in pollution problems. Rejecting this claim, GM released a statement saying that the case was "a matter of interpretation" of complex regulations, but that it had "worked extremely hard to resolve the matter and avoid litigation."

According to EPA and Justice Department officials, the $11 million civil penalty was the third largest penalty in a pollution case, the second largest such penalty under the Clean Air Act, and the largest involving motor vehicle pollution. This was also the first case of a court ordering an automobile recall to reduce pollution rather than to improve safety or dependability.

Government officials said that in 1990 a new computer chip was designed for the engine controls of Cadillac Seville and Deville models. This was in response to car owners' complaints that these cars tended to stall when the climate control system was running. The chips injected additional fuel into the engine whenever this system was running. But this resulted in tailpipe emissions of carbon dioxide well in excess of the regulations.

Although the cars are usually driven with the climate control system running, tests used for certifying the meeting of emission standards were conducted when the system was not running. This was standard practice for emission tests throughout the automotive industry.

However, EPA officials argued that under the Clean Air Act, GM should have informed them that the Cadillac's design was changed in a way that would result in violating pollution standards under normal driving conditions. In 1970, the officials said, automobile manufacturers were directed not to get around testing rules by designing cars that technically pass the tests but that nevertheless cause avoidable pollution. GM's competitors, the officials contended, complied with that directive.

A GM spokesperson said that testing emissions with the climate control running was not required because "it was not in the rules, not in the regulations; it's not in the Clean Air Act." However, claiming that GM discovered the problem in 1991, Justice Department environmental lawyer Thomas P. Carroll objected to GM's continued inclusion of the chip in the 1992–1995 models: "They should have gone back and re-engineered it to improve the emissions."

In agreeing to recall the vehicles, GM said it now had a way of controlling the stalling problem without increasing pollution. This involves "new fueling calibrations," GM said, and it "should have no adverse effect on the driveability of the vehicles involved."

What responsibilities did GM engineers have in regard to either causing or resolving the problems with the Cadillac Seville and Deville models?

CASE 5

Cartex

Ben is assigned by his employer, Cartex, to work on an improvement to an ultrasonic range-finding device. While working on the improvement, he gets an idea for a modification of the equipment that might be applicable to military submarines. If this is successful, it could be worth a lot of money to his company. However, Ben is a pacifist and does not want to contribute in any way to the development of military hardware. So Ben neither develops the idea himself nor mentions it to anybody else in the company. Ben has signed an agreement that all inventions he produces on the job are the property of the company, but he does not believe the agreement applies to his situation because (1) his idea is not developed and (2) his superiors know of his antimilitary sentiments. Yet he wonders if he is ethically right in concealing his idea from his employers.

An interesting historical precedent: Leonardo Da Vinci recorded in his journal that he had discovered how to make a vessel that can move about underwater—a kind of submarine. However, he refused to share this idea with others on the grounds that he feared it would be used for immoral purposes. "I do not publish or divulge on account of the evil nature of men who would practice assassinations at the bottom of the seas, by breaking the ships in their lowest parts and sinking them together with the crews who are in them."[6]

CASE 6

Citicorp[7]

William LeMessurier was understandably proud of his structural design of the 1977 Citicorp building in downtown Manhattan. He had resolved a perplexing problem in a very innovative way. A church had property rights to a corner of the block on which the 59-story building was to be constructed. LeMessurier proposed constructing the building *over* the church, with four supporting columns located at the center of each side of the building rather than in the four corners. The first floor began the equivalent of nine stories above ground, thus allowing ample space for the church. LeMessurier used a diagonal bracing design that transferred weight to the columns, and he added a tuned mass damper with a 400-ton concrete block floating on oil bearings to reduce wind sway.

In June 1978, LeMessurier received a call from a student at a nearby university who said his professor claimed the Citicorp building's supporting columns should be on the corners instead of midway between them. LeMessurier replied that the professor did not understand the design problem, adding that the innovative design made it even more resistant to quartering, or diagonal, winds. However, since the New York City building codes required calculating the effects of only 90-degree winds, no one actually worked out calculations for quartering winds. Then he decided that it would be instructive for his own students to wrestle with the design problem.

This may have been prompted by not only the student's call but also a discovery LeMessurier had made just 1 month earlier. While consulting on a building project in Pittsburgh, he called his home office to find out what it would cost to weld the joints of diagonal girders similar to those in the Citicorp building. To his surprise, he learned that the original specification for full-penetration welds was not followed. Instead, the joints were bolted. However, since this still more than

adequately satisfied the New York building code requirements, LeMessurier was not concerned.

However, as he began to work on calculations for his class, LeMessurier recalled his Pittsburgh discovery. He wondered what difference bolted joints might make to the building's ability to withstand quartering winds. To his dismay, LeMessurier determined that a 40 percent stress increase in some areas of the structure would result in a 160 percent increase in stress on some of the building's joints. This meant that the building was vulnerable to total collapse if certain areas were subjected to a "16-year storm" (i.e., the sort of storm that could strike Manhattan once every 16 years). Meanwhile, hurricane season was not far away.

LeMessurier realized that reporting what he had learned could place both his engineering reputation and the financial status of his firm at substantial risk. Nevertheless, he acted quickly and decisively. He drew up a plan for correcting the problem, estimated the cost and time needed for rectifying it, and immediately informed Citicorp owners of what he had learned. Citicorp's response was equally decisive. LeMessurier's proposed course of action was accepted and corrective steps were immediately undertaken. As the repairs neared completion in early September, a hurricane was reported moving up the coast in the direction of New York. Fortunately, it moved harmlessly out over the Atlantic Ocean, but not without first causing considerable anxiety among those working on the building, as well as those responsible for implementing plans to evacuate the area should matters take a turn for the worse.

Although correcting the problem cost several million dollars, all parties responded promptly and responsibly. Faced with the threat of increased liability insurance rates, LeMessurier's firm convinced its insurers that because of his responsible handling of the situation, a much more costly disaster may have been prevented. As a result, the rates were actually reduced.

Identify and discuss the ethical issues this case raises.

CASE 7

Disaster Relief[8]

Among the 24 recipients of the John D. and Catherine T. MacArthur Foundation Fellowships for 1995 was Frederick C. Cuny, a disaster relief specialist. The fellowship program is commonly referred to as a "genius program," but it is characterized by MacArthur executives as a program that rewards "hard-working experts who often push the boundaries of their fields in ways that others will follow."[9] The program, says Catherine Simpson, director of the awards program, is meant to serve as "a reminder of the importance of seeing as broadly as possible, of being willing to live outside of a comfort zone and of keeping your nerve endings open."[10]

Cuny's award was unusual in two respects. First, at the time the award was announced, his whereabouts were unknown, and it was feared that he had been executed in Chechnya. Second, he was a practicing engineer. Most MacArthur awards go to writers, artists, and university professors.

Ironically, although honored for his engineering achievements, Cuny never received a degree in engineering. Initially planning to graduate from the ROTC program at Texas A & M as a Marine pilot, he had to drop out of school in his second year due to poor grades. He transferred to Texas A & I, Kingsville, to continue his ROTC coursework, but his grades suffered there as well. Although he never became a Marine pilot, he worked effectively with Marine corps officers later in Iraq and Somalia.[11]

In Kingsville, Cuny worked on several community projects after he dropped out of school. He found his niche in life working in the barrios with poor Mexicans in Kingsville and formulated some common sense guidelines that served him well throughout his career. As he moved into disaster relief work, he understood immediately that the aid had to be designed for those who were in trouble in ways that would leave them in the position of being able to help themselves. He learned to focus on the main problem in any disaster to better understand how to plan the relief aid. Thus, if the problem was shelter, the people should be shown how to rebuild their destroyed homes in a better fashion than before. Similar approaches were adopted regarding famine, drought, disease, and warfare.

The first major engineering project Cuny worked on was the Dallas–Ft.Worth airport. However, attracted to humanitarian work, he undertook disaster relief work in Biafra in 1969. Two years later, at age 27, he founded the Intertect Relief and Reconstruction Corporation in Dallas. Intertect describes itself as a professional firm providing specialized services and technical assistance in all aspects of natural disaster and refugee emergency management—mitigation, preparedness, relief, recovery, reconstruction, resettlement—including program design and implementation, camp planning and administration, logistics, vulnerability analysis, training and professional development, technology transfer, assessment, evaluation, networking and information dissemination."[12]

Intertect also prides itself for its "multidisciplinary, flexible, innovative, and culturally-appropriate approach to problem-solving."[13] Obviously, such an enterprise requires the expertise of engineers. But it also must draw from social services, health and medical care professionals, sociology, anthropology, and other areas.

Fred Cuny was apparently comfortable working across disciplines. As an undergraduate he also studied African history. So, it is understandable that he would take a special interest in the course of the conflict between the Nigerian and Biafran governments in the late 1960s. In 1969, he announced to the Nigerian minister of the interior, "I'm from Texas. I'm here to study the war and try to suggest what can be done to get in humanitarian aid when it's over."[14] Rebuffed by the minister, Cuny then flew to Biafra and helped organize an airlift that provided short-term assistance to the starving Biafrans.

Cuny learned two important lessons from his Biafran work. First, food distribution in disaster relief often pulls people from their homes and working areas to distribution centers in towns and airports.

Cuny commented, "The first thing I recognized was that we had to turn the system around and get people back into the countryside away from the airfield." Second, Cuny realized that public health is a major problem—one that can effectively be addressed only through careful planning. This requires engineering efforts to, for example, build better drains, roads, dwellings, and so on. At the same time, Cuny realized that relatively few engineers were in relief agencies: hence the founding of Intertect. Concerned to share his ideas with others, in 1983 Cuny published *Disasters and Development* (Oxford University Press), which provides a detailed set of guidelines for planning and providing disaster relief. A major theme of his book is that truly helpful relief requires careful study of local conditions in order to provide long-term assistance.

Despite its small size, since its founding in 1971, Intertect has been involved in relief projects in nearly 70 different countries during Cuny's career. His work came to the attention of wealthy Hungarian philanthropist George Soros, who provided him with funding to work on a number of major disaster relief projects.

An especially daring project was the restoration of water and heat to a besieged section of Sarajevo in 1993.[15] Modules for a water filtration system were specially designed to fit into a C-130 airplane that was flown from Zagreb (Croatia's capital) into Sarajevo. (Cuny commented that there were only 3 inches to spare on each side of the storage area.) In order to get the modules unnoticed through Serbian checkpoints, they had to be unloaded in less than 10 minutes.

Clearly, the preparation and delivery of the modules required careful planning and courage in execution. However, prior to that someone had to determine that such a system could be adapted to the circumstances in Sarajevo. When Cuny and his associates arrived in Sarajevo, for many the only source of water was from a polluted river. The river could be reached only by exposing oneself to sniper fire, which had already injured thousands and killed hundreds. Thus, residents risked their lives to bring back containers of water whose contaminated contents posed additional risks. Noting that Sarajevo had expanded downhill in recent years, and that the newer water system had to pump water uphill to Old

Town Sarajevo, the Cuny team concluded that there must have been an earlier system for Old Town.[16] They located a network of old cisterns and channels still in good working order, thus providing them with a basis for designing and installing a new water filtration plant. This $2.5 million project was funded by the Soros Foundation, which also provided $2.7 million to restore heat for more than 20,000 citizens of Sarajevo.

Cuny told author Christopher Merrill, "We've got to say, 'If people are in harm's way, we've got to get them out of there. The first and most important thing is saving lives. Whatever it takes to save lives, you do it, and the hell with national sovereignty.'"[17] This philosophy lay behind his efforts to save 400,000 Kurds in northern Iraq after Operation Desert Storm, in addition to thousands of lives in Sarajevo; however, this may be what cost him his own life in Chechnya in 1995.

Perhaps Cuny's single most satisfying effort was in northern Iraq immediately following Operation Desert Storm. As soon as Iraq signed the peace treaty, Saddam Hussein directed his troops to attack the Shiites in the south and the Kurds in the north. The 400,000 Kurds fled into the mountains bordering Turkey, where the Turks prevented them from crossing the border. Winter was coming and food was scarce. President Bush created a no-fly zone over northern Iraq and directed the Marine Corps to rescue the Kurds in what was called "Operation Provide Comfort." The Marine general in charge hired Fred Cuny as a consultant, and Cuny quickly became, in effect, second in command of the operation.

When Operation Provide Comfort was regarded as no longer necessary, the Kurds held a farewell celebration at which the full Marine battalion marched before joyous crowds, with one civilian marching in the first row—Fred Cuny. Cuny had an enlargement of a photo of that moment hung over his desk in Dallas. The photo has the signature of the Marine general who led the parade.

Asked about his basic approach to disaster relief, Cuny commented: "In any large-scale disaster, if you can isolate a part that you can understand you will usually end up understanding the whole system."[18] In the case of Sarajevo, the main problems seemed to center around water and heat. So this is what Cuny and associates set out to address. In preparing for disaster relief work, Cuny was from the outset struck by the fact that medical professionals and materials are routinely flown to international disasters, but engineers and engineering equipment and supplies are not. So, his recurrent thought was, "Why don't you officials give first priority to, say, fixing the sewage system, instead of merely stanching the inevitable results of a breakdown in sanitary conditions?"[19]

It is unusual for engineers to receive the sort of public attention Fred Cuny did. We tend to take for granted the good work that engineers do. Insofar as engineers "make the news," more likely than not this is when an engineering disaster has occurred, a product is subjected to vigorous criticism, or an engineer has blown the whistle. Fred Cuny's stories are largely stories of successful humanitarian ventures.

Fred Cuny's untimely, violent death was tragic. In April 1995, while organizing a field hospital for victims in the conflict in Chechnya, Cuny, two Russian Red Cross doctors, and a Russian interpreter disappeared. After a prolonged search, it was concluded that all four were executed. Speculation is that Chechens may have been deliberately misinformed that the four were Russian spies. Cuny's article in the *New York Review of Books* titled "Killing Chechnya" was quite critical of the Russian treatment of Chechnya, and it gives some indication of why his views might well have antagonized Russians.[20] Already featured in the *New York Times,* the *New Yorker Magazine,* and the *New York Review of Books,* Cuny had attained sufficient national recognition that his disappearance received widespread attention and immediate response from President Clinton and government officials. Reports on the search for Cuny and colleagues regularly appeared in the press from early April until August 18, 1995, when his family finally announced that he was now assumed dead.

Many tributes have been made to the work of Fred Cuny. Pat Reed, a colleague at Intertect, was quoted soon after Cuny's disappearance: "He's one of the few visionaries in the emergency management field. He really knows what he's doing. He's not just some cowboy."[21] At the Moscow press conference calling an end to the search, Cuny's son Chris said, "Let it be known to all nations and humanitarian organizations that Russia was responsible for the death of one of the world's great humanitarians."[22] William

Shaw-cross fittingly concludes his article, "A Hero for Our Time," as follows:

> At the memorial meeting in Washington celebrating Fred's life it was clear that he had touched people in a remarkable way. He certainly touched me; I think he was a great man. The most enduring memorials to Fred are the hundreds of thousands of people he has helped—and the effect he has had, and will have, on the ways governments and other organizations try to relieve the suffering caused by disasters throughout the world.

AN AFTERWORD

It is certainly appropriate to make special note of extraordinary individuals such as Frederick C. Cuny for special praise. His life does seem heroic. However, we would do well to remember that even heroes have helpers. Cuny worked with others, both at Intertect and at the various other agencies with whom Intertect collaborated. There are unnamed engineers in Sarajevo with whom he worked. For example, his Sarajevo team was able to locate the old cisterns and channels through the assistance of local engineers (and historians).[23] Local engineers assisted in installing the water filtration system.

Furthermore, once the system was installed, the water had to be tested for purity. Here, a conflict developed between local engineers (as well as Cuny and specialists from the International Rescue Committee) and local water safety inspectors who demanded further testing. Convinced that they had adequately tested the water, the local engineers, Cuny, and the International Rescue Committee were understandably impatient. However, the cautious attitude of the water safety experts is understandable as well. Muhamed Zlatar, deputy head of Sarajevo's Institute for Water, commented, "The consequences of letting in polluted water could be catastrophic. They could be worse than the shelling. We could have 30,000 people come down with stomach diseases, and some of them could die."[24] Without presuming who might have been right, we might do well to remember Fran Kelsey, the FDA official who, in 1962, refused to approve thalidomide until further testing was done. That is, in our rush to do good, caution should not be thrown to the winds.

Identify and discuss the ethical issues raised by the story of Frederick C. Cuny.

CASE 8

Electric Chair

Thanks in part to Theodore Bernstein, retired University of Wisconsin professor of electrical and computer engineering, apparently the electric chair is disappearing.[25] Once regarded as a more humane way of executing someone than beheading or hanging, the electric chair itself has a questionable history. For instance, the Death Penalty Information Center classifies 10 of the 149 electrocutions of the past 25 years as botched. Although, as Bernstein says, "You give enough shocks, you can kill anybody," it is not clear how much is enough—or too much.

Having spent three decades studying the effects of electricity on the human body, Bernstein has frequently testified in court and in hearings in an effort to help defendants avoid being placed in the electric chair. He comments,

> The substance of my testimony is pretty much always the same. I tell the court that most of the work on the electric chair was done with a seat-of-the-pants approach. The electrical design is poor. Every state has a different sequence of shocks. Many of the states use old equipment, and they don't test it very well. They'll have in the notebook or the protocols, "Check the equipment," or "Check the electrodes." What does that mean? They need to be more specific.[26]

The problem, says Bernstein, is that electrocution has always been controlled by people without background in biomedical engineering. This is also reflected in its beginnings in the late 19th century. Believing that the alternating current (AC) system of his competitor, George Westinghouse, was more dangerous than his own system of direct current (DC), Thomas Edison recommended the AC system for the electric chair.

Not wanting his company's reputation to be tied to the electric chair, Westinghouse provided funding to William Kemmler's attorneys in their effort to stop their client from becoming the first person executed in an electric chair. Edison testified that an electric chair that used alternating current would cause minimal suffering and instantaneous death. Although Kemmler's attorneys got Edison to admit that he knew little about the structure of the human body or conductivity in the brain, Edison's claims carried the day. According to Bernstein, Edison's "reputation made more of an impression than did his bioelectrical ignorance."[27]

Not only was Kemmler the first person executed in an electric chair but also he was the first person whose execution by electricity required more than one application of current, the second of which caused vapor and smoke to be emitted from Kemmler's body. Witnesses were dismayed by what they saw, with one physician commenting that using an electric chair "can in no way be regarded as a step in civilization."[28] According to Bernstein, a basic problem was that executioners knew very little about how electrocution causes death—and, he notes, executioners know little more even today.

Does electrocution "fry the brain"? Bernstein comments: "That's a lot of nonsense. The skull has a very high resistance, and current tends to flow around it." Actually, he says, electrocution usually causes cardiac arrest, and this may not be painless— and it may not be fatal on the first try.

Discuss the ethical issues surrounding Theodore Bernstein's chosen area of research and his role as a witness in the courtroom and legal hearings.

CASE 9

Fabricating Data[29]

INTRODUCTION

In recent years, the National Science Foundation (NSF), the National Institutes of Health (NIH), the Public Health Services (PHS), the Office of Scientific Integrity, and various scientific organizations such as the National Academy of Sciences have spent considerable time and effort in trying to agree on a definition of *scientific misconduct*. A good definition is needed in developing and implementing policies and regulations concerning appropriate conduct in research, particularly when federal funding is involved. This is an important area of concern because although serious scientific misconduct may be infrequent, the consequences of even a few instances can be widespread.

Those cases that reach the public's attention can cause considerable distrust among both scientists and the public, however infrequent their occurrence. Like lying in general, we may wonder which scientific reports are tainted by misconduct, even though we may be convinced that relatively few are tainted. Furthermore, scientists depend on each other's work in advancing their own. Building one's work on the incorrect or unsubstantiated data of others infects one's own research, and the chain of consequences can be quite lengthy as well as very serious. This is as true of honest or careless mistakes as it is of the intentional distortion of data, which is what *scientific misconduct* is usually restricted to. Finally, of course, the public depends on the reliable expertise of scientists in virtually every area of health, safety, and welfare.

Although exactly what the definition of scientific misconduct should include is a matter of controversy, all proposed definitions include the fabrication and falsification of data and plagiarism. As an instance of fraud, the fabrication of data is a particularly blatant form of misconduct. It lacks the subtlety of questions about interpreting data that pivot around whether the data have been "fudged" or "manipulated." Fabricating data is making it up, or *faking* it. Thus, it is a clear instance of a lie, a deliberate attempt to deceive others.

However, this does not mean that fabrications are easy to detect or handle effectively once they are detected; and this adds considerably to the mischief and harm they can cause. Two well-known cases illustrate this, both of which feature ambitious, and apparently successful, young researchers.

THE DARSEE CASE[30]

Dr. John Darsee was regarded as a brilliant student and medical researcher at the University of Notre Dame (1966–1970), Indiana University (1970–1974), Emory University (1974–1979), and Harvard University (1979–1981). He was regarded by faculty at all four institutions as a potential "all-star" with a great research future ahead of him. At Harvard, he

reportedly often worked more than 90 hours a week as a research fellow in the Cardiac Research Laboratory headed by Dr. Eugene Braunwald. In less than 2 years at Harvard, he was first author of seven publications in very good scientific journals. His special area of research concerned the testing of heart drugs on dogs.

All of this came to a sudden halt in May 1981 when three colleagues in the Cardiac Research Laboratory observed Darsee labeling data recordings "24 seconds," "72 hours," "one week," and "two weeks." In reality, only minutes had transpired. Confronted by his mentor Braunwald, Darsee admitted the fabrication, but he insisted that this was the only time he had done this, and that he had been under intense pressure to complete the study quickly. Shocked, Braunwald and Darsee's immediate supervisor, Dr. Robert Kroner, spent the next several months checking other research conducted by Darsee in their lab. Darsee's research fellowships were terminated, and an offer of a faculty position was withdrawn. However, he was allowed to continue his research projects at Harvard for the next several months (during which time Braunwald and Kroner observed his work very closely).

Hopeful that this was an isolated incident, Braunwald and Kroner were shocked again in October. A comparison of results from four different laboratories in a National Heart, Lung, and Blood Institute Models Study revealed an implausibly low degree of invariability in data provided by Darsee. In short, his data looked "too good." Since these data had been submitted in April, there was strong suspicion that Darsee had been fabricating or falsifying data for some time. Subsequent investigations seemed to indicate questionable research practices dating back as far as his undergraduate days.

What were the consequences of John Darsee's misconduct? Darsee, we have seen, lost his research position at Harvard, and his offer of a faculty position was withdrawn. The NIH barred him from NIH funding or serving on NIH committees for 10 years. He left research and went into training as a critical care specialist. However, the cost to others was equally, if not more, severe. Harvard-affiliated Brigham and Women's Hospital became the first institution that NIH ever required to return funds ($122,371) because of research involving fraudulent data. Braunwald and colleagues had to spend several months investigating Darsee's research rather than simply continuing the work of the Cardiac Research Laboratory. Furthermore, they were severely criticized for carrying on their own investigation without informing NIH of their concerns until several months later. The morale and productivity of the laboratory were damaged. A cloud of suspicion hung over all the work with which Darsee was associated. Not only was Darsee's own research discredited but also, insofar as it formed an integral part of collaborative research, a cloud was thrown over published research bearing the names of authors whose work was linked with Darsee's.

The months of outside investigation also took others away from their main tasks and placed them under extreme pressure. Statistician David DeMets played a key role in the NIH investigation. Years later, he recalled the relief his team experienced when their work was completed:[31]

> For the author and the junior statistician, there was relief that the episode was finally over and we could get on with our careers, without the pressures of a highly visible misconduct investigation. It was clear early on that we had no room for error, that any mistakes would destroy the case for improbable data and severely damage our careers. Even without mistakes, being able to convince lay reviewers such as a jury using statistical arguments could still be defeating. Playing the role of the prosecuting statisticians was very demanding of our technical skills but also of our own integrity and ethical standards. Nothing could have adequately prepared us for what we experienced.

Braunwald notes some positive things that have come from the Darsee case. In addition to alerting scientists to the need for providing closer supervision of trainees and taking authorship responsibilities more seriously, the Darsee incident contributed to the development of guidelines and standards concerning research misconduct by PHS, NIH, NSF, medical associations and institutes, and universities and medical schools. However, he cautions that no protective system is able to prevent all research misconduct. In fact, he doubts that current provisions could have prevented Darsee's misconduct, although

they might have resulted in earlier detection. Furthermore, he warns that good science does not thrive in an atmosphere of heavy "policing" of one another's work:[32]

> The most creative minds will not thrive in such an environment and the most promising young people might actually be deterred from embarking on a scientific career in an atmosphere of suspicion. Second only to absolute truth, science requires an atmosphere of openness, trust, and collegiality.

Given this, it seems that William F. May is right in urging the need for a closer examination of character and virtue in professional life.[33] He says that an important test of character and virtue is what we do when no one is watching. The Darsee case and Braunwald's reflections seem to confirm this.

Many who are caught having engaged in scientific misconduct plead that they were under extreme pressure, needing to complete their research in order to meet the expectations of their lab supervisor, to meet a grant deadline, to get an article published, or to survive in the increasingly competitive world of scientific research. Although the immediate stakes are different, students sometimes echo related concerns: "I knew how the experiment should have turned out, and I needed to support the right answer"; "I needed to get a good grade"; "I didn't have time to do it right; there's so much pressure." Often these thoughts are accompanied by another—namely that this is only a classroom exercise and that, of course, one will not fabricate data when one becomes a scientist and these pressures are absent. What the Darsee case illustrates is that it is naive to assume such pressures will vanish. Therefore, the time to begin dealing with the ethical challenges they pose is now, not later (when the stakes may be even higher).

THE BRUENING CASE[34]

In December 1983, Dr. Robert Sprague wrote an 8-page letter, with 44 pages of appendices, to the National Institute of Mental Health documenting the fraudulent research of Dr. Stephen Breuning.[35] Breuning fabricated data concerning the effects psychotropic medication has on mentally retarded patients. Despite Breuning's admission of fabricating data only 3 months after Sprague sent his letter, the case was not finally resolved until July 1989. During that 5½-year interval, Sprague was a target of investigation (in fact, he was the first target of investigation), he had his own research endeavors severely curtailed, he was subjected to threats of lawsuits, and he had to testify before a U.S. House of Representatives committee. Most painful of all, Sprague's wife died in 1986 after a lengthy bout with diabetes. In fact, his wife's serious illness was one of the major factors prompting his "whistle-blowing" to NIH. Realizing how dependent his diabetic wife was on reliable research and medication, Sprague was particularly sensitive to the dependency that the mentally retarded, clearly a vulnerable population, have on the trustworthiness of not only their caregivers but also those who use them in experimental drug research.

Writing 9 years after the closing of the Bruening case, Sprague obviously has vivid memories of the painful experiences he endured and of the potential harms to participants in Bruening's studies. However, he closes the account of his own experiences by reminding us of other victims of Bruening's misconduct—namely psychologists and other researchers who collaborated with Bruening without being aware that he had fabricated data.

Dr. Alan Poling, one of those psychologists, writes about the consequences of Bruening's misconduct for his collaborators in research. Strikingly, Poling points out that between 1979 and 1983, Bruening was a contributor to 34 percent of all published research on the psychopharmacology of mentally retarded people. For those not involved in the research, initial doubts may, however unfairly, be cast on all these publications. For those involved in the research, efforts need to be made in each case to determine to what extent, if any, the validity of the research was affected by Bruening's role in the study. Even though Bruening was the only researcher to fabricate data, his role could contaminate an entire study. In fact, however, not all of Bruening's research did involve fabrication. Yet, convincing others of this is a time-consuming, demanding task. Finally, those who cited Bruening's publications in their own work may also suffer "guilt by association." As Poling points out, this is especially unfair in those instances in which Bruening collaborations with others involved no fraud at all.

THE ISSUES

The Darsee and Bruening cases raise a host of ethical questions about the nature and consequences of scientific fraud:

- What kinds of reasons are offered for fabricating data?
- Which, if any, of those reasons are *good* reasons—that is, reasons that might *justify* fabricating data?
- Who is likely to be harmed by fabricating data? Does actual harm have to occur in order for fabrication to be ethically wrong?
- What responsibilities does a scientist or engineer have for checking the trustworthiness of the work of other scientists or engineers?
- What should a scientist or engineer do if he or she has reason to believe that another scientist or engineer has fabricated data?
- Why is honesty in research important to the scientific and engineering communities?
- Why is honesty in research important for the public?
- What might be done to diminish the likelihood that research fraud occurs?

READINGS

For readings on scientific integrity, including sections on the fabrication of data and a definition of scientific misconduct, see Nicholas Steneck, *ORI Introduction to Responsible Conduct in Research* (Washington, DC: Office of Research Integrity, 2004); *Integrity and Misconduct in Research* (Washington, DC: U.S. Department of Health and Human Services, 1995); *On Being a Scientist*, 2nd ed. (Washington, DC: National Academy Press, 1995); and *Honor in Science* (Research Triangle Park, NC: Sigma Xi, The Scientific Research Society, 1991).

CASE 10

Gilbane Gold

The fictional case study presented in the popular videotape *Gilbane Gold* focuses on David Jackson, a young engineer in the environmental affairs department of ZCORP, located in the city of Gilbane.[36] The firm, which manufactures computer parts, discharges lead and arsenic into the sanitary sewer of the city. The city has a lucrative business in processing the sludge into fertilizer, which is used by farmers in the area.

To protect its valuable product, Gilbane Gold, from contamination by toxic discharges from the new high-tech industries, the city has imposed highly restrictive regulations on the amount of arsenic and lead that can be discharged into the sanitary sewer system. However, recent tests indicate that ZCORP may be violating the standards. David believes that ZCORP must invest more money in pollution-control equipment, but management believes the costs will be prohibitive.

David faces a conflict situation that can be characterized by the convergence of four important moral claims. First, David has an obligation as a good employee to promote the interests of his company. He should not take actions that unnecessarily cost the company money or damage its reputation. Second, David has an obligation—based on his personal integrity, his professional integrity as an engineer, and his special role as environmental engineer—to be honest with the city in reporting data on the discharge of the heavy metals. Third, David has an obligation as an engineer to protect the health of the public. Fourth, David has a right, if not an obligation, to protect and promote his own career.

The problem David faces is this: How can he do justice to all of these claims? If they are all morally legitimate, he should try to honor all of them, and yet they appear to conflict in the situation. David's first option should be to attempt to find a creative middle way solution, despite the fact that the claims appear to be incompatible in the situation. What are some of the creative middle way possibilities?[37]

One possibility would be to find a cheap technical way to eliminate the heavy metals. Unfortunately, the video does not directly address this possibility. It begins in the midst of a crisis at ZCORP and focuses almost exclusively on the question of whether David Jackson should blow the whistle on his reluctant company. For a detailed exploration of some creative middle way alternatives, see Michael Pritchard and Mark Holtzapple, "Responsible Engineering: *Gilbane Gold* Revisited," *Science and Engineering*, 3, no. 2, April 1997, pp. 217–231.

Another avenue to explore in *Gilbane Gold* is the attitudes toward responsibility exhibited by the various characters in the story. Prominent, for example, are David Jackson, Phil Port, Diane Collins, Tom Richards, Frank Seeders, and Winslow Massin. Look at the transcript (available at www.niee.org/pd.cfm?pt= Murdough). What important similarities and differences do you find?

CASE 11

Green Power?[38]

The growing consensus among scientists that carbon emissions are contributing to global warming is also beginning to have a significant impact on local energy policies and projects. For example, Fort Collins, Colorado, has a Climate Wise energy program to go with its official motto, "Where renewal is a way of life." Local reduction of carbon emissions is one of the city's global aims.

At the same time, local communities such as Fort Collins have continued, if not growing, energy needs. AVA Solar and Powertech Uranium are proposing ways of helping to meet these needs. Working with Colorado State University, AVA has developed a manufacturing process to make electricity-producing solar panels. Solar energy has popular appeal and is typically given high marks in regard to "green" technology. Local critics, however, have some worries about the AVA project. The process uses cadmium, which raises concerns about cancer. AVA's director of strategic planning, Russ Kanjorski, acknowledges that the use of cadmium will call for careful environmental monitoring, particularly in the discharge of water, and that monitoring practices are still in the developmental stage.

Powertech Uranium proposes drilling for uranium, which can be used to create nuclear power. Nuclear power promises to reduce carbon emissions, but it lacks solar power's popularity. Although Governor Bill Ritter, Jr., is strongly committed to what he calls "the new energy economy," this does not favor uranium mining. In fact, there are long-term, unresolved scientific and technological worries about extracting, processing, and disposing of uranium.

Complicating matters is that both projects seem to have great economic potential for the companies and the local economy. As Kirk Johnson states, "There is no doubt that new money is chasing new energy."

Meanwhile, Johnson observes, local environmentalists such as Dan Bihn are genuinely puzzled. Bihn is an electrical engineer and environmental consultant on the Fort Collins Electric Utilities Board. Johnson quotes Bihn as saying "I think nuclear needs to be on

the table, and we need to work through this thing and we can't just emotionally react to it." What is Bihn's emotional reaction to Powertech's proposal? "Deep down inside," he told Johnson, "my emotional reaction is that we should never do this."

Lane Douglas, a spokesperson for Powertech and its Colorado land and project manager, urges that its company's proposal be judged on facts, not prejudice. "The science will either be good science or it won't," Douglas says. "We're just saying give us a fair hearing."

Local citizens such as Ariana Friedlander are striving to be consistent in evaluating the proposals. Skeptical about uranium mining, she adds, "But we shouldn't be giving the other guys a pass because they're sexy right now."

Discuss the ethical issues raised by the Fort Collins circumstances. What responsibilities do engineers have in regard to issues like these? When Dan Bihn says we shouldn't *just* emotionally react to these issues, do you think he is saying that he should *ignore* his own emotional reaction? (Why do you suppose he characterizes this as "deep down inside"?) What do you think Lane Douglas has in mind by appealing to "good science" in resolving the issues about uranium mining? Do you think "good science" alone can provide the answers?

CASE 12

Greenhouse Gas Emissions[39]

On November 15, 2007, the Ninth Circuit Court of Appeals in San Francisco rejected the Bush administration's fuel economy standards for light trucks and sport utility vehicles. The three-judge panel objected that the regulations fail to take sufficiently into account the economic impact that tailpipe emissions can be expected to have on climate change. The judges also questioned why the standards were so much easier on light trucks than passenger cars. (The standards hold that by 2010 light trucks are to average 23.5 mpg, whereas passenger cars are to average 27.5 mpg.)

Although it is expected that an appeal will be made to the U.S. Supreme Court, this ruling is one of several recent federal court rulings that urge regulators

to consider the risk of climate change in setting standards for carbon dioxide and other heat-trapping gas emissions from industry.

Patrick A. Parenteau, Vermont Law School environmental law professor, is quoted as saying, "What this says to me is that the courts are catching up with climate change and the law is catching up with climate change. Climate change has ushered in a whole new era of judicial review."[40]

One of the judges, Betty B. Fletcher, invoked the National Environmental Policy Act in calling for cumulative impacts analyses explicitly taking into account the environmental impact of greenhouse gas emissions. Acknowledging that cost-benefit analysis may appropriately indicate realistic limits for fuel economy standards, she insisted that "it cannot put a thumb on the scale by undervaluing the benefits and overvaluing the costs of more stringent standards."

Finally, Judge Fletcher wrote, "What was a reasonable balancing of competing statutory priorities 20 years ago may not be a reasonable balancing of those priorities today."

Given recent court trends, what implications are there for the responsibilities (and opportunities) of engineers working in the affected areas?

CASE 13

"Groupthink" and the Challenger *Disaster*

The video *Groupthink* presents Irving Janis's theory of "groupthink" in the form of a case study of the 1986 *Challenger* disaster (discussed in Chapters 1 and 7). As we indicate in Chapter 7, Janis characterizes "groupthink" as a set of tendencies of cohesive groups to achieve consensus at the expense of critical thinking.

View the video and then discuss the extent to which you agree with the video's suggestion that groupthink could have been a significant factor leading up to the *Challenger* disaster. (This video is available from CRM Films, McGraw-Hill Films, 1221 Avenue of the Americas, New York, NY 10020. 1-800-421-0833.)

CASE 14

Halting a Dangerous Project

In the mid 1980s, Sam was Alpha Electronics' project leader on a new contract to produce manufactured weaponry devices for companies doing business with NATO government agencies.[41] The devices were advanced technology land mines with electronic controls that could be triggered with capacitor circuits to go off only at specified times, rather than years later when children might be playing in old minefields. NATO provided all the technical specifications and Alpha Electronics fulfilled the contract without problems. However, Sam was concerned that one new end user of this device could negate the safety aspects of the trigger and make the land mines more dangerous than any others on the market.

After the NATO contract was completed, Sam was dismayed to learn that Alpha Electronics had signed another contract with an Eastern European firm that had a reputation of stealing patented devices and also of doing business with terrorist organizations. Sam halted the production of the devices. He then sought advice from some of his colleagues and contacted the U.S. State Department's Office of Munitions Controls. In retrospect, he wishes he had also contacted the Department of Commerce's Bureau of Export Administration, as well as the Defense Department. He ruefully acknowledges that the issue would have been brought to a close much more quickly.

The contract that Sam unilaterally voided by his action was for nearly $2 million over 15 years. Sam noted that no further hiring or equipment would have been needed, so the contract promised to be highly profitable. There was a $15,000 penalty for breaking the contract.

On the basis of global corporate citizenship, it was clear that Alpha Electronics could legally produce the devices for the NATO countries but not for the Eastern European company. The Cold War was in full swing at that time.

On the basis of local corporate citizenship, it was clear that Alpha Electronics had to consider the expected impact on local communities. In particular, there was no guarantee regarding to whom the Eastern European company would be selling the devices and how they would end up being used.

Sam took matters into his own hands without any foreknowledge of how his decision would be viewed by his company's upper management, board of directors, or fellow workers, many of whom were also company stockholders. Happily, Sam was never punished for his unilateral action of halting production.

He recently retired from Alpha Electronics as a corporate-level vice president. He was especially gratified by the number of Alpha employees who were veterans of World War II, the Korean War, and the Vietnam War who thanked him for his action.

Sam strongly believed his action was the right thing to do, both for his company and for the public welfare. What ideas typically covered in an engineering ethics course might support that conviction?

CASE 15

Highway Safety Improvements[42]

David Weber, age 23, is a civil engineer in charge of safety improvements for District 7 (an eight-county area within a midwestern state). Near the end of the fiscal year, the district engineer informs David that delivery of a new snow plow has been delayed, and as a consequence the district has $50,000 in uncommitted funds. He asks David to suggest a safety project (or projects) that can be put under contract within the current fiscal year.

After a careful consideration of potential projects, David narrows his choice to two possible safety improvements. Site A is the intersection of Main and Oak Streets in the major city within the district. Site B is the intersection of Grape and Fir Roads in a rural area.

Pertinent data for the two intersections are as follows:

	Site A	Site B
Main road traffic (vehicles/day)	20,000	5,000
Minor road traffic (vehicles/day)	4,000	1,000
Fatalities per year (3-year average)	2	1
Injuries per year (3-year average)	6	2
PD* (3-year average)	40	12
Proposed improvement	New signals	New signals
Improvement cost	$50,000	$50,000

*PD refers to property damage-only accidents.

A highway engineering textbook includes a table of average reductions in accidents resulting from the installation of the types of signal improvements David proposes. The tables are based on studies of intersections in urban and rural areas throughout the United States during the past 20 years.

	Urban	Rural
Percent reduction in fatalities	50	50
Percent reduction in injuries	50	60
Percent reduction in PD	25	−25*

*Property damage-only accidents are expected to increase because of the increase in rear-end accidents due to the stopping of highspeed traffic in rural areas.

David recognizes that these reduction factors represent averages from intersections with a wide range of physical characteristics (number of approach lanes, angle of intersection, etc.), in all climates, with various mixes of trucks and passenger vehicles, various approach speeds, various driving habits, and so on. However, he has no special data about sites A and B that suggest relying on these tables is likely to misrepresent the circumstances at these sites.

Finally, here is additional information that David knows:

1. In 1975, the National Safety Council (NSC) and the National Highway Traffic Safety Administration (NHTSA) both published dollar scales for comparing accident outcomes, as shown below:

	NSC	NHTSA
Fatality	$52,000	$235,000
Injury	3,000	11,200
PD	440	500

A neighboring state uses the following weighting scheme:

Fatality	9.5 PD
Injury	3.5 PD

2. Individuals within the two groups pay roughly the same transportation taxes (licenses, gasoline taxes, etc.).

Which of the two site improvements do you think David should recommend? What is your rationale for this recommendation?

CASE 16

Hurricane Katrina

As we have noted in the text, until approximately 1970 nearly all engineering codes of ethics held that the engineer's first duty is fidelity to his or her employer and clients. However, soon after 1970, most codes insisted that "Engineers shall hold paramount the safety, health, and welfare of the public." Whatever may have precipitated this change in the early 1970s, recent events—ranging from the collapse of Manhattan's Twin Towers on September 11, 2001, to the collapse of a major bridge in Minneapolis/St. Paul on August 1, 2007— make apparent the vital importance of this principle. The devastation wreaked by Hurricane Katrina along the Gulf of Mexico coastline states of Louisiana, Mississippi, and Alabama in late August 2005 is also a dramatic case in point.

Hardest hit was Louisiana, which endured the loss of more than 1,000 lives, thousands of homes, damage to residential and nonresidential property of more than $20 billion, and damage to public infrastructure estimated at nearly $7 billion. Most severely damaged was the city of New Orleans, much of which had to be evacuated and which suffered the loss of more than 100,000 jobs. The city is still reeling, apparently having permanently lost much of its population and only slowly recovering previously habitable areas.

At the request of the U.S. Army Corp of Engineers (USACE), the American Society of Civil Engineers (ASCE) formed the Hurricane Katrina External Review Panel to review the comprehensive work of USACE's Interagency Performance Evaluation Task Force. The resulting ASCE report, *The New Orleans Hurricane Protection System: What Went Wrong and Why,* is a detailed and eloquent statement of the ethical responsibilities of engineers to protect public safety, health, and welfare.[43]

The ASCE report documents engineering failures, organizational and policy failures, and lessons learned for the future. Chapter 7 of the report ("Direct Causes of the Catastrophe") begins as follows:[44]

> What is unique about the devastation that befell the New Orleans area from Hurricane Katrina—compared to other natural disasters—is that much of the destruction was the result of engineering and engineering-related policy failures.

From an engineering standpoint, the panel asserts, there was an underestimation of soil strength that rendered the levees more vulnerable than they should have been, a failure to satisfy standard factors of safety in the original designs of the levees and pumps, and a failure to determine and communicate clearly to the public the level of hurricane risk to which the city and its residents were exposed. The panel concludes,[45]

> With the benefit of hindsight, we now see that questionable engineering decisions and management choices, and inadequate interfaces within and between organizations, all contributed to the problem.

This might suggest that blame-responsibility is in order. However, the panel chose not to pursue this line, pointing out instead the difficulty of assigning blame:[46]

> No one person or decision is to blame. The engineering failures were complex, and involved numerous decisions by many people within many organizations over a long period of time.

Rather than attempt to assign blame, the panel used the hindsight it acquired to make recommendations about the future. The report identifies a set of critical actions the panel regards as necessary. These actions fall under one of four needed shifts in thought and approach:[47]

- Improve the understanding of risk and firmly commit to safety.

- Repair the hurricane protection system.
- Reorganize the management of the hurricane protection system.
- Insist on engineering quality.

The first recommended action is that safety be kept at the forefront of public priorities, preparing for the possibility of future hurricanes rather than allowing experts and citizens alike to fall into a complacency that can come from the relative unlikelihood of a repeat performance in the near future.

The second and third recommendations concern making clear and quantifiable risk estimates and communicating them to the public in ways that enable nonexperts to have a real voice in determining the acceptability or unacceptability of those risks.

The next set of recommendations concern replacing the haphazard, uncoordinated hurricane protection "system" with a truly organized, coherent system. This, the panel believes, calls for "good leadership, management, and someone in charge."[48] It is the panel's recommendation that a high-level licensed engineer, or a panel of highly qualified, licensed engineers, be appointed with full authority to oversee the system:[49]

> The authority's overarching responsibility will be to keep hurricane-related safety at the forefront of public priorities. The authority will provide leadership, strategic vision, definition of roles and responsibilities, formalized avenues of communication, prioritization of funding, and coordination of critical construction, maintenance, and operations.

The panel's seventh recommendation is to improve interagency coordination. The historical record thus far, the panel maintains, is disorganization and poor mechanisms for interagency communication:[50]

> Those responsible for maintenance of the hurricane protection system must collaborate with system designers and constructors to upgrade their inspection, repair, and operations to ensure that the system is hurricane-ready and flood-ready.

Recommendations 8 and 9 relate to the upgrading and review of design procedures. The panel points out that "ASCE has a long-standing policy that recommends independent external peer review of public works projects where performance is critical to public safety, health, and welfare."[51] This is especially so where reliability under emergency conditions is critical, as it clearly was when Hurricane Katrina struck. The effective operation of such an external review process, the panel concludes, could have resulted in a significant reduction in the amount of (but by no means all) destruction in the case of Hurricane Katrina.

The panel's final recommendation is essentially a reminder of our limitations and a consequent ethical imperative to "place safety first":[52]

> Although the conditions leading up to the New Orleans catastrophe are unique, the fundamental constraints placed on engineers for any project are not. Every project has funding and/or schedule limitations. Every project must integrate into the natural and man-made environment. Every major project has political ramifications.
>
> In the face of pressure to save money or to make up time, engineers must remain strong and hold true to the requirements of the profession's canon of ethics, never compromising the safety of the public.

The panel concludes with an appeal to a broader application of the first Fundamental Canon of ASCE's Code of Ethics. Not only must the commitment to protect public safety, health, and welfare be the guiding principle for New Orleans' hurricane protection system but also "it must be applied with equal rigor to every aspect of an engineer's work—in New Orleans, in America, and throughout the world."[53]

Reading the panel's report in its entirety would be a valuable exercise in thinking through what ASCE's first Fundamental Canon requires not only regarding the Hurricane Katrina disaster but also regarding other basic responsibilities to the public that are inherent in engineering practice.

A related reading is "Leadership, Service Learning, and Executive Management in Engineering: The Rowan University Hurricane Katrina Recovery Team," by a team of engineering students and faculty advisors at Rowan University.[54] In their abstract, the authors identify three objectives for the Hurricane Katrina Recovery Team Project:

> The main objective is to help distressed communities in the Gulf Coast Region. Second, this

project seeks to not only address broader social issues but also leave a tangible contribution or impact in the area while asking the following questions: What do we as professional engineers have as a responsibility to the communities we serve, and what do we leave in the community to make it a better, more equitable place to live? The last objective is the management team's successful assessment of the experience, including several logistical challenges. To this end, this article seeks to help other student-led projects by relaying our service learning experience in a coherent, user-friendly manner that serves as a model experience.

CORPORATE RESPONSES

Supportive corporate responses to the Katrina hurricane were swift. By mid-September 2005, more than $312 million worth of aid had been donated by major corporations, much of it by those with no plants or businesses in the afflicted areas.[55] Engineers have played a prominent role in these relief efforts, as they did after the 9/11 Twin Towers attack and the Asian tsunami disaster. Hafner and Deutsch comment,[56]

> With two disasters behind them, some companies are applying lessons they have learned to their hurricane-related philanthropy. GE is a case in point. During the tsunami, the company put together a team of 50 project engineers—experts in portable water purification, energy, health care, and medical equipment.
>
> After Hurricane Katrina, GE executives took their cues from Jeffrey R. Immelt, GE's chief executive, and reactivated the same tsunami team for New Orleans. "Jeff told us, 'Don't let anything stand in the way of getting aid where it's needed,'" said Robert Corcoran, vice president for corporate citizenship.

Discuss how, with corporate backing, engineers who subscribe to Fred Cuny's ideas about effective disaster relief in his *Disasters and Development* (Oxford University Press, 1983) might approach the engineering challenges of Katrina.

C A S E   1 7

Hyatt Regency Walkway Disaster

Approximately 4 years after its occurrence, the tragic 1981 Kansas City Hyatt Regency walkway collapse was in the news again. The collapse of two suspended walkways in the lobby claimed the lives of 114 people and injured 200 more while they were attending a dance at the hotel. A November 16, 1985, *New York Times* article reported the decision of Judge James B. Deutsch, an administrative law judge for Missouri's administrative hearing commission.[57] Judge Deutsch found the hotel's structural engineers guilty of gross negligence, misconduct, and unprofessional conduct.

Judge Deutsch is quoted as saying that the project manager displayed "a conscious indifference to his professional duties as the Hyatt project engineer who was primarily responsible for the preparation of design drawings and review of shop drawing for that project."[58] The judge also cited the chief engineer's failure to closely monitor the project manager's work as "a conscious indifference to his professional duties as an engineer of record."[59]

The American Society for Civil Engineers (ASCE) may have influenced this court ruling. Just before the judge made his decision, ASCE announced a policy of holding structural engineers responsible for structural safety in their designs. This policy reflected the recommendations of an ASCE committee that convened in 1983 to examine the disaster.

The court case shows that engineers can be held responsible not only for their own conduct but also for the conduct of others under their supervision. It also holds that engineers have special *professional* responsibilities.

Discuss the extent to which you think engineering societies should play the sort of role ASCE apparently did in this case. To what extent do you think practicing engineers should support (e.g., by becoming members) professional engineering societies's attempts to articulate and interpret the ethical responsibilities of engineers?

The Truesteel Affair is a fictionalized version of circumstances similar to those surrounding the Hyatt Regency walkway collapse. View this video and discuss the ethical issues it raises. (This film is available from Fanlight Productions, 47 Halifax St., Boston, MA 02130. 1-617-524-0980.)

For a detailed account of the walkway collapse, see "Hyatt Regency Walkway Collapse," Engineering.com, October 24, 2006. Also, see "Hyatt Regency Walkway Collapse (Texas A&M University Engineering Ethics Cases)" Online Ethics Center for Engineering, February 16, 2006, National Academy of Engineering, www .onlineethics.org/Resources/Cases/hyatt_walkway.aspx.

C A S E   1 8

Hydrolevel[60]

"A conflict of interest is like dirt in a sensitive gauge," one that can not only soil one person's career but also taint an entire profession.[61] Thus, as professionals, engineers must be ever alert to signs of conflict of interest. The case of the *American Society of Mechanical Engineers (ASME) v. Hydrolevel Corporation* shows how easily individuals, companies, and professional societies can find themselves embroiled in expensive legal battles that tarnish the reputation of the engineering profession as a whole.

In 1971, Eugene Mitchell, vice president for sales at McDonnell and Miller, Inc., located in Chicago, was concerned about his company's continued dominance in the market for heating boiler low-water fuel cutoff valves that ensure that boilers cannot be fired without sufficient water in them because deficient water could cause an explosion.

Hydrolevel Corporation entered the low-water cutoff valve market with an electronic low-water fuel supply cutoff that included a time delay on some of its models. Hydrolevel's valve had won important approval for use from Brooklyn Gas Company, one of the largest installers of heating boilers. Some Hydrolevel units added the time-delay devices so the normal turbulence of the water level at the electronic probe would not cause inappropriate and repeated fuel supply turn-on and turn-off. Mitchell believed that McDonnell and Miller's sales could be protected if he could secure an interpretation stating that the Hydrolevel time delay on the cutoff violated the ASME B-PV code. He referred to this section of the ASME code: "Each automatically fired steam or vapor system boiler shall have an automatic low-water fuel cutoff, so located as to automatically cut off the fuel supply when the surface of the water falls to the lowest visible part of the water-gauge glass."[62] Thus, Mitchell asked for an ASME interpretation of the mechanism for operation of the Hydrolevel device as it pertained to the previously mentioned section of the code. He did not, however, specifically mention the Hydrolevel device in his request.

Mitchell discussed his idea several times with John James, McDonnell and Miller's vice president for research. In addition to his role at McDonnell and Miller, James was on the ASME subcommittee responsible for heating boilers and had played a leading role in writing the part of the boiler code that Mitchell was asking about.

James recommended that he and Mitchell approach the chairman of the ASME Heating Boiler Subcommittee, T. R. Hardin. Hardin was also vice president of the Hartford Steam Boiler Inspection and Insurance Company. When Hardin arrived in Chicago in early April on other business, the three men went to dinner at the Drake Hotel. During dinner, Hardin agreed with Mitchell and James that their interpretation of the code was correct.

Soon after the meeting with Hardin, James sent ASME a draft letter of inquiry and sent Hardin a copy. Hardin made some suggestions, and James incorporated Hardin's suggestions in a final draft letter. James's finalized draft letter of inquiry was then addressed to W. Bradford Hoyt, secretary of the B-PV Boiler and Pressure Vessel Committee.

Hoyt received thousands of similar inquiries every year. Since Hoyt could not answer James's inquiry with a routine, prefabricated response, he directed the letter to the appropriate subcommittee chairman, T. R. Hardin. Hardin drafted a response without consulting the whole subcommittee, a task he had authorization for if the response was treated as an "unofficial communication."

Hardin's response, dated April 29, 1971, stated that a low-water fuel cutoff must operate immediately.

Although this response did not say that Hydrolevel's time-delayed cutoff was dangerous, McDonnell and Miller's salesmen used Hardin's conclusion to argue against using the Hydrolevel product. This was done at Mitchell's direction.

In early 1972, Hydrolevel learned of the ASME letter through one of its former customers who had a copy of the letter. Hydrolevel then requested an official copy of the letter from ASME. On March 23, 1972, Hydrolevel requested an ASME review and ruling correction.

ASME's Heating and Boiler Subcommittee had a full meeting to discuss Hydrolevel's request, and it confirmed part of the original Hardin interpretation.

James, who had replaced Hardin as chairman of the subcommittee, refrained from participating in the discussion but subsequently helped draft a critical part of the subcommittee's response to Hydrolevel. The ASME response was dated June 9, 1972.

In 1975, Hydrolevel filed suit against McDonnell and Miller, Inc., ASME, and the Hartford Steam Boiler Inspection and Insurance Company, charging them with conspiracy to restrain trade under the Sherman Antitrust Act.

Hydrolevel reached an out-of-court settlement with McDonnell and Miller and Hartford for $750,000 and $75,000, respectively. ASME took the case to trial. ASME officials believed that, as a society, ASME had done nothing wrong and should not be liable for the misguided actions of individual volunteer members acting on their own behalf. After all, ASME gained nothing from such practices. ASME officials also believed that a pretrial settlement would set a dangerous precedent that would encourage other nuisance suits.

Despite ASME arguments, however, the jury decided against ASME, awarding Hydrolevel $3.3 million in damages. The trial judge deducted $800,000 in prior settlements and tripled the remainder in accordance with the Clayton Act. This resulted in a decision of $7,500,000 for Hydrolevel.

On May 17, 1982, ASME's liability was upheld by the second circuit. The Supreme Court, in a controversial 6-3 vote, found ASME guilty of antitrust violations. The majority opinion, delivered by Justice Blackmun, read as follows:

> ASME wields great power in the nation's economy. Its codes and standards influence the policies of numerous states and cities, and has been said about "so-called voluntary standards" generally, its interpretation of guidelines "may result in economic prosperity or economic failure, for a number of businesses of all sizes throughout the country," as well as entire segments of an industry.... ASME can be said to be "in reality an extragovernmental agency, which prescribes rules for the regulation and restraint of interstate commerce." When it cloaks its subcommittee officials with the authority of its reputation, ASME permits those agents to affect the destinies of businesses and thus gives them power to frustrate competition in the marketplace.[63]

The issue of damages was retried in a trial lasting approximately 1 month. In June, the jury returned a verdict of $1.1 million, which was tripled to $3.3 million. Parties involved were claiming attorney's fees in excess of $4 million, and a final settlement of $4,750,000 was decreed.

Following the decision, ASME revised it's procedures as follows:

> In the wake of the Hydrolevel ruling, the Society has changed the way it handles codes and standards interpretations, beefed up its enforcement and conflict-of-interest rules, and adopted new "sunset" review procedures for its working bodies.
>
> The most striking changes affect the Society's handling of codes and standards interpretations. All such interpretations must now be reviewed by at least five persons before release; before, the review of two people was necessary. Interpretations are available to the public, with replies to nonstandard inquiries published each month in the Codes and Standards section of ME or other ASME publications. Previously, such responses were kept between the inquirer and the involved committee or subcommittee. Lastly, ASME incorporates printed disclaimers on the letterhead used for code interpretations spelling out their limitations: that they are subject to change should additional information become available and that individuals have the right to appeal interpretations they consider unfair.
>
> Regarding conflict-of-interest, ASME now requires all staff and volunteer committee members to sign statements pledging their adherence to a comprehensive and well-defined set of guidelines regarding potential conflicts. Additionally,

the Society now provides all staff and volunteers with copies of the engineering code of ethics along with a publication outlining the legal implications of standards activities.

Finally, the Society now requires each of its councils, committees, and subcommittees to conduct a "sunset" review of their operations every 2 years. The criteria include whether their activities have served the public interest and whether they have acted cost-effectively, in accordance with Society procedures.[64]

Conflict-of-interest cases quickly become complicated, as the following questions illustrate:

- How could McDonnell and Miller have avoided the appearance of a conflict of interest? This applies to both Mitchell and James.
- What was T. R. Hardin's responsibility as chair of the B-PV Code Heating Boiler Subcommittee? How could he have handled things differently to protect the interests of ASME?
- What can engineering societies do to protect their interests once a conflict of interest is revealed?
- Was the final judgment against ASME fair? Why or why not?
- Have ASME's revised conflict-of-interest procedures addressed the problems fully? Why or why not?

CASE 19

Incident at Morales

Incident at Morales is a multistage video case study developed by the National Institute for Engineering Ethics (NIEE). It involves a variety of ethical issues faced by the consulting engineer of a company that is in a hurry to build a plant so that it can develop a new chemical product that it hopes will give it an edge on the competition. Issues include environmental, financial, and safety problems in an international setting.

Interspersed between episodes are commentaries by several engineers and ethicists involved in the production of the video. Information about ordering the video is available from the NIEE or the Murdough Center for Engineering Ethics (www.niee.org/pd.cfm?pt= Murdough). The full transcript of the video and a complete study guide are available online from the Murdough Center.

CASE 20

Innocent Comment?

Jack Strong is seated between Tom Evans and Judy Hanson at a dinner meeting of a local industrial engineering society. Jack and Judy have an extended discussion of a variety of concerns, many of which are related to their common engineering interests. At the conclusion of the dinner, Jack turns to Tom, smiles, and says, "I'm sorry not to have talked with you more tonight, Tom, but Judy's better looking than you."

Judy is taken aback by Jack's comment. A recent graduate from a school in which more than 20 percent of her classmates were women, she had been led to believe that finally the stereotypical view that women are not as well suited for engineering as men was finally going away. However, her first job has raised

some doubts about this. She was hired into a division in which she is the only woman engineer. Now, even after nearly 1 year on the job, she has to struggle to get others to take her ideas seriously. She wants to be recognized first and foremost as a good engineer. So, she had enjoyed "talking shop" with Jack. But she was stunned by his remark to Tom, however innocently it might have been intended. Suddenly, she saw the conversation in a very different light. Once again, she sensed that she was not being taken seriously enough as an engineer.

How should Judy respond to Jack's remark? Should she say anything? Assuming Tom understands her perspective, what, if anything, should he say or do?

CASE 21

Late Confession

In 1968, Norm Lewis was a 51-year-old doctoral candidate in history at the University of Washington.[65] While taking his final exam in the program, he excused himself to go to the bathroom, where he looked at his notes. For the next 32 years, Lewis told no one. At age 83, he decided to confess, and he wrote to the president of the university admitting that he had cheated and that he had regretted it ever since.

Commenting on the case, Jeanne Wilson, president of the Center for Academic Integrity remarked, "I think there is an important lesson here for students about the costs of cheating. He has felt guilty all these years, and has felt burdened by this secret, believing that he never really earned the degree he was awarded." Wilson's position is that the University of Washington should not take action against Lewis, given his confession, his age, and the fact that, after all, he did complete his coursework and a dissertation.

But, she added, "On the other hand, I think an institution might feel compelled to revoke the degree if we were talking about a medical or law degree or license, or some other professional field such as engineering or education, and the individual were younger and still employed on the basis of that degree or license."

Discuss the ethical issues this case raises, both for Dr. Lewis and for University of Washington officials. Evaluate Jeanne Wilson's analysis, especially as it might apply to engineers.

CASE 22

Love Canal[66]

INTRODUCTION

Degradation of the environment resulting from human activity is certainly not a phenomenon of recent origin. As early as the 15th century, long before the beginning of the industrial revolution, London was already being plagued by noxious air pollution resulting from the burning of coal and wood. However, the extent of the effect of environmental pollution was greatly increased following the end of World War II by the exponential expansion of industrial activity in developed nations, employing vast quantities of fossil fuels and synthetic chemicals. Today's environmental concerns are regional, national, and global, as well as local.

The ongoing educational, social, and political movement, which has raised the consciousness of people in the United States and throughout the world about environmental concerns, began in the early 1960s. Its initiation is often attributed to the popular response to *Silent Spring,* the eloquent book by marine biologist Rachel Carson about the dire effects of the overuse of pesticides and other chemical poisons, which was published in 1962. The ensuing environmental movement has spawned numerous local, regional, national, and international organizations—many rather militant—that have used numerous tactics to press their demands for the preservation of clean air, pure water, and unspoiled land. In response to these demands, legislative bodies have enacted all manner of regulations and numerous agencies have been charged with the task of environmental protection.

This increase in environmental activity has been accompanied by much controversy. Entrepreneurs, property owners, industrial workers, politicians, scientists, and people in all other walks of life differ with regard to the relative value they accord to the benefits and costs associated with restrictions on freedom of action designed to protect the environment. A wide variety of ethics and values issues arise in the course of attempting to balance such demands as property rights and the entrepreneurial freedom to pursue profits against the ecological need to curtail those rights and restrict that freedom.

One of the most contentious environmental issues has been how to respond to the discovery of many thousands of hazardous toxic dumps that have resulted from decades of virtually unrestricted disposal of toxic industrial waste. This issue was first widely publicized as a result of the health emergency declared by the New York State Department of Health in 1978 in response to shocking revelations about the problems caused by improper waste disposal in the now infamous Love Canal dump site. The actions and reactions of the corporation that disposed of the waste in question, public officials, residents, the media, and scientists involved in the Love Canal controversy serve as excellent illustrations of many of the ethics issues associated with efforts to protect the public from environmental pollution.

BACKGROUND

During the late 19th century, numerous canals were built by entrepreneurs to unify waterways into efficient shipping systems. One such canal was begun in 1894 by venture capitalist William Love in the Niagara Falls area of New York State. Within a few years, an economic depression undermined Love's financial plans and the partially completed project was abandoned.

Dubbed "Love Canal" by the local residents, it was used as a swimming hole and an ice rink. In 1942, faced with the need for a place to dispose of toxic waste from the manufacture of chlorinated hydrocarbons and caustics, the Hooker Electrochemical Corporation (currently Hooker Chemical and Plastics, a subsidiary of Occidental Petroleum Corporation) leased the canal as a waste dump. In 1947, Hooker bought the canal and the surrounding land. Between 1942 and 1950, more than 21,000 tons of chemicals, including such potent toxins as benzene, the pesticide lindane, polychlorinated dioxins, PCBs, and phosphorous, were deposited in the canal, which Hooker had lined with cement. Having exhausted the canal's potential as a waste dump, Hooker then installed an impermeable cap that was supposed to prevent water from entering and promoting seepage of the toxins, and the former canal disappeared from view beneath a layer of fill.

In the early 1950s, the local school board was confronted with the need to build a new school to accommodate an increasing population of children. The board knew that Hooker was anxious to get rid of the Love Canal property and began making inquiries. Hooker has claimed that it resisted and warned the board of education that the buried chemicals made the site inappropriate for school construction. The property sale was consummated for $1.00 in 1953, but the company asserts that it gave in because the board would otherwise have taken the land by eminent domain. Whether Hooker was as reluctant as it says it was and as assertive in cautioning the board about the hazards is impossible to determine. Existing minutes of the meetings in question do not fully support Hooker's version of the proceedings, and none of the board members are still alive. What is clear is that the deed that was negotiated contains a clause exempting Hooker from any "claim, suit, or action" due to future human exposure to the buried chemicals.

An elementary school was built in the middle of the property and the surrounding land was sold by the school board to developers who built 98 homes along the former canal banks and approximately 1,000 additional houses in the Love Canal neighborhood. The construction of the school, houses, and associated utilities resulted in the breaching of parts of the canal's cap and its cement walls.

THE CASE

The first known case of exposure to the buried toxins occurred in 1958 when three children suffered chemical burns from waste that had resurfaced at the former canal site. Both Hooker Chemical and city officials were officially informed, but neither the Niagara Falls Health Department nor any other public agency took any action in response to that event or to numerous other complaints during the next 20 years. Hooker's records reveal that it investigated the initial incident and several other reports and quickly became convinced that the very large reservoir of toxins was not likely to be contained. Hooker did nothing to convey this knowledge to the Love Canal homeowners, who had never been informed about the nature of the potential hazard. In testimony two decades later, Hooker acknowledged that its failure to issue a warning was due to concern that this might be interpreted as liability for possible harm despite the clause in their property sales deed.

By 1978, occupants of the homes in the area had begun to organize what was to become the Love Canal

Homeowners Association (LCHA), under the highly competent and aggressive leadership of Lois Gibbs. Investigative newspaper reporter Michael Brown helped publicize the plight of the many deeply concerned local residents who had encountered evidence of toxins resurfacing in or around their property. Chemicals had been observed in the form of viscous fluids seeping into both yards and basements, pervasive odors in homes, and a stench emanating from storm sewer openings.

Love Canal soon became the first hazardous waste site to be featured in TV news reports and to get front-page headline billing in newspapers and magazines in New York State and nationally. Embarrassed by the past failure of officials to respond to the clear indications of a serious problem, both the New York State Department of Health (NYSDH) and the EPA quickly became involved. Tests soon revealed a wide variety of noxious chemicals in the air in Love Canal homes and an excess frequency of miscarriages among women living in homes adjacent to the former canal site. A public health emergency was declared on August 2, 1978, by the New York State Commissioner of Health. A few days later, Governor Hugh Carey announced that New York State would purchase the 239 homes nearest to the canal and assist the displaced families in relocating. These abandoned homes were fenced in and work was soon begun on a plan to construct an elaborate drainage system including trenches, wells, and pumping stations to prevent further outward migration of the toxins.

These initial actions, which quickly followed the emergence of Love Canal as a national "cause célèbre," ultimately cost the state and federal governments in excess of $42 million. Public officials quickly recognized that a continued preemptive response to potential health problems at Love Canal was likely to exceed available emergency funds in the state's coffers. Furthermore, it was known that thousands of other toxic waste sites existed throughout the country that might pose similar threats to numerous other communities. Thus, it is not surprising that the concerns and demands of the owners of the 850 homes outside the inner evacuated circle were not to be satisfied by either state or federal officials in a similar manner.

The NYSDH did conduct a survey study of the residents in the remaining homes, which led to an announcement in early fall that the rest of the neighborhood was safe, posing no increased health risk. As subsequently revealed, this assurance had been based on only one health issue examined by the survey. The department had concluded that the miscarriage rate in the homes beyond the fence did not exceed normal rates—a conclusion based on a methodology that was subsequently seriously questioned. The many other possible health effects of chemical exposure had not entered into the NYSDH evaluation.

Citing the fact that chemical seepage was evident beyond the evacuated area and that families living there appeared to be experiencing unusual health problems, members of the LCHA rejected the department's assurances. They demanded more definitive studies, and when they did not get a satisfactory response from either the NYSDH or the EPA, they sought scientific aid from outside the government's environmental health establishment.

Beverly Paigen, a cancer research scientist who worked for the NYSHD Roswell Park Memorial Institute in nearby Buffalo, agreed to volunteer her services in an unofficial capacity. Her professional interests included the variation among individuals in their responses to chemical toxins and she anticipated that in addition to helping the Love Canal residents, her involvement might also result in identifying appropriate subjects for her research work. Dr. Paigen designed a survey aimed at investigating several potential effects of exposure to chemicals. She used a different set of assumptions about the mechanism and likely path of the flow of the dissolved toxins that seeped out of the canal. Based on her model, Dr. Paigen found that miscarriages were significantly higher among women living in homes most likely to be in the path of the chemical plume. She also found much higher than normal rates of birth defects and evidence of serious nervous system toxicity as well as elevated incidences of asthma and urological problems for residents of these homes.

In early November 1978, Dr. Paigen presented the results of her "unofficial" research to her NYSDH superiors. After a delay of 3 months, the new New York State Commissioner of Health publicly announced that after reevaluating its own data it also found excess miscarriages and birth defects in homes in previously "wet" regions of the Love Canal neighborhood and promised additional studies of

Dr. Paigen's other findings. However, the action taken in response to these results puzzled and dismayed both the residents and Dr. Paigen. Families with children younger than 2 years of age or with women who could prove they were pregnant were to be relocated at state expense but only until the youngest child reached the age of 2 years. Women who were trying to become pregnant, or those who thought they were in the early stages of pregnancy when the fetus is most sensitive to toxins but who could not yet prove they were pregnant with tests available at that time, were denied permission to join the group that was evacuated.

During the next 1½ years, the frustration and the militancy of the LCHA members increased as the additional studies promised by the commissioner failed to materialize. On the federal-level EPA lawyers had become convinced by media reports and public appeals from Love Canal residents claiming a variety of toxin-related illnesses that hundreds of additional families should be moved away. They sought a court order from the Department of Justice requiring Hooker Chemical to pay for the relocations. When the Justice Department responded by demanding evidence that the inhabitants who remained in the Love Canal neighborhood were at risk, the EPA commissioned a quick "pilot" study to determine whether residents had suffered chromosome damage that could be attributed to chemical exposure. This study, which was to subsequently receive much criticism from the scientific community both because of its specific design and because, at the time, chromosome studies were notoriously difficult to interpret, did provide the type of evidence the EPA was seeking. On the basis of finding "rare chromosomal aberrations" in 11 of 36 subjects tested, the scientist who performed the study concluded that inhabitants of the area were at increased risk for a variety of adverse health outcomes.

On May 19, 1980, when two EPA representatives went to the LCHA office in one of the evacuated homes to announce the results of the chromosome study, they were greeted by irate homeowners who proceeded to lock them in the office for 5 hours until FBI agents arrived and demanded their release. This tactic, which received the anticipated media coverage, had the desired effect. With the intervention of high-ranking officials in the Executive Branch, and undoubtedly with the support of President Carter,

funds were made available for the relocation of several hundred additional Love Canal families.

A conclusion that can clearly be drawn from this and many subsequent environmental controversies is that politics, public pressure, and economic considerations all take precedence over scientific evidence in determining the outcome. Another aspect of the Love Canal case that is characteristic of such events is that the victims, although hostile to Hooker Chemical, directed most of their rage at an indecisive, aloof, often secretive and inconsistent public health establishment.

Lawsuits against Occidental Petroleum Corporation, which bought Hooker Chemical in 1968, were initiated by both the state of New York and the U.S. Justice Department to cover costs of the cleanup and the relocation programs and also by more than 2,000 people who claimed to have been personally injured by the buried chemicals. In 1994, Occidental agreed to pay $94 million to New York in an out-of-court settlement, and the following year the federal case was settled for $129 million. Individual victims have thus far won in excess of $20 million from the corporation.

In early 1994, it was announced that the cleanup of the condemned homes in Love Canal had been completed and it was safe to move back to the area. The real estate company offering the inexpensive refurbished homes for sale had chosen to rename the area "Sunrise City."

READINGS AND RESOURCES

A wealth of written and audiovisual material is available on Love Canal and other environmental controversies. Searching the electronic catalogue of any public or academic library or using an Internet search engine should prove very fruitful.

For a colorful discussion of the early events in the Love Canal case by the investigative reporter who initiated the media coverage of the issue, and for a personal version of the events by the woman who organized the LCHA and went on to become a national leader of citizen's toxic waste organizing, see

Michael Brown, *Laying Waste* (New York: Pantheon, 1979).

Lois Gibbs, *Love Canal: My Story*, as told to Murray Levine (Albany: State University of New York Press, 1981).

For a thought-provoking article that focuses on the political and ethical dimensions of the case by the scientist who volunteered her services to the Love Canal residents, see

Beverly Paigen, "Controversy at Love Canal," *The Hastings Center Report*, June 1982, pp. 29–37.

For a report written by the public health, transportation, and environmental agencies of New York State, see

New York State Department of Health, Office of Public Health, "Love Canal, a Special Report to the Governor and Legislature," with assistance of New York State Department of Transportation and New York State Department of Environmental Conservation (Albany, NY: New York State Department of Health, Office of Public Health, 1981).

For two additional perspectives on the controversy, see

Adeline Levine, *Love Canal: Science, Politics and People* (Lexington, MA: Lexington Books, 1982).

L. Gardner Shaw, Citizen Participation in Government Decision Making: The Toxic Waste Threat at Love Canal, Niagara Falls, New York (Albany: State University of New York, Nelson A. Rockefeller Institute of Government, 1983).

For articles published in science news journals, see

Barbara J. Culliton, "Continuing Confusion over Love canal," *Science*, 209, August 19, 1980, pp. 1002–1003.

"Uncertain Science Pushes Love Canal Solutions to Political, Legal Arenas," *Chemical & Engineering News*, August 11, 1980, pp. 22–29.

For comments on the plan to rehabilitate, rename, and repopulate the Love Canal neighborhood, see

Rachel's Hazardous Waste News, 133, June 13, 1989.

For a highly informative collection of essays, comments, and analysis on a wide variety of issues in environmental ethics, see

D. Van Deveer and C. Pierce, *Environmental Ethics and Policy Book* (Belmont, CA: Wadsworth, 1994).

THE ISSUES

The following are significant questions of ethics and values raised by this case:

• Beverly Paigen, the research scientist who volunteered her services to the Love Canal residents, commented in reference to her differences with her superiors in the NYSDH, "I thought our differences could be resolved in the traditional scientific manner by examining protocols, experimental design, and statistical analysis. But I was to learn that actual facts made little difference in resolving our disagreements— the Love Canal controversy was predominantly political in nature, and it raised a series of questions that had more to do with values than science." Consider the differences in the values that might be of greatest importance to a Love Canal resident, the New York State Commissioner of Health, a scientist doing research sanctioned by either the New York State Department of Environmental Conservation or the EPA, an independent scientist (like Dr. Paigen) who was doing volunteer research for the residents, and a typical citizen of the state of New York. In what respects might these value differences lead them to conflicting decisions about what should have been done in response to the Love Canal disaster and how to do it?

• Is it reasonable to demand that the ethical duty of public officials is to respond to an environmental problem by objectively examining the scientific facts and the potential hazards to local residents, independent of economic and political considerations?

• One of the charges raised against the NYSDH and the health commissioner was that the public health establishment would not divulge the details of the studies that led to its decisions, held many closed meetings, and even refused to reveal the names of members who served on consultation panels it established. Do you think that there might be an ethical justification for such public agencies to refuse public access to such information? If so, does this seem to apply to the Love Canal situation?

• Another accusation was that state employees sympathetic to the Love Canal residents were harassed and punished. For example: Dr. Paigen's ability to raise funds for her research work was curtailed by the Roswell Park Memorial Institute, causing the professional staff to charge the administration with scientific censorship; her mail arrived opened and taped shut; her office was searched; and when she was subjected to a state income tax audit, she discovered newspaper clippings about her Love Canal activities in the auditor's file. In addition, when William Friedman, who had been the Department of Environmental Conservation's regional director, pressed state officials to take a less conservative approach to protecting the health of Love Canal residents, he was promptly demoted to staff engineer. This type of reaction by the political power structure seems morally indefensible, but it is by no means unique to the Love Canal case.

• Another values issue is the extent of evidence needed to justify action to protect public health. In order for the scientific community to accept as fact research showing that a specific health effect is caused by a particular agent, the statistical analysis of the data must indicate with more than 95 percent certainty that the observed effect could not occur by chance. This high but clearly arbitrary standard has been adopted to protect the integrity of the body of accepted scientific facts. But should public health officials demand, as they often do, the same standard before taking action? For example, if evidence shows that there is an 80 percent chance that exposure to some chemical in the environment may cause a serious adverse health effect, should health officials refuse to inform the public of the risk or take action to prevent exposure until further studies—which may take months or even years—raise the certainty of the causal relationship to 95 percent?

• It is common in environmental controversies for those who believe they are at risk to become distrustful of public officials in charge of investigating their concerns. This was certainly the case in the Love Canal controversy. It is unusual for a citizens group to be able to obtain the volunteer services of an independent expert with qualifications like those of Dr. Paigen and they are not likely to have the financial resources necessary to hire their own consultant. Furthermore, although Dr. Paigen was able to provide valuable scientific services, she was unable to gain access to and assess much of the evidence that the public officials used as the basis for their decisions. Dr. Paigen and others have suggested that the ethical solution to this problem is to provide public funds to groups such as the LCHA with which they can hire their own experts and which they can use to hire a qualified advocate who will be given access to all public data and a voice in the decision-making process.

• The Hooker Chemical Company did not violate any then-existing specific environmental regulations by disposing of toxic waste in Love Canal or by selling the land to the school board. However, the courts have found Hooker financially liable for the harm that was the ultimate result of their disposal practices. This decision was largely based on the judgment that Hooker possessed the scientific expertise to be able to anticipate that dumping waste chemicals in the canal was likely to result in a public health threat. It was also argued that Hooker acted irresponsibly by not informing the public of the risks it discovered in 1958. Should corporations be required to use their knowledge to avoid activities that may cause public harm?

• In recent years, the issues of environmental justice and equity have been raised within the environmental movement. Minority populations, and poor people in general, have produced persuasive data showing that they are far more likely to be exposed to environmental pollution from factories or waste disposal facilities than more affluent white people. In the Love Canal case, the initial neighborhood population was neither poor nor did it have a high percentage of minority members. Of course, those who chose to live there were not aware of the pollution risk. It is likely, however, that the inexpensive houses now being offered to induce people to move back into the area after remediation is supposed to have made it safe will attract primarily the poor. One proposal that has been put forth in response to demand for environmental justice is to provide some form of reward to those who live in neighborhoods where exposure to environmental toxins is significantly higher than average. Would this be an ethical practice? What other steps might be taken to promote environmental equity in an ethical manner?

• In our society, environmental risks are generally evaluated in economic terms. However, the assignment of economic value to human health, a pristine forest, or a smog-free vista is surely not an objective exercise. What other means might be used to evaluate environmental risks and benefits?

• We generally assign value to things in anthropogenic terms. We consider how humans will be affected by an activity that will cause pollution or degrade an ecosystem. Some environmental ethicists have proposed that we should adopt a biocentric perspective in which living things and natural objects are assigned intrinsic value independent of human concerns. How do you respond to the assertion that nature does not exist solely for the purpose of being exploited by humans?

Although there is no explicit mention of engineers in this case study, it is not difficult to imagine that engineers, too, were involved in the events resulting in the creation of the Love Canal hazard, as well as in the cleanup. Discuss the types of responsibilities that engineers have in regard to the prevention of hazards such as this from occurring in the future. What, if any, public roles might they play in helping the public understand what is at stake and how the issues should be addressed?

CASE 23

Member Support by IEEE

In the mid-1970s, the New York City Police Department operated an online computerized police car dispatching system called SPRINT. Upon receiving a telephoned request for police assistance, a dispatcher would enter an address into a computer and the computer would respond within seconds by displaying the location of the nearest patrol car. By reducing the response time for emergency calls, the SPRINT system probably saved lives.

In 1977, another system, PROMIS, was being considered by New York City prosecutors using the same host computer as that for SPRINT. The PROMIS system would provide names and addresses of witnesses, hearing dates, the probation statuses of defendants, and other information that would assist prosecutors or arresting officers who wanted to check the current status of apprehended perpetrators. This project was being managed by the Criminal Justice Coordinating Council, or Circle Project, a committee of high-level city officials that included the deputy mayor for criminal justice, the police commissioner, and Manhattan District Attorney Robert Morgenthau as chairman.

The committee employed a computer specialist as project director, who in turn hired Virginia Edgerton, an experienced system analyst, as senior information scientist to work under his supervision. Soon after being employed, Edgerton expressed concern to the project director about the possible effect on SPRINT's response time from loading the computer with an additional task, but he instructed her to drop the matter. Edgerton then sought advice from her professional society, the Institute of Electrical and Electronics Engineers (IEEE).

After an electrical engineering professor at Columbia University agreed that her concerns merited further study, she sent a memorandum to the project director requesting a study of the overload problem. He rejected the memorandum out of hand, and Edgerton soon thereafter sent copies of the memorandum with a cover letter to the members of the Circle Project's committee. Immediately following this, Edgerton was discharged by the project director on the grounds that she had, by communicating directly with the committee members, violated his orders. He also stated that the issues she had raised were already under continuing discussion with the police department's computer staff, although he gave no documentation to support this claim.

The case was then investigated by the Working Group on Ethics and Employment Practices of the Committee on the Social Implications of Technology (CSIT) of the IEEE, and subsequently by the newly formed IEEE Member Conduct Committee. Both groups agreed that Edgerton's actions were fully justified. In 1979, she received the second IEEE–CSIT Award for Outstanding Service in the Public Interest. After her discharge, Edgerton formed a small company selling data-processing services.[67]

Discuss the supporting role played by IEEE in this case. Does this provide electrical and electronic engineers an ethical basis for joining or supporting IEEE?

CASE 24

Moral Development[68]

The introduction of ethics into engineering education raises an important question about moral education: Shouldn't a student's introduction to ethics occur much earlier than the college level? The answer to this question is "yes, it should," and in fact, whether formally or informally, it does—in the home, in religious upbringing, on the playground, and in the schools. However, as children move into adulthood, their moral background needs to be adapted to new and more complex settings, such as the engineering workplace. This means that young engineers still have much to learn about ethics. Still, the importance of one's moral upbringing for addressing the ethical challenges facing professionals should not be underestimated.

Children's introduction to ethics, or morality, occurs rather early. They argue with siblings and playmates about what is fair or unfair. The praise and blame they receive from parents, teachers, and others encourage them to believe that they are capable of some degree of responsible behavior. They are both recipients and dispensers of resentment, indignation, and other morally reactive attitudes. There is also strong evidence that children, even as young as age 4 years, seem to have an intuitive understanding of the difference between what is merely conventional (e.g., wearing certain clothes to school) and what is morally important (e.g., not throwing paint in another child's face).[69] Therefore, despite their limited experience, children typically have a fair degree of moral sophistication by the time they enter school.

What comes next is a gradual enlargement and refinement of basic moral concepts—a process that, nevertheless, preserves many of the central features of those concepts. All of us can probably recall examples from our childhood of clear instances of fairness, unfairness, honesty, dishonesty, courage, and cowardice that have retained their grip on us as paradigms, or clear-cut illustrations, of basic moral ideas. Philosopher Gareth Matthews states,[70]

> A young child is able to latch onto the moral kind, bravery, or lying, by grasping central paradigms of that kind, paradigms that even the most mature and sophisticated moral agents still count as

paradigmatic. Moral development is … enlarging the stock of paradigms for each moral kind; developing better and better definitions of whatever it is these paradigms exemplify; appreciating better the relation between straightforward instances of the kind and close relatives; and learning to adjudicate competing claims from different moral kinds (classically the sometimes competing claims of justice and compassion, but many other conflicts are possible). This makes it clear that, although a child's moral start may be early and impressive, there is much conflict and confusion that needs to be sorted through. It means that there is a continual need for moral reflection, and this does not stop with adulthood, which merely adds new dimensions.

Nevertheless, some may think that morality is more a matter of subjective feelings than careful reflection. However, research by developmental psychologists such as Jean Piaget, Lawrence Kohlberg, Carol Gilligan, James Rest, and many others provides strong evidence that important as feelings are, moral reasoning is a fundamental part of morality as well.[71] Piaget and Kohlberg, in particular, performed pioneering work showing that there are significant parallels between the cognitive development of children and their moral development. Many of the details of their accounts have been hotly disputed, but a salient feature that survives is that moral *judgment* involves more than just feelings. Moral judgments (e.g., "Smith acted wrongly in fabricating the lab data") are amenable to being either supported or criticized by *good reasons*.

Kohlberg's account of moral development has attracted a very large following among educators, as well as an increasing number of critics. He characterizes development in terms of an invariable sequence of six stages.[72] The first two stages are highly self-interested and self-centered. Stage 1 is dominated by the fear of punishment and the promise of reward. Stage 2 is based on reciprocal agreements ("You scratch my back, and I'll scratch yours"). The next two stages are what Kohlberg calls conventional morality. Stage 3 rests on the approval and disapproval of friends and peers. Stage 4 appeals to "law and order" as necessary for social cohesion and order. Only the last two stages embrace what Kohlberg calls critical, or postconventional, morality. In these two stages, one acts on self-chosen principles that can be used to evaluate the appropriateness of responses in the first four stages. Kohlberg has been criticized for holding that moral development proceeds in a rigidly sequential manner (no stage can be skipped, and there is no regression to earlier stages); for assuming that later stages are more adequate morally than earlier ones; for being male biased in overemphasizing the separateness of individuals, justice, rights, duties, and abstract principles at the expense of equally important notions of interdependence, care, and responsibility; for claiming that moral development follows basically the same patterns in all societies; for underestimating the moral abilities of younger children; and for underestimating the extent to which adults employ critical moral reasoning. We do not attempt to address these issues here.[73] Nevertheless, whatever its limitations, Kohlberg's theory makes some important contributions to our understanding of moral education. By describing many common types of moral reasoning, it invites us to be more reflective about how we and those around us typically do arrive at our moral judgments. It invites us to raise critical questions about how we

should arrive at those judgments. It encourages us to be more autonomous, or critical, in our moral thinking rather than simply letting others set our moral values for us and allowing ourselves to accept without any questions the conventions that currently prevail. It brings vividly to mind our self-interested and egocentric tendencies and urges us to employ more perceptive and consistent habits of moral thinking. Finally, it emphasizes the importance of giving reasons in support of our judgments.

For a provocative presentation of Kohlberg's theory of moral development, see the video *Moral Development* (CRM Educational Films, McGraw-Hill Films, 1221 Avenue of the Americas, New York, NY. 1-800-421-0833). This video simulates the famous Milgram experiments on obedience, in which volunteers are led to believe that they are administering shocks to other volunteers in an experiment on learning and punishment. Kohlberg's theory is used to characterize the different kinds of responses of volunteers to instructions to administer shocks. Viewers can use this video as a stimulus for reflecting on their own and others' responses to moral challenges. Engineers can also ask the question of whether there are any ethical problems in assisting someone to develop the types of equipment needed to conduct experiments like Milgram's.

CASE 25

Oil Spill?[74]

Peter has been working with the Bigness Oil Company's local affiliate for several years, and he has established a strong, trusting relationship with Jesse, manager of the local facility. The facility, on Peter's recommendations, has followed all of the environmental regulations to the letter, and it has a solid reputation with the state regulatory agency. The local facility receives various petrochemical products via pipelines and tank trucks, and it blends them for resale to the private sector.

Jesse has been so pleased with Peter's work that he has recommended that Peter be retained as the corporate consulting engineer. This would be a significant advancement for Peter and his consulting firm, cementing Peter's steady and impressive rise in the firm. There is talk of a vice presidency in a few years.

One day, over coffee, Jesse tells Peter a story about a mysterious loss in one of the raw petrochemicals he receives by pipeline. Sometime during the 1950s, when operations were more lax, a loss of one of the process chemicals was discovered when the books were audited. There were apparently 10,000 gallons of the chemical missing. After running pressure tests on the pipelines, the plant manager found that one of the pipes had corroded and had been leaking the chemical into the ground. After stopping the leak, the company sank observation and sampling wells and found that the product was sitting in a vertical plume, slowly diffusing into a deep aquifer. Because there was no surface or groundwater pollution off the plant property, the plant manager decided to do nothing. Jesse thought that somewhere under the plant there still sits this plume, although the last tests from the sampling wells showed that the concentration of the chemical in the groundwater within 400 feet of the surface was essentially zero. The wells were capped, and the story never appeared in the press.

Peter is taken aback by this apparently innocent revelation. He recognizes that state law requires him to report all spills, but what about spills that occurred years ago, where the effects of the spill seem to have dissipated? He frowns and says to Jesse, "We have to report this spill to the state, you know."

Jesse is incredulous. "But there *is* no spill. If the state made us look for it, we probably could not find it; and even if we did, it makes no sense whatever to pump it out or contain it in any way."

"But the law says that we have to report...," replies Peter.

"Hey, look. I told you this in confidence. Your own engineering code of ethics requires client confidentiality. And what would be the good of going to the state? There is nothing to be done. The only thing that would happen is that the company would get into trouble and have to spend useless dollars to correct a situation that cannot be corrected and does not need remediation."

"But...."

"Peter, let me be frank. If you go to the state with this, you will not be doing anyone any good—not the company, not the environment, and certainly not your own career. I cannot have a consulting engineer who does not value client loyalty."

What are the ethical issues in this case? What factual and conceptual questions need to be addressed? How do you think Peter should deal with this situation?

CASE 26

Peter Palchinsky: Ghost of the Executed Engineer[75]

Peter Palchinsky grew up in Russia in the late 19th century. He was paid a small stipend by the tsarist government to attend St. Petersburg School of Mines. He supplemented this small income by working summers in factories, railroads, and coal mines. This impressed on him the importance of paying close attention to the living conditions of workers.

After graduating in 1901, Palchinsky was assigned by the government to an investigative team studying methods of increasing coal production in the Ukraine's Don River basin to support Russia's growing industrialization. He visited the living quarters of the miners and found barracks with no space between bunks and cracks in the walls so wide that snow blew over the workers as they slept. Underpaid, the workers also suffered from poor health and low morale. His report on these conditions marked the start of his pioneering work in the developing field of industrial engineering.

However, because of this report, Palchinsky was sentenced to 8 years of house arrest in Irkutsk, Siberia, charged with working with anarchists to overthrow the tsarist government. Nevertheless, he continued to be used by tsarist officials as a consultant because his recommendations led to increased production whenever they were followed. After 3 years of house arrest, Palchinsky and his wife escaped to western Europe, where he continued his work on increasing the productivity of workers and published multivolume studies on facility planning for the governments of Holland, Italy, and France. He was recognized in 1913, at the age of 38, as one of the leading and most productive engineers in Europe. Through the efforts of his wife, he was pardoned so that he could return to Russia.

For the next 3 years, Palchinsky served as a consultant to the tsarist government while establishing several engineering organizations. After the overthrow of the tsars in February 1917, he worked for the Russian provisional government. Following the Bolshevik Revolution in October 1917, Palchinsky and other officers of the provisional government were imprisoned. A number of these officials were executed, but Lenin was persuaded to use Palchinsky's skills for the good of the Bolshevik government. This began a decade of Palchinsky consultancies interrupted by stays in Siberian gulags for his outspoken views that conflicted with Soviet doctrine regarding engineering projects.

Palchinsky was especially critical of Stalin's massive engineering projects, complaining about careless disregard of both engineering and humanitarian issues. Stalin's projects included the world's largest hotel, university, steel mill, power plant, and canal. In the latter project alone, it is estimated that more than 5,000 slave laborers lost their lives and were buried in the foundations of the canal.

Palchinsky's planning studies for what was to be the world's largest dam and supplier of electricity in Dneprostroi opposed the government's final plan. All of his engineering and humanitarian warnings were ignored, and the dam never met its objectives. Palchinsky was next asked to do a planning study for a complex of blast furnaces and steel finishing mills in Magnitogorsk, designed to be the largest such facility in the world. Again, he called attention to many government engineering and humanitarian shortcomings. These warnings were ignored, and Palchinsky was sent back to Siberia. Slave labor was used to build the steel mill, which never came close to meeting its objectives.

In 1929, on Stalin's orders, Palchinsky was secretly taken from his prison and shot. In secret files uncovered as the result of the *glasnost* policy in Russia in the early 1990s, Palchinsky wrote that no government regime could survive the Bolshevik's inhumanity. He predicted that the Russian government would fall before the end of the 20th century (which it did). During the 1920s, the number of engineers decreased from approximately 10,000 to 7,000, with most simply disappearing. Peter Palchinsky sacrificed his life during this time fighting for the engineering and humanitarian concerns in which he believed.

Loren Graham's *Ghost of the Executed Engineer* portrays Palchinsky as a visionary and prophetic engineer. The "ghost" of Palchinsky, Graham suggests, can be seen in the Soviet Union's continued technological mistakes in the 60 years following his death, culminating in the 1986 Chernobyl nuclear disaster and the dissolution of the Soviet Union in 1991.

Ironically, although praising Palchinsky for his integrity, forthrightness, and vision, Graham concludes his book with a mixed verdict:[76]

> It is quite probably that Palchinsky's execution resulted from his refusal, even under torture, to confess to crimes he did not commit. Palchinsky always prided himself on being a rational engineer. One can question whether his final act was rational, but one cannot question its bravery.

Discuss whether it can be rational to be willing to die rather than confess to crimes to which one has not committed. (Those familiar with Plato's *Crito* might compare Palchinsky's situation with that of Socrates, who also gave up his life rather than compromise his integrity.) How much personal sacrifice should one be willing to make to maintain one's professional integrity?

CASE 27

Pinto[77]

In the late 1960s, Ford designed a subcompact, the Pinto, that weighed less than 2,000 pounds and sold for less than $2,000. Anxious to compete with foreign-made subcompacts, Ford brought the car into production in slightly more than 2 years (compared with the usual 3½ years). Given this shorter time frame, styling preceded much of the engineering, thus restricting engineering design more than usual. As a result, it was decided that the best place for the gas tank was between the rear axle and the bumper. The differential housing had exposed bolt heads that could puncture the gas tank if the tank were driven forward against them upon rear impact.

In court, the crash tests were described as follows:[78]

> These prototypes as well as two production Pintos were crash tested by Ford to determine, among other things, the integrity of the fuel system in rear-end accidents.... Prototypes struck from the rear with a moving barrier at 21-miles-per-hour caused the fuel tank to be driven forward and to be punctured, causing fuel leakage.... A production Pinto crash tested at 21-miles-per-hour into a fixed barrier caused the fuel tank to be torn from the gas tank and the tank to be punctured by a bolt head on the differential housing. In at least

one test, spilled fuel entered the driver's compartment.

Ford also tested rear impact when rubber bladders were installed in the tank, as well as when the tank was located above rather than behind the rear axle. Both passed the 20-mile-per-hour rear impact tests.

Although the federal government was pressing to stiffen regulations on gas tank designs, Ford contented that the Pinto met all applicable federal safety standards at the time. J. C. Echold, director of automotive safety for Ford, issued a study titled "Fatalities Associated with Crash Induced Fuel Leakage and Fires."[79] This study claimed that the costs of improving the design ($11 per vehicle) outweighed its social benefits. A memorandum attached to the report described the costs and benefits as follows:

Benefits	
Savings	180 burn deaths, 180 serious burn injuries, 2,100 burned vehicles
Unit cost	$200,000 per death, $67,000 per injury, $700 per vehicle
Total benefits	180 × $200,000 plus 180 × $67,000 plus 2100 × $700 = $49.15 million
Costs	
Sales	11 million cars, 1.5 million light trucks
Unit cost	$11 per car, $11 per truck
Total costs	11,000,000 × $11 plus 1,500,000 × $11 = $137 million

The estimate of the number of deaths, injuries, and damage to vehicles was based on statistical studies. The $200,000 for the loss of a human life was based on an NHTSA study, which estimated social costs of a death as follows:[80]

Component	1971 Costs
Future productivity losses	
Direct	$132,000
Indirect	41,300
Medical costs	
Hospital	700
Other	425
Property damage	1,500
Insurance administration	4,700
Legal and court	3,000
Employer losses	1,000
Victim's pain and suffering	10,000
Funeral	900
Assets (lost consumption)	5,000
Miscellaneous accident cost	200
Total per fatality	$200,725

Discuss the appropriateness of using data such as these in Ford's decision regarding whether or not to make a safety improvement in its engineering design. If you believe this is not appropriate, what would you suggest as an alternative? What responsibilities do you think engineers have in situations like this?

CASE 28

Profits and Professors

A *Wall Street Journal* article reports:

High-tech launches from universities frequently can't get off the ground without a steady supply of students, who are often the most talented and the most willing to toil around the clock. But intense schedules on the job can keep students from doing their best academic work. And when both student and teacher share a huge financial incentive to make a company a success, some professors might be tempted to look the other way when studies slip or homework gets in the way.[81]

In some instances, the article claims, students seriously consider leaving school before completing their degrees in order to devote themselves more fully to work that is financially very attractive.

In 1999, Akamai won the MIT Sloan eCommerce Award for Rookie of the Year, an award to the startup company that seems most likely to dominate its field. The article comments,

> No company has been more closely tied to MIT. The firm has its roots in a research project directed by Mr. Leighton [Computer Systems Engineering professor at MIT] about 3 years ago. Daniel Lewin, one of Mr. Leighton's graduate students, came up with a key idea for how to apply algorithms, or numerical instructions for computers, to Internet congestion problems.[82]

Soon, Mr. Leighton and Mr. Lewin teamed up to form Akamai, hiring 15 undergraduates to help code the algorithms.

They tried to separate their MIT and Akamai responsibilities. Mr. Leighton advised Mr. Lewin to get a second professor to co-sign his master's thesis "because he worried about the appearance of conflict in his supervising Mr. Lewin's academic work while also pursuing a business venture with him." It turns out that the co-signer was someone involved in Mr. Lewin's original research project, who sometime after the completion of Mr. Lewin's thesis became a part-time research scientist at Akamai.

Akamai continues to rely heavily on MIT students as employees. However, it does not hire students full-time before they have completed their undergraduate degree. Still, the opportunities seem very attractive. According to the article, Luke Matkins took a summer job with Akamai in the summer after his sophomore year. By age 21, prior to completing his degree, he was making $75,000 a year and was given 60,000 shares of stock estimated to be worth more than $1 million.

Mr. Matkins grades suffered because his work left him too little time to complete all of his homework assignments. However, he apparently has no regrets: "Mr. Matkins says the prospect of being a millionaire by his senior year is 'very cool.' He loves MIT, but in many ways, he says, Akamai has become his real university. 'There are different ways to learn stuff,' he says. 'I've learned more at Akamai than I would in a classroom.'"[83]

The article notes that Mr. Lewin's doctoral dissertation will be based on his work at Akamai, although he'll probably need permission from the Akamai board of directors to use some of the material. The article concludes, "He will also probably need approval from Akamai's chief scientist, Mr. Leighton, who, it turns out, is his PhD adviser."[84]

Identify and discuss the ethical issues that the previous account raises.

CASE 29

Pulverizer

Fred is a mechanical engineer who works for Super Mulcher Corporation. It manufactures the Model 1 Pulverizer, a 10-hp chipper/shredder that grinds yard waste into small particles that can be composted and blended into the soil. The device is particularly popular with homeowners who are interested in reducing the amount of garden waste deposited in landfills.

The chipper/shredder has a powerful engine and a rapidly rotating blade that can easily injure operators if they are not careful. During the 5 years the Model 1 Pulverizer has been sold, there have been 300 reported accidents with operators. The most common accident occurs when the discharge chute gets plugged with shredded yard waste, prompting the operator to reach into the chute to unplug it. When operators reach in too far, the rotating blades can cut off or badly injure their fingers.

Charlie Burns, president of Super Mulcher, calls a meeting of the engineers and legal staff to discuss ways to reduce legal liability associated with the sale of the Model 1 Pulverizer. The legal staff suggest several ways of reducing legal liability:

• Put bright yellow warning signs on the Model 1 Pulverizer that say, "Danger! Rapidly rotating blades. Keep hands out when machine is running!"

• Include the following warning in the owner's manual: "Operators must keep hands away from the rotating blades when machine is in operation."

• State in the owner's manual that safe operation of the Model 1 Pulverizer requires a debris collection bag placed over the discharge chute. State that operators are not to remove the debris collection bag while the Model 1 Pulverizing is running. If the discharge chute plugs, the owner is instructed to turn off the Model 1 Pulverizer, remove the debris collection bag, replace the debris collection bag, and restart the engine.

From operating the Model 1 Pulverizer, Fred knows the discharge chute has a tendency to plug. Because the machine is difficult to restart, there is a great temptation to run the unit without the debris collection bag—and to unplug the discharge chute while the unit is still running.

For each of the following scenarios, discuss the various ways Fred attempts to resolve the problem:

Scenario 1: Fred suggests to his engineering colleagues that the Model 1 Pulverizer should be redesigned so it does not plug. His colleagues reply that the company probably cannot afford the expense of reengineering the Model 1, and they conclude

that the legal staff's recommendations should be sufficient. Dissatisfied, in his spare time Fred redesigns the Model 1 Pulverizer and solves the plugging problem in an affordable way.

Scenario 2: Fred says nothing to his colleagues about the impracticality of requiring the machine to be run with the debris collection bag. He accepts the legal staff's advice and adds the warning signs and owner's manual instructions. No changes are made in the design of the Model 1 Pulverizer.

Scenario 3: Fred suggests to his engineering colleagues that they try to convince management that the Model 1 Pulverizer should be redesigned so that it does not plug. They agree and prepare a redesign plan that will cost $50,000 to implement. Then they take their plan to management.

CASE 30

Reformed Hacker?

According to John Markoff's "Odyssey of a Hacker: From Outlaw to Consultant," John T. Draper is attempting to become a "white-hat" hacker as a way of repaying society for previous wrongdoing.[85] In the early 1970s, Draper became known as "Cap'n Crunch" after discovering how to use a toy whistle in the Cap'n Crunch cereal box to access the telephone network in order to get free telephone calls. While serving time in jail for his misdeeds, he came up with the early design for EasyWriter, IBM's first word-processing program for its first PC in 1981. However, says Markoff, in subsequent years Draper used his skills to hack into computer networks, became a millionaire, lost jobs, and experienced homelessness. Now, however, Draper has been enlisted to help operate an Internet security software and consulting firm that specializes in protecting the online property of

corporations. Draper says, "I'm not a bad guy." However, realizing there are bound to be doubters, he adds, "But I'm being treated like a fox trying to guard the hen house." SRI International's computer security expert Peter Neumann summarizes the concern:

> Whether black hats can become white hats is not a black-and-white question. In general, there are quite a few black hats who have gone straight and become very effective. But the simplistic idea that hiring overtly black-hat folks will increase your security is clearly a myth.

Discuss the ethical issues this case raises. What might reasonably convince doubters that Draper has, indeed, reformed? Are customers of the consulting firm entitled to know about Draper's history and his role at the firm?

CASE 31

Resigning from a Project

In 1985, computer scientist David Parnas resigned from an advisory panel of the Strategic Defense Initiative Organization (SDIO).[86] He had concluded that

SDI was both dangerous and a waste of money. His concern was that he saw no way that any software program could adequately meet the requirements of a good SDI system.[87] His rationale for resigning rested on three ethical premises.[88] First, he must accept responsibility for his own actions rather than rely on others to decide for him. Second, he must not ignore or turn away from ethical issues. In Parnas's case, this means asking whether what he is doing is of any benefit to society. Finally, he "must make sure that I am solving the real problem, not simply providing short-term satisfaction to my supervisor."

However, Parnas did more than resign from the panel. He also undertook public opposition to SDI. This was triggered by the failure of SDIO and his fellow panelists to engage in scientific discussion of the technical problems he cited. Instead, Parnas says, he received responses such as "The government has decided; we cannot change it." "The money will be spent; all you can do is make good use of it." "The system will be built; you cannot change that." and "Your resignation will not stop the program."[89] To this, Parnas replied,

It is true, my decision not to toss trash on the ground will not eliminate litter. However, if we are to eliminate litter, I must decide not to toss trash on the ground. We all make a difference.

As for his part, Parnas regarded himself as having a responsibility to help the public understand why he was convinced that the SDI program could not succeed, thus enabling them to decide for themselves.[90]

Parnas's concerns did not stop with SDI. He also expressed concerns about research in colleges and universities:[91]

Traditionally, universities provide tenure and academic freedom so that faculty members can speak out on issues such as these. Many have done just that. Unfortunately, at U.S. universities there are institutional pressures in favor of accepting research funds from any source. A researcher's ability to attract funds is taken as a measure of his ability.

Identify and discuss the ethical issues raised by David Parnas. Are there other ethical issues that should be discussed?

CASE 32

Responsible Charge[92]

Ed Turner graduated from Santa Monica College (a 2-year school) with an associate degree in 1961. He worked for 8 years for the City of Los Angeles in its engineering department and took the professional Engineer in Training exam in California. As a result, he received a Civil Engineering/Professional Engineering license in the state of Idaho. To get his license, he had to work under the direction of already licensed supervisors and be strongly recommended for licensure by all of them. Because he did not have a BS degree in engineering from an accredited school, his experience had to be exemplary.

In the late 1960s, Turner moved to the city of Idaho Falls and went to work for the Department of Public Works. As a licensed professional engineer in 1980, he had sign-off authority for all engineering work done in the city. His problems with the city started when he refused to approve some engineering designs for public works projects. One such project omitted the sidewalk, requiring students to walk in street traffic on their way to

school. The public works director and mayor responded to his refusal by demoting him and moving him out of his office to a new and smaller work area. They appointed an unlicensed nonengineer as city engineering administrator to replace him and sign off on all engineering work. This was in violation of Idaho state law.

Turner stayed on that new job as long as he could to keep an eye on engineering work in the city and because he needed an income to support his family. Finally, he was dismissed, and he and his wife had to sort potatoes and do custodial work in order to survive and to finance a court appeal.

The Idaho Job Service Department approved his request for unemployment insurance coverage, but the city of Idaho Falls succeeded in getting that ruling reversed. The Idaho Industrial Commission eventually overturned the city's ruling, and Turner ultimately received his unemployment insurance.

Turner and the American Engineering Alliance (AEA) of New York managed to obtain the support of

22 states in his case against Idaho Falls for wrongful discharge and for not having responsible charge of engineering work. The Idaho State Board of Professional Engineers and the National Society of Professional Engineers (NSPE) also supported him, as did the ASME, the ASCE, the AEA, as well as several other important professional societies. Ed's wife, Debra, played a significant role throughout the 4-year litigation. In addition to keeping the court files in order, she was on the witness stand and was cross-examined by the city's lawyers.

Many individuals cognizant of the issues involved, including one of the authors of this text, volunteered their services to Turner on a pro bono basis and submitted depositions. However, the depositions were not admitted by the Idaho Falls city court that was hearing the case, and the case was thrown out of the court because the papers submitted to the Idaho Falls judge were late and on the wrong forms.

Fortunately, the story does have a happy ending. On the advice of many, and with a new lawyer, Ed's former lawyer was sued for malpractice at a court in another city. In order for a malpractice suit to be successful, the jury must first vote that the original case was winnable, and then it must separately determine that there was malpractice involved. Turner won both those decisions, with the court admonishing the government of Idaho Falls that it had violated state law. Although the settlement was large, after legal fees and taxes were paid, it was clear that Turner was not, in his words, "made whole." But he resumed practicing as a licensed professional civil engineer and happy that he was able to contribute to his profession and to public safety. It is noteworthy that in response to the devastation caused by Hurricane Katrina in 2005, Ed and his wife Debra spent months doing volunteer work in Alabama to provide aid to its victims.

CASE 33

Scientists and Responsible Citizenry

As a young man, Harrison Brown (1917–1986) played a prominent role in the Manhattan Project at the University of Chicago and Oak Ridge. In 1943, he became assistant director of chemistry for the Oak Ridge Plutonium Project. During the very few years it took to develop the atomic bomb, Brown and many of his fellow research scientists had serious and deep discussions of their responsibilities as scientists. After the bomb was used in 1945, Brown immediately wrote a book, *Must Destruction Be Our Destiny* (Simon & Schuster, 1946), in which he articulated his concerns and those of his colleagues. An ardent advocate for the establishment of an international body that could peaceably control the spread and possible use of atomic weapons, in the space of 3 months in 1946 he gave more than 100 speeches throughout the country presenting the basic arguments of his book.

It is noteworthy that on the jacket of this book, Albert Einstein is quoted as saying the following:

> One feels that this book is written by a man who is used to responsible work. It gives a clear, honest, and vivid description of the atom bomb as a weapon of war, objective and without any

exaggeration. It gives a clear discussion, free of rhetoric, of the special international problems and the possibilities for their solution. Everyone who reads this book carefully will be enabled—and one hopes stimulated—to contribute to a sensible solution of the present dangerous situation.

It is also noteworthy that the subtitle of *Must Destruction Be Our Destiny* is *A Scientist Speaks as a Citizen*. This subtitle reflects the modesty, yet firmness of conviction, with which Brown undertook his effort to communicate his concerns to the public. He was very sensitive to the claim that scientists should restrict themselves to questions of science. Without crediting scientists with special expertise regarding the social or political implications of science and technology, he responded by pointing out that scientists working on the atomic bomb had the advantage of knowing about the potential uses and consequences of this weapon some time before the general public did, and they had given this much careful thought. Convinced that the "man in the street" needs to be well informed before presenting social and political opinions about matters of great importance, Brown held that scientists have a responsibility to acquire and communicate needed information to lay audiences so that they are able to exercise better judgment.

As for himself, Brown said in his preface, "I have written as a man in the street, as an ordinary citizen, possessing primarily the fundamental desires to live freely, comfortably, and unafraid." Implicit here is the notion that *this* ordinary citizen also possessed information needed by all other ordinary citizens— information that, he was convinced, would enable them to join hands with those scientists who "have had the advantage of months and years to become acquainted with the problems and to think of them as would any reasonably literate and sensitive persons." He added, "As scientists we have indicated the problems—as citizens we have sought the answers."

Of course, Harrison Brown the scientist and Harrison Brown the ordinary citizen were one and the same person. He also chose to pursue a career at the California Institute of Technology, holding joint appointments in the geology and humanities divisions. In other words, he deliberately chose an interdisciplinary path in higher education. This is further reflected in his joining the Emergency Committee of Atomic Scientists as Vice Chair (with Albert Einstein serving as Chair) in 1947, his role as editor-in-chief of *The Bulletin of Atomic Scientists,* his service as foreign secretary of the National Academy of Sciences (1962–1974), and his service as science advisor to the presidential campaigns of Adlai Stevenson and Robert Kennedy.

Apparently, Harrison Brown's commitments as citizen–scientist did not interfere with his commitments to "pure science." He continued his scientific studies on meteorites, along with work in mass spectroscopy, thermal diffusion, fluorine and plutonium chemistry, geochemistry, and planetary structure. In 1947, at age 30, he became the youngest scientist ever to receive the annual award for making "the most notable contribution to science," based on his report, "Elements in Meteorites and the Earth's Origins." In 1952, he received the American Chemical Society's Award in Pure Chemistry.

In his second book, *The Challenge of Man's Future* (Viking Press, 1954), and in subsequent writings throughout the next three decades, Harrison Brown argued that technological advancement, population growth, the desire for increased living standards throughout the world, and limited food, mineral, and energy resources call for urgent consideration by scientists and ordinary citizens alike. Convinced that we have the power, intelligence, and imagination to deal with the challenges posed by these developments, he insisted, however, that this "necessitates an understanding of the relationships between man, his natural environment, and his technology."

The comments of three Nobel Prize winners were quoted on the jacket of this second book. One of them, Albert Einstein, said,

> We may well be grateful to Harrison Brown for this book on the condition of mankind as it appears to an erudite, clear-sighted, critically appraising scientist.... The latest phase of technical–scientific progress, with its fantastic increase of population, has created a situation fraught with problems of hitherto unknown dimensions.... This objective book has high value.

Harrison Brown died in 1986. Twenty years later, Harvard University's John Holdren, Teresa and John Heinz Professor of Environmental Policy and Director of the Program on Science, Technology, and Public Policy in the John F. Kennedy School of Government, recalled reading *The Challenge of Man's Future* years before as a high school student. In a speech titled, "Science, Technology, and the State of the Word: Some Reflections after September 11," he said that prior to reading that book and C. P. Snow's *The Two Cultures,* his ambition was to become the chief design engineer at Boeing. Moved by these books, he decided that, instead, he wanted to "work on the great problems of the human condition that sit at the intersection of disciplines, the intersection of the natural sciences and the social sciences where science, technology, and the public policy come together" (www.spusa.org/pubs/speeches/holdrenspeech.html).

At the outset of his speech, Holdren said that he would be sharing his reflections in the way he thought Harrison Brown would if he were still alive—focusing on what we can now (and should have been able to earlier) clearly understand about the relationships among science, technology, and the state of the world prior to September 11, 2001. Most important, he indicated that he would be talking "in terms of what socially responsible scientists and technologists should be striving to contribute to these issues, not just the issues in the aftermath of September 11th but the still wider ones at this immensely important intersection of science and technology and the human condition."

CASE 34

Sealed Beam Headlights

It is important to realize that engineering success typically requires the collaborative efforts of engineers rather than simply the efforts of one individual. An early safety problem in the automotive industry was the unreliability of headlights due to the fact that they were inadequately protected from moisture and the resulting rusting. In the late 1930s, a group of General Electric engineers worked together to develop the sealed beam headlight, which promised to reduce sharply the number of fatalities caused by night driving.[93] To accomplish this, it was necessary to involve engineers in collaborative research, design, production, economic analysis, and governmental regulation. Although the need for headlight improvement was widely acknowledged, there was also widespread skepticism about its technical and economic feasibility. By 1937, the GE team provided the technical feasibility of the sealed beam headlight. However, the remaining task was to persuade car builders and designers to cooperate with each other in support of the innovation, as well as to convince regulators of its merits.

Given this skepticism, there is little reason to suppose that the GE engineers were simply doing what they were told—namely to develop a more adequate headlamp. Apparently, the consensus was that this could not be done, so the engineers had to overcome considerable resistance. This was no ordinary task, as evidenced by the remarks of another engineer of that era:

> The reaching of the consensus embodied in the specifications of the sealed beam headlamp is an achievement which commands the admiration of all who have any knowledge of the difficulties that were overcome. It is an achievement not only in illuminating engineering, but even more in safety engineering, in human engineering, in the art of cooperation.[94]

The difficulties faced by this group of engineers should remind us that enthusiasm for desirable ends needs to be tempered with realism. Other demands and constraints may discourage undertaking such projects. Nevertheless, looking for opportunities to accomplish such ends, as well as taking advantage of these opportunities when they arise, is desirable. Discuss the abilities and qualities of character that contribute to the success of projects such as the sealed beam headlight. Can you think of other examples of collaborative engineering success?

CASE 35

Service Learning[95]

Current Accreditation Board for Engineering and Technology (ABET) requirements for accredited engineering programs in the United States include helping students acquire "an understanding of the ethical characteristics of the engineering profession and practice."[96] ABET 2000 more specifically requires engineering programs to demonstrate that their graduates also understand the impact of engineering in a global and social context, along with a knowledge of current issues related to engineering. The recent surge of interest in service learning in engineering education presents students with creative, hands-on possibilities to meet these ABET expectations.

Service learning involves combining community service and academic study in ways that invite reflection on what one learns in the process. Given ABET 2000's requirement that students be involved in a "major design experience" that includes ethical factors in addition to economic, environmental, social, and political factors, the idea of service learning in engineering may be especially promising. But this idea is important for another reason. Much of the engineering ethics literature dwells on the negative—wrongdoing, its prevention, and appropriate sanctioning of misconduct. These will always be fundamental concerns. However, there is more to engineering ethics. There is the more positive side that focuses on doing one's work responsibly and well—whether in the workplace or in community service.

Given the common association of engineering ethics with wrongdoing and its prevention, it might be asked whether community service should be regarded as a part of engineering ethics at all. However, it is not uncommon for other professions to include pro bono service as an important feature of their professional ethics. This is based in large part on the recognition that professions provide services that may be needed by anyone but which not everyone can afford or gain easy access to. Medical and legal services readily come to mind. But this is no less true of engineering.

Is this acknowledged in engineering codes of ethics? It is in at least two—those of the NSPE and the ASCE. Emphasizing the crucial impact that engineering has on the public, the Preamble of NSPE's Code of Ethics for Engineers states that engineering "requires adherence to the highest principles of ethical conduct on behalf of the public, clients, employers, and the profession." Following this, the code lists as its first Fundamental Canon that engineers are to hold paramount the safety, health, and welfare of the public in the performance of their professional duties. Under section III. Professional Obligations, provision 2 reads, "Engineers shall at all times strive to serve the public interest." Subsection a under this obligation reads, "Engineers shall seek opportunities to be of constructive service in civic affairs and work for the advancement of the safety, health, and well-being of their community."

Noteworthy here is the assertion that engineers are to seek opportunities to be of service to the community. Furthermore, there is no qualifier, "in the performance of their professional duties." This suggests that engineers' obligations in regard to public well-being are not restricted to their responsibilities within their place of employment.

The first Fundamental Canon of ASCE's code reads, "Engineers shall hold paramount the safety, health, and welfare of the public and shall strive to comply with the principles of sustainable development in the performance of their professional duties." Subsection e, directly under this, reads, "Engineers should seek opportunities to be of constructive service in civic affairs and work for the advancement of the safety, health, and well-being of their communities, and the protection of the environment through the practice of sustainable development." Subsection f reads, "Engineers should be committed to improving the environment by adherence to the principles of sustainable development so as to enhance the quality of life of the general public."

Although the NSPE and ASCE provisions are rather broadly stated, they do provide a rationale for concluding that, at least from the perspective of two major professional engineering societies, community service is an important feature of engineering ethics.

Many worry that students today are part of a "me-generation." At the same time, however, there has been a marked increase in student interest in volunteer work. Until fairly recently, there has not been a strong correlation between students' academic pursuits and the types of volunteer work they undertake. Noting this lack of correlation, organizations such as Campus Compact have made concerted efforts to encourage the development of academic programs that explicitly encourage students to seek volunteer work related to their course of academic study and to reflect quite self-consciously on the connections.[97]

Academic areas such as teacher education and the health care professions immediately suggest themselves as candidates for service learning programs. Students preparing to become teachers can offer tutorial or mentoring services to the schools, students in nursing programs can volunteer their services to nursing homes or other health care facilities, and so on. But engineering students, even early on in their programs, can volunteer tutorial services to the schools, particularly in areas of computer science, math, science, and technology that are relevant to engineering. For example, while at the University of South Alabama, Edmund Tsang's Introduction to Mechanical Engineering course included a service learning project.[98] Engineering student teams worked with the Mobile school system and its Southeastern Consortium for Minorities in Engineering program. Students in this class designed equipment for teachers and middle school students that illustrated basic principles of motion, energy, and force and mathematical modeling.

To illustrate the potential value of service learning projects for both students and those who benefit from their projects, it is helpful to discuss an example in some detail. This was a project undertaken some years ago by a group of electrical engineering students at Texas A & M in Tom Talley's senior design course.[99] This course was intended to help prepare students for the challenges in project design and management that they will confront in industry. In this case, the students were also introduced to community service.

Team members were undecided about what project to undertake until Tom Talley shared with them a letter he had received from the Brazos Valley Rehabilitation Center. The letter identified a need for an Auditory Visual Tracker (AVIT) to help in evaluating and training visual skills in very young children with disabilities. Most students, Talley said, end up only building a working prototype. However, in this case, he pointed out, "The students took on the project knowing that it was larger and potentially more expensive for them to produce than might be expected of a typical project."

"We like that it was a project that was going to be genuinely used," said team member Robert D. Siller, "It wasn't going to just end up in a closet. It's actually helping someone." Myron Moodie added, "When we presented the AVIT to the center, we got to see some of the kids use it. It was worth it watching the way the children like it." However, completion of the project was anything but easy. One complication was that the team was interdisciplinary. It included a student from management, which meant that the team was introduced to the project management environment, giving the endeavor a more industry-like flavor than was typical of projects in Talley's design class. To further complicate matters, the management student was seriously injured in a car accident during the semester; but she was able to continue in the project. By the end of the semester, the project was not quite completed. However, the students were so committed to providing a usable AVIT for the rehabilitation center that they stayed on after the semester.

What seems obvious from student comments is that they found the service aspect of their experience very rewarding. Whether this encouraged them to continue to seek out community service opportunities once they were fully employed engineers can be, of course, only a matter for speculation. Another matter for speculation is that this experience speaks positively about the kinds of engineers these students could be expected to become in their places of employment. Tom Talley, at least, was quite optimistic. He said, "They clearly went above and beyond—that's Aggie spirit. Someone is going to get some fine young engineers." This comment can be taken to include what can be expected from these students both as engineers in the workplace and as civic-minded contributors to the public good.

This particular kind of project—one taken to completion and one involving direct interaction with those being helped—can enhance students' understanding and appreciation of responsibilities they have both on the job and in community service. In this case, the project went well beyond designing a prototype; everything worked out well. However, this required very careful attention to the specific needs of the center's staff and the children who were in need of assistance. This is a very important lesson in responsible engineering, whether volunteer or work related.

From a service learning perspective, two limitations of this example should be noted. First, although the students apparently did reflect on the significance of the service aspects of their experience, this was not a specific objective of the project. Service learning is distinguished by it's deliberate combining of service and study: "One of the characteristics of service learning that distinguishes it from volunteerism is its balance between the act of community service by participants and reflection on that act, in order both to provide better service and to enhance the participants' own learning."[100] This project was not simply an instance of volunteerism; it was a class project. However, it was a project primarily in engineering design and, from the perspective of the class, only incidentally did it involve community service. Nevertheless, this is the sort of project that could be undertaken with the full service learning objectives in mind; many of those objectives were, in fact, fulfilled even though this was not part of the official class agenda.

Second, a point related to the first, the AVIT project stood virtually alone. There may have been other projects that lent themselves to service learning objectives that were undertaken by students in Tom Talley's design class or in other design classes at Texas A & M. But service learning in engineering as a planned, coordinated activity requires a much more sustained effort. A second example illustrates this point.

An early service learning program in engineering, the student-initiated Case Engineering Support Group (CESG) at Case Western Reserve University was founded in 1990 as a nonprofit engineering service organization composed of engineering students who "design and build custom equipment to assist the disabled in therapy or normal daily activities."[101] According to the CESG brochure, the equipment is given to individuals at therapy centers at no cost. CESG has received donations of equipment from industry, financial support from the National Science Foundation and the Case Alumni Association, legal services from Case's Law School Clinic, and cooperation and support from the medical and health care community in Cleveland.

In CESG's first year, 18 students completed 6 projects. During the 1995–1996 academic year, 120 students completed 60 projects, as well as follow-up work on previous projects. At that time, CESG supported four major programs:[102]

- Custom Product Development Program: working with faculty members designing, manufacturing, and providing at no cost to individuals adaptive devices and equipment to help them gain a higher level of independent living skills; working with physicians and physical, occupational, and speech therapists in adapting, modifying, and providing devices and equipment.

- Technology Lender Program: repairing and adapting donated computer equipment and designing specialized software for those with special communication, vocational, or educational needs.

- Toy Modification Program: providing specially adapted toys to families of children with disabilities and to hospitals, and presenting related workshops to junior and senior high school students to stimulate interest in engineering as a career.

- Smart Wheelchair Project: working with the Cleveland Clinic Foundation's Seating/Wheeled Mobility Clinic, Invacare Corporation, and engineers at the NASA Lewis Research Center to design, modify, and improve the 'smart wheelchair,' which is fit with special sensors and artificial intelligence routines.

Recent years have seen the rapid growth of service learning programs in engineering. The *International Journal for Service Learning in Engineering* was launched in 2006. This periodical provides detailed accounts of service learning projects written by faculty and students. Learn and Serve America's National Service-Learning Clearinghouse provides a comprehensive list of web resources on service learning in engineering, as well as a list of print resources (www.servicelearning.org). Three web references warrant special mention here:

Engineers Without Borders (www.ewb-usa.org). Established in 2000, this is a national, nonprofit organization that offers help developing areas throughout the world with their engineering needs. It has the goal of "involving and training a new kind of internationally responsible engineering student." This website lists all the EWB-USA registered student chapters, along with their websites. EWB-USA also has a *Wikipedia* entry (http://en.wikipedia.org). It is identified as a member of the "Engineers Without Borders" international network. EWB-USA's projects typically involve the design and construction of water, sanitation, energy, and shelter systems in projects initiated by and completed with the host communities. According to the *Wikipedia* entry, "These projects are initiated by, and completed with, contributions from the host community, which is trained to operate the systems without external assistance. In this way, EWB-USA ensures that its projects are appropriate and self-sustaining."

Engineering Projects in Community Service (EPICS) National Program (http://epicsnational.ecn.purdue .edu). EPICS is described as integrating "highly mentored, long-term, large-scale, team-based, multidisciplinary design projects into the undergraduate engineering curriculum.... Teams work closely with a not-for-profit organization in the community to define, design, build, test, deploy, and support projects that significantly improve the organization's ability to serve the community."

Service-Learning in Engineering: A Resource Guide-book (www.compact.org/publications). Developed by William Oaks and published by Campus Compact, this guidebook introduces the idea of service learning in engineering and provides models from the EPICS program, course descriptions and syllabi, and evaluation tools. It can be downloaded from the Campus Compact website.

CASE 36

Shortcut?

Bruce Carson's civil engineering firm has a contract with the state to specify the route of a new road connecting two major cities. Bruce determines that the shortest workable path will save 20 minutes from what would otherwise be a 2-hour trip, but it would require the state to destroy a farm house that has been in the Jones family for 150 years. Bruce visits the Jones family to get some idea of what it would cost the state to purchase their home and the land immediately surrounding it.

Not surprisingly, the prospect of losing the home their family has maintained for the past 150 years is very upsetting to the family. "What's 20 minutes compared to 150 years of family tradition?" objects Robert Jones, who has lived in the farmhouse the entire 63 years of his life. The family insists that no amount of money would tempt them to sell their home to the state, or to anyone else for that matter.

Bruce knows that one option would be for the state to exercise "eminent domain" and condemn the farmhouse. Should he recommend this to the state? Why or why not?

CASE 37

"Smoking System"[103]

Philip Morris Companies reported testing a microelectronic cigarette holder that eliminates all smoke except that exhaled by the smoker. Battery powered, it is expected to cost approximately $50. The result of years of research, it cost approximately $200 million to develop.

Tentatively called the Accord, the device uses cigarettes that are 62 millimeters long (compared with the standard 85 millimeters). Users will have to remember to recharge the Accord's battery (a 30-minute process, but extra batteries can be purchased). A cigarette is inserted into the 4-inch long, 1½-inch wide device. A microchip senses when the cigarette is puffed and transmits powers to eight heating blades. A display shows the remaining battery charge and indicates how many puffs are left in the eight-puff cigarette. The device also contains a catalytic converter that burns off residues.

Supporters of this product say it will be welcomed by smokers who currently refrain from smoking in their homes or cars for the sake of nonsmoking family members, guests, and passengers. Although smokers will inhale the same amount of tar and nicotine as from conventional "ultralight" cigarettes, 90 percent of second-hand smoke will be eliminated. Furthermore, the same smoking restriction rules in public places will apply to the device.

Critics claim that the Accord will simply reinforce addiction to cigarettes. Richard A. Daynard, chair of the Tobacco Products Liability Project at Boston's Northeastern University School of Law, an anti-tobacco organization, asks, "Who would use an expensive and cumbersome thing like this if they weren't hooked? There is something grim and desperate about it. This is hardly the Marlboro Man, getting on his horse and checking the battery." He also expresses concern that children might be encouraged to smoke since the Accord would enable them to hide smoking from their parents. However, Philip Morris replies that the Accord has a locking device for parents. Consider the following questions:

• Imagine that it is several years ago and you have just received your engineering degree. You are in search of your first job. You are invited to interview with a research division of Philip Morris that is about to begin research to develop the Accord. Would you have any reservations about accepting such a position? Discuss.

• If you have some reservations, would the fact that this job pays $10,000 more per year than any other

offer you have convince you to take the Philip Morris offer?

• Assuming you took the job, what kinds of ethical concerns might you have about how the device should be designed? For example, would you agree that it should have a locking device?

CASE 38

Software for a Library[104]

A small library seeks a software system to catalogue its collection and keep records of materials checked out of the library. Currently, the records of who has checked out what, when materials are due, and the like are kept in a file drawer behind the check-out desk. These records are confidential. Patrons are assured that these records are not accessible to anyone other than library personnel. But, of course, drawers can be opened when no one is looking. What assurance is there that the software systems under consideration will provide as much, if not greater, security? Assuming that no one in the library is a software

specialist, the library has no alternative but to place its trust in someone who presumably has the requisite expertise. How concerned should that expert be (again, bearing in mind that even the best system is not completely sleuthproof)? Furthermore, what assurance has the library that it is not being oversold or undersold in general? To what extent should software specialists be concerned with determining precisely what the various needs of the library are—and to try to meet those needs rather than offer more than is necessary in order to secure greater profit or less than is needed in order to come in with a lower bid?

CASE 39

Sustainability

Scientists, engineers, and the government are publicly expressing urgent concern about the need to address the challenges of sustainable scientific and technological development. Global warming, for example, raises concern about glacial meltdown and consequent rising ocean levels threatening coastal cities. A related concern is the lowering of levels of freshwater in the American West as a result of lowered levels of accumulated mountain snow. In Joe Gertner's "The Future Is Drying Up," Nobel laureate Steven Chu, director of the Lawrence Berkeley National Laboratory, is cited as saying that even optimistic projections for the second half of the 21st century indicate a 30 to 70 percent drop in the snowpack level of the Sierra Nevada, provider of most of northern California's water.[105] Gertner goes on to discuss other likely freshwater problems that will have to be faced by Western states as a result of both global warming and the consumption needs

and demands of an increasing population. He also outlines some of the efforts of engineers to address these problems aggressively now rather than wait until it is too late to prevent disaster.[106]

We noted in Chapter 9 that most engineering society codes of ethics do not make direct statements about the environmental responsibilities of engineers. However, in 2007 the NSPE joined the ranks of engineering societies that do. Under section III. Professional Obligations, provision 2 reads, "Engineers shall at all times strive to serve the public interest." Under this heading, there is a new entry, d: "Engineers are encouraged to adhere to the principles of sustainable development in order to protect the environment for future generations." Footnote 1 addresses the conceptual question of what is meant by "sustainable development": "'Sustainable development' is the challenge of meeting human needs for natural resources, industrial products, energy, food, transportation, shelter, and effective waste management while conserving and protecting environmental quality and the natural resource base essential for future development."

Although this definition of sustainable development leaves many fundamental conceptual and value questions in need of further analysis (e.g., What are human needs? What is meant by "environmental quality"?), it provides a general framework for inquiry. It also identifies a variety of fundamental areas of concern (e.g., food, transportation, and waste management). Of course, responsibilities in these areas do not fall only on engineers. Government officials, economists, business leaders, and the general citizenry need to be involved as well. Thus, a basic question relates to how those who need to work together might best do so and what role engineers might play. We offer three illustrations for discussion. The first is an early effort to involve students from different disciplines in a project that supports sustainable development. The second is the recent proliferation of centers and institutes for sustainability on college campuses throughout the country. The third is service learning opportunities in support of sustainable design and development.

RENEWABLE ENERGY[107]

Dwayne Breger, a civil and environmental engineer at Lafayette College, invited junior and senior engineering, biology, and environmental science students to apply to be on an interdisciplinary team to design a project that would make use of farmland owned by Lafayette College in a way that supports the college mission. Twelve students were selected for the project: two each from civil and environmental engineering, mechanical engineering, chemical engineering, and Bachelor of Arts in engineering, plus three biology majors and one in geology and environmental geosciences. These students had minors in such areas as economics and business, environmental science, chemistry, government, and law. The result of the project was a promising design for a biomass farm that could provide an alternative, renewable resource for the campus steam plant.[108]

Professor Breger regards projects such as this as providing important opportunities for students to involve themselves in work that contributes to restructuring our energy use toward sustainable resources. ABET's *Engineering Criteria* 2000 for evaluating engineering programs includes the requirement that engineering programs demonstrate that their graduates have "an understanding of professional and ethical responsibility," "the broad education necessary to understand the impact of engineering solutions in a global and societal context," and "a knowledge of contemporary issues." Criterion 4 requires that students have "a major design experience" that includes consideration of the impact on design of such factors as economics, sustainability, manufacturability, ethics, health, safety, and social and political issues.[109] Discuss how the Lafayette College project might satisfy criterion 4, especially the ethical considerations.

ACADEMIC CENTERS FOR SUSTAINABILITY

Historically, joint research in colleges and universities is done within separate disciplines rather than in collaboration with other disciplines. Thus, biologists collaborate with other biologists, chemists with other chemists, economists with other economists, and political scientists with other political scientists. The recent emergence of centers and institutes for sustainability represents a significant and important break from that tradition.

In September 2007, the Rochester Institute of Technology initiated the Golisano Institute for Sustainability.[110] Noting that it is customary for new programs to be run by just one discipline, Nabil Nasr, the institute director, comments, "But the problem of sustainability cuts across economics, social elements, engineering, everything. It simply cannot be solved by one discipline, or even by coupling two disciplines."[111]

Dow Chemical has recently given the University of California at Berkeley $10 million to establish a sustainability center. Dow's Neil Hawkins says, "Berkeley has one of the strongest chemical engineering schools in the world, but it will be the M.B.A.'s who understand areas like microfinance solutions to drinking water problems."[112] The center is in Berkeley's Center for Responsible Business, directed by Kellie A. McElhaney. Commercialization of research undertaken by students and professors is expected. However, McElhaney notes, "Commercialization takes forever if the chemical engineers and the business types do not coordinate. So think how much easier it will be for chemistry graduates to work inside a company if they already know how to interact with the business side."[113]

Discuss how considerations of ethics might enter into the collaborative efforts of centers and institutes for sustainability.

SERVICE LEARNING OPPORTUNITIES

The first two issues of the recently launched *International Journal for Service Learning* feature three articles promoting the notion that service learning projects can provide hands-on opportunities to undertake sustainable design and development. In "Service Learning in Engineering and Science for Sustainable Development," Clarion University of Pennsylvania physicist Joshua M. Pearce urges that undergraduates should have opportunities to become involved in projects that apply appropriate technologies for sustainable development.[114] Especially concerned with alleviating poverty in the developing world, Pearce argues,

> The need for development is as great as it has ever been, but future development cannot simply follow past models of economic activity, which tended to waste resources and produce prodigious pollution. The entire world is now paying to clean up the mess and enormous quantities of valuable resources have been lost for future generations because of the Western model of development. For the future, the entire world population needs ways to achieve economic, social, and environmental objectives *simultaneously*.

He cites successful projects in Haiti and Guatemala that make use of readily available materials in the locales in which they have been undertaken.

In "Learning Sustainable Design through Service," Stanford University PhD students Karim Al-Khafaji and Margaret Catherine Morse present a service learning model based on the Stanford chapter of Engineers for a Sustainable World to teach sustainable design.[115] They illustrate this model in discussing a Stanford project in the Andaman Islands that focused on rebuilding after the December 26, 2004, earthquake and tsunami. Behind such projects is a student-led course, "Design for a Sustainable World," that seeks to

- Develop students' iterative design skills, project management and partnership-building abilities, sustainability awareness, cultural sensitivity, empathy, and desire to use technical skills to promote peace and human development.
- Help developing communities ensure individuals' human rights via sustainable, culturally appropriate, technology-based solutions.
- Increase Stanford University's stewardship of global sustainability.[116]

In "Sustainable Building Materials in French Polynesia," John Erik Anderson, Helena Meryman, and Kimberly Porsche, graduate students at the University of California at Berkeley's Department of Civil and Environmental Engineering, provide a detailed, technical description of a service learning project designed to assist French Polynesians in developing a system for the local manufacturing of sustainable building materials.[117]

CASE 40

Testing Water ... and Ethics

The video *Testing Water ... and Ethics* is a fictional portrayal of a young engineer facing his first professional dilemma. He attempts to solve the problem by treating it as analogous to a design problem in engineering. He also employs the method of seeking a creative middle way. This video is available from the Institute for Professional Practice, 13 Lanning Road, Verona, NJ 07044-2511 (phone, 1-888-477-2723; e-mail, Bridge2PE@aol.com).

CASE 41

Training Firefighters[118]

Donald J. Giffels, civil engineer and president of a large engineering consulting firm, was puzzled by the design of a government facility to train firefighters dealing with fire crashes of airplanes. His firm was under contract to do the civil engineering work for installing equipment at the facility. Because it contaminates the soil, jet fuel had recently been replaced by liquid propane for simulating crash fires. However, Giffels was concerned about a lack of design specificity in a number of areas crucial to safety (e.g., sprinkler systems, safeguards against flashbacks, fuel quantity, and fuel controls). Furthermore, no design analysis was submitted. Giffels concluded that none existed. However, none of this fell within the direct responsibility of Giffels's firm, whose contract was simply to do the civil engineering work required for installation.

Nevertheless, Giffels concluded that his firm could not simply let this go. He contacted the designers and asked them how they could justify putting their professional seal of approval on the design. They replied, "We don't need to. We're the government." Giffels agreed, but he persisted (to the point, he suspects, of making a pest of himself). Noting that it is easy to be a minimalist (e.g., stay within the law), Giffels worried that one might nevertheless fail to fulfill a responsibility to society. He contacted another engineering firm that had installed a similar design at

10 sites. It, too, he said, had been concerned about safety when looking at the designs. It contacted a mechanical engineering firm, asking it to do a design study. This request was turned down because of liability fears. So, the civil engineering firm asked the government agency to write a letter absolving it of any responsibility in case of mishaps due to the inadequate design.

While not contesting the legality of this firm's way of dealing with the problem, Giffels insisted that this was not the correct way to proceed. His company refused to proceed with the installation until the safety issues were adequately addressed. The government agency agreed to bring in three other firms to deal with the concerns. Giffels firm's contract was modified to provide assurances that the safety issues would be addressed. Giffels stresses the importance of being able to communicate effectively about these matters—a communication responsibility. Good communication, he says, is essential to getting others on board.

Although successful in his efforts to ensure safety, Giffels says that this is not a story that would receive press notice. However, *not* resisting, he insists, might well have resulted in press coverage—such as from the deaths of firefighters going through their simulations.

Discuss the ethical challenges facing Giffels and his strategy in dealing with them.

CASE 42

TV Antenna[119]

Several years ago, a TV station in Houston decided to strengthen its signal by erecting a new, taller (1,000-foot) transmission antenna in Missouri City, Texas. The station contracted with a TV antenna design firm to design the tower. The resulting design employed twenty 50-foot segments that would have to be lifted into place sequentially by a jib crane that moved up with the tower. Each segment required a lifting lug to permit that segment to be hoisted off the flatbed delivery truck and then lifted into place by the crane. The

actual construction of the tower was done by a separate rigging firm that specialized in such tasks.

When the rigging company received the 20th and last tower segment, it faced a new problem. Although the lifting lug was satisfactory for lifting the segment horizontally off the delivery truck, it would not enable the segment to be lifted vertically. The jib crane cable interfered with the antenna baskets at the top of the segment. The riggers asked permission from the design company to temporarily remove the antenna baskets and were refused. Officials at the design firm said that the last time they gave permission to make similar changes, they had to pay tens of thousands of dollars to repair the antenna baskets (which had been damaged on removal) and to remount and realign them correctly.

The riggers devised a solution that was seriously flawed. They bolted an extension arm to the tower section and calculated the size of the required bolts based on a mistaken model. A sophomore-level engineering student who had taken a course in statics could have detected the flaw, but the riggers had no engineers on their staff. The riggers, knowing they lacked engineering expertise, asked the antenna design company engineers to review their proposed solution. The engineers again refused, having been ordered by company management not only not to look at the drawings but also not to visit the construction site during the lifting of the last segment. Management of the design firm feared that they would be held liable if there were an accident. The designers also failed to suggest to the riggers that they should hire an engineering consultant to examine their lifting plans.

When the riggers attempted to lift the top section of the tower with the microwave baskets, the tower fell, killing seven men. The TV company was taping the lift of the last segment for future TV promotions, and the videotape shows the riggers falling to their death.

Consider how you would react to watching that tape if you were the design engineer who refused to look at the lifting plans or if you were the company executive who ordered the design engineer not to examine the plans.

To take an analogy, consider a physician who examines a patient and finds something suspicious in an area outside her specialty. When asking advice from a specialist, the physician is rebuffed on the grounds that the specialist might incur a liability. Furthermore, the specialist does not suggest that the patient should see a specialist.

What conceptions of responsibility seemed most prevalent in this case? Can you suggest other conceptions that might have helped avoid this tragedy?

CASE 43

Unlicensed Engineer[120]

Charles Landers, former Anchorage assemblyman and unlicensed engineer for Constructing Engineers, was found guilty of forging partner Henry Wilson's signature and using his professional seal on at least 40 documents. The falsification of the documents was done without Wilson's knowledge, who was away from his office when they were signed. Constructing Engineers designs and tests septic systems. The signed and sealed documents certified to the Anchorage city health department that local septic systems met city wastewater disposal regulations. Circuit Judge Michael Wolverton banned Landers for 1 year from practicing as an engineer's, architect's, or land surveyor's assistant. The judge also sentenced him to 20 days in jail, 160 hours of community service, $4,000 in fines, and 1 year of probation. Finally, Landers was ordered to inform property owners about the problems with the documents, explain how he would rectify the problem, and pay for a professional engineer to review, sign, and seal the documents.

Assistant Attorney General Dan Cooper had requested the maximum penalty: a 4-year suspended sentence and $40,000 in fines. Cooper argued that "the 40 repeated incidents make his offense the most serious within the misuse of an engineer's seal." This may have been the first time a case like this was litigated in Alaska. The Attorney General's office took on the case after seeking advice from several professional engineers in the Anchorage area.

According to Cooper, Landers said he signed and sealed the documents because "his clients needed something done right away." (The documents were needed before proceeding with property transactions.) Lander's attorney, Bill Oberly, argued that his client should be sentenced as a least offender since public health and safety were not really jeopardized—subsequent review of the documents by a professional engineer found no violations of standards (other than forgery and the misuse of the seal). The documents were resubmitted without needing changes.

However, Judge Wolverton contended that Lander's actions constituted a serious breach of public trust.

The public, he said, relies on the word of those, like professional engineers, who are entrusted with special responsibilities: "Our system would break down completely if the word of individuals could not be relied upon."

The judge also cited a letter from Richard Armstrong, chairman of the Architects, Engineers, and Land Surveyors Board of Registration for Alaska's Department of Commerce and Economic Development. Armstrong said,

> Some of the reasons for requiring professional engineers to seal their work are to protect the public from unqualified practitioners; to assure some

minimum level of competency in the profession; to make practicing architects, engineers, and land surveyors responsible for their work; and to promote a level of ethics in the profession. The discovery of this case will cast a shadow of doubt on other engineering designed by properly licensed individuals.

Identify and discuss the ethically important elements in this case. How relevant is it that subsequent review showed that none of the falsified documents needed to be changed? (Although Judge Wolverton did not impose the maximum penalty, he did not treat Landers as a least offender.)

CASE 44

Where Are the Women?[121]

Although women have become more prevalent in engineering schools during the past few decades, they still make up only approximately 20 percent of engineering school undergraduates in the United States. Even this percentage is somewhat misleading. Women are more prevalent in some engineering fields than others. For example, more than 30 percent of the undergraduates in chemical engineering departments are women, but only 13 percent of the undergraduates in mechanical engineering and electrical engineering are women.[122] Eighteen percent of all engineering PhDs are awarded to women. There are even fewer women faculty in engineering schools. The higher the faculty rank, the fewer women there are. At the top rank of full professor, less than 5 percent are women.[123] This means that engineering students in the United States are taught and

mentored almost exclusively by males, that there are few women faculty serving as role models for female students, and that engineering more generally remains dominated by men.

As interesting comparisons, women receive 57 percent of all baccalaureate degrees in the United States and 55 percent of all social science PhDs, women make up at least 50 percent of the students in medical and law schools, and 28 percent of full professors in the social sciences are women.[124] Therefore, what is happening in engineering schools? No doubt, there are a number of contributing factors to the fact that there are so few women in engineering. But many common beliefs about women and academic advancement in engineering prove to be without merit when the evidence is examined.

Belief	Evidence
1. Women are not as good in mathematics as men.	Female performance in high school mathematics now matches that of males.
2. It is only a matter of time before the issue of "underrepresentation" on faculties is resolved; it is a function of how many women are qualified to enter these positions.	Women's representation decreases with each step up the tenure track and academic leadership hierarchy, even in fields that have had a large proportion of women doctorates for 30 years.

(Continued)

Belief	Evidence (Continued)
3. Women are not as competitive as men. Women do not want jobs in academe.	Similar proportions of men and women with science and engineering doctorates plan to enter postdoctoral study or academic employment.
4. Women and minorities are recipients of favoritism through affirmative action programs.	Affirmative action is meant to broaden searches to include more women and minority group members but not to select candidates on the basis of race or sex, which is illegal.
5. Academe is a meritocracy.	Although scientists like to believe that they "choose the best" based on objective criteria, decisions are influenced by factors—including biases about race, sex, geographic location of a university, and age—that have nothing to do with the quality of the person or work being evaluated.
6. Changing the rules means that standards of excellence will be deleteriously affected.	Throughout a scientific career, advancement depends on judgments of one's performance by more senior scientists and engineers. This process does not optimally select and advance the best scientists and engineers because of implicit bias and disproportionate weighting of qualities that are stereotypically male. Reducing these sources of bias will foster excellence in science and engineering fields.
7. Women faculty are less productive than men.	The publication productivity of women science and engineering faculty has increased during the past 30 years and is now comparable to that of men. The critical factor affecting publication productivity is access to institutional resources; marriage, children, and elder care responsibilities have minimal effects.
8. Women are more interested in family than in careers.	Many women scientists and engineers persist in their pursuit of academic careers despite severe conflicts between their roles as parents and as scientists and engineers. These efforts, however, are often not recognized as representing the high level of dedication to their careers they represent.
9. Women take more time off due to childbearing, so they are a bad investment.	On average, women take more time off during their early careers to meet caregiving responsibilities, which fall disproportionately to women. However, by middle age, a man is likely to take more sick leave than a woman.
10. The system as currently configured has worked well in producing great science; why change it?	The global competitive balance has changed in ways that undermine America's traditional science and engineering advantages. Career impediments based on gender, racial, or ethnic bias deprive the nation of talented and accomplished researchers.[125]

Recently, a number of academic researchers have attempted to separate the myths from the facts about why so few women hold senior-level and leadership engineering positions. One plausible explanation is that slight disparities accumulate over time to disadvantage women and advantage men. Subconscious expectations tied to gender (gender schemas) are an important source of these disparities. We expect, for example, men to be the primary earners and women to be the primary providers of child care. A full range of studies on the influence of gender schemas in assessments of professional competence shows quite convincingly that over time, gender schemas contribute significantly to female engineering faculty being consistently underrated and male engineering faculty being consistently overrated.[126] Gender schemas are held unconsciously by both men and women and subtly influence perceptions and judgments made about one another.[127] Experimental data show, for example, that letters of reference for professional women tend to be shorter and to contain twice as many doubt-raisers (e.g., "she has a somewhat challenging personality"), more grindstone adjectives (e.g., "hardworking" or "conscientious"), and fewer standout adjectives (e.g., "brilliant") as letters for men.[128] Other studies show that women tend to feel less entitled to high salaries and less confident in their mathematical abilities even when their actual performance levels equal those of male peers. Men are expected to be strong and assertive (leaders) and women to be nurturing listeners. As a result, women holding positions of leadership often must work harder to demonstrate actual leadership.

Because most of the faculty and administrators at engineering schools, both male and female, genuinely wish to advance and promote more women, focusing on gender schemas is especially relevant to advancing women in engineering fields. Virginia Valian, a researcher on gender schemas, makes this point. She writes, "The moral of the data on gender schemas is that good intentions are not enough; they will not guarantee the impartial and fair evaluation that we all hold as an ideal."[129] As engineering schools attempt to recruit and advance more women, it is important to assess the ways in which and the degree to which harmful gender schemas serve as barriers to women's advancement. At some institutions, such as the University of Michigan, such efforts have involved conducting gender schema workshops, forming focus groups, conducting interviews, and collecting survey data to assess the prevalence of gender schemas contributing to underrating women faculty in science, technology, engineering, and mathematics fields.[130]

One hypothesis is that once the harmful implicit schemas are made explicit, we can begin to address them at individual, departmental, and institutional levels and, at the very least, decrease their harmful impact. Identify and discuss some of the subtle expectations both men and women have about gender. How do these gender schemas influence the advancement and promotion of women in engineering? Can you think of any examples from your own experience of men being advantaged and women being disadvantaged as a result of gender schemas?

CASE 45

XYZ Hose Co. [131]

Farmers use anhydrous ammonia to fertilize their fields. The anhydrous ammonia reacts violently with water, so care must be exercised in disbursing it. Farmers' cooperatives rent anhydrous ammonia in pressurized tanks equipped with wheels so the tanks can be pulled by tractors. The farmers also rent or purchase hoses that connect the tanks to perforated hollow blades that can be knifed through the soil to spread the ammonia. Leaks from the hose are potentially catastrophic.

For years, the industry standard hose was made of steel-meshed reinforced rubber, which was similar in construction to steel-reinforced automobile tires. Two separate trade associations had established these industry-wide standards.

Approximately 15 years ago, a new, heavy-duty plastic became available that could replace the steel in the hoses. The plastic-reinforced hoses were less expensive, lighter, and easier to process than the steel-braided rubber. The new hose met the industry standards. One company, the XYZ Hose Company, began marketing the plastic-reinforced hose to farmers. Officials of XYZ knew, as a result of tests by a consultant at a nearby state agricultural college, that the plastic did not react immediately to the anhydrous ammonia; however, over the years the plastic did degrade and lose some of its mechanical properties. Accordingly, they put warnings on all the hoses they manufactured, indicating that they should be replaced periodically.

After the product had been on the market a few years, several accidents occurred in which the XYZ hoses ruptured during use and blinded and severely injured the farmers using them. Litigation followed, and XYZ argued in its defense that the farmers had misused the hoses and not heeded the replacement warnings. This defense was unsuccessful, and XYZ made substantial out-of-court settlements.

XYZ has since dropped this product line and placed advertisements in farmers' trade journals and producers' cooperatives newsletters asking farmers to turn in their XYZ hoses for full refunds. The advertisements state that the hoses are "obsolete," not that they are unsafe.

Identify and discuss the ethical issues this case raises, paying special attention to relevant, key ideas presented in this chapter. What are the relevant facts? What factual, conceptual, and application issues are there? What methods for resolving these issues might be used?

CASE 46

The 2010 Loss of the Deepwater Horizon and the Macondo Well Blowout

The Deepwater Horizon was a $340 million semisubmersible deep water drilling rig owned and operated by Transocean. Transocean was contracted by British Petroleum (BP) to drill the 18,360 ft Macondo well in about 5000 feet of water in the Gulf of Mexico about 40 miles off the coast of Louisiana. Deepwater Horizon drilling operations, at a cost of about $1 million per day for a planned 51 days, began at the Macondo well in February 2010, taking over operations started in October 2009 by another rig, and ended on April 20, 2010 with an explosion and fire which resulted in the loss of 11 lives (out of 126 workers on the rig at the time), the sinking of the rig, and a prolonged uncontrolled release of oil and gas from the wellhead. Efforts to control the well have been unsuccessful for months, resulting in what is thought to be the largest oil spill in US history. Well owner BP has pledged a $20 billion fund for cleanup and compensations, although the total cost of the disaster will not be known for months or years.

House Committee on Energy and Commerce hearings in the weeks following the disaster have focused attention on several aspects of the drilling and completion operations that suggest owner BP repeatedly cut corners to reduce costs with several risky design decisions. What follows is from testimony to the committee as summarized in a June 14, 2010 letter from the Committee Chairman Henry Waxman to BP CEO Tony Hayward that outlines five areas where questionable decisions were made by BP managers and engineers seemingly favoring economy over safety.[132] These areas were well design, the number of

centralizers used in cementing the final string of casing, a decision not to require a cement bond log, abbreviated mud circulation prior to cementing the final string of casing, and a decision not to use a lockdown sleeve.

- *Well Design* A critical decision in the design of the Macondo well was to use a full string casing in the final 1192 ft of the wellbore rather than the more conservative liner/tieback casing design. Full string casing is faster and therefore less expensive than the liner/tieback casing design, but does not offer as much redundancy in the control of gas in the annular space surrounding the casing, and it may have failed to meet Minerals Management Service (MMS) regulations. This conscious decision by BP in the final days before the blowout reduced the cost of the well completion by several million dollars, but with a reduction in safety against blowout.
- *Centralizers* Centralizers are annular spacers that center the casing in the borehole prior to cementing to improve displacement of mud by the cement slurry. When casing is not centered in the wellbore, American Petroleum Institute (API) Recommended Practice 65 says that mud will not effectively be displaced by the slurry, which can result in weak or porous cement seals, leading to gas leakage and the risk of blowout. BP chose to use six centralizers on the final 1192 ft of casing despite predictions by the contractor Halliburton that 21 centralizers were required to reduce the risk of a gas flow problem from "severe" to

"minor." An additional 15 centralizers were located, but evidently the time required to get them to the rig, 10 hours, represented an unacceptable delay, so the decision was made to use only the six available centralizers.

- *Cement Bond Log* This standard nondestructive test is designed to detect if any mud inclusions or other problems have caused voids or channels in the cement seal, reducing the integrity of the cement seal. MMS regulations may have required such a test on the Macondo well. BP flew a Schlumberger crew to the rig on April 18 to stand by to perform such a test, but dismissed them on April 20. A cement bond test on the Macondo well would have taken about 9–12 hours, and the discovery of any voids in the cement would have led to further delay.

- *Mud Circulation* Before the cement slurry is placed in the annular region, displacing the mud to form the annular seals, it is good practice to circulate the mud to remove cuttings, gas bubbles, and decrease the viscosity of the mud to allow better cement flow and mud displacement. API guidelines recommend circulating the greater of 1.5 annular volumes of mud or 1.0 casing volume, at a minimum. Circulating this much mud takes time, perhaps as much as 12 hours on the Macondo well, and BP chose to circulate a much smaller amount, 261 barrels of mud.

- *Casing Hanger Lockdown Sleeve* BP had not installed a casing hanger lockdown sleeve (LDS) designed to lock the wellhead and casing in the seal assembly at the seafloor. This may have just been a delay while waiting for MMS approval of a design change, but the end result was that an LDS not installed at the time of the April 20 blowout. LDS devices represent another safety feature against blowouts by preventing the casing from rising up and damaging the wellhead seal.

In at least the first four of these questions raised by the committee, it appears that BP engineers' and managers' design decisions represented the faster (cheaper) and less conservative (riskier) alternatives, in some cases reversing an initial design decision using the safer alternative. Well Team Leader John Guide reportedly reversed Drilling Engineering Team Leader John Walz's

decision to order the additional 15 centralizers because of the 10-hour delay for delivery. In this process, Guide reportedly made use of a "risk/reward equation," but the details of that decision are not yet public knowledge. The "risk/reward" approach is a management tool commonly used in making investment and stock trading decisions, and is not engineering terminology, which strongly suggests that this critical engineering decision was made by an individual with management training and background using investment/stock trading logic, most likely without appropriate engineering consideration of public health, safety, and welfare. Whether there will be evidence presented of rational engineering decision making behind these five critical design decisions is yet to be learned. For now it must be questioned whether these decisions were made appropriately as "proper engineering decisions" (PED) or "proper management decisions" (PMD).

It also appears that the personnel in the BP chain of command responsible for these questionable decisions did not include many, if any, registered professional engineers, which raises another very important question about BP's operation. While the rules of the Texas State Board of Professional Engineers (and probably those of other gulf states) do not require professional registration of Houston-based individuals holding these jobs (an "industry exemption" in Texas allows individuals who work for industrial employers without offering services to the public to practice engineering without being licensed), the apparent absence or scarcity of licensed engineers in this chain of command raises questions about the level of experience and professionalism behind the decisions.

One comment in the House Committee letter, attributed to BP Drilling Engineer Brian Morel, suggests BP discounted or ignored a contractor's quantitative simulations that indicated the use of only six centralizers would not ensure a safe cement job. Morel's e-mail to the contractor said, "We have 6 centralizers, we can run them in a row, spread out, or any combination of the two. It's a vertical hole, so *hopefully* the pipe stays centralized due to gravity … it's too late to get any more product on the rig. Our only option is to rearrange placement of these centralizers" (emphasis added). The essence of engineering is the reliance on accurate quantitative simulations to develop safe designs, yet Morel's comment suggests that the decision relied on good fortune rather than calculated safety. One would expect an experienced professional engineer would have not made or accepted a decision with this stated basis. The industry exemption to engineering registration requirements, or the overreliance on that exemption by some corporate employers involved in this incident, deserves some of the blame for this disaster.

Finally, the oversight by the MMS comes into question. Many aspects of the design process appear to have been approved without challenge by the MMS or justification by BP. The choice of a single string of casing instead of the safer liner/tieback casing was approved the same day it was requested.

CASE 47

Units, Communications, and Attention to Detail—the Loss of the Mars Climate Orbiter

The Mars Climate Orbiter was a 629 kg Mars satellite launched by NASA on December 11, 1998 with a mission to map the Martian surface and atmosphere for about 2 years and serve as a communications relay station for future Mars landers for about 3 additional years. The Orbiter was lost during entry into Martian orbit; it is presumed to have burned up during atmospheric entry or overheated and skipped into space.

The following, taken from the official report of the investigation into the loss of the Climate Orbiter, indicates the probe was inserted into Mars orbit much lower in the atmosphere than designed because of cumulative navigation errors resulting from the use of data in English units provided by a contractor in onboard calculations requiring metric units.[133]

> At the time of Mars insertion, the spacecraft trajectory was approximately 170 kilometers lower than planned. As a result, MCO either was destroyed in the atmosphere or re-entered heliocentric space after leaving Mars' atmosphere. The Board recognizes that mistakes occur on spacecraft projects. However, sufficient processes are usually in place on projects to catch these mistakes before they become critical to mission success. Unfortunately for MCO, the root cause was not caught by the processes in-place in the MCO project.
>
> A summary of the findings, contributing causes and MPL recommendations are listed below. These are described in more detail in the body of this report along with the MCO and MPL observations and recommendations.
>
> Root Cause: Failure to use metric units in the coding of a ground software file, "Small Forces," used in trajectory models.

In addition the report lists eight contributing causes, including inadequate communications between project elements, inadequate staffing, and inadequate training.

CASE 48

Expensive Software Bug—the Loss of the Mars Polar Lander

On December 3, 1999, 11 months after its launch, the Mars Polar Lander communications with NASA halted abruptly during descent to the Martian surface. Subsequent investigations identified several possible failure mechanisms but focused on a coding error in one line of software. It is theorized that the programming error allowed the system to misinterpret vibrations of the craft's extended landing gear as touchdown on the Martian surface, triggering a premature shutdown of

the braking rockets and a subsequent free fall of about 130 ft, which destroyed the lander.

Some interpret this failure as an outcome of increasingly complex computer programs and believe that NASA's testing of large and complex codes cannot always identify and prevent all possible errors. It has been suggested that too often testing is done to demonstrate that the codes work as intended when all input is within an expected range of "normal" operations, but not enough testing is done to ascertain possible outcomes whenever operational parameters vary into abnormal territory.

Leveson[134] cites several aspects of software design, testing, and operations that have contributed to recent aerospace failures or incidents, including:

- Overconfidence and overreliance on digital automation
- Not understanding the risks associated with the software
- Confusing reliability and safety a tendency of computer scientists in general?
- Overrelying on redundancy (redundancy influences reliability more than safety)
- Assuming risk decreases over time (Therac-25)
- Ignoring warning signs in software incidents (related to what has been called "normalization of deviance")
- Inadequate cognitive engineering

- Inadequate specifications—specifications sometimes include what the software was supposed to do, but no mention of what it **must not** do (Mars Polar Lander)
- Flawed review process (Mars Polar Lander)
- Inadequate System Safety Engineering
- Violation of basic safety engineering practices in the digital parts of the system—software engineers are almost never taught these principles (Mars Polar Lander)
- Software reuse without appropriate safety analysis
- Unnecessary complexity and software functions—Creeping featurism (Keep it simple, stupid!)
- Operational personnel not understanding the automation
- Test and simulation environments that do not match the operational environment (Fly what you test and test what you fly!)
- Deficiencies in safety-related information collection and use

CASE 49

A Construction Inspector's Responsibility in Collapsed Cantilevered Balcony

No engineer was involved in the project, which is common for residential structures like this one, but the same ideas about ethical responsibility in design and construction oversight apply to engineers with these responsibilities.

In 2004, two visitors to a recently constructed Central Texas lakeside residence walked out onto a third-floor balcony to enjoy the new view of Inks Lake, but the balcony collapsed and both fell more than 20 feet, which caused serious injuries.[135] The cantilevered balcony had been attached to a ledger board that was nailed to the structure by the framing subcontractor instead of bolted as specified by the architect. The ledger board separated from the structure under dead load plus a very light live load (the two visitors). The architect designed the structure, including the balconies, and oversaw the construction but did not inspect the finished balcony closely enough to detect the deviation from his plans and specifications.

The architect's contract required that he sign off on the contractor's pay applications as assurance that "the quality of workmanship and materials used conforms with the contract documents." But the contract also said that, "The architect shall not be required to make exhaustive or continuous on-site inspections to check the quality or quantity of the work."

The legal argument centered on whether the architect should have done more to inspect the structure, with the plaintiffs arguing that he was contracted to "observe construction" and "endeavor to guard the owner against defects and deficiencies" in addition to providing his design services. The defendant architect argued that his inspection could not be detailed for that fee and that he had properly discharged his responsibility for construction observation.

A general counsel for the Texas Society of Architects wrote, "unless the project's owner retains the architect to provide more extensive services, the architect's on-site duties are limited and do not include exhaustive or continuous on-site inspections to check the quality of the construction work performed by the contractor.... The architect cannot be expected to guarantee the quality of the contractor's work, however, unless the architect has agreed to provide the additional services that would be necessary to enable the architect to provide that assurance."

In our assessment, the construction error that occurred was egregious, and because of the criticality of the cantilevered balcony components, this construction error should not have gone undetected by any reasonable inspection by a professional architect or engineer with ANY responsibility for oversight of structural construction.

The original design has not been questioned, but it called for joist hangers that were not used by the framing subcontractor to secure the joists to the ledger board and bolts to secure the ledger board to the structure. Instead nails were used. But even the original design was likely inadequate. Joist hangers are not designed to carry a moment as in this cantilevered application. Had the joist hangers been used

and had the ledger board been more securely fastened to the structure with the bolts originally specified, the failure would likely have occurred between joist and ledger, rather than between ledger and structure, and perhaps with more than two people on the structure. A more reasonable design would involve joists that penetrate into the structure and are secured to parallel floor/ceiling joists that allow them to develop the required moment capacity at the wall, and it is not clear whether this design was an alternative that was also rejected by the general or framing contractor.

The lesson here is that the professional engineer (or architect) has a moral responsibility, even where there is no clear legal responsibility, to prevent problems like this from developing in projects in which he or she has a significant role. In engineered projects, there must be a contractual arrangement allowing appropriate construction inspection engineering efforts, and the most critical design details such as the one in question here should have the highest priority for the construction inspector.

CASE 50

Computer Programs and Moral Responsibility— The Therac-25 Case

Medical linear accelerators (linacs) create high energy beams that can destroy tumors with minimal damage to surrounding healthy tissue. For relatively shallow tissue, accelerated electrons are used; for deeper tissue, the electron beam is converted into X-ray photons.[136] In the mid-1970s, Atomic Energy of Canada Limited (AECL) developed a radical new "double-pass" accelerator that needs much less space to develop the required energy levels because it folds the long physical mechanism required to accelerate electrons. Using this double-pass mechanism, AECL designed the Therac-25, which also had the economic advantage over the Therac-20 and other predecessor machines of combining electron and photon acceleration in one machine. The Therac-25 was also different in another way: the software had more responsibility for insuring patient safety than in previous machines. The earlier Therac-20, for example, had independent protective circuits

for monitoring electron-beam scanning, plus mechanical interlocks for ensuring safe operation.

Eleven Therac-25 machines were installed in the United States and Canada between 1985 and 1987, and six accidents involving massive overdoses occurred. The first overdose occurred at the Kennestone Regional Oncology Center in 1985. When the machine turned on, the patient felt a "tremendous force of heat ... this red-hot sensation." When the technician came in, the patient said, "You burned me." The technician said this was not possible. Later, the patient's shoulder (the area of treatment) "froze," and she experienced spasms. The doctors could provide no satisfactory explanation for an obvious radiation burn. Eventually, the patient's breast had to be removed because of radiation burns, and she was in constant pain. The manufacturer and operators of the machine refused to believe that it could have been caused by the Therac-25. A lawsuit was settled out of court, and other Therac-25 users were not informed that anything untoward had happened.

The second accident occurred at the Ontario Cancer Foundation in Hamilton, Ontario. When the machine shut down on the command to deliver the dose, the operator was not concerned, having become accustomed to frequent malfunctions with no harmful consequences. After the treatment was finally administered, however, the patient described a burning sensation in the treatment area. The patient died four months later of an extremely virulent cancer, but an autopsy revealed that a total hip replacement would have been necessary because of the radiation overexposure. AECL could not reproduce the malfunction that occurred at the Hamilton facility, but it altered the software, claiming an improvement over the old system by five orders of magnitude—a claim that was probably exaggerated.

The third accident occurred at Yakima Valley Memorial Hospital in 1985 in Yakima, Washington. After treatment, the patient developed an excessive reddening of the skin, which the hospital staff eventually attributed to "cause unknown." The patient was in constant pain, which was relieved by surgery, and did not die from the radiation. The fact that three similar incidents had occurred with this equipment did not trigger investigation by the manufacturer or government agencies.

The fourth accident occurred in 1986 at the East Texas Cancer Center (ETCC) in Tyler, Texas. Upon attempting to administer the dose, the machine shut down with a "Malfunction 54" error message. The patient said he felt like he had received an electric shock or that someone had poured hot coffee on his back. He began to get up from the treatment table to ask for help, but at that moment the operator hit the "P" key to proceed with treatment. The patient said he felt like his arm was being shocked by electricity and that his hand was leaving his body. He went to the treatment room door and pounded on it. The operator was shocked and immediately opened the door for the patient, who appeared shaken and upset. Unknown to anyone at the time, the patient had received a massive overdose. He died from complications of the overdose five months after the accident.

One local AECL engineer and one from the home office in Canada came to investigate. They were unable to reproduce Malfunction 54. One local AECL engineer explained that it was not possible to overdose a patient. AECL engineers also said that AECL knew of no accidents involving radiation overexposure by Therac-25, even though AECL must surely have been aware of the Hamilton and Yakima incidents. The AECL engineers suggested that an electrical problem might be to blame, but further investigation by ETCC ruled out this possibility.

The fifth incident also occurred at ETCC, this time on April 11, 1986. Upon being given the command to administer the dose, the Therac-25 again registered the Malfunction 54 message, made some loud noises, and shut down. The patient said he heard a sizzling sound, felt "fire" on the side of his face and saw a flash of light. Agitated, he asked, "What happened to me, what happened to me?" He died from the overdose on May 1, 1986.

If not for the efforts of Fritz Hager, the Tyler hospital physicist, the understanding of the software problems might have come much later. Mr. Hager was eventually able to elicit the Malfunction 54 message, determining that the speed of the data entry was the key factor in producing the error condition. After explaining this to AECL, the firm was finally able to produce the condition on its own. This seemed to suggest that the particular coding error was not as important as the fact that there was an unsafe design of the software and the lack of any backup hardware safety mechanisms.

The sixth accident occurred also at Yakima Valley Hospital in January 1987. The patient reported "feeling a burning sensation" in the chest and died in April from complications related to the overdose. After the second Yakima accident, the US Food and Drug Administration concluded that the software alone could not be relied upon to ensure the safe operation of the machine. The initiatives for identifying the problems with the Therac-25 came from users, not the manufacturer, which was slow to respond. The medical staff on the user side were also slow to recognize the problem.

BLAME-RESPONSIBILITY: CORPORATE RESPONSIBILITY

This tragic story illustrates irresponsible actions on both the corporate and individual levels. Yet the investigators of the accidents did not wish "to criticize the manufacturer of the equipment or anyone else."[137]

Philosopher Helen Nissenbaum believes that this reluctance to assign blame, either to organizations or groups, is not unusual. Rather, "accountability is systematically undetermined in our computerized society—which, given the value of accountability to society, is a disturbing loss."[138] She believes further that "if not addressed, this erosion of accountability will mean that computers are 'out of control' in an important and disturbing way."[139] Even if Nissenbaum's claims are extreme, it is probably true that the increased usage of computers have raised in an especially urgent way the problem of responsibility or accountability, and that the issue must be addressed.

Let us first consider the issue of blame-responsibility, as described in Chapter 3, on the corporate level. What is the blame-responsibility (if any) that can be assigned to such corporate entities as AECL, Yakima Valley Memorial Hospital, and the East Texas Cancer Center?

We saw in Chapter 3 that corporations can be causes of harm by way of specific corporate policies (or the absence of corporate policies), corporate decisions, management decisions, and a corporate culture. We noted that there are some relatively strong arguments that organizations such as corporations can be morally responsible agents like people. Whether or not they can be morally responsible agents, they can still be (1) criticized for harms, (2) asked to make reparations for harms, and (3) assessed as in need of reform. Let us look at specific issues in the Therac-25 case that might lead to blame-responsibility on the corporate level.

1. One design flaw in the Therac-25 was the absence of hardware safety backups. Earlier versions of the machine had such backups, and if they had been present in the later version, some (or all) of the accidents might not have occurred. Although this design flaw may have been simply the fault of the individual engineers, it may have resulted from the fact that some of the engineers at AECL apparently did not have proper training in systems engineering. This, in turn, may have been the result of a failure of AECL management and company policy with respect to the training of AECL engineers.
2. AECL evidently did not have adequate testing and an adequate quality assurance program. This deficiency may also have been a major factor in

producing the accidents, and these failures should probably be attributed to management and perhaps to corporate policies and a corporate culture that did not sufficiently value both testing and quality assurance.

3. AECL made exaggerated claims for the safety of the Therac-25. Technicians were led to believe that the machines could not possibly administer an overdose, and this was probably one reason the technicians were also insufficiently responsive to patient complaints. The exaggerated claims for safety may have also been partially responsible for the fact that physicians were slow to recognize the radiation burns. These problems could well be attributable to a corporate culture that was excessively concerned for sales.
4. AECL was slow in responding to reports of accidents and in informing other users of the malfunctions of the Therac-25. Bad management decisions and, again, a corporate culture that was overly concerned with sales and insufficiently concerned with safety were probably at least partly to blame.
5. The monitoring equipment in at least one of the medical facilities (the east Texas Cancer center) was not properly functioning, and this may have played a part in the injuries to patients. There may have been a deficiency with management and perhaps with a corporate culture that was not sufficiently oriented toward the highest standards of safety.

These examples strongly suggest that at least AECL deserves moral criticism for the injuries and deaths to patients. AECL could be asked to make reparations for harms (and may be legally liable for such reparations) and is in need of internal reform. The East Texas Cancer Center may also be open to criticisms, although on a far more limited basis.

BLAME-RESPONSIBILITY: INDIVIDUAL RESPONSIBILITY

The Therac-25 accidents were not caused by any single individual. In Chapter 3, however, we saw that in situations involving collective action and inaction, there are principles that give direction for assigning blame-responsibility. The principle of responsibility for action in groups states: in a situation in which harm has been produced by collective action, the degree of responsibility of each member of the group depends on the extent to which the member caused the action by some action reasonably avoidable on his part. The principles of responsibility for inaction in a group states: in a situation in which a harm has been produced by collective inaction, the degree or responsibility of each member of the group depends on the extent to which the member could reasonably be expected to have tried to prevent the action.

We have also seen that blame-responsibility can be the result of malicious intent, recklessness, or negligence. The following enumeration is probably best understood as a list of various types of negligence and therefore as types of inaction for which those who are involved bear some degree of blame-responsibility, depending on the causal importance of their inaction in the harms.

We also saw that negligence involves the following four factors: (1) the existence of a standard of conduct, (2) a failure of conformity to these standards, (3) a reasonably close causal connection between the conduct and resulting harm, and (4) a resulting actual loss or damage to the interests of another person. One of the problems with attributing negligence in computer-related incidents is that the standards of conduct (or "due care") are sometimes insufficiently developed and made public. Nevertheless, we believe that there are implicit standards that warrant the attribution of blame-responsibility with respect to the following groups of individuals.

1. As we have noted, one of the design flaws in the Therac-25 was the absence of the hardware safety backups that the earlier machines had. If the backups had been present, some (or all) of the accidents might not have occurred. Although this design flaw may have been partly attributable to management and company policies that did not place enough emphasis on systems engineering, it may also be attributable to professional negligence that was the fault of the individual engineers involved. The accidents might not have occurred if the hardware backups had been present. Insofar as the professional negligence is the fault of the individual engineers, they bear considerable responsibility for the accidents. The negligence here was the failure of engineers to investigate more fully the dangers associated with a system with no hardware backups and the resulting failure to incorporate these backups into their design.

2. The manufacturing personnel who built the faulty microswitch that controlled the position of the turntable on which the patients were placed were important causal agents in some of the accidents, especially the one at the Ontario Cancer Foundation. The standard account gives little information about the reasons for this fault, but perhaps we can best attribute it to negligence involved in the building of the faulty equipment. If the patients had been properly positioned, they might not have suffered radiation burns, but we shall see that there were other causal factors present. So we can say that the manufacturing personnel should be held partially responsible.

3. The programmers were also partially responsible for harm to patients. There were errors in programming and obscure error messages. There appeared to be considerable negligence on the part of the programmers, and their errors apparently were directly causally responsible in part for the harms. It should be said on behalf of the programmers, however, that there are usually "bugs" in programs, and the programmers may not have had sufficient training to be aware of the dangers of leaving all of the responsibility for safety to the computer programs.

4. Evidently, the user manuals were inadequately written. There was no explanation, for example, of the Malfunction 54 error message. The absence of proper instructions was clearly a factor in the accidents. Had the operators known how to respond to error messages, they might have been able to avoid some of the accidents. Here again there appeared to be negligence that was causally related to the accidents. Manual writers can only write what they are given, however, and we do not know what information they were given. So we cannot, without further information, know just how much blame-responsibility the manual writers should bear.

5. In some of the accidents, technicians may not have been sufficiently aware of the possibility of radiation burns, and they sometimes seemed shockingly insensitive to patient distress. This again is a type of negligence that may have played some part in the harm done to patients. In defense of the

technicians, however, two considerations are relevant. First, both of these faults can probably be attributed in part to the AECL claims that radiation burns were not possible and to the limited knowledge that was at the disposal of the technicians. Second, technician negligence probably was a minor factor in the actual harm done. Therefore the causal relationship of technician negligence to actual harm done was probably minimal.

6. In several cases, physicians seemed slow to recognize that overexposure had occurred. This is also a type of professional negligence. Again, however, two considerations in defense of the physicians are relevant. First, whether lives would have been saved if treatments for radiation burns have been more prompt is not clear. Second, one reason for the physicians' tardiness might have been the excessive claims of AECL that overexposure was not possible. Still, physicians in radiation-treatment facilities should be alert to the possibility of radiation burns.

As this analysis shows, the major blame-responsibility for the injuries and deaths from the Therac-25 lies with AECL on both the individual and corporate levels. There was probably negligence on the part of both management and individuals at AECL. Furthermore, there was probably also a corporate culture that encouraged irresponsible action. Finally, the negligence had a strong causal relationship to the injuries and deaths.

It would be interesting to speculate on the impediments to responsibility (outlined in Chapter 7) that explain the problems at AECL. AECL was apparently plagued by a corporate culture in which managers focused excessively on profit and sales to the exclusion of other considerations such as safety. This may have been a type of microscopic vision. Managers may have also engaged in self-deception, convincing themselves that the reports of injuries and malfunctions of the Therac-25 were not significant, would not be repeated, and were not the result of any fundamental faults of the machine itself.

Individual negligence on the part of engineers and programmers may have been partly the result of self-interest because any insistence on greater attention to safety considerations might have resulted in disfavor by managers. We have already pointed out that engineers may have been affected by ignorance because of their insufficient training in systems engineering. Finally, group-think may have played a part in the behavior of engineers and programmers. Perhaps a "can-do" mentality and an emphasis on avoiding delays in getting the product on the market inhibited individuals from making objections based on safety considerations.

MAINTAIN ACCOUNTABILITY IN A COMPUTERIZED SOCIETY

Helen Nissenbaum has made several suggestions about ways to maintain accountability in a computerized society, two of which seem especially valuable.[140] One suggestion is that standards of care should be promoted in computer science and computer engineering. Guidelines for producing safer and more reliable computer systems should be widely promulgated and adhered to by computer professionals. Not only should such standards result in greater safety and reliability, but also the existence of such standards should make it easier to identify those who should be held responsible and liable for failures. We have already mentioned one such standard, namely, that computer programs should not bear the sole responsibility for safety.

A second suggestion is that strict liability should be imposed for defective customer-oriented software and for software that has a considerable impact on society. Strict liability implies the manufacturer is responsible for any harm caused by a defective product, regardless of whether the fault can be assigned to the producer of the product. Strict liability would help to ensure that victims are properly compensated, and it would send a strong message to the producers of software that they should be vitally concerned with the safety of the public. As an example of the current situation in which the producers of software assume no responsibility for the safety of their product, according to Nissenbaum, Apple Computer makes the following statement:

> Apple makes no warranty or representation, either expressed or implied, with respect to software, its quality, performance, merchantability, or fitness for a particular purpose. As a result, this software is sold "as is," and you, the purchaser, are assuming the entire risk as to its quality and performance.

These evasions are problematic from an ethical standpoint. As the Therac-25 case illustrates, people can be harmed and even killed by computer mishaps.

Some people have objected to Nissenbaum's suggestions. One objection is that, although software engineering has standards for software-development processes, there are few standards for software products. Furthermore, setting product standards has turned out to be difficult. So Nissenbaum's first suggestion may be hard to implement. Nissenbaum's second suggestion is also somewhat impractical, according to some critics. Software may not be sufficiently mature to qualify for strict liability, they argue. Nevertheless, some computer scientists are sympathetic with Nissenbaum's suggestions, believing that they point the way to necessary reforms.

C A S E   5 1

Roundabouts[141]

Roadway intersections present several engineering challenges. Consider, for instance, that in 2009, 20.8 percent of roadway fatalities in the United States occurred at intersections, or were in some way intersection related.[142] Signaled intersections are problematic for drivers, since a good deal of attention and thought may be required to traverse a busy intersection. Drivers must decide quickly when and how to proceed, especially when facing a changing light, or when navigating multiple traffic lanes. Consider as well that stop-and-go traffic, such as traffic at a busy intersection, increases automobile emissions significantly and results in traffic congestion. Both of these issues raise significant problems for engineers, since safety and efficiency are primary engineering concerns.

Roundabouts provide an elegant solution to many of these problems. Roundabouts are circular intersections designed to allow vehicles to traverse in any direction, often without ever coming to a complete halt. The process of traversing a roundabout is very straightforward, with drivers simply following the one-way circular roadway to their chosen exit without having to worry about changing lights or multiple turning lanes. In addition, because cars must travel in a fairly tight circle, drivers are forced to reduce their speed. These two factors together make accidents, both vehicular and pedestrian, less likely. The design of the roundabout also helps to prevent some of the most dangerous kinds of accidents, such as "T-bone" collisions, in which a vehicle passing through a standard intersection is struck by another vehicle moving perpendicular to it. It is therefore unsurprising that a study by the Insurance Institute for Highway Safety found that replacing standard intersections mediated by stop signs or signals with roundabout intersections resulted in an a 37 percent overall reduction in intersection collisions, and a full 90 percent reduction in fatal collisions.[143]

In addition to safety improvements, roundabout intersections are also more efficient. Unlike at standard intersections, vehicles are not required to decelerate and accelerate repeatedly, but can usually proceed without stopping. This enhances fuel economy, and also reduces traffic delays associated with standard intersection designs. Roundabouts can also typically handle traffic using fewer lanes than signaled intersections, typically making them smaller. Finally, roundabouts are *financially* efficient. Because no signals are employed, maintenance and electrical costs are significantly reduced. Given these benefits, the roundabout looks like an engineer's dream—a simple, low cost design which provides holistic improvements in safety and efficiency. The story is complicated, however, by the needs of visually impaired pedestrians.

Navigating intersections is already a challenge for blind and visually impaired pedestrians, for obvious reasons. However, it is fairly easy to provide accessible crossing for them at signaled intersections. Many signaled intersections are equipped with crossing assistance systems that provide audible cues to help visually impaired individuals know when to cross. Even intersections mediated by stop signs can be effectively navigated by careful attention to the sounds of oncoming vehicles. Roundabouts, however, are much more challenging for the visually impaired. Audible crossing assistance is untenable at roundabouts, since there is typically no traffic signal with which to integrate such a system. Even worse, the fact that traffic in a roundabout is constant means that auditory cues of oncoming traffic are very easily lost in the din of vehicles moving around the circular roadway. These factors, in combination with the orientation challenges posed by the unusual geometry of roundabout crossings, make navigating a roundabout on foot much more dangerous for the visually impaired.[144]

However, someone might ask, "Why should the concerns of the visually impaired be of any great significance here? After all, visually impaired individuals represent a small minority of the overall population. Surely the inconvenience of finding an alternative route for the disabled is a small price to pay for all the benefits roundabouts provide in terms of general safety and efficiency." One answer is the Americans with Disabilities Act (ADA). The ADA mandates that all transportation facilities be equally accessible to both able-bodied and disabled citizens. Failure to comply with the ADA can be quite costly, with legal damages between $55,000 and $110,000 being standard.[145]

But, even without considering the ADA, concerns of professional ethics exist that are relevant to these issues. Commitment to safety is a ubiquitous feature of professional engineering codes of conduct. While the visually impaired are, indeed, a minority in the United States, their safety is, nevertheless, threatened by standard roundabout design. Equality and accessibility are also strongly valued by American culture at large. Insofar as engineers are required to consider the values of the public who utilize what they design, such strong values should be respected.

These conflicting interests of safety, efficiency, financial risk, and equal access make roundabouts a difficult issue for engineers. Should we therefore abandon the idea, and rely only on standard sign and signal mediated intersections? Perhaps. However, one might also look at the issues surrounding access for the visually impaired as an opportunity for further innovation. And, indeed, much work has been done in developing roundabouts that retain the benefits described above while also providing easier access for the disabled. Many ideas have been explored, but two in particular serve to draw attention to the interplay of conflicting interests in this case.

Solution #1: Pedestrian-actuated signals

One potential solution to some of the issues discussed above is to introduce traffic signals at standard roundabouts that are typically inactive, and that can be activated by the presence of a pedestrian. This kind of system would provide safer passage for the visually impaired, while minimizing the congestion effects incurred by more traditional signaling systems. However, introducing such a system also incurs an increase in expense not associated with standard roundabout designs.

Solution #2: Raised crosswalks

A particularly elegant solution to the problems raised by the odd geometry of roundabout crosswalks is to raise the crosswalk and provide tactile cues (such as ridges) to help keep visually impaired pedestrians on the right path. Raised crosswalks are a relatively inexpensive solution, and have the added benefit of slowing traffic, resulting in an overall safer intersection.

QUESTIONS FOR FURTHER THOUGHT

1. What reasons other than legal concerns might motivate an engineer to attend to the needs of the visually impaired?
2. Studies indicate that drivers are much less likely to yield to pedestrians in crosswalks at intersections without traffic signals.[146] What does this mean for the second solution discussed above?
3. Should engineers be responsible for ensuring that their designs are accessible to individuals who are both visually *and* hearing impaired? Why or why not?
4. Fuel-efficient electric and gas/electric hybrid vehicles produce very little sound at normal driving speeds, and are thus difficult for the visually impaired to detect. Does this raise problems for engineers similar to those raised by roundabouts? In what ways are these problems similar? In what ways are they different?

REFERENCES

"ADA Enforcement," The US Department of Justice, US Department of Justice, December 8, 2011, http:// www.ada.gov/enforce.htm.

"Intersection Safety," Federal Highway Administration, US Department of Transportation, Federal Highway Administration, June 21, 2012, http://safety .fhwa.dot.gov/ intersection/.

"Pedestrian Access to Modern Roundabouts: Design and Operation Issues for Pedestrians who are Blind," United States Access Board, US Access Board, June 21, 2012, http:// www.access-board .gov/research/roundabouts/bulletin.htm.

"Pedestrian Access to Roundabouts: Assessment to Motorists' Yielding to Visually Impaired Pedestrians and Potential Treatments to Improve Access," Federal Highway Administration, US Department of Transportation, Federal Highway Administration, May 2006, June 21, 2012, http:// www.fhwa.dot.gov/publications/research/safety/.

"Roundabout Benefits," Washington State Department of Transportation, Washington State Department of Transportation, June 21, 2012, http://www .wsdot.wa.gov/Safety/roundabouts/benefits.htm.

CASE 52

Interface[147]

Ray C. Anderson was, by his own account, the very picture of a successful American industrialist. He risked everything to found a company (Interface, a carpeting manufacturer), and as a result of hard work and his own intense competitiveness, the company flourished. But then something very unusual happened. In August of 1994, Anderson convened a task force whose role was to evaluate his company's environmental impact. The task he put before this group was a difficult one. Anderson summed it up in this way:

> We're going to push the envelope until we no longer take anything the earth can't easily renew. We're going to keep pushing until all our products are made from recycled or renewable materials. And we're not going to *stop* pushing until all our waste is biodegradable or recyclable, until nothing we make ends up as pollution. No gases up a smokestack, no dirty water out a pipe, no piles of carpet scraps to the dump. *Nothing.* (Anderson 2009, p. 16–17)

These are, by most standards, radical goals, and certainly not those we typically associate with the world of bottom-line capitalism. Even more surprisingly, Anderson was not an environmentalist. He was driven to start his company by an intense competitiveness, and a desire to succeed in business. So what happened? Why did Anderson's vision for the future of his company shift so suddenly, and so radically, from a

vision unconcerned with the ethics of pollution and consumption of resources to a vision which deeply incorporates these issues? The answer to this question is illuminating, perhaps especially to employees attempting to affect change in managerial attitudes towards ethical concerns.

Before his "conversion," Anderson was, by his own admission, largely ignorant of his company's impact on the environment. This was fine by him. He writes:

> … after two decades of what can only be called spectacular success, it didn't bother me a bit that Interface consumed enough energy each year to light and heat a city. Or that we and our suppliers transformed more than a billion pounds of petroleum-derived raw materials into carpet tiles for offices and hospitals, airports and hotels, schools, universities, and stores all around the world. So what, if each day just one of my plants sent *six tons* of carpet trimmings to the local landfill? What happened to it there? I had no idea. Why should I? It was someone else's problem, not mine. That's what landfills were for. In fact, our belching smokestacks, our gushing effluent pipes, our mountains of waste (all completely legal), were tangible proof that business was good. They meant jobs. They meant orders coming in, products going out, and money in the bank. (Anderson 2009, p. 8)

This changed, though, when Jim Hartzfeld, an engineer from the Interface's research division, relayed a question from a sales associate, "Some customers want to know what Interface is doing for the environment. How should we answer?" It is unrealistic, although appealing, to imagine that this simple question could singlehandedly spark such a monumental shift in the ethical trajectory of a company like Interface; Anderson was already aware that customers were concerned about the environmental practices at the company. But Hartzfeld's question was at least enough to get the proverbial ball rolling, and what's more, he kept at it. Anderson describes his own attitude towards the problem as nervous, and unsure. He was content to pass the responsibility for handling the problem on to others. But Hartzfeld continued to press him, encouraging him not only to convene the task force responsible for identifying the company's environmental impact, but also to carefully define the scope of its project in a speech to the committee's members.

It's important to note, too, that the question Hartzfeld asked was not obviously an ethical one. The "hook" for Anderson was not the notion that his company might be causing harm to the environment, but that this harm was of concern for his clients. He writes: "I wasn't about to ignore any customer's concerns or to turn my back on any piece of business. If we didn't answer the question Jim had relayed, I knew we stood to lose other sales." By making it clear that concrete, financially important factors were involved, Hartzfeld forced Anderson to genuinely consider the issue, rather than brush it off as being of no importance to his concerns as a businessman. This led Anderson to read *The Ecology of Commerce*, a book by environmentalist and entrepreneur Paul Hawken. It is there that Anderson seems to have found revelation.

Importantly, though, the content of the book that was most compelling to Anderson was not about the inherent goodness of stewardship of natural resources. He was already familiar with these worries and had dismissed them—believing, in his words, that "as technology improves, we'll get better and more efficient at supplying whatever the market demands." Anderson's credence in this "article of faith" seems to suggest, again, that his motivations and attitudes were typically capitalist. He had no special sympathies for the idea that, regardless of the demands of the market,

corporations should be responsible consumers of resources. The mere fact that corporations were egregious polluters and consumers of finite resources was of little concern. Had that been the only message present in Hawken's book, Anderson would likely not have been swayed. If things needed to change, the market would make them change. But Hawken also presented a discussion of overconsumption, and it is here that Anderson's assumptions were fundamentally challenged. He had not before considered the fact that the resources demanded by market concerns might one day *just run out*. This prospect caused him to, in essence, broaden the scope of what he took to be the concerns of a business. Where there is a danger of overconsumption of resources, it is paramount to the success of any industrial enterprise to change the way it consumes those resources. This revelation, says Anderson, led him to radically question the practices of his company, leading to the wide-ranging environmental policies outlined above.

So what can we learn from Anderson's case? Taking him as being fairly representative of the financially minded leads to some optimistic conclusions. Anderson was not initially hostile to environmental issues, but merely ambivalent, despite being by his own description concerned primarily with financial interests. He characterizes his ambivalence as being largely due to ignorance of the relevant issues. Taking him as a representative case, then, indicates that inattention to ethical problems by management may typically be linked to a failure to understand or appreciate those problems, rather than a general disdain for ethical conduct, or the belief that ethical and financial interests are always at odds. This should be encouraging to the ethical engineer. Despite appearances, corporate management is not always hostile to ethical concerns.

Anderson's ignorance was not ignorance of the material facts of Interface's environmentally important conduct, but rather a failure to appreciate the impact of this conduct on the potential future of his company, and the world at large. Narrowness of vision of this sort may often play an important role in preventing managers from fully appreciating the ethical concerns of their employees. Part of the role of engineers, like all expert professionals, is to help inform the scope of their employer's vision. It appears that, at least in cases like Anderson's, such education can affect real change.

The initial push to evaluate Interface's environmental impact came from low-level employees through standard channels. This illustrates the importance of communication between employees, especially experts, and management. Again, what seems an intentional oversight on the part of management may, in fact, be the unintentional consequence of having not fully appreciated all relevant concerns. The fact that Hartzfeld was able to effectively transmit the concerns of a low-level sales associate to the highest level of the company was crucial to the overhaul of the company's environmental vision.

The impact of the employee input was heightened due to the fact that clients hung in the balance. This illustrates the effectiveness of generating concern for ethical interests when those interests are presented as financially relevant. This pressure (again, from employees of the company) forced Anderson to consider environmental issues, which led him to read Hawken's book, the source of his "revelation." This illustrates an important interplay between financial interests and "abstract" general ethical interests in motivating a change in managerial policy. Anderson's initial concern with the loss of potential clients led him to fully consider the ethical ramifications of his company's wasteful behavior.

Broadly, the upshot of this case seems to be that upper level management can, in some cases, be expected to change its mind when supplied with the right information. As experts, it is the role of engineers to acquaint their employers with reality and it seems, at least in cases such as Anderson's, that such an acquaintance can go a long way towards encouraging managerial support of ethical conduct. Practically, this should encourage engineers to be vocal and straightforward with their ethical concerns, but also sensitive to any related financial matters, since addressing these interests can serve as an inroad with management, forcing them to more deeply consider the concerns of their employees.

It may also be important to note that Anderson seems to be an exceptional case, and that it is perhaps unrealistic to expect all managers to behave in precisely the same way. However, although it may well be the case that Anderson was not a typical businessman, this is not because he had any particular sympathies with environmentalism prior to his conversion. The difference between Anderson and more typical cases is not (or at least not obviously) a difference in motivation. That being the case, studying his account may lead to insight as to how typical management, with typically managerial motivations, might be convinced of the importance of ethical concerns.

QUESTIONS FOR FURTHER THOUGHT

1. Is Anderson really representative of industrialists in general? If not, what differentiates him from the norm? What is it about our standard conception of corporate management which makes behavior like Anderson's so surprising?
2. Imagine that you are an engineer employed by a manufacturing company, and you learn that some of the company's manufacturing processes could result in the contamination of local water supplies. What does the case of Ray Anderson tell you about the kinds of strategy to employ when bringing this issue to the attention of your managers?

REFERENCES

Anderson, Ray. "The Power of One Good Question," *Confessions of a Radical Industrialist: Profits, People, Purpose—Doing Business by Respecting the Earth*, New York: St. Martin's Press, 2009, pp. 20–28.

NOTES

1. Steven Weisskoph, "The Aberdeen Mess," *Washington Post Magazine,* January 15, 1989.

2. *The Aberdeen Three,* a case prepared under National Science Foundation grant number DIR-9012252. The principal investigators were Michael J. Rabins, Charles E. Harris, Jr., Charles Samson, and Raymond W. Flumerfelt. The complete case is available at the Texas A & M Engineering Ethics website (http://ethics.tamu.edu).

3. Case study prepared by Ryan Pflum, MA philosophy student at Western Michigan University.

4. Case study prepared by Ryan Pflum.

5. This account is based on John H. Cushman, Jr., "G.M. Agrees to Cadillac Recall in Federal Pollution Complaint," *New York Times,* December 1, 1995, pp. A1 and A12.

6. Leonardo Da Vinci, *The Notebooks of Leonardo Da Vinci,* vol. I, Edward MacCurdy, ed. (New York: George Braziller, 1939), p. 850. Cited in Mike Martin and Roland Schinzinger, *Ethics in Engineering,* 3rd ed. (New York: McGraw-Hill, 1996), p. 246.

7. This account is based on Joe Morgenstern, "The Fifty-Nine Story Crisis," *The New Yorker Magazine,* May 29, 1995, 49–53. For more on William LeMessurier and the Citicorp building, see the Online Ethics Center for Engineering (http://www.onlineethics.org/CMS/profpractice/exemp.index.aspx).

8. Much of what follows is based on Michael S. Pritchard, "Professional Responsibility: Focusing on the Exemplary," *Science and Engineering Ethics,* 4, 1998, pp. 230–233. In addition to sources cited here, there is an excellent PBS *Frontline* documentary on Cuny, "The Lost American." This is available at PBS Video, P.O. box 791, Alexandria, VA 22313-0791. There is a wealth of additional information on Cuny online at http://www.pbs.org/wgbh/pages/frontline/shows/cuny/bio/chron.html. Also, Cuny is featured as a moral leader on the Online Ethics Center for Engineering.

9. Karen W. Arenson, "Missing Relief Expert Gets MacArthur Grant," *New York Times,* June 13, 1995, p. A12.

10. Ibid.

11. Scott Anderson's gripping account of Frederick Cuny's life portrays him as a person with many foibles and shortcomings who still managed to save the lives of thousands threatened by man-made and natural disasters. See Scott Anderson, *The Man Who Tried to Save the World: The Dangerous Life and Mysterious Disappearance of Fred Cuny* (New York: Doubleday, 1999).

12. From Intertect's corporate brochure.

13. Ibid.

14. Quoted in William Shawcross, "A Hero of Our Time," *New York Review of Books,* Nov. 30, 1995, p. 35. The next paragraph is based on Shawcross's article.

15. The following is based on Chuck Sudetic, "Small Miracle in a Siege: Safe Water for Sarajevo," *New York Times,* January 10, 1994, pp. A1 and A7.

16. This account is based on "The Talk of the Town," *The New Yorker,* 69, no. 39, Nov. 22, 1993, pp. 45–46.

17. Anderson, *The Man Who Tried to Save the World,* p. 120.

18. Ibid.

19. Ibid. This expresses a thought attributed to Cuny.

20. Frederick C. Cuny, "Killing Chechnya," *The New York Review of Books,* April 6, 1995, pp. 15–17.

21. Marilyn Greene, "Texas Disaster Relief 'Visionary' Vanishes on Chechnya Mission," *USA Today,* May 10, 1995, p. A10.

22. Shawcross, "A Hero of Our Time," p. 39.

23. "Talk of the Town," p. 46.

24. Sudetic, "Small Miracle in a Siege," p. A7.

25. John Allen, "The Switch," *On Wisconsin,* Fall 2001, pp. 38–43.

26. Ibid., p. 42.

27. Ibid., p. 41.

28. Ibid.

29. These case studies were written by Theodore D. Goldfarb and Michael S. Pritchard for their *Ethics in the Science Classroom* (http://www.onlineethics.org). This text is a product of two National Science Foundation grants on teaching ethics in the science classroom: SBR-9601284 and SBR-932055.

30. Sources for information on the Darsee case include Sharen Begley, with Phyllis Malamud and Mary Hager, "A Case of Fraud at Harvard," *Newsweek,* February 4, 1982, pp. 89–92; Richard Knox, "The Harvard Fraud Case: Where Does the Problem Lie?" *Journal of the American Medical Association,* 249, no. 14, April 3, 1983, pp. 1797–1807; Walter W. Stewart, "The Integrity of the Scientific Literature," *Nature,* 325, January 15, 1987,

pp. 207–214; Eugene Braun-wald, "Analysing Scientific Fraud," *Nature*, 325, January 15, 1987, pp. 215–216; and Eugene Brunwald, "Cardiology: The John Darsee Experience," in David J. Miller and Michel Hersen, eds., *Research Fraud in the Behavioral and Biomedical Sciences* (New York: Wiley, 1992), pp. 55–79.

31. David DeMets, "Statistics and Ethics in Medical Research," *Science and Engineering Ethics*, 5, no. 1, January 1999, p. 111. At the 1994 Teaching Research Ethics for Faculty Workshop at Indiana University's Poynter Center, DeMets recounted in great detail the severe challenge she and his team of statisticians faced in carrying out their investigation.

32. Eugene Braunwald, "Cardiology: The John Darsee Experience," in David J. Miller and Michel Hersen, eds., *Research Fraud in the Behavioral and Biomedical Sciences* (New York: Wiley, 1992), pp. 55–79.

33. William F. May, "Professional Virtue and Self-Regulation," in Joan Callahan, ed., *Ethical Issues in Professional Life* (New York: Oxford University Press, 1988), p. 408.

34. For readings on the Bruening case, see Robert L. Sprague, "The Voice of Experience," *Science and Engineering Ethics*, 4, no. 1, 1998, p. 33; and Alan Poling, "The Consequences of Fraud," in Miller and Hersen, pp. 140–157.

35. Robert L. Sprague, "The Voice of Experience," *Science and Engineering Ethics*, Vol. 4, 1, 1998, p. 33.

36. This video was produced by the National Society for Professional Ethics (Alexandria, VA) in 1989. Information about obtaining it can be found at the Murdough Center for Engineering Ethics website, http://www.niee.org/pd.cfm?pt= Murdough. This website also contains the entire transcript for this video.

37. One would be able to find a cheap technical way to eliminate the heavy metals. Unfortunately, the video does not directly address this possibility. It begins in the midst of a crisis at ZCORP and focuses almost exclusively on the question of whether David Jackson should blow the whistle on his reluctant company. For a detailed exploration of some creative middle way alternatives, see Michael Pritchard and Mark Holtzapple, "Responsible Engineering: *Gilbane Gold* Revisited," *Science and Engineering*, 3, no. 2, April 1997, pp. 217–231.

38. This case is based on Kirk Johnson, "A Deeply Green City Confronts Its Energy Needs and Nuclear Worries," *New York Times,* November 19, 2007 (http://www.nytimes.com/2007/11/19/us/19collins.html?th=&emc=).

39. This case is based on Felicity Barringer and Micheline Maynard, "Court Rejects Fuel Standards on Trucks," *New York Times,* Nov. 16, 2007 (http://www.nytimes.com/2007/11/16/business/16fuel.html?th&emc=th).

40. Ibid.

41. We first learned of this true case (with names changed) from Sam's daughter, who was an honor student in two of the authors' engineering ethics classes and a member of a team of students from that class that competed in the College Ethics Bowl competition held at Loyola/Mary-mount College in Los Angeles. She suggested that the team present a case based on her father's experience. The team won the competition with its discussion of the case described here (which has been reviewed by "Sam" for accuracy).

42. This is an adaptation of a case developed by James Taylor, Civil Engineering, Notre Dame University.

43. ASCE Hurricane Katrina External Review Panel, *The New Orleans Hurricane Protection System: What Went Wrong and Why* (Reston, VA: American Society for Civil Engineers, 2007). Available at http://www.asce.org/static/hurricane/erp.cfm.

44. Ibid., p. 47.

45. Ibid., p. 61.

46. Ibid.

47. Ibid., p.73.

48. Ibid., p. 79.

49. Ibid.

50. Ibid.

51. Ibid., p. 81.

52. Ibid., p. 82.

53. Ibid., p. 82.

54. Jacqueline Finger, Joseph Lopez, III, Christopher Barallus, Matthew Parisi, Fred Rohs, John Schmalzel, Amrinder Kaur, DeMond S. Miller, and Kimberly Rose, "Leadership, Service Learning, and Executive Management in Engineering: The Rowan University Hurricane Katrina Recovery Team," *International Journal for Service Learning in Engineering*, 2, no. 2, Fall 2007.

55. Katie Hafner and Claudia H. Deutsch, "When Good Will Is Also Good Business," *New York*

Times, September 14, 2005 (http://nytimes.com).

56. Ibid.

57. William Robbins, "Engineers are Held at Fault in '81 Hotel Disaster," Special to the *New York Times,* November 16, 1985, Section 1, p. 28.

58. Ibid.

59. Ibid.

60. This account is drawn from R. W. Flumerfelt, C. E. Harris, M. J. Rabins, and C. H. Samson, eds., *Introducing Ethics Case Studies into Required Undergraduate Engineering Courses,* NSF Grant no. DIR-9012252, November 1992. The full version is available at the Texas A & M Engineering Ethics website (http://ethics.tamu.edu).

61. Paula Wells, Hardy Jones, and Michael Davis, *Conflicts of Interest in Engineering,* Module Series in Applied Ethics, Center for the Study of Ethics in the Professions, Illinois Institute of Technology (Dubuque, IA: Kendall/Hunt, 1986), p. 20.

62. American Society of Mechanical Engineers, Boiler and Pressure Vessel Code, section IV, paragraph HG-605a.

63. Charles W. Beardsley, "The Hydrolevel Case—A Retrospective," *Mechanical Engineering,* June 1984, p. 66.

64. Ibid., p. 73.

65. This case is based on an article that appeared in *The Seattle Times,* July 24, 2000.

66. This case study was written by Theodore D. Goldfarb and appeared in Theodore D. Goldfarb and Michael S. Pritchard, *Ethics in the Science Classroom* (http://www.onlineethics.org). It is a product of two National Science Foundation grants on teaching ethics in the science classroom: SBR-9601284 and SBR-932055.

67. This case is based on Stephen H. Unger's account in *Controlling Technology: Ethics and the Responsible Engineer* (New York: Holt, Rinehart & Winston, 1994), pp. 27–30.

68. Much of this account is adapted from Theodore D. Goldfarb and Michael S. Pritchard for their *Ethics in the Science Classroom* (http://www.onlineethics.org). This text is a product of two National Science Foundation grants on teaching ethics in the science classroom: SBR-9601284 and SBR-932055.

69. See Richard A. Shweder, Elliot Turiel, and Nancy C. Much, "The Moral Intuitions of the Child," in John H. Flavell and Lee Ross, eds., *Social Cognitive Development: Frontiers and Possible Futures* (Cambridge, UK: Cambridge University Press, 1981), p. 288.

70. Gareth Matthews, "Concept Formation and Moral Development," in James Russell, ed., *Philosophical Perspectives on Developmental Psychology* (Oxford: Basil Blackwell, 1987), p. 185.

71. For balanced, accessible discussions of recent findings in moral development, see William Damon, *The Moral Child* (New York: Free Press, 1988); and Daniel K. Lapsley, *Moral Psychology* (Boulder, CO: Westview Press, 1996).

72. See, for example, Lawrence Kohlberg, *The Philosophy of Moral Development: Essays on Moral Development,* Vol. 1 (San Francisco: Harper & Row, 1981).

73. Michael Pritchard has written extensively on many of them elsewhere. See his *On Becoming Responsible* (Lawrence: University Press of Kansas, 1991); *Reasonable Children* (Lawrence: University Press of Kansas, 1996); and "Kohlbergian Contributions to Educational Programs for the Moral Development of Professionals," *Educational Psychology Review,* 11, no. 4, 1999, pp. 397–411. James Rest, Muriel Bebeau, Darcia Narvaez, and Stephen Thoma have developed what they call a neo-Kohlbergian account. They identify three "schemas": personal interest, maintaining norms, and postconventional. In general, these three schemas correlate significantly with Kohlberg's three basic levels of moral development. However, they maintain that a much higher percentage of adults meet their postconventional criteria than Kohlberg suggests meet his postconventional level. See Rest et al., *Postconventional Moral Thinking* (Mahwah, NJ: Erlbaum, 1999); and their essays in *Educational Psychology Review,* 11, no. 4, 1999.

74. This case was developed by P. Aarne Vesilind, Department of Civil and Environmental Engineering at Duke University.

75. This account is based on Loren Graham's *The Ghost of the Executed Engineer: Technology and the Fall of the Soviet Union* (Cambridge, MA: Harvard University Press, 1993).

76. Ibid., p. 106.

77. Information for this case is based on a case study prepared by Manuel Velasquez, "The Ford Motor Car," in Manuel Velasquez, *Business Ethics: Concepts and Cases,* 3rd ed. (Englewood Cliffs, NJ: Prentice-Hall, 1992), pp. 110–113.

78. *Grimshaw v. Ford Motor Co.*, app., 174 Cal. Rptr. 348, p. 360.

79. This is reported in Ralph Drayton, "One Manufacturer's Approach to Automobile Safety Standards," *CTLA News*, VIII, no. 2 (February 1968), p. 11.

80. Mark Dowie, "Pinto Madness," *Mother Jones*, September/October 1977, p. 28.

81. Amy Docker Marcus, "MIT Students, Lured to New Tech Firms, Get Caught in a Bind," *The Wall Street Journal*, June 24, 1999, pp. A1, A6.

82. Ibid., p.A6.

83. Ibid.

84. Ibid.

85. John Markoff, "Odyssey of a Hacker: From Outlaw to Consultant," *New York Times*, January 29, 2001.

86. David Lorge Parnas, "SDI: A Violation of Professional Responsibility," in Deborah Johnson, ed., *Ethical Issues in Engineering* (Englewood Cliffs, NJ: Prentice-Hall, 1991), pp. 15–25. This case is based on Pritchard's discussion in "Computer Ethics: The Responsible Professional," in James A. Jaksa and Michael S. Pritchard, eds., *Responsible Communication: Ethical Issues in Business, Industry, and the Professions* (Cresskill, NJ: Hampton Press, 1996), pp. 146–148.

87. Ibid., p. 17.

88. Ibid., p. 15.

89. Ibid., p. 25.

90. Parnas was convinced that the public, when informed, would agree with his conclusions about the SDI program. For a contrary view, see the debate between David Parnas and Danny Cohen, "Ethics and Military Technology: Star Wars," in Kristen Shrader-Frechette and Laura Westra, eds., *Technology and Values* (New York: Rowman & Littlefield, 1997), pp. 327–353.

91. Ibid.

92. This account is based on the authors' conversations with Ed Turner as well as information available at http://www.responsiblecharge.com.

93. This account is based on G. P. E. Meese, "The Sealed Beam Case," *Business & Professional Ethics*, 1, no. 3, Spring 1982, pp. 1–20.

94. H. H. Magsdick, "Some Engineering Aspects of Headlighting," *Illuminating Engineering*, June 1940, p. 533, cited in Meese, p. 17.

95. Much of this case is adapted from Michael S. Pritchard, "Service-Learning and Engineering Ethics," *Science and Engineering Ethics*, 6,

2000, pp. 413–422. An earlier version of this article is available at the Online Ethics Center (http://www.onlineethics.org/CMS/edu/resources/servicelearning.aspx).

96. Accreditation Board for Engineering and Technology, *Fifty-Third Annual Report*, 1985, p. 98.

97. Campus Compact supports the development of service learning programs throughout the country. For an early statement of its efforts, see Timothy Stanton, *Integrating Public Service with Academic Study* (Providence, RI: Campus Compact, Brown University, 1989).

98. Edmund Tsang, "Why Service Learning? And How to Integrate It into a Course in Engineering," in Kathryn Ritter-Smith and John Salt-marsh, eds., *When Community Enters the Equation: Enhancing Science, Mathematics and Engineering Education through Service-Learning* (Providence, RI: Campus Compact, Brown University, 1998). Currently at Western Michigan University as associate dean in the College of Engineering & Applied Sciences, Tsang continues his work in service learning. He has also edited *Projects that Matter: Concepts and Models for Service-Learning in Engineering*, Vol. 14 (Washington, DC: American Association for Higher Education, 2000). Service learning is appropriate throughout both undergraduate and graduate programs in engineering. This is well illustrated by Kevin Passino, Professor of Electrical and Computing Engineering at Ohio State University. In addition to founding the student-centered Engineers for Community Service at his university, he is developing international service learning projects for PhD students. See Kevin Passino, "Educating the Humanitarian Engineer," *Science Engineering Ethics*, vol. 15, no. 4, 2009, pp. 577–600.

99. This account is based on a conversation with Tom Talley and Dave Wylie's, "AVIT Team Helps Disabled Children," *Currents* (Texas A & M University), Summer 1993, p. 6.

100. *Research Agenda for Combining Service and Learning in the 1990s* (Raleigh, NC: National Society for Internships and Experiential Education, 1991), p. 7.

101. CESG brochure.

102. CESG Strategic Plan Draft: 1997–2000, pp. 1–2.

103. This case is based on Glenn Collins, "What Smoke? New Device Keeps Cigarettes in a

'Box'," *New York Times,* October 23, 1997, pp. A1, C8.

104. Case presented by Pritchard in "Computer Ethics: The Responsible Professional," pp. 144–145.

105. Joe Gertner, "The Future Is Drying Up," *New York Times Magazine,* October 21, 2007.

106. One is environmental engineer Bradley Udall, son of U.S. Congressman Morris Udall and nephew of Stewart Udall, Secretary of the Interior under Presidents John F. Kennedy and Lyndon Johnson.

107. From Michael S. Pritchard, "Professional Responsibility: Focusing on the Exemplary," *Science and Engineering Ethics,* 4, 1998, p. 224.

108. See the May 1997 report by the Biomass Energy Design Project Team, "Design and Feasibility Study of a Biomass Energy Farm at Lafayette College as a Fuel Source for the Campus Steam Plant."

109. Accreditation Board for Engineering and Technology, *Engineering Criteria 2000,* 3rd ed. (Baltimore: Author, 1997). See also http://www.abet.org/eac2000html.

110. This case is based on Claudia H. Deutsch, "A Threat So Big, Academics Try Collaboration," *New York Times,* December 25, 2007 (http://www.nytimes.com/2007/12/25/business/25sustain.html?8br).

111. Ibid.

112. Ibid.

113. Ibid.

114. Joshua M. Pearce, "Service Learning in Engineering and Science for Sustainable Development," *International Journal for Service Learning in Engineering,* 1, No. 1, Spring 2006.

115. Karim Al-Khafaji and Margaret Catherine Morse, "Learning Sustainable Design through Service," *International Journal for Service Learning in Engineering,* 1, No. 1, Spring 2006.

116. Ibid., quoted from the article.

117. John Erik Anderson, Helena Meryman, and Kimberly Porsche, "Sustainable Building Materials in French Polynesia," *International Journal for Service Learning in Engineering,* 2, No. 2, Fall 2007.

118. From Michael S. Pritchard, "Professional Responsibility: Focusing on the Exemplary," *Science and Professional Ethics, 4,* 1998, pp. 225–226. This is based on Donald J. Giffels's commentary on Pritchard's speech, "Education for Responsibility: A Challenge to Engineers and Other Professionals," presented at the Third Annual Lecture in Ethics in Engineering, Center for Academic Ethics, Wayne State University, April 19, 1995.

119. This case is presented in greater detail, complete with an instructor's guide and student handouts, in R. W. Flumerfelt, C. E. Harris, M. J. Rabins, and C. H. Samson, eds, *Introducing Ethics Case Studies into Required Undergraduate Engineering Courses,* final report to NSF on grant no. DIR-9012252, November 1992, pp. 231–261. The case is available at the Texas A & M Engineering Ethics website (http://ethics.tamu.edu/).

120. This case is based on Molly Galvin, "Unlicensed Engineer Receives Stiff Sentence," *Engineering Times,* 16, no. 10, October 1994, pp. 1 and 6.

121. This discussion was researched and authored by Peggy DesAutels, a philosopher at University of Dayton who has special interests in gender and engineering issues.

122. 2001 statistics from the National Science Foundation, http://www.nsf.gov/statistics/wmpd.

123. 2003 statistic reported in *Beyond Bias and Barriers: Fulfilling the Potential of Women in Academic Science and Engineering* (Washington, DC: National Academies Press, 2006), pp. 14–17. This report was produced by the Committee on Maximizing the Potential of Women in Academic Science and Engineering and the Committee on Science, Engineering, and Public Policy, National Academy of Sciences, National Academy of Engineering, and Institute of Medicine of the National Academies.

124. 2003 statistic reported in *Beyond Bias and Barriers: Fulfilling the Potential of Women in Academic Science and Engineering,* pp. 14–17.

125. This table is modified from a table in *Beyond Bias and Barriers: Fulfilling the Potential of Women in Academic Science and Engineering,* pp. 5–6.

126. *Beyond Bias and Barriers: Fulfilling the Potential of Women in Academic Science and Engineering,* pp. 158–159.

127. Virginia Valian, "Beyond Gender Schemas: Improving the Advancement of Women in Academia," *Hypatia* 20, no. 3, Summer 2005, pp. 198–213.

128. F. Trix and C. Psenka, "Exploring the Color of Glass: Letters of Recommendation for Female and Male Medical Faculty," *Discourse and Society,* 14, 2003, pp. 191–220.

129. Valian, p. 202.

130. NSF ADVANCE Project at the University of Michigan (http://www.umich.edu/~advproj).

131. This case is supplied by an engineering colleague who was an expert witness in the case. We have given the company the fictitious name of "XYZ." For a more complete account, see R. W. Flumerfelt, C. E. Harris, M. J. Rabins, and C. H. Samson, *Introducing Ethics Case Studies into Required Undergraduate Engineering Courses,* pp. 287–312.

132. Waxman, Henry A., Chairman, Committee on Energy and Commerce, June 14, 2010, letter to Tony Hayward, CEO, BP PLC. Found online July 16, 2012 at http://tenc.net/a/ltr-to-hayward.pdf.

133. Mars Climate Orbiter Mishap Investigation Board, Phase 1 Report, Arthur G. Stephenson, Chairman, George C. Marshall Space Flight Center, November 10, 1999. 44 pp.

134. Leveson, Nancy G., The Role of Software in Recent Aerospace Accidents, Aeronautics and Astronautics Department, Massachusetts Institute of Technology, Cambridge, MA (undated paper found at http://sunnyday.mit.edu/accidents/issc01.pdf on 2/15/2011).

135. Harwell, Barry, "Austin architect, civic leader Black ensnared in legal battle over balcony collapse," *Austin American-Statesman,* September 11, 2010.

136. This account is a summary of a much longer account: Nancy G. Leveson and Clark S. Turner, "An Investigation of the Therac-25 Accidents" in Johnson and Nissenbaum, pp. 474–514.

137. Leveson and Turner, p. 474.

138. Johnson and Nissenbaum, p. 526

139. Ibid., p. 526.

140. Ibid., p. 536.

141. Case study prepared by Jeremy Dillon, graduate research assistant, Western Michigan University.

142. "Intersection Safety."

143. "Roundabout Benefits."

144. "Pedestrian Access to Modern Roundabouts: Design and Operation Issues for Pedestrians who are Blind."

145. "ADA Enforcement."

146. "Pedestrian Access to Roundabouts: Assessment to Motorists' Yielding to Visually Impaired Pedestrians and Potential Treatments to Improve Access."

147. Case study prepared by Jeremy Dillon, graduate research assistant, Western Michigan University.

APPENDIX

Codes of Ethics

IN THIS APPENDIX, the code of the National Society of Professional Engineers (NSPE) is printed, and web sources for most of the other major engineering codes are provided, together with a few comments on features of the codes that are worth particular notice. The NSPE code has been selected for inclusion for two primary reasons. First, membership in the NSPE is open to all professional engineers, regardless of their particular engineering discipline, such as electrical, mechanical, or civil engineering. For this reason, the code is in principle applicable to all engineers. This feature distinguishes the NSPE code from the codes of those professional societies that are open only to members of a particular engineering discipline. Electrical engineers, for example, might not be especially interested in the code of mechanical or civil engineering, but they should be interested in the provisions of the NSPE code since they are potential members of this organization. Second, the NSPE code is a very complete code and in general is representative of the other codes. Codes do, however, address the ethical problems that arise in their particular branch of engineering, and there may be some differences in the codes because of this. Codes may also differ because of the special "culture" of the professional societies.

Because the NSPE code is printed here in full and is in general representative of engineering codes of ethics, several features of the code deserve mention:

- The highest ethical obligation of engineers is to the "safety, health, and welfare of the public." Virtually every engineering code contains similar wording and makes it clear that the obligation to the public takes priority over obligations to clients or employers.
- Engineers must also act for clients or employers as "faithful agents or trustees," with the implicit understanding that this obligation is subordinate to the obligation to the public.
- Engineers must practice only in their areas of competence.
- Engineers must act objectively, truthfully, and in a way that avoids deception and misrepresentation, especially to the public. This includes avoiding bribes or other actions that might compromise an engineer's professional integrity.

- Engineers are encouraged (not required) to participate in civic affairs, such as career guidance for youth, and not only to promote or "work for the advancement of the safety, health, and well-being of their community."
- Engineers are encouraged (not required) to adhere to the principles of sustainable development in order to protect the environment for future generations. In an endnote, sustainable development is defined as "meeting human needs ... while conserving and protecting environmental quality and the natural resource base essential for human development." Increasingly, codes are making reference to the concept of sustainable development as well as the obligation to protect the environment.
- Finally, engineers have an obligation to other engineers and to the engineering profession. The obligation to other engineers requires them to refrain from such activities as untruthfully criticizing the work of other engineers and to give credit to other engineers when appropriate. The obligation to the engineering profession requires them to conduct their work (and their advertising) with dignity as well as according to ethical standards.

NSPE CODE OF ETHICS FOR ENGINEERS[1]

Preamble

Engineering is an important and learned profession. As members of this profession, engineers are expected to exhibit the highest standards of honesty and integrity. Engineering has a direct and vital impact on the quality of life for all people. Accordingly, the services provided by engineers require honesty, impartiality, fairness, and equity, and must be dedicated to the protection of the public health, safety, and welfare. Engineers must perform under a standard of professional behavior that requires adherence to the highest principles of ethical conduct.

I. Fundamental Canons

Engineers, in the fulfillment of their professional duties, shall:

1. Hold paramount the safety, health, and welfare of the public.
2. Perform services only in areas of their competence.
3. Issue public statements only in an objective and truthful manner.
4. Act for each employer or client as faithful agents or trustees.
5. Avoid deceptive acts.
6. Conduct themselves honorably, responsibly, ethically, and lawfully so as to enhance the honor, reputation, and usefulness of the profession.

II. Rules of Practice

1. Engineers shall hold paramount the safety, health, and welfare of the public.

   a. If engineers' judgment is overruled under circumstances that endanger life or property, they shall notify their employer or client and such other authority as may be appropriate.
   b. Engineers shall approve only those engineering documents that are in conformity with applicable standards.

    c. Engineers shall not reveal facts, data, or information without the prior consent of the client or employer except as authorized or required by law or this Code.

    d. Engineers shall not permit the use of their name or associate in business ventures with any person or firm that they believe is engaged in fraudulent or dishonest enterprise.

    e. Engineers shall not aid or abet the unlawful practice of engineering by a person or firm.

    f. Engineers having knowledge of any alleged violation of this Code shall report thereon to appropriate professional bodies and, when relevant, also to public authorities, and cooperate with the proper authorities in furnishing such information or assistance as may be required.

2. Engineers shall perform services only in the areas of their competence.

    a. Engineers shall undertake assignments only when qualified by education or experience in the specific technical fields involved.

    b. Engineers shall not affix their signatures to any plans or documents dealing with subject matter in which they lack competence, nor to any plan or document not prepared under their direction and control.

    c. Engineers may accept assignments and assume responsibility for coordination of an entire project and sign and seal the engineering documents for the entire project, provided that each technical segment is signed and sealed only by the qualified engineers who prepared the segment.

3. Engineers shall issue public statements only in an objective and truthful manner.

    a. Engineers shall be objective and truthful in professional reports, statements, or testimony. They shall include all relevant and pertinent information in such reports, statements, or testimony, which should bear the date indicating when it was current.

    b. Engineers may express publicly technical opinions that are founded upon knowledge of the facts and competence in the subject matter.

    c. Engineers shall issue no statements, criticisms, or arguments on technical matters that are inspired or paid for by interested parties, unless they have prefaced their comments by explicitly identifying the interested parties on whose behalf they are speaking, and by revealing the existence of any interest the engineers may have in the matters.

4. Engineers shall act for each employer or client as faithful agents or trustees.

    a. Engineers shall disclose all known or potential conflicts of interest that could influence or appear to influence their judgment or the quality of their services.

    b. Engineers shall not accept compensation, financial or otherwise, from more than one party for services on the same project, or for services pertaining to the same project, unless the circumstances are fully disclosed and agreed to by all interested parties.

    c. Engineers shall not solicit or accept financial or other valuable consideration, directly or indirectly, from outside agents in connection with the work for which they are responsible.

d. Engineers in public service as members, advisors, or employees of a governmental or quasi-governmental body or department shall not participate in decisions with respect to services solicited or provided by them or their organizations in private or public engineering practice.

e. Engineers shall not solicit or accept a contract from a governmental body on which a principal or officer of their organization serves as a member.

5. Engineers shall avoid deceptive acts.

a. Engineers shall not falsify their qualifications or permit misrepresentation of their or their associates' qualifications. They shall not misrepresent or exaggerate their responsibility in or for the subject matter of prior assignments. Brochures or other presentations incident to the solicitation of employment shall not misrepresent pertinent facts concerning employers, employees, associates, joint venturers, or past accomplishments.

b. Engineers shall not offer, give, solicit, or receive, either directly or indirectly, any contribution to influence the award of a contract by public authority, or which may be reasonably construed by the public as having the effect or intent of influencing the awarding of a contract. They shall not offer any gift or other valuable consideration in order to secure work. They shall not pay a commission, percentage, or brokerage fee in order to secure work, except to a bona fide employee or bona fide established commercial or marketing agencies retained by them.

III. Professional Obligations

1. Engineers shall be guided in all their relations by the highest standards of honesty and integrity.

a. Engineers shall acknowledge their errors and shall not distort or alter the facts.

b. Engineers shall advise their clients or employers when they believe a project will not be successful.

c. Engineers shall not accept outside employment to the detriment of their regular work or interest. Before accepting any outside engineering employment, they will notify their employers.

d. Engineers shall not attempt to attract an engineer from another employer by false or misleading pretenses.

e. Engineers shall not promote their own interest at the expense of the dignity and integrity of the profession.

2. Engineers shall at all times strive to serve the public interest.

a. Engineers are encouraged to participate in civic affairs; career guidance for youths; and work for the advancement of the safety, health, and well-being of their community.

b. Engineers shall not complete, sign, or seal plans and/or specifications that are not in conformity with applicable engineering standards. If the client or employer insists on such unprofessional conduct, they shall notify the proper authorities and withdraw from further service on the project.

c. Engineers are encouraged to extend public knowledge and appreciation of engineering and its achievements.

    d. Engineers are encouraged to adhere to the principles of sustainable develop-ment* in order to protect the environment for future generations.

3. Engineers shall avoid all conduct or practice that deceives the public.

    a. Engineers shall avoid the use of statements containing a material misrepre-sentation of fact or omitting a material fact.

    b. Consistent with the foregoing, engineers may advertise for recruitment of personnel.

    c. Consistent with the foregoing, engineers may prepare articles for the lay or technical press, but such articles shall not imply credit to the author for work performed by others.

4. Engineers shall not disclose, without consent, confidential information concern-ing the business affairs or technical processes of any present or former client or employer, or public body on which they serve.

    a. Engineers shall not, without the consent of all interested parties, promote or arrange for new employment or practice in connection with a specific project for which the engineer has gained particular and specialized knowledge.

    b. Engineers shall not, without the consent of all interested parties, participate in or represent an adversary interest in connection with a specific project or proceeding in which the engineer has gained particular specialized knowledge on behalf of a former client or employer.

5. Engineers shall not be influenced in their professional duties by conflicting interests.

    a. Engineers shall not accept financial or other considerations, including free engineering designs, from material or equipment suppliers for specifying their product.

    b. Engineers shall not accept commissions or allowances, directly or indirectly, from contractors or other parties dealing with clients or employers of the engineer in connection with work for which the engineer is responsible.

6. Engineers shall not attempt to obtain employment or advancement or profes-sional engagements by untruthfully criticizing other engineers, or by other improper or questionable methods.

    a. Engineers shall not request, propose, or accept a commission on a contingent basis under circumstances in which their judgment may be compromised.

    b. Engineers in salaried positions shall accept part-time engineering work only to the extent consistent with policies of the employer and in accordance with ethical considerations.

    c. Engineers shall not, without consent, use equipment, supplies, laboratory, or office facilities of an employer to carry on outside private practice.

---

*"Sustainable development" is the challenge of meeting human needs for natural resources, industrial products, energy, food, transportation, shelter, and effective waste management while conserving and protecting environmental quality and the natural resource base essential for future development.
—As Revised July 2007

7. Engineers shall not attempt to injure, maliciously or falsely, directly or indirectly, the professional reputation, prospects, practice, or employment of other engineers. Engineers who believe others are guilty of unethical or illegal practice shall present such information to the proper authority for action.

   a. Engineers in private practice shall not review the work of another engineer for the same client, except with the knowledge of such engineer, or unless the connection of such engineer with the work has been terminated.
   b. Engineers in governmental, industrial, or educational employ are entitled to review and evaluate the work of other engineers when so required by their employment duties.
   c. Engineers in sales or industrial employ are entitled to make engineering comparisons of represented products with products of other suppliers.

8. Engineers shall accept personal responsibility for their professional activities, provided, however, that engineers may seek indemnification for services arising out of their practice for other than gross negligence, where the engineer's interests cannot otherwise be protected.

   a. Engineers shall conform with state registration laws in the practice of engineering.
   b. Engineers shall not use association with a nonengineer, a corporation, or partnership as a "cloak" for unethical acts.

9. Engineers shall give credit for engineering work to those to whom credit is due, and will recognize the proprietary interests of others.

   a. Engineers shall, whenever possible, name the person or persons who may be individually responsible for designs, inventions, writings, or other accomplishments.
   b. Engineers using designs supplied by a client recognize that the designs remain the property of the client and may not be duplicated by the engineer for others without express permission.
   c. Engineers, before undertaking work for others in connection with which the engineer may make improvements, plans, designs, inventions, or other records that may justify copyrights or patents, should enter into a positive agreement regarding ownership.
   d. Engineers' designs, data, records, and notes referring exclusively to an employer's work are the employer's property. The employer should indemnify the engineer for use of the information for any purpose other than the original purpose.
   e. Engineers shall continue their professional development throughout their careers and should keep current in their specialty fields by engaging in professional practice, participating in continuing education courses, reading in the technical literature, and attending professional meetings and seminars.

"By order of the United States District Court for the District of Columbia, former Section 11(c) of the NSPE Code of Ethics prohibiting competitive bidding, and all policy statements, opinions, rulings or other guidelines interpreting its scope, have been rescinded as unlawfully interfering with the legal right of engineers, protected under the antitrust laws, to provide price information to prospective clients;

accordingly, nothing contained in the NSPE Code of Ethics, policy statements, opinions, rulings or other guidelines prohibits the submission of price quotations or competitive bids for engineering services at any time or in any amount."

Statement by NSPE Executive Committee

In order to correct misunderstandings which have been indicated in some instances since the issuance of the Supreme Court decision and the entry of the Final Judgment, it is noted that in its decision of April 25, 1978, the Supreme Court of the United States declared: "The Sherman Act does not require competitive bidding." It is further noted that as made clear in the Supreme Court decision:

1. Engineers and firms may individually refuse to bid for engineering services.
2. Clients are not required to seek bids for engineering services.
3. Federal, state, and local laws governing procedures to procure engineering services are not affected, and remain in full force and effect.
4. State societies and local chapters are free to actively and aggressively seek legislation for professional selection and negotiation procedures by public agencies.
5. State registration board rules of professional conduct, including rules prohibiting competitive bidding for engineering services, are not affected and remain in full force and effect. State registration boards with authority to adopt rules of professional conduct may adopt rules governing procedures to obtain engineering services.
6. As noted by the Supreme Court, "nothing in the judgment prevents NSPE and its members from attempting to influence governmental action…"

NOTE: In regard to the question of application of the Code to corporations vis-à-vis real persons, business form or type should not negate nor influence conformance of individuals to the Code. The Code deals with professional services, which services must be performed by real persons. Real persons in turn establish and implement policies within business structures. The Code is clearly written to apply to the Engineer, and it is incumbent on members of NSPE to endeavor to live up to its provisions. This applies to all pertinent sections of the Code.

1420 King Street
Alexandria, Virginia 22314-2794
703/684-2800 • Fax: 703/836-4875
www.nspe.org

Publication date as revised: July 2007, Publication #1102

AMERICAN INSTITUTE OF CHEMICAL ENGINEERS (AIChE)

www.aiche.org/About/Code.asps
The AIChE code requires members to "never tolerate harassment" and to "treat fairly all colleagues and co-workers." It states that members "shall" pursue the positive goal of "using their knowledge and skill for the enhancement of human welfare." Also, members "shall" protect the environment.

AMERICAN SOCIETY OF CIVIL ENGINEERS (ASCE)

www.asce.org/inside/codeofethics.cfm

The ASCE code contains a number of statements about obligations to protect the environment and to adhere to the principles of sustainable development. These obligations are characterized as something engineers "should" (not "shall") adhere to in their professional work.

AMERICAN SOCIETY OF MECHANICAL ENGINEERS, ASME INTERNATIONAL

www.asme.org/NewsPublicPolicy/Ethics/Ethics_Center.cfm

The ASME code is divided into two parts. The Fundamental Principles and Fundamental Canons are in one document, and the ASME Criteria for Interpretation of the Canons are in another document. The first of the three Fundamental Principles states that engineers "use their knowledge and skills for the enhancement of human welfare."

ASSOCIATION FOR COMPUTING MACHINERY (ACM)

Short version: www.acm.org/about/se-code#short
Full version: www.acm.org/about/se-code#full

The ACM code for "software engineering" has a more informal tone than the other codes and tends to use a different vocabulary from the other codes. According to the code, the "public interest" takes priority over the interests of the employer. Software "shall" not only be safe but also should "not diminish quality of life, diminish privacy, or harm the environment." The "ultimate effect" of work in software engineering should be "the public good." When appropriate, software engineers "shall" also "identify, document, and report significant issues of social concern."

INSTITUTE OF ELECTRICAL AND ELECTRONICS ENGINEERS (IEEE)

www.ieee.org/web/membership/ethics/code_ethics.html

According to the code, members recognize "the importance of our technologies in affecting the quality of life throughout the world." Members agree to "accept responsibility in making decisions consistent with the safety, health, and welfare of the public, and to disclose promptly factors that might endanger the public or the environment." They also agree to "improve the understanding of technology, its appropriate application, and potential consequences." Finally, members agree to "treat fairly all persons regardless of such factors as race, religion, gender, disability, age, or national origin."

INSTITUTE OF INDUSTRIAL ENGINEERS (IIE)

www.iienet2.org/Details.aspx?id=299

In addition to providing Fundamental Principles and Fundamental Canons of its own, the IIE also endorses the Canon of Ethics provided by the Accreditation Board for Engineering and Technology. The Fundamental Principles state that engineers uphold and advance the integrity, honor, and dignity of the engineering profession by (among other things) "using their knowledge and skill for the enhancement of human welfare." The Fundamental Principles and Fundamental Canons make no mention of the environment.

NOTE

1. Reprinted by permission of the National Society of Professional Engineers (NSPE), www.nspe.org.

Alger, P. L., Christensen, N. A., and Olmstead, S. P. *Ethical Problems in Engineering* (New York: Wiley, 1965).

Allen, A. L. "Genetic Privacy: Emerging Concepts and Values," in M. Rothstein, ed., *Genetic Secrets* (New Haven, CT: Yale University Press, 1997), pp. 36–59.

———. "Privacy," in H. LaFollette, ed., *Oxford Handbook of Practical Ethics* (Oxford: Oxford University Press, 2003), pp. 485–513.

Alpern, K. D. "Moral Responsibilities for Engineers," *Business and Professional Ethics Journal*, 2, no. 2, 1983, pp. 39–48.

Anand, S., and Sen, A. *Development as Freedom* (New York: Anchor Books, 1999).

———. "The Income Component of the Human Development Index," *Journal of Human Development*, 1, no. 1, 2000, pp. 83–106.

Anderson, R. M., Perrucci, R., Schendel, D. E., and Trachtman, L. E. *Divided Loyalties: Whistle-Blowing at BART* (West Lafayette, IN: Purdue Research Foundation, 1980).

Anderson, S. *The Man Who Tried to Save the World* (New York: Doubleday, 1999).

Baase, S. *A Gift of Fire: Social, Legal and Ethical Issues in Computers and the Internet* (Hoboken, NJ: Wiley, 2004).

Baier, K. *The Moral Point of View* (Ithaca, NY: Cornell University Press, 1958).

Bailey, M. J. *Reducing Risks to Life: Measurement of the Benefits* (Washington, DC: American Enterprise Institute for Public Policy Research, 1980).

Baille, C., Pawley, A. L., and Riley, D., eds. *Engineering and Social Justice in the University* (West Lafayette, IN: Purdue University Press, 2012).

Baker, D. "Social Mechanics for Controlling Engineers' Performance," in Albert Flores, ed., *Designing for Safety: Engineering Ethics in Organizational Contexts* (Troy, NY: Rensselaer Polytechnic Institute, 1982).

Baram, M. S. "Regulation of Environmental Carcinogens: Why Cost–Benefit Analysis May Be Harmful to Your Health," *Technology Review*, 78, July–August 1976.

Baron, M. *The Moral Status of Loyalty* (Dubuque, IA: Center for the Study of Ethics in the Professions and Kendall/Hunt, 1984).

Baum, R. J. "Engineers and the Public: Sharing Responsibilities," in D. E. Wueste, ed., *Professional Ethics and Social Responsibility* (Lanham, MD: Rowman & Littlefield, 1994).

———. *Ethics and Engineering* (Hastings-on-Hudson, NY: Hastings Center, 1980).

———, and Flores, A., eds. *Ethical Problems in Engineering*, vols. 1 and 2 (Troy, NY: Center for the Study of the Human Dimensions of Science and Technology, Rensselaer Polytechnic Institute, 1978).

Baxter, W. F. *People or Penguins: The Case for Optimal Pollution* (New York: Columbia University Press, 1974).

Bayles, M. D. *Professional Ethics*, 2nd ed. (Belmont, CA: Wadsworth, 1989).

Bazelon, D. L. "Risk and Responsibility," *Science*, 205, July 20, 1979, pp. 277–280.

Beauchamp, T. L. *Case Studies in Business, Society and Ethics*, 2nd ed. (Englewood Cliffs, NJ: Prentice-Hall, 1989).

Bellah, R., Madsen, R., Sullivan, W. M., Swidler, A., and Tipton, S. M. *Habits of the Heart: Individualism and Commitment in American Life* (New York: Harper & Row, 1985).

Belmont Report: Ethical Principles and Guidelines for Protection of Human Subjects of Biomedical and Behavioral Research, publication no. OS 78-00f12 (Washington, DC: DHEW, 1978).

Benham, L. "The Effects of Advertising on the Price of Eyeglasses," *Journal of Law and Economics,* 15, 1972, pp. 337–352.

Benjamin, M. *Splitting the Difference: Compromise in Ethics and Politics* (Lawrence: University Press of Kansas, 1990).

Black, B. "Evolving Legal Standards for the Admissibility of Scientific Evidence," *Science,* 239, 1987, pp. 1510–1512.

Blackstone, W. T. "On Rights and Responsibilities Pertaining to Toxic Substances and Trade Secrecy," *Southern Journal of Philosophy,* 16, 1978, pp. 589–603.

Blinn, K. W. *Legal and Ethical Concepts in Engineering* (Englewood Cliffs, NJ: Prentice-Hall, 1989).

Board of Ethical Review, NSPE. *Opinions of the Board of Ethical Review,* vols. I–VII (Arlington, VA: NSPE Publications, National Society of Professional Engineers, various dates).

Boeyink, D. "Casuistry: A Case-Based Method for Journalists," *Journal of Mass Media Ethics,* Summer 1992, pp. 107–120.

Bok, S. *Common Values* (Columbia: University of Missouri Press, 1995).

——. *Lying: Moral Choice in Public and Private Life* (New York: Vintage Books, 1979).

Borgmann, A. *Technology and the Character of Contemporary Life: A Philosophical Inquiry* (Chicago: University of Chicago Press, 1984).

Bowyer, K., ed. *Ethics and Computing,* 2nd ed. (New York: IEEE Press, 2001).

Broad, W., and Wade, N. *Betrayers of the Truth* (New York: Simon & Schuster, 1982).

Bucciarelli, L. L. *Designing Engineers* (Cambridge, MA: MIT Press, 1994).

Buchanan, R. A. *The Engineers: A History of the Engineering Profession in Britain, 1750–1914* (London: Jessica Kingsley Publishers, 1989).

Cady, J. F. *Restricted Advertising and Competition: The Case of Retail Drugs* (Washington, DC: American Enterprise Institute, 1976).

Callahan, D., and Bok, S. *Ethics Teaching in Higher Education* (New York: Plenum Press, 1980).

Callahan, J. C., ed. *Ethical Issues in Professional Life* (New York: Oxford University Press, 1988).

Callon, M., and Law, J. "Agency and the Hybrid Collectif," *South Atlantic Quarterly,* 94, 1995, 481–507.

Cameron, R., and Millard, A. J. *Technology Assessment: A Historical Approach* (Dubuque, IA: Center for the Study of Ethics in the Professions and Kendall/Hunt, 1985).

Carson, T. L. "Bribery, Extortion, and the 'Foreign Corrupt Practices Act,'" *Philosophy and Public Affairs,* 14, no. 1, 1985, pp. 66–90.

Chadwick, R., ed. *Ethics and the Professions* (Aldershot, UK: Avebury, 1994).

Chalk, R., Frankel, M., and Chafer, S. B. *AAAS Professional Ethics Project: Professional Ethics Activities of the Scientific and Engineering Societies* (Washington, DC: American Association for the Advancement of Science, 1980).

Childress, J. F., and Macquarrie, J., eds. *The Westminster Dictionary of the Christian Church* (Philadelphia, PA: Westminster Press, 1986).

Cohen, R. M., and Witcover, J. *A Heartbeat Away: The Investigation and Resignation of Vice President Spiro T. Agnew* (New York: Viking Press, 1974).

Columbia Accident Investigation Board (CAIB). *The CAIB Report,* vols. I–VII. Available at www.caib.us/.

Cranor, C. F. "The Problem of Joint Causes for Workplace Health Protections [1]," *IEEE Technology and Society Magazine,* September 1986, pp. 10–12.

——. *Regulating Toxic Substances: A Philosophy of Science and the Law* (New York: Oxford University Press, 1993).

Curd, M., and May, L. *Professional Responsibility for Harmful Actions* (Dubuque, IA: Center for the Study of Ethics in the Professions and Kendall/Hunt, 1984).

Davis, M. "Avoiding the Tragedy of Whistleblowing," *Business and Professional Ethics Journal,* 8, no. 4, 1989, pp. 3–19.

——. "Better Communication between Engineers and Managers: Some Ways to Prevent Many Ethically Hard Choices," *Science and Engineering Ethics,* 3, 1997, pp. 184–193.

——. "Conflict of Interest," *Business and Professional Ethics Journal,* Summer 1982, pp. 17–27.

——. "Explaining Wrongdoing," *Journal of Social Philosophy,* 20, Spring–Fall 1988, pp. 74–90.

——. "Is There a Profession of Engineering?" *Science and Engineering Ethics,* 3, no. 4, 1997, pp. 407–428.

———. *Profession, Code and Ethics* (Burlington, VT: Ashgate, 2002).

———. *Thinking Like an Engineer* (New York: Oxford University Press, 1998).

———. "Thinking Like an Engineer: The Place of a Code of Ethics in the Practice of a Profession," *Philosophy and Public Affairs*, 20, no. 2, Spring 1991, pp. 150–167.

———. "The Usefulness of Moral Theory in Practical Ethics: A Question of Comparative Cost (A Response to Harris)," *Teaching Ethics*, 10, no. 1, 2009, pp. 69–78.

———, Pritchard, M. S., and Werhane, P. "Case Study in Engineering Ethics: 'Doing the Minimum,'" *Science and Engineering Ethics*, 7, no. 2, April 2001, pp. 286–302.

———, and Stark, A., eds. *Conflicts of Interest in the Professions* (New York: Oxford University Press, 2001).

De George, R. T. "Ethical Responsibilities of Engineers in Large Organizations: The Pinto Case," *Business and Professional Ethics Journal*, 1, no. 1, Fall 1981, pp. 1–14.

Donaldson, T., and Dunfee, T. W. *Ties that Bind: A Social Contracts Approach to Business Ethics* (Boston, MA: Harvard Business School Press, 1999).

———. "Toward Unified Conception of Business Ethics: Integrative Social Contract Theory," *Academy of Management Review*, 19, no. 2, 1994, pp. 152–184.

Douglas, M., and Wildavsky, A. *Risk and Culture* (Berkeley, CA: University of California Press, 1982).

Dusek, V. *Philosophy of Technology: An Introduction* (Malden, MA: Blackwell, 2006).

Eddy, E., Potter, E., and Page, B. *Destination Disaster: From the Tri-Motor to the DC-10* (New York: Quadrangle Press, 1976).

Elbaz, S. W. *Professional Ethics and Engineering: A Resource Guide* (Arlington, VA: National Institute for Engineering Ethics, 1990).

Engineering Times (NSPE). "AAES Strives towards Being Unified" and "U.S. Engineer: Unity Elusive," 15, no. 11, November 1993.

Ermann, M. P., Williams, M. B., and Shauf, M. S. *Computers, Ethics, and Society*, 2nd ed. (New York: Oxford University Press, 1997).

Ethics Resource Center and Behavior Resource Center. *Ethics Policies and Programs in American Business* (Washington, DC: Ethics Resource Center, 1990).

Evan, W., and Manion, M. *Minding the Machines* (Upper Saddle River, NJ: Prentice-Hall, 2002).

Faden, R. R., and Beauchamp, T. L. *A History and Theory of Informed Consent* (New York: Oxford University Press, 1986).

Fadiman, J. A. "A Traveler's Guide to Gifts and Bribes," *Harvard Business Review*, July–August 1986, pp. 122–126, 130–136.

Feenberg, A. *Questioning Technology* (New York: Routledge, 1999).

Feinberg, J. "Duties, Rights and Claims," *American Philosophical Quarterly*, 3, no. 2, 1966, pp. 137–144.

Feliv, A. G. "The Role of the Law in Protecting Scientific and Technical Dissent," *IEEE Technology and Society Magazine*, June 1985, pp. 3–9.

Fielder, J. "Organizational Loyalty," *Business and Professional Ethics Journal*, 11, no. 1, 1991, pp. 71–90.

———. "Tough Break for Goodrich," *Journal of Business and Professional Ethics*, 19, no. 3, 1986.

———, and Birsch, D., eds. *The DC-10* (New York: State of New York Press, 1992).

Firmage, D. A. *Modern Engineering Practice: Ethical, Professional and Legal Aspects* (New York: Garland STPM, 1980).

Fledderman, C. B., *Engineering Ethics*, 4th ed., (Englewood Cliffs, NJ: Prentice-Hall, 2011).

Flores, A., ed. *Designing for Safety* (Troy, NY: Rensselaer Polytechnic Institute, 1982).

———. *Ethics and Risk Management in Engineering* (Boulder, CO: Westview Press, 1988).

———. *Professional Ideals* (Belmont, CA: Wadsworth, 1988).

———, and Johnson, D. G. "Collective Responsibility and Professional Roles," *Ethics*, 93, April 1983, pp. 537–545.

Florman, S. C. *Blaming Technology: The Irrational Search for Scapegoats* (New York: St. Martin's, 1981).

———. *The Civilized Engineer* (New York: St. Martin's, 1987).

———. *The Existential Pleasures of Engineering* (New York: St. Martin's, 1976).

———. "Moral Blueprints," *Harper's Magazine*, 257, no. 1541, October 1978, pp. 30–33.

Flumerfelt, R. W., Harris, C. E., Jr., Rabins, M. J., and Samson, C. H., Jr. *Introducing Ethics Case Studies into Required Undergraduate Engineering Courses*, Report on NSF Grant DIR-9012252 (November 1992).

Ford, D. F. *Three Mile Island: Thirty Minutes to Meltdown* (New York: Viking Press, 1982).

Frankel, M., ed. *Science, Engineering, and Ethics: State of the Art and Future Directions,* Report of an American Association for the Advancement of Science Workshop and Symposium (February 1988).

Fredrich, A. J. *Sons of Martha: Civil Engineering Readings in Modern Literature* (New York: American Society of Civil Engineers, 1989).

French, P. A. *Collective and Corporate Responsibility* (New York: Columbia University Press, 1984).

Friedman, M. "The Social Responsibility of Business Is to Increase Its Profits," *New York Times Magazine,* September 13, 1970.

Garrett, T. M., et al. *Cases in Business Ethics* (New York: Appleton Century Crofts, 1968).

General Dynamics Corporation. *The General Dynamics Ethics Program Update* (St. Louis: Author, 1988).

Gert, B. *Common Morality* (New York: Oxford University Press, 2004).

———. "Moral Theory, and Applied and Professional Ethics," *Professional Ethics,* 1, nos. 1 and 2, Spring–Summer 1992, pp. 1–25.

Gewirth, A. *Reason and Morality* (Chicago: University of Chicago Press, 1978).

Glantz, P., and Lipton, E. *City in the Sky … The Rise and Fall of the World Trade Centers* (New York: Times Books/Holt, 2003).

———. "The Height of Ambition," *New York Times Magazine,* September 8, 2002, section 6, p. 32.

Glazer, M. "Ten Whistleblowers and How They Fared," *Hastings Center Report,* 13, no. 6, 1983, pp. 33–41.

———. *The Whistleblowers: Exposing Corruption in Government and Industry* (New York: Basic Books, 1989).

Glickman, T. S., and Gough, R. *Readings in Risk* (Washington, DC: Resources for the Future, 1990).

Goldberg, D. T. "Turning in to Whistle Blowing," *Business and Professional Ethics Journal,* 7, 1988, pp. 85–99.

Goldman, A. H. *The Moral Foundations of Professional Ethics* (Totowa, NJ: Rowman & Littlefield, 1979).

Goodin, R. E. *Protecting the Vulnerable* (Chicago: University of Chicago Press, 1989).

Gorlin, R. A., ed. *Codes of Professional Responsibility,* 2nd ed. (Washington, DC: Bureau of National Affairs, 1990).

Gorman, M. E., Mehalik, M. M., and Werhane, P. *Ethical and Environmental Challenges to Engineering* (Upper Saddle River, NJ: Prentice-Hall, 2000).

Graham, L. *The Ghost of an Executed Engineer* (Cambridge, MA: Harvard University Press, 1993).

Gray, M., and Rosen, I. *The Warning: Accident at Three Mile Island* (New York: Norton, 1982).

Greenwood, E. "Attributes of a Profession," *Social Work,* July 1957, pp. 45–55.

Gunn, A. S., and Vesilind, P. A. *Environmental Ethics for Engineers* (Chelsea, MI: Lewis, 1986).

Harris, C. E. *Applying Moral Theories,* 5th ed. (Belmont, CA: Wadsworth, 2006).

———. "Engineering Responsibilities in Lesser- Developed Nations: The Welfare Requirement," *Science and Engineering Ethics,* 4, no. 3, July 1998, pp. 321–331.

———. "Is Moral Theory Useful in Practical Ethics," *Teaching Ethics,* 10, no. 1, 2009, pp. 51–68.

———. "Response to Michael Davis: The Cost is Minimal and Worth it," *Teaching Ethics,* 10, no. 1, 2009, pp. 79–86.

———, Pritchard, M. S., and Rabins, M. J. *Practicing Engineering Ethics* (New York: Institute of Electrical and Electronic Engineers, 1997).

Heilbroner, R., ed. *In the Name of Profit* (Garden City, NY: Doubleday, 1972).

Herkert, J. "Future Directions in Engineering Ethics Research: Microethics, Macroethics and the Role of Professional Societies," *Science and Engineering Ethics,* 7, no. 3, July 2001, pp. 403–414.

Hick, J. *Disputed Questions in Theology and the Philosophy of Religion* (New Haven, CT: Yale University Press, 1986).

Howard, J. L. "Current Developments in Whistleblower Protection," *Labor Law Journal,* 39, no. 2, February 1988, pp. 67–80.

Hunter, T. "Engineers Face Risks as Expert Witnesses," *Rochester Engineer,* December 1992.

Hynes, H. P. "Women Working: A Field Report," *Technology Review,* November–December 1984.

Jackall, R. "The Bureaucratic Ethos and Dissent," *IEEE Technology and Society Magazine,* June 1985, pp. 21–30.

———. *Moral Mazes: The World of Corporate Managers* (New York: Oxford University Press, 1988).

Jackson, I. *Honor in Science* (New Haven, CT: Sigma Xi, 1986).

Jaksa, J. A., and Pritchard, M. S. *Communication Ethics: Methods of Analysis,* 2nd ed. (Belmont, CA: Wadsworth, 1994).

James, G. G. "Whistle Blowing: Its Moral Justification," in W. M. Hoffman and R. E. Frederick, eds.,

Business Ethics, 3rd ed. (New York: McGraw-Hill, 1995), pp. 290–301.

Jamshidi, M., Shahinpoor, M., and Mullins, J. H., eds. *Environmentally Conscious Manufacturing: Recent Advances* (Albuquerque, NM: ECM Press, 1991).

Janis, I. *Groupthink,* 2nd ed. (Boston, MA: Houghton Mifflin, 1982).

Johnson, D. G. *Computer Ethics,* 3rd ed. (Upper Saddle River, NJ: Prentice-Hall, 2001).

——. *Ethical Issues in Engineering* (Englewood Cliffs, NJ: Prentice-Hall, 1991).

——, and Nissenbaum, H. *Computer Ethics and Social Policy* (Upper Saddle River, NJ: Prentice-Hall, 1995).

——, and Snapper, J. W., eds. *Ethical Issues in the Use of Computers* (Belmont, CA: Wadsworth, 1985).

Johnson, E. "Treating Dirt: Environmental Ethics and Moral Theory," in T. Regan, ed., *Earthbound: New Introductory Essays in Environmental Ethics* (New York: Random House, 1984).

Jonsen, A. L., and Toulmin, S. *The Abuse of Casuistry* (Berkeley, CA: University of California Press, 1988).

Jurmu, J. L., and Pinodo, A. "The OSHA Benzene Case," in T. L. Beauchamp, ed., *Case Studies in Business, Society, and Ethics,* 2nd ed. (Englewood Cliffs, NJ: Prentice-Hall, 1989), pp. 203–211.

Kahn, S. "Economic Estimates of the Value of Life," *IEEE Technology and Society Magazine,* June 1986, pp. 24–31.

Kant, I. *Foundations of the Metaphysics of Morals, with Critical Essays* (R. P. Wolff, ed.) (Indianapolis, IN: Bobbs-Merrill, 1969).

Kemper, J. D. *Engineers and Their Profession,* 3rd ed. (New York: Holt, Rinehart & Winston, 1982).

Kettler, G. J. "Against the Industry Exemption," in J. H. Shaub and K. Pavlovic, eds., *Engineering Professionalism and Ethics* (New York: Wiley–Interscience, 1983), pp. 529–532.

Kipnis, K. "Engineers Who Kill: Professional Ethics and the Paramountcy of Public Safety," *Business and Professional Ethics Journal,* 1, no. 1, 1981.

Kline, A. D. "On Complicity Theory," *Science and Engineering Ethics,* 12, 2006, pp. 257–264.

Kolhoff, M. J. "For the Industry Exemption …," in J. H. Shaub and K. Pavlovic, eds., *Engineering Professionalism and Ethics* (New York: Wiley–Interscience, 1983).

Kroes, P., and Bakker, M., eds. *Technological Development and Science in the Industrial Age* (Dordrecht, The Netherlands: Kluwer, 1992).

Kuhn, S. "When Worlds Collide: Engineering Students Encounter Social Aspects of Production," *Science and Engineering Ethics,* 1998, pp. 457–472.

Kultgen, J. *Ethics and Professionalism* (Philadelphia, PA: University of Pennsylvania Press, 1988).

——. "Evaluating Codes of Professional Ethics," in W. L. Robison, M. S. Pritchard, and J. Ellin, eds., *Profits and Professions* (Clifton, NJ: Humana Press, 1983), pp. 225–264.

Ladd, J. "Bhopal: An Essay on Moral Responsibility and Civic Virtue," *Journal of Social Philosophy,* XXII, no. 1, Spring 1991.

——. "The Quest for a Code of Professional Ethics," in R. Chalk, M. S. Frankel, and S. B. Chafer, eds., *AAAS Professional Ethics Project: Professional Ethics Activities of the Scientific and Engineering Societies* (Washington, DC: American Association for the Advancement of Science, 1980).

Ladenson, R. F. "Freedom of Expression in the Corporate Workplace: A Philosophical Inquiry," in W. L. Robison, M. S. Pritchard, and J. Ellin, eds., *Profits and Professions* (Clifton, NJ: Humana Press, 1983), pp. 275–285.

——. "The Social Responsibilities of Engineers and Scientists: A Philosophical Approach," in D. L. Babcock and C. A. Smith, eds., *Values and the Public Works Professional* (Rolla: University of Missouri–Rolla, 1980).

——, Choromokos, J., d'Anjou, E., Pimsler, M., and Rosen, H. *A Selected Annotated Bibliography of Professional Ethics and Social Responsibility in Engineering* (Chicago: Center for the Study of Ethics in the Professions, Illinois Institute of Technology, 1980).

LaFollette, H. *Oxford Handbook of Practical Ethics* (Oxford: Oxford University Press, 2003).

——. *The Practice of Ethics* (Oxford: Blackwell, 2007).

Langewiesche, W. "Columbia's Last Flight," *The Atlantic,* 292, no. 4, November 2003, pp. 58–87.

Larson, M. S. *The Rise of Professionalism* (Berkeley, CA: University of California Press, 1977).

Latour, B. *Science in Action: How to Follow Scientists and Engineers through Society* (Cambridge, MA: Harvard University Press, 1987).

Layton, E. T., Jr. *The Revolt of the Engineers: Social Responsibility and the American Engineering Profession* (Baltimore, MD: John Hopkins University Press, 1971, 1986).

Leopold, A. *A Sand County Almanac* (New York: Oxford University Press, 1966).

Lichtenberg, J. "What Are Codes of Ethics for?" in M. Coady and S. Bloch, eds., *Codes of Ethics and the Professions* (Melbourne, Australia: Melbourne University Press, 1995), pp. 13–27.

Litai, D. *A Risk Comparison Methodology for the Assessment of Acceptable Risk,* Ph.D. dissertation, Massachusetts Institute of Technology, Cambridge, MA, 1980.

Lockhart, T. W. "Safety Engineering and the Value of Life," *Technology and Society (IEEE),* 9, March 1981, pp. 3–5.

Lowrance, W. W. *Of Acceptable Risk* (Los Altos, CA: Kaufman, 1976).

Luebke, N. R. "Conflict of Interest as a Moral Category," *Business and Professional Ethics Journal,* 6, no. 1, 1987, pp. 66–81.

Luegenbiehl, H. C. "Codes of Ethics and the Moral Education of Engineers," *Business and Professional Ethics Journal,* 2, no. 4, 1983, pp. 41–61.

———. "Whistleblowing," in C. Mitchum, ed., *Encyclopedia of Science, Technology, and Ethics* (Detroit, MI: Thomson, 2005).

Lunch, M. F. "Supreme Court Rules on Advertising for Professions," *Professional Engineer,* 1, no. 8, August 1977, pp. 41–42.

Lynch, W. T., and Kline, R. "Engineering Practice and Engineering Ethics," *Science, Technology and Human Values,* 25, 2000, pp. 223–231.

MacIntyre, A. *After Virtue* (Notre Dame, IN: University of Notre Dame Press, 1984).

———. "Regulation: A Substitute for Morality," *Hastings Center Report,* February 1980, pp. 31–41.

———. *A Short History of Ethics* (New York: Macmillan, 1966).

Magsdick, H. H. "Some Engineering Aspects of Headlighting," *Illuminating Engineering,* June 1940, p. 533.

Malin, M. H. "Protecting the Whistleblower from Retaliatory Discharge," *Journal of Law Reform,* 16, Winter 1983, pp. 277–318.

Mantell, M. I. *Ethics and Professionalism in Engineering* (New York: Macmillan, 1964).

Margolis, J. "Conflict of Interest and Conflicting Interests," in T. Beauchamp and N. Bowie, eds., *Ethical Theory and Business* (Englewood Cliffs, NJ: Prentice-Hall, 1979), pp. 361–372.

Marshall, E. "Feynman Issues His Own Shuttle Report Attacking NASA Risk Estimates," *Science,* 232, June 27, 1986, p. 1596.

Martin, D. *Three Mile Island: Prologue or Epilogue?* (Cambridge, MA: Ballinger, 1980).

Martin, M. W. *Everyday Morals* (Belmont, CA: Wadsworth, 1989).

———. *Meaningful Work* (New York: Oxford University Press, 2000).

———. "Personal Meaning and Ethics in Engineering," *Science and Engineering Ethics,* 8, no. 4, October 2002, pp. 545–560.

———. "Professional Autonomy and Employers' Authority," in A. Flores, ed., *Ethical Problems in Engineering,* vol. 1 (Troy, NY: Rensselaer Polytechnic Institute, 1982), pp. 177–181.

———. "Rights and the Meta-Ethics of Professional Morality," and "Professional and Ordinary Morality: A Reply to Freedman," *Ethics,* 91, July 1981, pp. 619–625, 631–622.

———. *Self-Deception and Morality* (Lawrence: University Press of Kansas, 1986).

———, and Schinzinger, R. *Engineering Ethics,* 4th ed. (New York: McGraw-Hill 2005).

Martin, M., and Schinzinger, R., *Introduction to Engineering Ethics,* 2nd ed. (New York: McGraw-Hill, 2009).

Mason, J. F. "The Technical Blow-by-Blow: An Account of the Three Mile Island Accident," *IEEE Spectrum,* 16, no. 11, November 1979, pp. 33–42.

May, W. F. "Professional Virtue and Self-Regulation," in J. L. Callahan, ed., *Ethical Issues in Professional Life* (New York: Oxford, 1988), pp. 408–411.

McCabe, D. "Classroom Cheating among Natural Science and Engineering Majors," *Science and Engineering Ethics,* 3, no. 4, 1997, pp. 433–445.

McIlwee, J. S., and Robinson, J. G. *Women in Engineering: Gender, Power, and Workplace Culture* (Albany, NY: State University of New York Press, 1992).

Meese, G. P. E. "The Sealed Beam Case," *Business and Professional Ethics Journal,* 1, no. 3, Spring 1982, pp. 1–20.

Meyers, C. "Institutional Culture and Individual Behavior: Creating the Ethical Environment," *Science and Engineering Ethics,* 10, 2004, p. 271.

Milgram, S. *Obedience to Authority* (New York: Harper & Row, 1974).

Mill, J. S. *Utilitarianism* (G. Sher, ed.) (Indianapolis, IN: Hackett, 1979).

———. *Utilitarianism, with Critical Essays* (S. Gorovitz, ed.) (Indianapolis, IN: Bobbs-Merrill, 1971).

Millikan, R. A. "On the Elementary Electrical Charge and the Avogadro Constant," *Physical Review,* 2, 1913, pp. 109–143.

Morgenstern, J. "The Fifty-Nine Story Crisis," *The New Yorker,* May 29, 1995, pp. 45–53.

Moriarity, G., *The Engineering Project: Its Nature, Ethics, and Promise* (University Park, PA: Pennsylvania State University Press, 2008).

Morrison, C., and Hughes, P. *Professional Engineering Practice: Ethical Aspects,* 2nd ed. (Toronto: McGraw-Hill Ryerson, 1988).

Murdough Center for Engineering Professionalism. *Independent Study and Research Program in Engineering Ethics and Professionalism* (Lubbock: College of Engineering, Texas Technological University, October 1990).

Murphy, C., and Gardoni, P. "The Acceptability and the Tolerability of Societal Risks," *Science and Engineering Ethics,* 14, no. 12, March 2008, pp. 77–92.

———. "Determining Public Policy and Resource Allocation Priorities for Mitigating Natural Hazards: A Capabilities-Based Approach," *Science & Engineering Ethics,* 13, no. 4, December 2007, pp. 489–504.

———. "The Role of Society in Engineering Risk Analysis: A Capabilities Approach," *Risk Analysis,* 26, no. 4, 2006, pp. 1073–1083.

Nader, R. "Responsibility and the Professional Society," *Professional Engineer,* 41, May 1971, pp. 14–17.

———, Petkas, P. J., and Blackwell, K. *Whistle Blowing* (New York: Grossman, 1972).

National Academy of Science, Committee on the Conduct of Science. *On Being a Scientist* (Washington, DC: National Academy Press, 1989).

New York Times. "A Post–September 11 Laboratory in High Rise Safety," January 23, 2003, p. A1.

Noonan, J. T. *Bribery* (New York: Macmillan, 1984).

Nussbaum, M. *Women and Human Development: The Capabilities Approach* (New York: Cambridge University Press, 2000).

———, and Glover, J., eds. *Women, Culture, and Development* (Oxford: Clarendon, 1995).

Okrent, D., and Whipple, C. *An Approach to Societal Risk Assessment Criteria and Risk Management,* Report UCLA-Eng-7746 (Los Angeles: UCLA School of Engineering and Applied Sciences, 1977).

Oldenquist, A. "Commentary on Alpern's 'Moral Responsibility for Engineers,'" *Business and Professional Ethics Journal,* 2, no. 2, Winter 1983.

Otten, J. "Organizational Disobedience," in A. Flores, ed., *Ethical Problems in Engineering,* vol. 1 (Troy, NY: Center for the Study of the Human Dimensions of Science and Technology, Rensselaer Polytechnic Institute, 1978), pp. 182–186.

Patton-Hulce, V. R. *Environment and the Law: A Dictionary* (Santa Barbara, CA: ABC Clio, 1995).

Peterson, J. C., and Farrell, D. *Whistleblowing: Ethical and Legal Issues in Expressing Dissent* (Dubuque, IA: Center for the Study of Ethics in the Professions and Kendall/Hunt, 1986).

Petroski, H. *Beyond Engineering: Essays and Other Attempts to Figure without Equations* (New York: St. Martin's, 1985).

———. *To Engineer Is Human: The Role of Failure in Successful Design* (New York: St. Martin's, 1982).

Petty, T. "Use of Corpses in Auto-Crash Test Outrages Germans," *Time,* December 6, 1993, p. 70.

Pfatteicher, S. K. A. *Lessons Amid the Ruble: An Introduction to Post-Disaster Engineering and Ethics* (Baltimore, MD: Johns Hopkins Press, 2010).

Philips, M. "Bribery," in Werhane, P., and D'Andrade, K., eds., *Profit and Responsibility* (New York: Edwin Mellon Press, 1985), pp. 197–220.

Pinkus, R. L. D., Shuman, L. J., Hummon, N. P., and Wolfe, H. *Engineering Ethics* (New York: Cambridge University Press, 1997).

Pletta, D. H. *The Engineering Profession: Its Heritage and Its Emerging Public Purpose* (Washington, DC: University Press of America, 1984).

Pritchard, M. S. "Beyond Disaster Ethics," *The Centennial Review,* XXXIV, no. 2, Spring 1990, pp. 295–318.

———. "Bribery: The Concept," *Science and Engineering Ethics,* 4, no. 3, 1998, pp. 281–286.

———. "Good Works," *Professional Ethics,* 1, nos. 1 and 2, Spring–Summer 1992, pp. 155–177.

———. *Professional Integrity: Thinking Ethically* (Lawrence, Kansas: University Press of Kansas, 2006).

———. "Professional Responsibility: Focusing on the Exemplary," *Science and Engineering Ethics,* 4, no. 2, 1998, pp. 215–233.

———. "Responsible Engineering: The Importance of Character and Imagination," *Science and Engineering Ethics,* 7, no. 3, 2001, pp. 391–402.

———, ed. *Teaching Engineering Ethics: A Case Study Approach,* National Science Foundation grant no. DIR-8820837 (June 1992).

———, and Holtzapple, M. "Responsible Engineering: Gilbane Gold Revisited," *Science and Engineering Ethics,* 3, no. 2, April 1997, pp. 217–231.

Rabins, M. J. "Teaching Engineering Ethics to Undergraduates: Why? What? How?" *Science and Engineering Ethics,* 4, no. 3, July 1998, pp. 291–301.

Rachels, J. *The Elements of Moral Philosophy,* 4th ed. (New York: Random House, 2003).

Raelin, J. A. *The Clash of Cultures: Managers and Professionals* (Boston, MA: Harvard Business School Press, 1985).

Rawls, J. *A Theory of Justice* (Cambridge, MA: Harvard University Press, 1971).

Relman, A. "Lessons from the Darsee Affair," *New England Journal of Medicine,* 308, 1983, pp. 1415–1417.

Richardson, H. "Specifying Norms," *Philosophy and Public Affairs,* 19, no. 4, 1990, pp. 279–310.

Ringleb, A. H., Meiners, R. E., and Edwards, F. L. *Managing in the Legal Environment* (St. Paul, MN: West, 1990).

Rogers Commission. *Report to the President by the Presidential Commission on the Space Shuttle Challenger Accident* (Washington, DC: Author, June 6, 1986).

Ross, W. D. *The Right and the Good* (Oxford: Oxford University Press, 1988).

Rostsen, G. H. "Wrongful Discharge Based on Public Policy Derived from Professional Ethics Codes," *American Law Reports,* 52, 5th 405.

Rothstein, M., ed. *Genetic Secrets* (New Haven, CT: Yale University Press, 1997).

Ruckelshaus, W. D. "Risk, Science, and Democracy," *Issues in Science and Technology,* 1, no. 3, Spring 1985, pp. 19–38.

Sagoff, M. "Where Ickes Went Right or Reason and Rationality in Environmental Law," *Ecology Law Quarterly,* 14, 1987, pp. 265–323.

Salzman, J., and Thompson, B. H., Jr. *Environmental Law and Policy* (New York: Foundation Press, 2003).

Scharf, R. C., and Dusek, V., eds. *Philosophy of Technology* (Malden, MA: Blackwell, 2003).

Schaub, J. H., and Pavlovic, K. *Engineering Professionalism and Ethics* (New York: Wiley–Interscience, 1983).

Schlossberger, E. *The Ethical Engineer* (Philadelphia, PA: Temple University Press, 1993).

———. "The Responsibility of Engineers, Appropriate Technology, and Lesser Developed Nations," *Science and Engineering Ethics,* 3, no. 3, July 1997, pp. 317–325.

Schrader-Frechette, K. S. *Risk and Rationality* (Berkeley, CA: University of California Press, 1991).

Schwing, R. C., and Albers, W. A., Jr., eds., *Societal Risk Assessment: How Safe Is Safe Enough?* (New York: Plenum Press, 1980).

Science and Engineering Ethics. Special Issue on Ethics for Science and Engineering-Based International Industries, 4, no. 3, July 1998, pp. 257–392.

Shapiro, S. "Degrees of Freedom: The Interaction of Standards of Practice and Engineering Judgment," *Science, Technology and Human Values,* 22, no. 3, Summer 1997.

Simon, H. A. *Administrative Behavior,* 3rd ed. (New York: Free Press, 1976).

Singer, M. G. *Generalization in Ethics* (New York: Knopf, 1961).

———, ed. *Morals and Values* (New York: Charles Scribner's Sons, 1977).

Singer, P. *Practical Ethics* (Cambridge, UK: Cambridge University Press, 1979).

Sismondo, S. *An Introduction to Science and Technology Studies* (Malden, MA: Blackwell, 2004).

Slovic, P., Fischoff, B., and Lichtenstein, S. "Rating the Risks," *Environment,* 21, no. 3, April 1969, pp. 14–39.

Solomon, R. C., and Hanson, K. R. *Above the Bottom Line: An Introduction to Business Ethics* (New York: Harcourt Brace Jovanovich, 1983).

Spinello, R. A. *Case Studies in Information and Computer Ethics* (Upper Saddle River, NJ: Prentice-Hall, 1997).

———, ed. *Cyber Ethics: Morality and Law in Cyberspace* (New York: Jones & Bartlett, 2003).

———. *Regulating Cyberspace* (Westport, CT: Quorum Books, 2002).

———, and Tavani, H. T., eds. *Readings in Cyber Ethics* (New York: Jones & Bartlett, 2001).

Starry, C. "Social Benefits versus Technological Risk," *Science,* 165, September 19, 1969, pp. 1232–1238.

Stone, C. *Where the Law Ends* (Prospect Heights, IL: Waveland Press, 1991).

Strand, P. N., and Golden, K. C. "Consulting Scientist and Engineer Liability," *Science and Engineering Ethics,* 3, no. 4, October 1997, pp. 347–394.

Sullivan, T. F. P., ed. *Environmental Law Handbook* (Rockdale, MD: Government Institutes, 1997).

Taeusch, C. F. *Professional and Business Ethics* (New York: Holt, 1926).

Tavani, H. T. *Ethics and Technology: Ethical Issues in Information and Communication Technology* (Hoboken, NJ: Wiley, 2004).

Taylor, P. W. "The Ethics of Respect for Nature," *Environmental Ethics,* 3, no. 3, Fall 1981, pp. 197–218.

———. *Principles of Ethics: An Introduction* (Encino, CA: Dickenson, 1975).

Thompson, P. "The Ethics of Truth-Telling and the Problem of Risk," *Science and Engineering Ethics,* 5, 1999, pp. 489–510.

Toffler, A. *Tough Choices: Managers Talk Ethics* (New York: Wiley, 1986).

Travis, L. A. *Power and Responsibility: Multinational Managers and Developing Country Concerns* (Notre Dame, IN: University of Notre Dame Press, 1997).

Unger, S. H. *Controlling Technology: Ethics and the Responsible Engineer,* 2nd ed. (New York: Holt, Rinehart & Winston, 1994).

————. "Would Helping Ethical Professionals Get Professional Societies into Trouble?" *IEEE Technology and Society Magazine,* 6, no. 3, September 1987, pp. 17–21.

Urmson, J. O. "Hare on Intuitive Moral Thinking," in S. Douglass and N. Fotion, eds., *Hare and Critics* (Oxford: Clarendon, 1988), pp. 161–169.

————. "Saints and Heroes," in A. I. Meldon, ed., *Essays in Moral Philosophy* (Seattle: University of Washington Press, 1958), pp. 198–216.

Vallero, P. A., and Vesilind, P. A. *Socially Responsible Engineering: Justice in Risk Management* (Hoboken, NJ: John Wiley & Sons, Inc., 2007).

van de Poel, I., and Lambèr, R., *Ethics, Technology, and Engineering: An Introduction* (Wiley-Blackwell, 2011).

Van de Poel, I., and van Gorp, A. C. "The Need for Ethical Reflection in Engineering Design," *Science, Technology and Human Values,* 31, no. 3, 2006, pp. 333–360.

Vandivier, R. "What? Me Be a Martyr?" *Harper's Magazine,* July 1975, pp. 36–44.

Vaughn, D. *The Challenger Launch Decision* (Chicago: University of Chicago Press, 1996).

Vaughn, R. C. *Legal Aspects of Engineering* (Dubuque, IA: Kendall/Hunt, 1977).

Velasquez, M. *Business Ethics,* 3rd ed. (Englewood Cliffs, NJ: Prentice-Hall, 1992).

————. "Why Corporations Are Not Responsible for Anything They Do," *Business and Professional Ethics Journal,* 2, no. 3, Spring 1983, pp. 1–18.

Vesilind, P. A. "Environmental Ethics and Civil Engineering," *The Environmental Professional,* 9, 1987, pp. 336–342.

————. *Peace Engineering: When Personal Values and Engineering Careers Converge* (Woodsville, NH: Lakeshore Press, 2005).

————, and Gunn, A. *Engineering, Ethics, and the Environment* (New York: Cambridge University Press, 1998).

Vogel, D. A. *A Survey of Ethical and Legal Issues in Engineering Curricula in the United States* (Palo Alto, CA: Stanford Law School, Winter 1991).

Wall Street Journal. "Executives Apply Stiffer Standards Than Public to Ethical Dilemmas," November 3, 1983.

Weil, V., ed. *Beyond Whistleblowing: Defining Engineers' Responsibilities,* Proceedings of the Second National Conference on Ethics in Engineering, March 1982.

————. *Moral Issues in Engineering: Selected Readings* (Chicago: Illinois Institute of Technology, 1988).

————. "Professional Standards: Can They Shape Practice in an International Context?" *Science and Engineering Ethics,* 4, no. 3, 1998, pp. 303–314.

Weisskoph, M. "The Aberdeen Mess," *Washington Post Magazine,* January 15, 1989.

Wells, P., Jones, H., and Davis, M. *Conflicts of Interest in Engineering* (Dubuque, IA: Center for the Study of Ethics in the Professions and Kendall/Hunt, 1986).

Werhane, P. *Moral Imagination and Management Decision Making* (New York: Oxford University Press, 1999).

Westin, A. F. *Individual Rights in the Corporation: A Reader on Employee Rights* (New York: Random House, 1980).

————. *Whistle Blowing: Loyalty and Dissent in the Corporation* (New York: McGraw-Hill, 1981).

Whitbeck, C. *Engineering Ethics in Practice and Research,* 2nd ed. (New York: Cambridge University Press, 2011).

————. "The Trouble with Dilemmas: Rethinking Applied Ethics," *Professional Ethics,* 1, nos. 1 and 2, Spring–Summer 1992, pp. 119–142.

Wilcox, J. R., and Theodore, L., eds. *Engineering and Environmental Ethics* (New York: Wiley, 1998).

Williams, B., and Smart, J. J. C. *Utilitarianism: For and Against* (New York: Cambridge University Press, 1973).

Wong, D. *Moral Relativity* (Berkeley, CA: University of California Press, 1984).